EMMETT DULANEY
SHEILA GRAVEN
ANGELA J.R. JONES
STEPHEN P. LOY

MCSD
TRAINING GUIDE

MICROSOFT ACCESS

MCSD Training Guide: Microsoft Access

By Emmett Dulaney, Sheila Graven, Angela J.R. Jones, and
Stephen P. Loy

Published by:
New Riders Publishing
201 West 103rd Street
Indianapolis, IN 46290 USA

© 1997 by New Riders Publishing

Printed in the United States of America 1 2 3 4 5 6 7 8 9 0

Library of Congress Cataloging-in-Publication Data

```
***CIP data available upon request***
```

ISBN: 1-56205-771-5

Warning and Disclaimer

Associate Publisher *David Dwyer*
Executive Editor *Mary Foote*
Managing Editor *Sarah Kearns*

Acquisitions Editor
Steve Weiss

Development Editor
Nancy Price-Warner

Project Editor
Christopher Morris

Copy Editors
Daryl Kessler, Audra McFarland

Technical Editor
Bob Reinsch

Software Product Developer
Steve Flatt

**Software Acquisitions and
Development**
Dustin Sullivan

Team Coordinator
Stacey Beheler

Manufacturing Coordinator
Brook Farling

Book Designer
Glenn Larsen

Cover Designer
Dan Armstrong

Cover Production
Casey Price

Director of Production
Larry Klein

Production Manager
Laurie Casey

Graphics Image Specialists
Steve Adams, Debi Bolhuis,
Kevin Cliburn, Sadie Crawford,
Wil Cruz, Tammy Graham,
Oliver Jackson

Production Analysts
Dan Harris, Erich J. Richter

Production Team
Kim Cofer, Maribeth Echard,
Michelle Mitchell, Elizabeth
SanMiguel, Lisa Stumpf

Indexer
Tim Wright

About the Authors

Emmett Dulaney is an MCSE, as well as a CNE, CNA, and LAN Server Engineer. A trainer for a national training company, Emmett is also a consultant for D S Technical Solutions and can be reached at edulaney@iquest.net.

Sheila Graven is a Microsoft Certified Professional and runs her own consulting business in suburban Chicago.

Angela J. Reeves Jones, MCPS, has been teaching people how to use things since high school, when she earned spare money by tutoring her peers through math and science classes. She received a B.S. in Theatre Arts from Northwestern University because of her heartfelt belief that people and emotions are more challenging than math and science. Upon graduation, however, the lure of puzzle-solving with computers (and earning a living wage) was greater than she could resist, so she began teaching end-user computing classes. In the process of training hundreds of people how to use Microsoft Access, she enjoyed consulting and developing enough to move into Access development full-time. She joined Apex Consulting Group of Northbrook, IL, as an analyst/developer of desktop database solutions for small businesses and corporate departments.

Stephen P. Loy is a senior consultant in client technology service for Whittman-Hart Inc., in Indianapolis, Indiana. He is currently working on his MCSE Certification.

About the Technical Editor

Bob Reinsch is an independent contractor, providing services as a Microsoft Certified Systems Engineer and Microsoft Certified Trainer. He has been working on personal computers and networks for almost 20 years, dating back to Commodore Pets with 16 KB of RAM. In his career, he has served as a network administrator on UNIX, Macintosh, Novell, and Windows NT networks. He has been working with Windows NT since 3.1 and has pursued certification since NT 3.5. He has been a trainer since 1994 and has worked with students from Boeing, Chase Manhattan Banks, John Hancock Companies, Cinergy, and the Department of Defense. He has taught classes from Portland, Oregon to Wiesbaden, Germany. Bob is husband to Dr. Lisa Friis, PhD, and father to Bonnie Reinsch, a beautiful baby girl who learned to whistle when she was eight months old.

Trademark Acknowledgments

All terms mentioned in this book that are known to be trademarks or service marks have been appropriately capitalized. New Riders Publishing cannot attest to the accuracy of this information. Use of a term in this book should not be regarded as affecting the validity of any trademark or service mark.

Dedications

From Emmett Dulaney
For Karen.

From Angela J. R. Jones
To Dan, for enabling me in my first step to Asimov.

From Stephen P. Loy
To my wife Angela, for her support, encouragement, and love.

Acknowledgments

I would like to thank Jack Belbot and Steve Weiss of Macmillan for keeping this project going, and Nancy Warner for keeping me on track.
—*Emmett Dulaney*

Many thanks to Karla Carter & Jim Scoltock—in different ways, you both gave me the opportunity to do this, mentored me as I learned, and rejoiced with me in my development. And a special thanks to Nancy Warner for her encouraging guidance, which helped the hours seem a little shorter.
—*Angela J. Reeves Jones*

Contents at a Glance

Table of Contents

Introduction

MCSD Training Guide: Microsoft Access is designed for advanced end-users and developers who are considering certification as a Microsoft Certified Solution Developer (MCSD). The Microsoft Access exam (Exam 70-69: "Microsoft Access for Windows 95 and the Microsoft Access Developer's Toolkit") tests your ability to design, develop, and implement solutions based on Microsoft Access for Windows 95. This will demonstrate to your customers and colleagues that you are fully qualified to design and develop superior custom solutions with Microsoft tools and technologies.

Who Should Read This Book

MCSD Training Guide: Microsoft Access is your one-stop shop. Everything you need to know to pass exam #70-69 is in this book, and it has been acknowledged by Microsoft as certified study material. You do not *need* to take a class in addition to buying this book to pass the exam. However, according to your personal study habits, you might benefit from taking a class in addition to buying the book, or buying this book as a supplement to a class.

This book also can help advanced users and administrators who are not studying for the MCSD exam but are looking for a single-volume reference on Microsoft Access for Windows 95 and the Microsoft Access Developer's Toolkit.

How This Book Helps You

This book takes you on a guided tour of all the areas covered by the MCSD "Microsoft Access for Windows 95 and the Microsoft Access Developer's Toolkit" exam and teaches you the specific skills you need to achieve your MCSD certification. You'll also find helpful hints, tips, real-world examples, exercises, and references to additional study materials. Specifically, this book is set up to provide you with the following assistance:

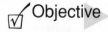

- ▶ **Organization.** This book is organized according to major exam topics (16 in all) and objectives. Every objective you need to know for the "Microsoft Access for Windows 95 and the Microsoft Access Developer's Toolkit" exam is covered in this book; we've included a margin icon like the one in the margin here to help you quickly locate these objectives in each chapter. There are references at different elements to direct you to the appropriate place in the book if you find you need to review certain sections.

- ▶ **Time-management guidance.** Pre-chapter quizzes are at the beginning of each chapter to test your knowledge of the objectives contained within that chapter. If you already know the answers to those questions, you can make a time-management decision accordingly.

- ▶ **Extensive practice test options.** Plenty of questions are placed at the end of each chapter to test your comprehension of material covered within that chapter. An answer list follows the questions so you can check your accuracy. These practice test options will help you decide what you already understand and what topics require extra review on your part.

You'll also get a chance to practice for the certification exams by using the test engine on the accompanying CD-ROM. The questions on the CD-ROM provide a more thorough and comprehensive look at what certification exams really are like. The CD-ROM includes the Microsoft Education and Certification Roadmap—a publication from Microsoft that provides a thorough outline of the certification process. The Roadmap Assessment Exam includes the best available examples of the kinds of questions you'll find on a certification exam. The Roadmap also includes the Planning Wizard, an online tool that helps you quickly map out a plan for achieving your certification goals.

 Note

> For a complete description of Macmillan's newly developed test engine, please see Appendix D, "All About TestPrep."
>
> For a complete description of what you can find on the CD-ROM, see Appendix C, "What's on the CD-ROM."

Most Roadmap Assessment Exams are based on specific product versions, and new elective exams are available on an ongoing basis. The Microsoft Education and Certification Roadmap is a quarterly publication. You can obtain updates of the Roadmap at any of the following locations:

Microsoft Education: Call (800) 636-7544

Internet: `ftp://ftp.microsoft.com/Services/MSEdCert`

World Wide Web: `http://www.microsoft.com/train_cert/default.htm`

CompuServe Forum: `GO MSEDCERT`

The enclosed CD-ROM also includes MCP Endeavor, an interactive practice test application (designed exclusively for Macmillan Publishing) that will help you prepare for the MCSD exams.

This book also can help you by serving as a desktop reference for information on Microsoft Access for Windows 95 and the Microsoft Access Developer's Toolkit.

Understanding What the Microsoft Access for Windows 95 and the Microsoft Access Developer's Toolkit Exam (#70-69) Covers

The "Microsoft Access for Windows 95 and the Microsoft Access Developer's Toolkit" certification exam goes beyond testing your knowledge of Microsoft Access Windows 95 and the Microsoft Access Developer's Toolkit. You should have a comprehensive understanding of application programming concepts and procedures, and be able to apply these skills to design, develop, and implement solutions based on Microsoft Access for Windows 95. Before taking the exam, you should be proficient in the job skills outlined in the following sections.

Working with Visual Basic for Applications

▶ Use Visual Basic for Applications loop statements.

▶ Given a scenario, use arithmetic, comparison, logical, concatenation, and pattern-matching operators.

▶ Create user-defined functions.

▶ Use common built-in functions.

▶ Declare variables in modules and procedures.

▶ Declare arrays, and initialize elements of arrays.

▶ Declare and use object variables and collections, and use their associated properties and methods.

▶ Declare symbolic constants, and make them available locally or publicly.

Database Design

▶ Apply basic concepts of normalization.

▶ Use the Cascade Update and Cascade Delete options.

Microsoft Access SQL

▶ Use Access SQL to write common queries.

▶ Refer to objects by using Access SQL.

▶ Use Union queries.

Programming with Objects

▶ Given a scenario, determine when to use Data Access objects.

▶ Differentiate between objects and collections.

▶ Write statements that access and modify database objects.

▶ Use Data Access objects and Microsoft Access objects.

▶ Select appropriate methods and property settings for use with specified objects.

Debugging and Error Handling

▶ Use the Errors collection and the Error object to trap errors.

▶ Use debugging tools to suspend program execution, and to examine, step through, and reset execution of code.

▶ Debug given code samples.

▶ Use the Debug window to monitor variable values.

▶ Write an error handler.

Working with Sets of Records

▶ Alter an Access SQL statement that is set for an existing QueryDef object.

▶ Implement transaction processing in a Workspace object.

▶ Use record locking.

▶ Identify the different Recordset object types.

▶ Differentiate between dynaset-type Recordset objects and snapshot-type Recordset objects.

▶ Manipulate data by using Recordset objects.

▶ Create Recordset objects.

▶ Write procedures that manipulate Recordset objects.

Working with Forms and Reports

▶ Choose which form-specific and report-specific properties to set.

▶ Choose which control properties to set.

▶ Assign event-handling procedures to controls in a form.

▶ Define and create form and report modules.

▶ Given sample code, identify the scope of a form or report module.

▶ Open multiple instances of a form, and refer to them.

▶ Use the Property Set and Property Let statements to assign values to form properties.

▶ Use form methods.

OLE Automation

▶ Control other applications by using OLE automation.

▶ Control Microsoft Access from other applications by using OLE automation.

Custom Controls

▶ Set properties for custom controls.

▶ Customize OLE controls.

Using Windows DLLs

▶ Properly declare Windows API functions.

▶ Use the ByVal and ByRef keywords.

Database Replication

▶ Use Visual Basic for Applications, Microsoft Access, Brief-case, or Replication Manager to make a database replicable.

▶ Use Replication Manager to view a synchronization schedule.

▶ Explain the purpose of the Replication ID.

▶ Explain how Replication Manager resolves synchronization conflicts.

▶ Identify the advantages of using replication for synchronization.

▶ Identify the changes that the Microsoft Jet Database Engine makes when it converts a nonreplicable database into a repli-cable database.

Implementing Database Security

▶ Analyze a scenario and recommend an appropriate type of security.

▶ Explain the steps for implementing security.

▶ Analyze code to ensure that it sets security options.

▶ Write code to implement security options.

Client/Server Application Development

▶ Given a scenario, decide whether to use SQL pass-through queries or Microsoft Access queries.

▶ Access external data by using ODBC.

▶ Trap errors that are generated by the server.

▶ Optimize connections.

▶ Optimize performance for a given client/server application.

Improving Database Performance

▶ Differentiate between single-field and multiple-field indexes.

▶ Optimize queries by using Rushmore technology.

▶ Restructure queries to allow faster execution.

▶ Optimize performance in distributed applications.

▶ Optimize performance for client/server applications.

Distributing an Application

▶ Prepare an application for distribution by using the Setup Wizard.

▶ Choose the best way to distribute a client/server application.

▶ Distribute OLE custom controls with an application.

▶ Provide online help in a Microsoft Access application.

Extending Microsoft Access

▶ Implement error handling in add-ins.

▶ Test and debug library databases.

▶ Describe the purpose of the USysRegInfo table.

Hardware and Software Needed

As a self-paced study guide, much of the book expects you to use Access for Windows 95 and follow along through the exercises while you learn. Microsoft designed Access for Windows 95 to operate in a wide range of actual situations, and the exercises in this book encompass that range.

Tips for the Exam

Remember the following tips as you prepare for the MCSD certification exams:

▶ **Read all the material.** Microsoft has been known to include material not specified in the objectives. This book has included additional information not required by the objectives in an effort to give you the best possible preparation for the examination, and for the real-world network experiences to come.

▶ **Complete the exercises in each chapter.** The exercise sections will help you gain experience using the Microsoft product. All Microsoft exams are experience-based and require you to have used the Microsoft product in a real networking environment. Exercises for each objective are placed toward the end of each chapter.

▶ **Complete all the questions in the "Review Questions" sections.** Complete the questions at the end of each chapter—they will help you remember key points. The questions are fairly simple, but be warned: some questions may have more than one answer.

▶ **Review the exam objectives in the Microsoft Education and Certification Roadmap.** Develop your own questions for each topic listed. If you can make and answer several questions for each topic, you should pass.

▶ **Complete the Roadmap Assessment Exam and visit the relevant topics in the MCP Endeavor application.** Do not make the mistake of trusting all the answers in the Assessment Exams—they're not always correct. Look at this not as a bug, but as a feature to test your knowledge; not only do you have to know you are right, you have to be sure about it, and you have to know why any one of the answers might be wrong.

Note

Although this book is designed to prepare you to take and pass the "Microsoft Access for Windows 95 and the Microsoft Access Developer's Toolkit" certification exam, there are no guarantees. Read this book, work through the exercises, and take the practice assessment exams.

When taking the real certification exam, make sure you answer all the questions before your time limit expires. Do not spend too much time on any one question. If you are unsure about an answer, answer the question as best you can and mark it for later review when you have finished all the questions. It has been said, whether correctly or not, that any questions left unanswered will automatically cause you to fail.

Remember, the object is not to pass the exam—it is to understand the material. Once you understand the material, passing the exam is simple. Knowledge is a pyramid: to build upward, you need a solid foundation. The Microsoft Certified System Developer program is designed to ensure that you have that solid foundation.

Good luck!

New Riders Publishing

The staff of New Riders Publishing is committed to bringing you the very best in computer reference material. Each New Riders book is the result of months of work by authors and staff who research and refine the information contained within its covers.

As part of this commitment to you, the NRP reader, New Riders invites your input. Please let us know if you enjoy this book, if you have trouble with the information or examples presented, or if you have a suggestion for the next edition.

Please note, however: New Riders staff cannot serve as a technical resource during your preparation for the Microsoft MCSD certification exams or for questions about software- or hardware-related problems. Please refer to the documentation that accompanies Microsoft Access for Windows 95 or to the applications' Help systems.

If you have a question or comment about any New Riders book, there are several ways to contact New Riders Publishing. We will respond to as many readers as we can. Your name, address, or phone number will never become part of a mailing list or be used for any purpose other than to help us continue to bring you the best books possible. You can write us at the following address:

New Riders Publishing
Attn: Publisher
201 W. 103rd Street
Indianapolis, IN 46290

If you prefer, you can fax New Riders Publishing at (317) 817-7448.

You also can send e-mail to New Riders at the following Internet address:

```
certification@mcp.com
```

NRP is an imprint of Macmillan Computer Publishing. To obtain a catalog or information, or to purchase any Macmillan Computer Publishing book, call (800) 428-5331.

Thank you for selecting *MCSD Training Guide: Microsoft Access*!

C h a p t e r

Working with Visual Basic for Applications

By the end of this chapter, you will be able to execute the following test objectives:

Objectives

- ▶ Use VBA loop statements

- ▶ Given a scenario, use arithmetic, comparison, concatenation, and pattern-matching operators

- ▶ Create user-defined functions

- ▶ Use common built-in functions

- ▶ Declare variables in modules and procedures

- ▶ Declare arrays and initialize elements of arrays

- ▶ Declare and use object variables and collections, and use their associated properties and methods

- ▶ Declare symbolic constants and make them available locally or publicly

Test Yourself! Before reading this chapter, test yourself to determine how much study time you will need to devote to this section.

1. Two people in the Sales Department have asked you, the computer expert, to settle a bet for them. They disagree about the highest order total in the company. Sam says that he had the highest order total ever, and it was $230,500. Michelle insists that she had a $250,000 order last year. Assuming that there is an OrderTotal field in your database, what function can you use to quickly determine that they are both wrong (the highest order total was actually $300,000)? If they also want to know who made that sale, what other function can you use to find out the SalesID?

2. The DateDue field in your Orders table needs to have a default value of 30 days after the BillDate. How would you write a function to calculate the DateDue? Where would you store the function so that users can access it from anywhere in the database?

3. In order to calculate TotalPrice, you must subtract Rebate from Price. However, Rebate is sometimes Null. How can you prevent TotalPrice from being Null, even if rebate is Null?

4. You need to declare a variable for Age. Age will always be calculated in years (whole numbers only), and it should be available only to the module basCalculations. How would you declare it, what name would you give it (use standard naming conventions), and what data type should it be?

5. An array Students() was declared and has 30 elements. You now need to add a 31st element, but you do not want to lose the original data. How can you accomplish this?

6. How can you determine how many TableDefs exist in your database?

7. You can never remember the value of Pi, and every time you need to use it in a calculation, you have to look it up. How can you avoid this problem?

Answers are located at the end of the chapter...

As you read this chapter, you learn about each Visual Basic for Applications (VBA) test objective described on the opening page. Access 7.0 and Access 97 now use Visual Basic for Applications (VBA) instead of Access Basic. Beginning with Office 97, all Office products use VBA. This means that you can use the same programming language in Access, Excel, Word, PowerPoint, and Project.

This chapter focuses on the basics of VBA: how and when it can be used, the syntax required, data types used, and so on. For the exam, be prepared to read code and predict the outcome. You should also be able to spot errors in code, whether due to incorrect syntax, the wrong data type, or incorrect keywords.

The exam tests your ability to read VBA code and determine the results. You must also be able to spot minor syntactical errors in code. You should be very familiar with variables, data types, and objects, and you should understand the scope and lifetime of variables. This section also covers your ability to work with collections (including DAO).

Storing Visual Basic Code in Modules

Before we go into detail about the specifics of Visual Basic for Applications, it is important that you understand where and how the code is written. The following sections discuss the different types of modules available in Visual Basic for Applications and the differences between them. Visual Basic for Applications code is stored in modules. In Access, there are three types of modules: standard modules, form modules, and report modules.

Standard modules are used to store subprocedures and user-defined functions, which are available to the entire application. Variables and constants that are stored in a public module are available to the entire application. They are also visible in the Object Browser.

Form and report modules contain all code to respond to events on the form or report (Event Procedures). In addition, Sub and Function procedures, which are related to the form or report, can be stored in the form or report module. Form and report modules are types of class modules.

Visual Basic for Applications code is written in units called *proce-dures*. A procedure contains a series of statements and methods that perform an operation or calculate a value. There are two types of procedures: sub and function.

Subprocedures are often written to respond to an event on a form or report. When the event occurs, the Event Procedure is triggered. A procedure cannot be nested within another procedure. However, you can call a procedure or a user-defined function within a procedure, and you can use a user-defined function in a procedure.

Using VBA Loop Statements

Loops are used to execute a block of code (or even a single line of code) more than once. There are four types of loops in VBA, each of which is used in different situations:

- ▶ Do...loop

- ▶ For Each...Next loop

- ▶ For...Next loop

- ▶ While...Wend loop

These loops, complete with examples, are described in the following sections.

Using Do... Loops

You use a Do...loop when you need to execute a block of code repeatedly until a certain condition is met. You do not need to know how many times the code executes.

A Do...loop uses a numeric or string expression that evaluates to either True or False. The statement continues to execute as long as the condition is True. If the condition is Null, it is treated as False, and the loop is exited. The condition can be tested at the beginning of the loop. If the condition evaluates to False, the code inside the loop never executes. Study the following example to see:

```
Do [{While ¦ Until} condition]
[statements]
[Exit Do]
[statements]
Loop
```

This example uses the Northwind database to evaluate whether "EOF" (end of file) is True. You often have to evaluate for EOF when using DAO in order to make sure you do not have to go beyond the end of the recordset. It loops through all the records in the Customers table until it reaches the end of the file. The data from the CompanyName field for each record is then printed in the debug window. See the following:

```
Dim db As DATABASE
Dim rs As Recordset

Set db = CurrentDb()
Set rs = db.OpenRecordset("Customers")

Do Until rs.EOF
Debug.Print rs![CompanyName]
rs.MoveNext
Loop
```

Alternately, the condition can be tested at the end of the code. This ensures that the statements will be executed at least once. This method uses the following syntax:

```
Do
[statements]
[Exit Do]
[statements]
Loop [{While } condition]
```

 Tip

> The While and Until commands can be used interchangeably. Use While if you want the statements executed while a condition is True. For example, Do While x < 10. Use Until if you want the statements to execute until a condition becomes True. For example, Do Until x >=10. Both statements produce the same results, so use whichever makes more sense to you.

Notice the use of the Exit Do command in the previous code snippet. Exit Do is used to immediately end a loop. There is no limit to the number of Exit Do statements you can use. When the Exit Do statement is executed, the code jumps to the statement immediately following the loop.

Several Do... loops can be nested within one another, resulting in *nested Do... loops*. When used within nested Do... loop statements, Exit Do causes the code to jump to the loop that is one nested level above the loop where it occurs.

Using For Each...Next Loops

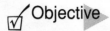 For Each...Next is a new loop structure (so it is quite likely that questions about it will be on the exam). You use the For Each...Next syntax when you want to execute a block of code for elements in an array or objects in a collection.

For Each...Next is faster and more efficient than the For...Next method. It is also much easier because you don't have to know how many objects are in your collection or array.

The syntax for For Each...Next loops is as follows:

```
For Each element In group
[statements]
[Exit For]
[statements]
Next [element]
```

The following code loops through each control on a form (frm-Loops). If the control is a label, it changes the font size to 14-pt.

```
Sub ChangeLabels()
    Dim ctl As Control
    Dim frm As Form
    Set frm = Forms!frmLoops

    For Each ctl In frm
        If ctl.ControlType = acLabel Then
            ctl.FontSize = 14
```

```
        End If
     Next ctl
End Sub
```

A variable is used to move through the elements of the collection or array. The element must be variant or an object variable; it cannot be a user-defined type. Typical elements in a group might be Controls, Forms, or Records.

The Group is the name of an object group or an array. The array cannot be a user-defined array because a variant cannot contain a user-defined type. Typical groups might be Recordset, Database, Forms, and so on.

Exit For provides an alternate way of exiting the loop. There is no limit to the number of Exit For statements that you can use in a loop. However, it can be used only in a For...Next or For Each...Next loop. Exit For transfers control to the statement following the Next statement. When used within nested For loops, Exit For transfers control to the loop that is one nested level above the loop where it occurs.

If you omit the counter in a Next statement, execution continues as if you had included it. However, if a Next statement appears before its corresponding For statement, an error occurs.

Using For...Next Loops

The For...Next loop repeats a group of statements a specified number of times. You must know how many times the code is to execute, and you supply a start value and an end value. If you do not want to increment the value by one (the default), you may specify a step increment. The step increment can be negative or positive, and it does not have to be a whole number.

The syntax for For...Next loops is as follows:

```
For counter = start To end [Step step]
[statements]
[Exit For]
```

```
[statements]
Next [counter]
```

Study the following example:

```
For X = 1 to 10
    X = X + 1
    Debug.Print X
Next X
```

The loop executes ten times. Once the loop starts and all statements in the loop have executed, one step is added to the counter. This causes X to increase by 1 (the default). At this point, either the statements in the loop execute again, or the loop is exited, depending on the value of X. Execution continues with the statement following the Next statement. For the exam, make sure that you can determine the value of a counter at any given point during code execution.

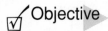 **Objective** Exit For is used in the same way as Exit Do. This statement provides a way to exit a For... loop. It can be used only in a For...Next or For Each...Next loop. Exit For transfers control to the statement following the Next statement. When used within nested For loops, Exit For transfers control to the loop that is one nested level above the loop where it occurs.

If you omit the counter in a Next statement, execution continues as if you had included it. If a Next statement appears before its corresponding For statement, an error occurs.

Using While...Wend Loops

The While...Wend loop executes a series of statements as long as a given condition is True. While...Wend is very similar to a Do loop, but it is slightly less flexible and less easy to read. A Do loop is usually preferred.

The syntax for While...Wend loops is as follows:

```
While condition
[statements]
Wend
```

Just like in the Do structure, if the condition in a While...Wend structure is Null, it is treated as False.

Comparing Loops

The Do... loop is the most efficient structure to use if you want statements to execute until (or while) a condition is True. The For Each...Next method is the most efficient way to move through the items in a collection or an array. In loops, if a condition is Null, it is treated as if it is False. For the exam, you must be able to recognize the syntax (keywords) of each structure. Also, you should be able to read loop structures and evaluate the value of variables used within the structures.

 Warning

Always test your code for endless loops. Make sure that the user always has some way to exit your code. If you have inadvertently created an endless loop, press Control + Break to halt execution, so that you can fix your code.

Understanding User-Defined Functions

User-defined functions are created as a procedure in a module. They are usually created in order to reuse a complex calculation. To avoid having to recreate the calculation every time you need it, you simply create the calculation in a function and then call the function, which supplies the required arguments. Every function returns a value. If the function is declared using the Public keyword, you can use it anywhere in your application in the same way you use a built-in function.

The syntax of a function is similar to an event procedure. However, you must use the keywords Function and End Function instead of Sub and End Sub.

The syntax for user-defined functions is as follows:

```
[Public ¦ Private] [Static] Function name [(arglist)] [As type]
    [statements]
    [name = expression]
```

```
     [Exit Function]
     [statements]
     [name = expression]
End Function
```

The following list outlines the arguments for user-defined functions:

Public. This determines the scope of the function. The Public keyword causes the procedure to be accessible to all other procedures in all modules. Functions are public by default.

Private. This determines the scope of the function. The Private keyword causes the Function procedure to be accessible only to other procedures in the module where it is declared.

Static. This argument determines the lifetime of the function. When the keyword Static is used to declare a function, it indicates that the Function procedure's local variables are preserved between calls. This only affects the local variables (which are declared within the function). Variables that are declared elsewhere in the application but are used within the function do not maintain their values.

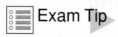 Exam Tip ▶

Watch out for this on the test. If Static is not used, the variables used in the function have no value when the function is not running.

Type. This is the data type of the value returned by the Function procedure. Type cannot be an array or a fixed-length string. However, it can be a variant that contains an array. It might be Byte, Boolean, Integer, Long, Currency, Single, Double, Date, String (except fixed-length), Object, Variant, or any user-defined type.

Arglist. This is a list of variables representing arguments that are passed to the Function procedure when it is called. Multiple variables are separated by commas.

Expression. The return value of the function.

The arglist has the following syntax:

```
[Optional][ByVal ¦ ByRef][ParamArray] varname[( )][As type]
```

The following are the arguments that make up the arglist argument:

Optional. Indicates that an argument is not required. If it is used, all subsequent arguments in arglist also must be optional and must be declared using the Optional keyword. Optional can't be used for any argument if ParamArray is used. All Optional arguments must be Variant.

ByVal. Indicates that the argument is passed by value. (Arguments passed by value cannot be changed by the function.)

ByRef. Indicates that the argument is passed by reference. This means that a pointer to argument is passed instead of a copy of the argument. When an argument is passed ByRef, its value can be changed.

ParamArray. Used only as the last argument in arglist, this indicates that the final argument is an Optional array of Variant elements. The ParamArray keyword enables you to provide an arbitrary number of arguments. It cannot be used with ByVal, ByRef, or Optional.

Type. Indicates the data type of the argument passed to the procedure; it might be Byte, Boolean, Integer, Long, Currency, Single, Double, Date, String (variable-length only), Object, Variant, a user-defined type, or an object type.

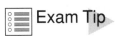 Exam Tip

The Optional keyword does not have to be used with the last argument. However, if it is used, all arguments that follow are optional. Optional cannot be used with ParamArray. Be aware of this for the exam. ParamArray *must* be the last argument used and it *cannot* be used with By Value, By Reference, or Optional. ParamArray must be a variant. Function procedures are Public by default. You can't define a Function procedure inside another Function, Sub, or Property procedure.

Exit Function Statement

You can use an unlimited number of Exit Function statements anywhere in a Function procedure. The Exit Function keywords cause an immediate exit from a Function procedure. Program execution continues with the statement following the statement that called the Function procedure.

After the function has been declared in a module, you can call it as you would a built-in function (by using the function name, followed by the argument list in parentheses) in an expression. It can appear on the left side of an expression. It also appears in the expression builder.

Return Values of Functions

If no value is assigned to the function name, the procedure returns the default value for the data type.

 Note

If your procedure refers to an undeclared variable that has the same name as another procedure (constant or variable), it is assumed that your procedure is referring to that module-level name. You must explicitly declare variables to avoid this kind of conflict. You can use an Option Explicit statement to force explicit declaration of variables.

Understanding Comparison, Logical, Concatenation, and Pattern-Matching Operators

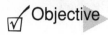 Objective

String operators are used to compare strings and numeric variables. Concatenation operators are used to join two strings together. Pattern-matching operators are used to search for data that matches a specific pattern. This section covers the use and syntax of each operator and provides an example of each. For the exam, you should be able to use each operator correctly and determine the result of an expression that uses one of these operators.

Comparison Operators

There are two types of comparison operators: string and numeric. *String* comparisons should be used only with string expressions. *Numeric* operators can be used to compare strings if the string can be converted to a number.

String Comparison Operators

Is and Like are used to compare strings. The expression evaluates to True or False.

The syntax for string comparison operators is as follows:

```
result = object1 Is object2
result = string Like pattern
```

The following is a list of the arguments for string comparison operator expressions:

Result. Any numeric variable

Expression. Any expression

Object. Any valid object name

String. Any string expression

Pattern. Any string expression or range of characters

You use Is when you are searching for an exact match. You use Like when you are searching for a pattern. For example, the following expression will find any records that contain the string "Smith" in the LastName field:

```
[LastName] Is "Smith"
```

On the other hand, the following expression will find "Smith," "Smuthers," and "Smiley":

```
[LastName] Like "Sm"*
```

Numeric Comparison Operators

You can use numeric comparison operators to compare two numeric expressions or to compare a numeric expression to a string expression that can be converted to a numeric value. If the string can be converted to a number, Visual Basic automatically converts the string. If you use a numeric comparison operator on a string that cannot be converted to a value, a Type-Mismatch error occurs. Table 1.1 lists the numeric comparison operators.

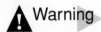 Warning

> Be careful when comparing two numbers of different data types. If a Currency is compared with a Single or Double, the Single or Double is converted to a Currency. This causes you to lose any fractional part of the Single or Double value less than 0.0001, and it *may cause two values to compare as equal when they are not.* When a Single is compared to a Double, the Double is rounded to the precision of the Single.

Table 1.1

Numeric Comparison Operators

Operator	Description
<	Less than
<=	Less than or equal to
>	Greater than
>=	Greater than or equal to
=	Equal to
<>	Not equal to

Logical Operators

The following logical operators are used to perform logic on two operators. For the exam, make sure you understand what caused each one to evaluate to True or False. You should be able to read code that uses a logical operator and determine whether it is True or False.

And

```
Result = expression1 And expression2
```

The result is True if and only if both parts are True. If either expression is Null, the result is Null.

If you are using And as part of the search criteria, Visual Basic will find only those records that meet *both* criteria. For example, the following will find only people who live in Chicago and are 23 years old:

```
[City] = "Chicago" AND [Age] = 23
```

Eqv

```
result = expression1 Eqv expression2
```

The result is True if both expressions are True or if both expressions are False.

Imp

```
result = expression1 Imp expression2
```

The result evaluates two values and returns a True value *unless* the first operand is True and the other is False. All other combinations result in False.

Not

```
result = Not expression
```

If the expression is True, the result evaluates to False. If the expression is False, the expression evaluates to True.

Not is often used to exclude criteria. For example, if you are searching for all customers except those in Cleveland, you can enter this criteria for the City field:

```
NOT "Cleveland"
```

Or

```
result = expression1 Or expression2
```

The result is True if either or both of the expressions are True.

Xor

```
result = expression1 Xor expression2
```

The result is True if one and only one of the expressions is True.

Concatenation Operators

Concatenation operators are used to join two strings together. For example, if First Name and Last Name are stored in two separate files, you can use the & operator to create a field that joins the data together. Although the + operator can be used as a concatenation operator, the & operator is preferred. For the exam, you must be able to evaluate an expression that uses a concatenation operator and determine its result.

The & Operator

The & operator joins two string expressions. You can use it with literal strings or with data in a variant or field. If one expression is Null, that expression is treated as a zero-length string. However, if both expressions are Null, the result is Null. An expression that is Empty is also treated as a zero-length string.

When joining two strings with the & operator, don't forget to include a space in quotation marks between the strings. For example, [FirstName]&[LastName] will produce "JoeSchmo." If you want a space between the names in the result, you use [FirstName] & " " & [LastName], which produces "Joe Schmo."

The + Operator

The + operator is used to sum two numbers. Although you can also use the + operator to concatenate two character strings, you should use the & operator for concatenation. When you use the

+ operator, you may not be able to determine whether addition or string concatenation will occur. For example, if one expression is a string and the other is a number, the + will concatenate, as shown here:

```
Dim strVariable as string
Dim intNumber as integer
strVariable = "First"
intNumber=1
X= strVariable + intNumber
X will equal First1.
```

Built-In Functions

Access has several hundred built-in functions. This section discusses some of the common functions (the ones that are most likely to show up on an exam). You should be familiar with how they work, what they are used for, the arguments they take (and the data types of those arguments), and the data types they return.

Domain Aggregate Functions

Aggregate functions are used to calculate statistical information about sets of records. Most domain aggregate functions have a standard counterpart (Dcount and Count, Davg and Avg, and so on). If you are performing statistical calculations from within a macro or module in Access, you must use the domain aggregate functions instead of their standard counterparts.

The good thing about these functions is that all domain aggregate functions have the same syntax. Therefore, after you learn the following syntax, you have basically learned how to use ten functions:

```
DFunction(expr, domain[, criteria])
```

 Objective

Here's a breakdown of the syntax:

> *Expr.* This is the field on which you want to perform the function. It can be the name of the field itself or a string expression identifying a field in a table or query in the database.

This expression can include the name of a table field, a control on a form, a constant, or a function. However, if it includes a function, that function *cannot* be another domain aggregate function. It can, however, be either a built-in or a user-defined function. Because this is a string expression, it must be enclosed in quotation marks.

Domain. This is the name of the table or query that contains the records on which you want to perform the domain aggregate function. Because this is a string expression, it must be enclosed in quotation marks.

Criteria. This argument is optional. It is used to restrict the range of data on which the domain aggregate function is performed. This is often equivalent to the WHERE clause in an SQL expression (but you do not use WHERE). If no criteria is supplied, the domain aggregate function is evaluated against all the records in the domain. If any field in the criteria is not in the domain, the function returns Null. Because this is a string expression, it must be enclosed in quotation marks. In addition, if a string is used within the criteria, that string must be enclosed in single quotation marks. Note that this is quite likely to be on the exam. See the following section for more information.

Using Quotation Marks in Domain Aggregate Functions

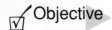 Objective

Each argument in a domain aggregate function must be enclosed in quotation marks. This is because Access must pass the string to the Microsoft Jet Database Engine. Before passing the criteria to the Jet Database Engine, Microsoft Access must evaluate any variables, concatenate them into a string, and then pass the entire criteria string to the Jet Database Engine.

If you embed a numeric variable, Microsoft Access evaluates the variable and simply concatenates the value into the string. However, if the variable is a text string, the resulting criteria string contains a string within a string. A string within a string must be identified by string delimiters (single quotation marks). If it's not, the Jet Database Engine won't be able to determine which part of the string is the value you want the string to use.

In other words, Jet needs to see the string in a format as follows:

```
"[FirstName] = 'Mary'"
```

In order to accomplish this, if the data for FirstName is contained in a variable (strName), you must make sure that there are single quotation marks around the string variable, as follows:

```
"[Last Name] = '" & strName & "'"
```

If this seems confusing, remember that the entire expression must be enclosed in quotation marks, and any string variables must be enclosed in single quotation marks. When trying to decipher criteria on the exam, it usually helps to try to "translate" the expression the way that Jet would. Evaluate the expression, and then concatenate the strings together. Make sure the result is acceptable to Jet.

Variables that contain numeric data do not need to be enclosed within quotation marks.

These rules also cover criteria in Find methods and SQL strings. Make sure that you are very familiar with them when you take the exam.

DAvg

Used to calculate the average of a set of values.

Records containing Null values are not included in the calculation of the average.

 Tip

> Although you can use either DAvg or Avg in a calculated field in a totals query, the results are very different. If you use DAvg, values are averaged before the data is grouped. If you use Avg, the data is grouped before values in the field expression are averaged.

For example, the following expression calculates the AvgPrice of items in the Inventory table:

```
AvgPrice = Davg ("[Price]","[Inventory]")
```

DCount

DCount is used to count the number of records returned.

 Tip

> Use Count, instead of DCount, in a query expression. The Count function has been optimized to speed counting of records in queries. You can set optional criteria to enforce any restrictions on the results. Use DCount when you must count records in a domain from within a code module or macro or in a calculated control.

The DCount function doesn't count records that contain Null values in the field referenced by expr, unless expr is the asterisk (*) wildcard character. If you include the wildcard character, DCount returns the total number of records, including those that contain Null:

```
DAvg(expr, domain[, criteria])
```

The following example counts the number of items in the inventory table that are more expensive than the AvgPrice (AvgPrice was calculated in the previous example):

```
X= DCount("[Price]", "Inventory","[Price] > AvgPrice"
```

DMin and DMax

These functions determine the minimum and maximum values in a specified set of records:

```
DMin(expr, domain[, criteria])
DMax(expr, domain[, criteria])
```

For example, if you want to locate the most- and least-expensive items in your inventory, you can use the DMax function as shown here:

```
MostExp = Dmax ("[Price]","[Inventory]")
LeastExp=Dmin ("[Price]","[Inventory]")
```

You can use DMin and DMax or Min and Max in a calculated field expression of a totals query. If you use DMin or DMax, values are evaluated before the data is grouped. If you use Min or Max, the data is grouped before values in the field expression are evaluated.

DLookup

DLookup is normally used to obtain the data from a field, which is not in the recordset. For example, suppose you have a report based on the Orders Table. The Orders Table contains a field called CustomerID, but you want to display the Customer's Name—which is stored in the Customers Table. You can use DLookup to find the customer's name based on the CustomerID.

 Tip

> Make sure that you supply criteria. If you don't supply a value for criteria, DLookup returns a random value in the domain.

If more than one field meets the criteria, DLookup returns the first occurrence.

 Tip

> Of course, all this is much easier (and much more efficient) if you simply base the report on a query of both tables. But that won't help you when you're asked about it on the exam.

Conversion Functions

Conversion functions are used to convert variables from one data type to another. Be careful when converting from a large data type to a smaller data type.

You can use data type conversion functions to prevent an operation from returning its default data type.

Each of the data type conversion functions uses the same syntax:

```
CFunction(expression)
```

An error occurs if the expression is outside of the range of the data type. For example, the following expression generates an error because a byte must be between 0 and 255:

```
Cbyte (-2 * 350)
```

Commonly Used Numeric Conversion Functions

Cbyte

CDbl

CCur

CInt

CLng

CInt differs from the Fix and Int functions, which truncate—rather than round—the fractional part of a number. When the fractional part is exactly 0.5, the CInt function always rounds it to the nearest even number. For example, 0.5 rounds to 0, and 1.5 rounds to 2.

CBool

This function converts any valid numeric or string expression to a Boolean value (True or False).

If an expression is 0, False is returned; otherwise, True is returned. If an expression can't be interpreted as a numeric value, a runtime error occurs.

CDate

Before using the CDate function, you should use the IsDate function (see the next section, "Date Functions") to determine whether the value can be converted to a date. CDate recognizes date formats according to the locale setting of your system. The correct order of day, month, and year may not be determined if it is provided in a format other than one of the recognized date settings. In addition, a long date format is not recognized if it also contains the day-of-the-week string.

Date Functions

This section lists some of the more commonly used date functions. Each date function manipulates data stored in a date field in some way. Many date functions extract a part of a date from a date field.

DatePart

DatePart returns a specific part of a date field. For example, if you need to return only the month from a date field that contains a complete date, you can use DatePart.

The syntax for DatePart is as follows:

```
DatePart(interval, date[, firstdayofweek[, firstweekofyear]])
```

The following is a list of the arguments for the DatePart function:

Interval. A string expression that represents the interval of time you want returned, such as hour, day, week, or month. See table 1.2 for valid settings.

Date. The date that you want to evaluate. This is normally the name of a date field in your recordset.

FirstDayofWeek. A constant that specifies the first day of the week. See table 1.3 for valid settings. This argument is optional. If FirstDayofWeek is not specified, Sunday is assumed. This argument affects only calculations that use the "w" and "ww" interval symbols.

FirstWeekofYear. A constant that specifies the first week of the year. If FirstWeekofYear is not specified, the first week is assumed to be the week of January 1st. See table 1.4 for valid settings.

Table 1.2

Intervals	
Setting	Description
Yyyy	Year
q	Quarter
m	Month
y	Day of year
D	Day
w	Weekday
ww	Week
h	Hour
n	Minute
s	Second

Table 1.3

FirstDayofWeek		
Constant	Value	Description
VbUseSystem	0	Use application setting if one exists; otherwise use NLS API setting
VbSunday	1	Sunday (default)
VbMonday	2	Monday
VbTuesday	3	Tuesday
VbWednesday	4	Wednesday
VbThursday	5	Thursday
VbFriday	6	Friday
VbSaturday	7	Saturday

Table 1.4

FirstDayofYear

Constant	Value	Description
VbUseSystem	0	Use application setting if one exists; otherwise use NLS API setting.
VbFirstJan1	1	Start with week in which January 1 occurs (default).
VbFirstFourDays	2	Start with the first week that has at least four days in the new year.
VbFirstFullWeek	3	Start with first full week of the year.

Writing Code for Multiple Years

If a date is enclosed by pound signs (as in #01/01/97#), the year becomes a permanent part of that date. However, if a date is enclosed in double quotation marks ("") and you omit the year ("01/01/"), the current year is inserted in your code each time the date expression is evaluated. This makes it possible to write code that can be used in different years.

The IsDate function determines whether or not a value can be converted to a date (see the earlier section, "CDate"). IsDate returns a Boolean value. If the value can be converted to a date, IsDate returns True. If it cannot be converted to a date, IsDate returns False. Here's an example:

```
IsDate(expression)
```

The expression argument can be any date or string expression that's recognizable as a date or time.

String Functions

The following functions enable you to manipulate strings. For the exam, you need to know the correct syntax for each string function and be able to determine the result of an expression that uses a string function.

Left, Right, and Mid

These functions return a specified number of characters from the left, right, or middle of a string. The syntax for the Left, Right, and Mid functions are as follows:

```
Left(string, length)
Right(string, length)
Mid(string, start[, length])
```

The following are the arguments for the Left, Right, and Mid functions:

> *String.* String expression from which the leftmost characters are returned. If string contains Null, Null is returned.

> *Start.* Use for Mid only. Character position in string at which the part to be taken begins. If Start is greater than the number of characters in string, Mid returns a zero-length string.

> *Length.* Numeric expression indicating how many characters to return. If the value is 0, a zero-length string is returned. If the value is greater than or equal to the number of characters in the string, the entire string is returned.

For example, imagine that you currently use an inventory code (Part-Num), which identifies a product first by its three-digit category code and then by its product number. In order to divide this information into two fields, you can use the Left function in this way:

```
Category=Left(PartNum,3)
```

This code returns the first three digits of the PartNum field. That data is then assigned to the Category variable.

These three functions are often used to split a Name field into three parts: First, Middle, and Last. For example, in order to extract "John" from a name field that contains "John P. Doe," you can use the following code:

```
FirstName: Left([Names],InStr(1,[Names]," ")-1)
```

The code you use to extract the "P." from "John P. Doe" gets a bit more complex (see the next section, "InStr," for more information):

```
MidName: Mid([Names],InStr(1,[Names],
➨"")+1,InStr(InStr(1,[Names]," ")+1,[Names]," ")-InStr(1,[Names],
➨""))
```

Finally, to extract "Doe" from "John P. Doe," you use this code:

```
Expr: Right(Trim([Names]),Len(Trim([Names]))-
➨InStr(InStr(1,[Names]," ")+1,[Names]," "))
```

InStr

This function returns the position of the first occurrence of one string within another. The syntax for the InStr function is as fol-. lows:

```
InStr([start, ]string1, string2[, compare])
```

The following are the arguments in the InStr function:

Start. Numeric expression that sets the starting position for each search. If Start is omitted, the search begins at the first character position. If Start contains Null, an error occurs. The Start argument is required if Compare is specified.

String1. String expression being searched.

String2. String expression sought.

Compare. Specifies the type of string comparison.

The Compare argument can be omitted, it can be 0 or 1, or it can be the value of the CollatingOrder property of a Field object. Specify 0 (default) to perform a binary comparison. Specify 1 to perform a textual, case-insensitive comparison. Specify the return value of the CollatingOrder property of a Field object if you want to sort or compare values from a database in the same way the database itself would. If Compare is Null, an error occurs. The Start argument is required if you specify Compare. If you omit Compare, the Option Compare setting determines the type of comparison.

Trim

Trim returns a copy of a string without leading spaces (LTrim), without trailing spaces (RTrim), or without either leading or trailing spaces (Trim).

The syntax for the Trim function is as follows:

```
LTrim(string)
RTrim(string)
Trim(string)
```

The string argument is any valid string expression. If string contains Null, Null is returned.

LCase and UCase

These functions are used to convert a string to lowercase and uppercase, respectively. The syntax for the LCase and UCase functions are:

```
LCase(string)
UCase(string)
```

The string argument is any valid string expression. If string contains Null, Null is returned.

Determining If Data Has Value

You can use the functions described in this section to determine if the data is Null, Empty, or missing. Remember Null and Empty have distinctly different meanings in VBA. For the exam, you must know the difference between these values and be able to determine when each value is assigned.

Null. No valid data.

Empty. No beginning value has been assigned to a variant variable.

IsNull

IsNull returns a Boolean value that indicates whether an expression contains no valid data (Null). The syntax for the IsNull function is as follows:

```
IsNull(expression)
```

The expression argument can be any numeric or string expression. If the expression is Null, IsNull returns True; if the expression is not Null, it returns False. If the expression contains more than one variable, IsNull evaluates to False if any one of the elements is Null.

IsEmpty

IsEmpty returns a Boolean value indicating whether a variable has been initialized. The syntax for the IsEmpty function is as follows:

```
IsEmpty(expression)
```

The expression argument can be any numeric or string expression (normally a variable name).

IsEmpty returns True if the variable is uninitialized or is explicitly set to Empty; otherwise, it returns False. False is always returned if the expression contains more than one variable.

IsMissing

IsMissing returns a Boolean value indicating whether an optional argument has been passed to a procedure. IsMissing returns True if no value has been passed for the specified argument; otherwise, it returns False. If IsMissing is used on a ParamArray argument, the function always returns False.

The syntax for the IsMissing function is as follows:

```
IsMissing(argname)
```

The argname argument can be the name of any optional procedure argument.

Miscellaneous Functions

The following functions are used often in VBA code and might appear on the exam.

Iif

This function is known as the "immediate if." It evaluates an expression. If the expression is True, Iif returns the truepart; if the expression is False, it returns the falsepart.

The syntax for the Iif function is as follows:

```
Iif(expr, truepart, falsepart)
```

The following are the arguments for the Iif function:

> *Expr.* Expression you want to evaluate
>
> *TruePart.* Value or expression returned if expr is True
>
> *FalsePart.* Value or expression returned if expr is False

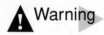 **Warning**

Iif always evaluates both truepart and falsepart, even though it returns only one of them. Because of this, you should watch for undesirable side effects. For example, if you're evaluating falsepart results in a Division by Zero error, an error occurs even if expr is True.

Iif is often used in conjunction with IsNull to convert Null expressions to 0 so that they can be used in a calculation. (Any calculation that contains a Null value results in Null.)

The following expression evaluates the Discount field. If Discount is Null, the expression assigns a value of 0 to DiscountValue. If it is not Null, the expression assigns the value of Discount to DiscountValue. This example illustrates the combination of the Iif function and the IsNull function:

```
DiscountValue= IIf ( IsNull ( [Discount] ) , 0, [Discount] )
```

This expression checks to make sure that Discount is not Null. If Discount is Null, the expression changes the value to 0; if it is not Null, the expression does not change the value of Discount. After you use this code, you can use DiscountValue in an expression, and you don't have to worry about a Null value. (Remember, a Null value anywhere in an expression causes the expression to evaluate to Null.)

Chr

This function returns the character associated with the specified character code. The syntax for the Chr function is as follows:

```
Chr(charcode)
```

For example, the following code results in the Return character:

```
Chr(13)
```

See the topic "Character Set" in the Help system for a complete list of characters.

LBound and UBound

These functions are used to determine the lower and upper bounds of an array. The syntax for the LBound and UBound functions are:

```
UBound(arrayname[, dimension])
LBound(arrayname[, dimension])
```

The following is a list of the arguments for the LBound and UBound functions:

> *ArrayName.* Name of the array variable; follows standard variable-naming conventions.

Dimension. A whole number indicating which dimension's upper bound is returned. Use 1 for the first dimension, 2 for the second, and so on. If Dimension is omitted, 1 is assumed.

For example, the following array has three dimensions:

```
MyArray(1 to 10, 3 to 5,4)
```

To determine the upper bound of the second dimension, you use this function:

```
Upper=Ubound(MyArray,2)
```

The variable Upper now has a value of 5, which is the upper bound of the second dimension of MyArray.

VarType

This function determines the way in which Access is storing the data in a variant. The syntax for the VarType function is as follows:

```
VarType(varname)
```

Varname cannot be a user-defined type. Any other data type is acceptable.

Declaring Variables in Modules and Procedures

Variables are declared in order to allocate space in memory for the data that the variable holds. Variables are either declared in the declarations section of a module (Module-level variables) or within a procedure (Procedure-level variables). Module-level variables are declared using either Dim or Public. Procedure-level variables are declared using Dim or Static (see the following).

This is the syntax you use for declaring variables:

```
Dim ¦ Public VariableName as DataType
```

When several variables are declared, they can be placed on the same line (separated by commas) with one Dim statement. Alternately, they can each have their own line and Dim statement. However, if they are declared on the same line, make sure that each variable has its own data type. For example, the following line declares sName and sCity as variants and sCountry as a string:

```
Dim sName, sCity, sCountry as String
```

To declare them each as a string, the statement should read like this:

```
Dim sName as String, sCity as String, sCountry as String
```

Or it can read as three lines, as shown here:

```
Dim sName as String
```

```
Dim sCity as String
```

```
Dim sCountry as String
```

Naming Variables

When choosing names for variables and constants, you must adhere to the following guidelines.

- ▶ Names must begin with a letter.
- ▶ Names can include letters, numbers, or underscore characters (_).
- ▶ You cannot include punctuation characters or spaces.
- ▶ Visual Basic keywords are forbidden.

Naming Standards

In addition to the rules listed previously, you should also be familiar with the *Hungarian* programming standards for objects and variables. This requires attaching a standard prefix to the name of the object or variable. The prefix identifies the data type of a variable and the object type of an object. Table 1.5 represents the naming conventions for variables and for some commonly used objects.

Table 1.5

Standard Naming Prefixes (Data Types)

Prefix	Data Type	Prefix	Data Type
byt	Byte	cur	Currency
f	Boolean	dat	Date
int	Integer	obj	Object
lng	Long	str	String
sng	Single	stf	String (fixed-length)
dbl	Double	var	Variant
app	Application	bas	Module
chk	Check Box	opt	OptionButton
cbo	Combo Box	fra	OptionGroup (frame)
cmd	Command Button	ole	ObjectFrame
dcm	DoCmd	rpt	Report
frm	Form	sfrm	SubForm
img	Image	srp	SubReport
Lbl	Label	txt	Text Box
Lst	List Box	tgl	Toggle Button

Explicit versus Implicit Declaration

If you use a variable that has not been declared, Access initializes the variable to a variant. This is known as implicit declaration. Variants are initialized with the value Empty the first time they are used.

To prevent implicit declaration of a variable, type the words **Option Explicit** at the top of the module. This requires that all variables in that module must be explicitly declared before use. Not only does this prevent you from forgetting to declare a variable, it also prevents spelling errors.

If you always want to use Option Explicit, you can check Require Variable Declaration in the Options dialog box (available via the Tools, Options command). This automatically places Option Explicit at the top of every module. It may take a little getting used to, but explicitly declaring variables is worth the effort.

Scope and Lifetime of Variables

The time during which a variable retains its value is known as its lifetime. Although the value of a variable usually changes during its lifetime, it always maintains value. When a variable goes out of scope, it no longer has a value.

When a procedure begins running, Microsoft Access initializes all variables that have been declared explicitly. Table 1.6 shows the initial value for each data type.

Table 1.6

Default Value of Data Type	
Data Type	Initial Value
Numeric	0
Variable-length string	""
Fixed-length string	00000 (Filled with)s)
Variant	Empty

Procedure-Level Variables

Procedure-level variables are variables that are declared within a procedure and are available only within that procedure. Procedure-level variables are declared using Dim or Static (see the section, "Using the Static Keyword to Retain the Value of a Variant," for more information about Static). A procedure-level variable cannot be declared with Public. A procedure-level variable declared with the Dim statement goes out of scope (has no value) when the procedure ends.

After it's initialized, a procedure-level variable remains in scope (retains its value) while the procedure runs. In addition, if the procedure calls other procedures, the variable remains in scope while those procedures are running as well. For the exam, make sure that you understand how long a variable retains its value.

Module-Level Variables

Module-level variables are declared in the declarations section of a module. The default scope for a module-level variable is Private. If the variable is declared using Dim, it is private (that is, available only to other procedures within that module). You can also declare the variable with the keyword Public. Variables declared in the declarations section of a module with Public are available anywhere in the application. Module-level variables retain their values until they are reset or until the database is closed.

Referencing from Another Database

Variables declared with the keyword Public are available to referencing databases, but they aren't available in the Object Browser. Public variables defined in a form module or report module are never visible outside the current database.

 Tip

> When you declare a variable, you are reserving space in memory for that variable. The data type determines how much space is allocated. If you do not specify a data type, the data type Variant is used.

VBA Data Types

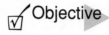 **Objective**

Table 1.7 lists the data types available in Visual Basic for Applications. It is very important that you know the size and range of each data type for the exam. Given a scenario, you must be able to recognize the best data type for the situation.

Table 1.7

Visual Basic Data Types

Data Type	Symbol	Storage Size	Range
Byte	None	1 byte	0 to 255
Boolean	None	2 bytes	True or False
Integer	%	2 bytes	–32,768 to 32,767
Long (long integer)	&	4 bytes	–2,147,483,648 to 2,147,483,647
Single (single-precision floating-point)	!	4 bytes	–3.402823E38 to –1.401298E–45 for negative values; 1.401298E–45 to 3.402823E38 for positive values
Double (double-precision floating-point)	#	8 bytes	–4.94065645841247E–324 for negative values; 4.94065645841247E–324 to 1.79769313486232E308 for positive values
Currency (scaled integer)	@	8 bytes	-922,337,203,685,477.5808 to 922,337,203,685,477.5807
Date	None	8 bytes	January 1, 100 to December 31, 9999
Object	None	4 bytes	Any Object reference
String (variable-length)	$	10 bytes + string length	0 to approximately 2 billion (approximately 65,400 for Microsoft Windows version 3.1 and earlier)
String (fixed-length)	None	Length of string	1 to approximately 65,400
Variant (with numbers)	None	16 bytes	Any numeric value up to the range of a Double
Variant (with characters)	None	22 bytes + string length	Same range as for variable-length string
User-defined (using Type)	None	Number required by elements	The range of each element is the same as the range of its data type

The Declaration Type characters in the preceding table can be used instead of the *as data type* statement.

Dim Name$ is the equivalent of Dim Name as String.

Variants

Variants are the most inefficient data types because they are large and slow. Using variants is slower than using other data types because Access has to track which *type* of data they hold at any given time in addition to the actual data. Try to avoid using variants in your code.

Empty versus Null Variants

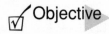

The value Empty denotes a Variant variable that hasn't been initialized (assigned an initial value). A Variant containing Empty is 0 if the variant is used in a numeric context; the variant is a zero-length string ("") if the variant is used in a string context. Empty is not the same as Null. Null indicates that the Variant variable intentionally contains no valid data.

Determining Data Type in a Variant

Use the built-in function VarType to determine how VBA stores the data in a variant. (See the section "Built-In Functions," earlier in this chapter.)

Using the Static Keyword to Retain the Value of a Variant

The Static statement can be used for an entire procedure or an individual variable. To declare a procedure as Static, type the statement Static before the name of the procedure. For example, you could type the following statement to declare the *entire* procedure as static:

```
Static Sub MySub()
```

Every variable declared within that procedure is static; it will retain its value for the lifetime of the application. For nonstatic procedures, storage space for variables is allocated each time the procedure is called, and storage space is released when the procedure is exited.

To declare a single variable as static, use the keyword Static when you declare the variable, as follows:

```
Static iCounter as Integer
```

When you use Static instead of Dim to declare a variable, the variable retains its value between procedures. Static variables do not lose their value until all code in the call tree has finished executing. (The call tree includes all modules that might be called by any procedure in the module code that is currently running.)

Declaring Arrays and Initializing Elements of Arrays

An array is a set of elements of the same data type. The array is a variable that acts as a container for the elements of the array. Think of an array as a single variable that can store many values. All members of the array must be of the same data type. By using an array, you can declare one variable for the entire group instead of declaring each element individually. This enables you to refer to the group as a whole.

If you need to refer to a specific element in an array, you can use that element's index number. Each element in the array has a unique index number to differentiate it from other elements in the array.

You declare an array as you do other variables, by using the Static, Dim, Private, or Public statement. The name of the array is followed by a list of the elements that an array can contain. These elements must be in parentheses.

For example, suppose you have a figure for monthly payroll expenses. Instead of declaring 12 variables, you can declare one array with 12 elements. Each element in an array contains one value.

The following statement declares the array variable curPayroll with 12 elements. By default, an array is indexed beginning with zero, so the upper bound of the array is 12 and not 11.

```
Dim curPayroll(11) as currency
    curPayroll(0)=$23,456,789        'January's payroll
    curPayroll(1)=$12,345,678        'February's payroll
```

This declares an array (curPayroll) which has 12 elements. The first element (January's payroll) has a value of $23,456,789.

By default, the number of elements is 0-based. That is why you use the number 11 to hold 12 elements.

Option Base

The default lower bound of an array is 0. This means that an array declared with "(4)" can contain five elements. However, you can change the default lower bound value to 1 for all arrays. To do this, place the statement "Option Base 1" at the top of a module. This can only be done at module level, and it only affects arrays contained within that module.

You can also specify the lower bound and upper bound values for each dimension of an array. For example, this statement declares an array "iStudents," which holds nine elements:

```
Dim iStudents (2 to 10) as integer
```

Multi-Dimensional Arrays

Arrays can have more than one dimension, and each dimension can have an upper bound and a lower bound. For example:

```
Dim iNumber (2 to 5, 1 to 10, 3) as integer
```

This statement declares a three-dimensional array. The first dimension (2 to 5) contains four elements. The second dimension (1 to 10) contains ten elements. The third dimension (3) contains four elements (assuming no Option Base statement was used). To determine the total size of the elements of a multi-dimensional array, multiply the sizes of all elements in the array. For example, to determine the size of the iNumber array previously listed, multiply $4 \times 3 \times 4$ to get a value of 48. (See the later section "Size of Arrays" to determine the total size of arrays.)

Dynamic Arrays

If you do not know how many elements will be needed in an array or if the number of elements will change, you can declare a *dynamic* array. You declare a dynamic array in the same way as a standard array, but you leave the arguments out of the parentheses, as follows:

```
Dim intMyArray() as integer
```

You can change the size of an array while your code is running by using the ReDim statement. The ReDim statement changes the number of dimensions of an array and defines the number of elements and the upper and lower bounds for each dimension. You can use the ReDim statement to change the dynamic array as often as you need. The following example uses a variable (intCount), which is the number of records in a recordset:

```
ReDim intMyArray(intCount)
```

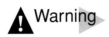 **Warning**

Make sure that you use ReDim to change the size of an array. If you declare a variable a second time with the Dim statement, it will cause a run-time error.

Be careful not to misspell the name of the array when you use the ReDim statement. You can use the ReDim statement to declare an array implicitly within a procedure. Even if the Option Explicit statement is included in the module, Visual Basic creates a second array.

Preserving Values

Each time you use the ReDim statement, you lose all the values stored in the array. In order to retain the existing data, you can use the Preserve keyword after the ReDim keyword in your declaration. However, when you use the Preserve keyword with a dynamic array, you can change only the upper bound of the last dimension. If you use the Preserve keyword with a dynamic array, you cannot change the number of dimensions.

```
ReDim Preserve intMyArray(intCount + 20)
```

Passing an Array to a Function or a Sub

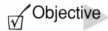 Objective

When passing an array to a function or sub, be sure to include the empty parentheses. For example, this function

```
Function ManipulateArrays(SomeArray as Variant)
    ...
End Function
```

can be called using the following syntax:

```
intNumber=ManipulateArray(MyArray())
```

In the preceding example, MyArray() must be enclosed in parentheses, and the empty parentheses must follow the name of the array.

Size of Arrays

Arrays require 20 bytes of memory plus four bytes for each array dimension (regardless of the data type of the array). In addition, you must add the number of bytes occupied by the data itself. The memory occupied by the data can be calculated by multiplying the number of data elements and the size of the elements. For example, the data in an array consisting of four Currency data elements of eight bytes each occupies 32 bytes. The 32 bytes the data requires plus the 24 bytes of overhead brings the total memory requirement for the array to 56 bytes.

GetRows() Method

You can use the GetRows() method of a recordset to copy data from the recordset into a variant variable. The array that this function creates is two-dimensional with enough space to hold the data from the recordset:

```
VarData = rs.GetRows(intRowsNeeded)
```

GetRows returns a two-dimensional array. The first subscript identifies the field and the second identifies the row number, as follows:

```
avarRecords(intField, intRecord)
```

The number of rows that GetRows() can obtain is limited by memory. Try to limit your fields and records in the recordset before using the GetRows() method.

 Note

> After a call to GetRows, the current record is positioned at the next unread row. That is, GetRows has an equivalent positioning effect to Move numrows.

Declaring and Using Object Variables and Collections

This section covers in detail object variables and collections: how they are used and their associated properties and methods. Although Chapter 4 "Programming with Objects," covers working with objects in greater detail, this section discusses objects as necessary for working with Visual Basic for Applications.

Understanding Object Variables

An object variable is a variable that refers to a Data Access Object (DAO) or to a user-interface object (such as a Form or Report). Unlike most variables, an object variable is really only a pointer to the actual object.

The following code declares two object variables, one for the Database and one for the Recordset:

```
Dim db as Database
Dim rs as Recordset
```

Set

Simply declaring the variable does not cause the variable to *point* to an object. Before the variable is set, it is simply a placeholder. The Set keyword is used to make the variable point to the object. The object to which the variable points to must already exist.

In the previous example, you declared object variables db and rs. The following example uses the Set keyword to point db to the Current Database and rs to a recordset called Customers within that database:

```
Set db = CurrentDb()
Set rs=db.OpenRecordset("Customers")
```

Lifetime of Object Variables

As soon as the variable goes out of scope, the reference to the object is destroyed. However, if necessary, you can clear the variable by setting it to nothing, as follows:

```
Set db = Nothing
Set rs= Nothing
```

Collections

Objects can contain collections, and collections can contain objects. For example, Database is an object of the Workspace collection, and TableDefinition is an object of the Database collection. Collections can be of different types, but objects within collections must be of the same type.

In Data Access Objects (DAO), the DBEngine object represents the Jet Database Engine. The DBEngine is the top-level object in the DAO hierarchy; it is not an element of any collection. Therefore, it is always the first reference required in DAO. The DBEngine contains two objects: Workspaces and Errors.

In order to refer to an object correctly, you must first refer to its parent:

```
DBEngine.ParentCollectionItem.ChildCollection("ChildObject")
```

ParentCollection is Workspaces, and ChildCollection refers to Databases. The object in this case is a particular object, such as a table, within that database.

Access provides several different methods for referring to Objects. Each of the following examples refers to a table named Customers in the open Database.

The most common method is the following:

```
DBEngine.Workspaces(0).Databases!Customers
```

If the name contains a nonstandard character, such as a space, the name should be in brackets as shown here:

```
DBEngine.Workspaces(0).Databases![Customer Information]
```

Or, you can use the following:

```
DBEngine.Workspaces(0).Databases("Customers")
```

The following method is similar, but it uses a variable to hold the table name:

```
Dim sName as String
sTable="Customers"
DBEngine.Workspaces(0).Databases(sTable)
```

The third method uses the ordinal position of the object within the database instead of a name. (The first number in a built-in collection is always 0.)

```
DBEngine.Workspaces(0).Databases(0)
```

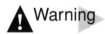 **Warning**

> Although Access begins numbering collections with 0, Microsoft Excel and Microsoft Graph both begin with 1. Don't confuse them if you are programming in Excel.

Referring to all levels of the object hierarchy can result in very long lines of code. Fortunately, Access provides default collections for most objects. This means you can write much simpler code (although it may not be quite as clear). For example, you can use either of the following lines of code to refer to a table definition:

```
DBEngine.Workspaces(0).Databases(0).TableDefs(0)
```

Or, you can use the following:

```
DBEngine(0)(0)(0)
```

Not only is the second line much shorter, but it actually runs *marginally* faster.

TableDef

The TableDefs Collection contains all the TableDefs in a database. A TableDef is a stored definition of a table. Use the OpenRecordset method of a TableDef to create a recordset based on a table. Use the CreateTableDef method to create a new TableDef.

The syntax for the CreateTable method is as follows:

```
Set variable = database.CreateTableDef([name[, attributes[,
source[, connect]]]])
```

The following is a list of the arguments for TableDef:

Variable. A variable declared as an object data type TableDef.

Database. The variable name of the Database object you want to use to create the new TableDef object.

Name. A String variable that uniquely names the new TableDef object. TableDef and QueryDef objects can't share the same name, nor can User and Group objects.

Attributes. A Long variable that indicates one or more characteristics of the new TableDef object. The data type of the setting or return value is Long.

Source. A String variable containing the name of a table in an external database that is the original source of the data. The source string becomes the SourceTableName property setting of the new TableDef object.

Connect. A String variable containing information about the source of an open database, a database used in a pass-through query, or an attached table.

QueryDef

The QueryDefs Collection contains all the QueryDefs in a database. It is very similar to a TableDef. The QueryDef object also has a Parameter collection, which enables you to specify parameters for a query.

To create a new QueryDef object, use the CreateQueryDef method.

The syntax for the QueryDef method is as follows:

```
Set querydef = database.CreateQueryDef([name][, sqltext])
```

The following is a list of the arguments for the QueryDef method:

Querydef. A variable of an object data type that references the QueryDef object you want to create.

Database. A variable of an object data type that references the open Database object that contains the new QueryDef.

Name. A string expression identifying the new QueryDef.

Sqltext. A string expression (a valid SQL statement) that defines the QueryDef. If you omit this argument, you can define the QueryDef by setting its SQL property before or after you append it to a collection.

Note

Queries executed from QueryDef objects run faster than queries specified by the OpenRecordset method because the Microsoft Jet Database Engine doesn't need to compile the query before executing it.

Using the Forms and Reports Collections

The Forms collection contains all open forms in a database. The Reports collection contains all open reports in a database.

Controls Collection

The Controls collection contains all the controls on a form or report. The Controls collection is a member of a Form or Report object. You can use the Controls collection to get or set information about any control on a form or report.

The following code sets the FontName and ForeColor for all labels on a form:

```
Sub SetLabelProperties()
    Dim frm As Form, ctl As Control
```

```
Set frm = Forms!Customers
' Enumerate Controls collection.
For Each ctl In frm.Controls
      ' Check to see if control is label.
      If ctl.ControlType = acLabel Then
            ' Set control properties.
            With ctl
                  .FontName = Arial
                  .ForeColor = 8388608
            End With
      End If
Next ctl
End Sub
```

Understanding Default Collections for DAO Objects

Table 1.8 lists the objects in Access and their default collections.

Table 1.8

Objects and Defualt Collections

Object	Default Collection
DBEngine	Workspaces
Workspace	Databases
Database	TableDefs
TableDef	Fields
Recordset	Fields
Index	Fields
Relation	Fields
QueryDef	Parameters
Group	Users
User	Groups
Container	Documents

Collection Properties

If you think of objects as nouns, properties can be considered adjectives. They are attributes of objects, and they can usually be retrieved and set.

For example, the following code retrieves the name of a TableDefinition and assigns the value to the variable strTable. This example assumes that the variable tdf has already been declared and set to a valid table object:

```
strTable=tdf.Name
```

 Note

For a complete list of the properties of objects and collections, please refer to Properties Reference in the Access Help file.

To refer to an object's property, use the following syntax:

```
object.property
```

Object usually refers to a variable that you have set to point to an object, such as a variable rs, which represents an open recordset.

Connect Property

This is a read/write property that applies to Database, QueryDef, and TableDef objects:

```
object.Connect = [databasetype;[parameters;]]
```

Use the Connect property to pass additional information to ODBC and certain ISAM drivers as needed. It isn't used for Jet Databases, except for those containing attached tables, to allow SQL pass-through queries.

Count Property

Every collection has a Count property. This is a Long Integer, which contains the number of items in the collection. If no objects are in the collection, the Count property = 0, *not* Null.

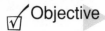 **Objective** The first item in a collection is assigned the number 0. Although Count always begins with 0, the Count property is always pointing at the next available object in the collection. Therefore, the Count property always reflects the actual number of objects present in that collection. However, if you are using the For...Next loop structure, you want to move only to the last item in a collection. The following code snippet shows the beginning of a loop, which loops through all items in the collection and stop at the last one:

```
For I = 0 to Databases.Count - 1
```

Methods

If an object is considered a noun, and a property is considered an adjective, a method can be considered a verb. Methods are actions that can be applied to objects.

 Note For a complete list of the properties of objects and collections, please refer to Methods Reference in the Access Help file.

The syntax for methods is very similar to the syntax for properties, which follows:

```
Rs.MoveLast
```

This code assumes that the variable rs has already been declared and set. The code causes the record pointer to move to the last record in the recordset.

Efficiency

If you are going to be referring to an object several times in your code, it is a good idea to declare a variable to represent that object and then refer to the variable. Not only is it easier to use rs (a commonly used object variable for a recordset) than to use the following line, but it is also faster to process:

```
DBEngine.Workspaces(0).Databases(0).Recordsets("Customers")
```

With…End With

Objective

If you are going to refer to more than one property or method of a variable, it is best to use the With…End With structure. When you use this structure, VBA has to call the variable only one time and then set or read several properties or use methods. Otherwise, it calls the variable, uses a method or sets or reads the properties, *releases* the variable (even though it is still initialized and still has value), calls it again, sets the property, and so on.

Imagine if your boss called you into her office and told you to start a new project (calling a method of the object). You leave her office and go back to your office (although you are still initialized and have value, you have been *released* from her office). As soon as you get to your desk, she calls you back into her office. This time she tells you that you must wear a suit to work (changing one of your properties). You then go back to your office, she calls you back again, and so on. This is not a very efficient way to work. It works the same way in VBA. If you are going to work with an object, call it into your office only once by using the With…End With statement.

To use the With…End With structure, simply type With and the name of the object or object variable. On the next line (which is normally indented to make it easier to read), set each property as you normally would, *omitting the name of the object or object variable.* You still need to include the dot that normally is placed after the object variable and before the property or method. On the last line, aligned with the original With, you must have End With so that VBA knows when it can release the object. Consider this example:

```
Dim rs as recordset
set rs =
DBEngine.Workspaces(0).Databases(0).Recordsets("Customers")
with rs
     .Update
     .MoveFirst
End With
```

Declaring Symbolic Constants

Constants are used to assign a meaningful name to a value. Constants are similar to variables, except that the value of a constant never changes. For example, suppose you have to refer to a company's commission rate. They have decided that it will *always* be 3.2041%. Instead of always referring to the number directly, you can declare it as a constant (conCmsn), and then you can simply refer to the constant.

The syntax for declaring symbolic constants is as follows:

```
Const ConstName as DataType
```

Constants are declared much the same way that variables are declared. Instead of using Dim or Static, you simply use the Const keyword and assign it a value like this:

```
const conPi as double =3.14
```

You can declare several constants on one line, separated by commas (just like variables). Don't forget to assign a data type to each constant, or it will be considered a variant. For example, the following code declares three constants. Notice that the data type was declared for each constant:

```
Con conAge as integer =21, conYearsExperience as Integer =2,
conSalary as Currency =250000
```

Valid Data Types for Constants

A constant can be any one of the following data types: Boolean, Byte, Integer, Long, Currency, Single, Double, Date, String, or Variant.

Scope

Constants have the same scope as variables. That is, a module-level constant (declared in the declarations section of a module) is Private, and a procedure-level constant is always Private. To make a procedure-level constant Public, use the Public keyword before the Constant keyword.

Lab Exercise

Exercise 1.1:   Arrays, Loops, and Functions

In this lab you create a user-defined function that uses ParamArray.

Objectives:

Create user-defined functions

Declare and use arrays

Change the size of an array during a procedure

Use a For...Next loop with arrays

Use the following functions: UBound and Chr

Time Estimate: 30 minutes

Steps:

1. Create a New Database (Lab One).

2. Create a module, basArraysLoopsFunctions.

3. In basArraysLoopsFunctions, create a Public function ComputePay.

4. ComputePay requires the following arguments: Employee as String, Rate as Currency, and Hours().

5. Declare the following variables:

   ```
   Dim X As Integer
   Dim TotalHours As Double
   Dim TotalCost As Currency
   ```

6. Use a For...Next loop to compute TotalHours.

   ```
   For X = 0 To UBound(HoursWorked)
       TotalHours = TotalHours + HoursWorked(X)
   Next X
   ```

7. Compute TotalCost by multiplying TotalHours by HoursWorked.

8. Display a message box that shows the Employee's name, hours worked, and TotalCost. (Hint: Use Chr(13) to create carriage returns in your message box to make it easier to read).

9. Test your function in the debug window:

```
? ComputeCost("Joe Schmo, 45.99,8,10,6,12,5)
```

Comments:

The completed lab can be found on the CD-ROM in the Lab One Database.

Reading Reference:

See the following sections for more information: "Using VBA Loop Statements," "Understanding User-Defined Functions," and "Declaring Variables in Modules and Procedures."

Review Questions

1. Which of the following expressions returns the value 2?

```
Dim mydate As Date
myDate = #2/24/36#
```

    A. x = DatePart("m", mydate)

    B. x = DatePart("month", mydate)

    C. x = DatePart(m, mydate)

    D. x = DatePart(month, mydate)

2. Which of the following lines of code finds the value "Jones" in the LastName field? Choose two.

```
Sub Proc1()
Dim X as Integer
Dim Y as Integer
X=X+1
Y=Y=1
End Sub

Sub Proc2()
Proc1
Proc1
Proc1
Intro=Y-X
Debug.Print Z
```

    A. [LastName]=Jones

    B. [LastName] = "Jones"

    C. [LastName] Like Jo*

    D. [LastName] Like "Jo"*

3. What will print in the Debug window after Proc2 executes?

    A. 0

    B. 5

    C. 3

    D. 1

4. Which of the following are valid settings for the option Base statements? Choose all that apply.

```
Public Sub MyIf()
Dim X as integer
X = 10
Iif (X >5 , X=X*2,X=X/0
Debug.Print X
```

    A. 2

    B. 1

    C. 0

    D. −1

5. What occurs after this procedure runs?

```
End Sub
```

    A. 20 appears in the debug window.

    B. 0 appears in the debug window.

    C. 10 appears in the debug window.

    D. Nothing appears in the debug window because X/0 would cause an error.

6. What appears in the last line of the debug window after this code executes?

```
Dim X as Integer
Dim Y as Integer
For x = 2 to 6
```

```
y = y + 2
If y >4 Then y=Y+1
If y>6 then exit for
Debug.Print y & " ," & "x"
Next X
```

  A. 4,3

  B. 7,4

  C. 7,6

  D. An error occurs. You cannot use & in the debug
      window.

7. What is the value of X after this code executes?

```
Dim MyArray(2 to 10, 7 to 10, 6)
    X=LBound(MyArray,2)
```

  A. 7

  B. 4

  C. 0

  D. 2

8. The Clients table has the fields City and Salary. Which ex-
    pression calculates the average salary of clients from Athens?

```
Dim strCity as String
strCity="Athens"
```

  A. AvgSalary=Davg("[Salary]","[Clients]","[City] =strCity")

  B. AvgSalary=Davg("[Salary]","[Clients]","[City] = '" strCity)

  C. AvgSalary=Davg("[Salary]","[Clients]","[City] =
      '"& strCity"'")

  D. AvgSalary=Davg([Salary],[Clients],[City] = ""& strCity &"")

9. What is the correct way to name a combo box?

    A. comboCompany

    B. cmbCompany

    C. cmCompany

    D. cboCompany

10. Which of the following constant declarations is valued? Choose all that apply.

    A. Const MyVariable = "Declaring constants is " & "Easy!"

    B. Const MyVariable = Chr(13)

    C. Const MyVariable =2 ^ 3

    D. Const MyVariable%= 32

11. Which of these statements shows the total number of tables in the database in the debug window?

    A. Debug.Print CurrentDB.TableDefs.Count

    B. Debug.Print CurrentDB.TableDefs.Count – 1

    C. Debug.Print CurrentDB.Table.Count

    D. Debug.Print CurrentDB.Tables.Count – 1

12. Which of the following statements correctly declares the variable as an integer? Choose all that apply.

    A. Dim X%

    B. Dim X

    C. Dim integer X

    D. Dim X as integer

13. Which of the following statements are *not* valid in Visual Basic? Choose two.

    A. Exit For

    B. End Loop

C. Next

D. GoTo Next

14. Which of the following lines of code completes this block?

```
With txtName
     .FontName=Arial
     .ForeColor=0
     .FontSize=12
```

A. Exit With

B. Next With

C. End With

D. Loop With

15. Suppose you have created the following function:

```
Public Function FuncArray(YourArray) as variant
```

How would you call this function and pass it the array MyArray, which has three elements?

A. FuncArray(MyArray)

B. FuncArray MyArray()

C. FuncArray (MyArray"(3)")

D. FuncArray(MyArrray(3))

16. Which of the following lines of code correctly declares a function?

A. Function MyFunction(By Val Name, Optional MyArg as string)

B. Function MyFunction (Name, ParamArray MyParam(), Age, Optional DateOfBirth)

C. Function MyFunction(Name, Age, Optional DateOfBirth)

D. Function MyFunction (Name, ByRef ParamArray MyParam()) as Date

17. Which of the following statements correctly declares a user-defined function? Choose two.

    A. Function MyFunction() as String*10

    B. Function MyFunction() as String

    C. Function MyFunction()

    D. Function MyFunction as String

18. Which of the following statements evaluates to True? Select all that apply.

```
Public Sub Test()
Dim x as integer, y as integer
X=10
Y=5
End Sub
```

    A. Imp(X=Y+Y,Y=X–Y)

    B. Eqv(Y>X, X=Y*3)

    C. Cbool(X–Y)

    D. X>Y AND Y+Y=X

19. Which of the following expressions returns 150? Choose all that are correct.

    A. MyNumber="100" & "50"

    B. MyNumber="100" + "50"

    C. MyNumber="1" & "50"

    D. MyNumber= 100 + 50

20. What is the value of Y when Stop executes?

```
Dim x As Integer
    Dim Y
    Public Sub Proc1()
        x = 10
        Stop
        Y = x + 1
    End Sub
```

A. Null

B. Nothing

C. 0

D. Empty

21. Which of the following keywords can be used to declare a variable in a module? Choose all that apply.

   A. Private

   B. Global

   C. Static

   D. Dim

22. An array, MyArray(), has been declared, and it contains 23 elements. Which statement adds a 24th element without losing the original data?

   A. ReDim Preserve MyArray(24)

   B. ReDim MyArray(24)

   C. ReDim Preserve MyArray(1)

   D. Preserve ReDim MyArray(23 + 1)

23. Which of the following statements releases the object variable frm from memory?

   A. Release frm

   B. Set frm= Null

   C. Set frm=Nothing

   D. Set frm=""

24. Which of the following expressions returns GHI?

```
Dim X as String
x= ABC DEF GHI JKL
```

   A. X=(Left,11)

   B. X=Mid(X,7,3)

  C. X=Mid(X,9,3)

  D. X=Mid(X,3,7)

Answers to Review Questions

1. A is correct. To return the month portion of a date, DatePart requires that you use the constant m, and it must be enclosed in quotes. You can learn about this concept in the section entitled "Understanding User-Defined Functions."

2. B and D are correct. In VBA, string expressions must always be enclosed in quotation marks. You can learn about this concept in the section entitled "Comparison Operators."

3. A is correct. A variable goes out of scope as soon as its procedure ends. Therefore, X and Y both have a value of 0 in Proc2. You can learn about this concept in the section entitled "Declaring Variables in Modules and Procedures."

4. B and C are correct. Option Base can be set to 0 (the default) or 1. You can learn about this concept in the section entitled "Declaring Arrays and Initializing Elements of Arrays."

5. D is correct. It evaluates both the truepart and the falsepart, even if the expression is True. Therefore, this expression causes an error. You can learn about this concept in the section entitled "Built-In Functions."

6. D is correct. After the first loop, Y=2 and X=2. After the second loop, Y=4 and X=3. During the third loop, Y is greater than 6, which causes the code to exit the loop before anything prints in the debug window. You can learn about this concept in the section entitled "Using VBA Loop Statements"

7. A is correct. The lower bound of the 2nd dimension of MyArray is 7. You can learn about this concept in the section entitled "Built-In Functions."

8. C is correct. Each expression in a Domain Aggregate function must be enclosed in quotation marks. Any string expressions (such as strCity) must also be enclosed within single quotation marks. You can learn about this concept in the section entitled "Domain Aggregate Functions."

9. D is correct. The correct prefix is cbo for a combo box. You can learn about this concept in the section entitled "Naming Variables."

10. D is correct. When declaring constants you may *not* use the following: string concatenation, intrinsic Access functions, or exponentation operators. You may use type declaration characters. You can learn about this concept in the section entitled "Declaring Symbolic Constants."

11. A is correct. Although the Count property begins with 0, count is always pointing at the next available object in a collection. Therefore, Count will always reflect the actual number of objects. You can learn about this concept in the section entitled "Collection Properties."

12. A and D are correct. The type declaration character % can be used, as well as the "as integer" statement. You can learn about this concept in the section entitled "Declaring Variables in Modules and Procedures."

13. B and D are correct. Exit For is the correct way to exit a For...Next loop before the loop ends naturally. End Loop is not a valid statement. Next is the keyword to place at the end of a block of code in a For...Next loop. You can learn about this concept in the section entitled "Comparing Loops."

14. C is correct. End With is the only option for ending a With block. You can learn about this concept in the section entitled "With...End With."

15. D is correct. When passing an array to a variable, you must include the parentheses and the number of elements in the array. You can learn about this concept in the section entitled "Declaring Arrays and Initializing Elements of Arrays."

16. C is correct. Optional arguments must be variants. ParamArray cannot be used with Optional, ByVal, or ByRef. You can learn about this concept in the section entitled "Understading User-Defined Functions."

17. B and C are correct. A function can return any data type except a fixed-length string or a variable. A function must

have parentheses, even if no arguments are enclosed. You can learn about this concept in the section entitled "Understanding User-Defined Functions."

18. B, C, and D are correct. Imp returns a True value only if the first statement is True and the other is False. Because both expressions are True, IMP returns False. EQV returns a True value when both expressions are True or when both expressions are False. You can learn about this concept in the section entitled "Comparison Operators."

19. C and D are correct. A and B both return 150 by concatenating the digits. C returns 150 using concatenation. D returns 150 by adding the two numbers together. You can learn about this concept in the section entitled "Concatenation Operators."

20. D is correct. When variables are initialized, they are assigned a default value. Variants are Empty, numeric variables are 0, Strings are an empty string "", and object variables are Nothing. You can learn about this concept in the section entitled "Scope and Lifetime of Variables."

21. A, C, and D are correct. The Global keyword cannot be used in a procedure. You can learn about this concept in the section entitled "Declaring Variables in Modules and Procedures."

22. A is correct. ReDim enables you to change the size of an array without losing the original data. You can learn about this concept in the section entitled "Dynamic Arrays."

23. C is correct. The keyword Nothing is used with object variables to clear the variable and release it from memory. You can learn about this concept in the section entitled "Understanding Object Variables."

24. C is correct. The Mid function takes the following arguments: string (x), starting position (9, because you must include spaces), and length (3). You can learn about this concept in the section entitled "Left, Right, and Mid."

Answers to Test Yourself Questions at Beginning of Chapter

1. Use Dmax to determine what the highest sale was. Use DLookup to then find the SalesID for that order. You can learn about this concept in the section entitled "Domain Aggregate Functions."

2. The function should add 30 days to the OrderDate.

```
Function CalcDate(OrderDate) as Date
    BillDate= OrderDate + 30
End Function
```

This function should be stored in a public module so that the user can access it from anywhere in the database. You can learn about this concept in the section entitled "Domain Aggregate Functions."

3. Use the Iif and IsNull functions:

```
[Price] –(Iif(IsNull([Rebate]),0,[Rebate]))
```

You can learn about this concept in the section entitled "Miscellaneous Functions."

4. Declare it in the Declarations section of module basCalculations:

```
Private bytAge as Byte
```

Age should be a byte because it will always be between 0 and 255. You can learn about this concept in the section entitled "Declaring Variables in Modules and Procedures."

5. You can change the size of an array by using ReDim. In order to preserve the original data, you must also use Preserve, as in ReDim Preserve Students(31). You can learn about this concept in the section entitled "Declaring Arrays and Intializing Elements of Arrays."

6. Use the Count property of the TableDefs collection to determine how many TableDefs exist in your database. You can learn about this concept in the section entitled "Collection Properties."

7. Declare Pi as a constant in a Public module. You can then simply refer to Pi when you need to use it in a calculation. You can learn about this concept in the section entitled "Declaring Variables in Modules and Procedures."

Chapter

Database Design

2

By the end of this chapter, you will be able to execute the following test objectives:

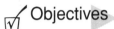 Objectives

▶ Apply the basic concepts of normalization

▶ Use the Cascade Update and Cascade Delete options

Test Yourself! Before reading this chapter, test yourself to determine how much study time you will need to devote to this section.

1. You are designing a database for a doctor's office, and its employees need to be able to keep track of each family and their visits. The doctor does not want to use an AutoNumber to create a primary key for the Patient table, and the office does not track patients by their Social Security numbers. The Patient table will be related to the Visits table, so that each visit can be recorded. You have decided to use the customer's telephone number as the primary key. What type of relationship should be established between the Patient table and the Visits table? What would you need to do if a patient changed her phone number?

2. How would you create a many-to-many relationship between two tables?

Answers are located at the end of the chapter...

As you read this chapter, you will learn about the database design test objectives described earlier. This chapter covers the design process and the rules that you must follow when designing a database. Although you must understand the concepts of normalization in order to answer the questions about database design, the exam will not ask questions about normalization theory. This topic is not usually covered extensively on the exam.

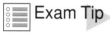 Exam Tip

There will be at least one question on the exam about how you use Access to apply the rules of normalization to your database. You must understand the different types of relationships between tables and how the relationships affect the data. You must also understand referential integrity, Cascade Updates, Cascade Deletes, and how these affect the data. The questions will usually give a scenario and several possible solutions. You must be able to choose the appropriate solution, and know why it is appropriate.

Understanding the Concepts of Normalization

 Objective

Normalization is the process of achieving the optimum design in a database. In order to achieve normalization, a database must meet the requirements of each of the three Normal Forms.

First Normal Form

First Normal Form requires that all column values be *atomic*, or indivisible. In other words, each column must store a single value, not a list of values.

In the Northwind database, for example, a customer can purchase many products in one order. Rather than have a Products column that contains a list of items purchased, there is a Product column that contains one product number. Figure 2.1 shows a table that is not in First Normal Form, because the Products column is not atomic.

Figure 2.1

This table is not in First Normal Form because of the format of the Products column.

Customer Number	DatePurchased	Products
132	2/3/97	Alice Mutton, Pavlova,Scottish Longbreads,
321	2/24/97	Chef Anton's Gumbo Mix, Sir Rodney's Maramalade,Mis
123	4/7/97	Teatime Chocolate Biscuists, Chang,Longlife Tofu
0		

In addition to requiring each column to be atomic, First Normal Form requires that groups of columns cannot be repeated. Because a customer can purchase many products in one order, a *many-to-many relationship* must be established between Orders and Products. A many-to-many relationship cannot be established directly; a *junction table* must be created to join the two tables. Figure 2.2 shows the Orders table after the Product column has been made atomic. However, it is still not in First Normal Form because the Product column is repeated three times.

Figure 2.2

This table is still not in First Normal Form because the Product column is repeated.

Customer Num	DatePurchased	Product1	Product2	Product3
123	4/7/97	Teatime Chocolate Biscuists	Chang	Longlife Tofu
321	2/24/97	Chef Anton's Gumbo Mix	Sir Rodney's M:	Mishi Kobe Niku
132	2/3/97	Alice Mutton	Pavlova	Scottish Longbreads
0				

Establishing a Junction Table

A junction table must have a composite primary key. The primary key of the junction table must contain the primary keys of the tables that you are joining. For example, in Northwind, OrderDetails is the junction table that joins Orders and Products. The primary key of the Orders table is OrderID, and the primary key of the Products table is ProductID. Therefore, the primary key of the junction table is made up of the foreign keys OrderID and ProductID. A *one-to-many relationship* is set up between Orders and OrderDetails and between Products and OrderDetails. This effectively creates a many-to-many relationship between Orders and Products. Figure 2.3 shows the relationship between Orders, OrderDetails, and Products. All three tables are in First Normal Form.

Figure 2.3

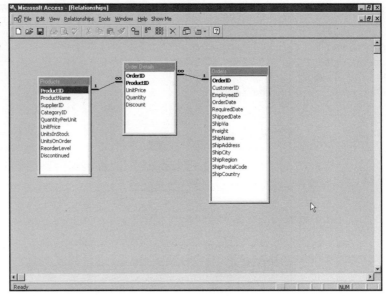

Splitting Tables

If a table is not in First Normal Form, it might need to be split
into two tables to achieve this. The easiest way to do this is to create two Make Table queries that create two separate tables. If
there are several repeating columns, you will have to use an Append query to add the data from each column to the new table.
Be sure to exclude Null values when appending this data.

Figure 2.4 shows an Append query that adds the data from the
ProductID2 field to the Order Details table. Originally, all of this
data was stored in the Orders table, which had a ProductID1, Pro-
ductID2, and ProductID3 column. The Order table was split into
two tables: Orders and Order Details. The Append query is used
to transfer the data from ProductID2 to the Product ID field of
the OrderDetails table.

Second Normal Form

Second Normal Form requires that a table be in First Normal
Form and that every non-key column of the table is fully dependent on the primary key. In other words, every field in the table
should relate directly to the primary key, and each table should
only be about one entity.

Figure 2.4

An Append query, which appends data to the Order Details table.

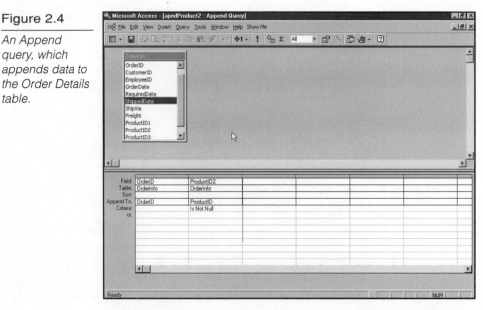

In order to achieve Second Normal Form, one table often has to be split into several tables. For example, if Northwind had originally been designed with an Order table that listed each product that had been purchased, that would have to be split into two tables: Orders and OrderDetails. Usually the easiest way to split a table is by using a Make Table query. When splitting a table, make sure that you can put it together again with a query! For example, because OrderDetails contains an OrderID for each order, a query based on these two tables could rejoin this information.

Third Normal Form

A table is in Third Normal Form if it is in Second Normal Form and if all non-key columns are mutually independent. The most common example of a dependent column is a calculation. Calculations should be stored in a query, form, or report, rather than a table.

There is another common dependency caused by duplicating information throughout a table. If, for example, the OrderDetails table stored information about the products purchased, such as description, this would break the rules for Third Normal Form. Because the description is actually dependent on the ProductID, it should be stored in the Products table.

Relationships

When creating a relationship between two tables, the fields that you are joining must be of the same data type if you want to enforce *referential integrity*. They do not have to have the same name. For example, you might join CustomerID in the Customer table to Customer in the Order table. As long as both fields have the same data type, the relationship could be created. If the tables already contain data, Access will check the data to make sure that none of the data violates the rules of referential integrity (see in the following sections) before creating the relationship.

Relationships created in the Relationship window (Tools, Relationships in the Database window) are global; the line representing the relationship will automatically appear whenever you base a query on those tables. A relationship established within a query is valid only within that query.

When you create a relationship between two tables, Access automatically assigns one of the following relationships between the tables, based upon the fields that you are joining.

One-to-Many

The most common relationship between tables in Access is a *one-to-many* relationship. This means that the primary key of one table is related to the foreign key of another table. (A key that refers to the primary key of another table is referred to as a *foreign key*.) For example, the relationship between Customers and Orders in the Northwind Database is based on CustomerID. CustomerID is the primary key in the Customers table, and a foreign key in the Orders table.

A one-to-many relationship can also be established between two tables, but it is not common. Tables are joined on the *primary key*.

Many-to-Many

Although Access does not support *many-to-many* relationships directly, they can be created through a junction table. See the earlier section "First Normal Form."

One-to-One

A *one-to-one* relationship is created when you join the primary key of one table to the primary key of another table.

Join Types

There are three join types in Access: inner, left-outer, and right-outer. When creating a relationship, you specify the join type by clicking on the Join Type button in the relationship window.

Join types are particularly important in queries. The join type determines which records will be included in the dynaset.

Inner Joins

The default relationship between tables in Access is an *inner join.* A query based on tables that have an inner join will include only records that have a match on *both* sides of the join. For example, if a customer was entered in the customer table, but had not yet placed an order (and therefore did not have an entry in the Order table), a query based on Customers and Orders would not include that customer in its dynaset.

Outer Joins

An *outer join* is created when you need to include all records from one table and only those from the related table that include the matching record. For example, if a dynaset needed to include all customers, regardless of whether or not they had placed an order, and the date of their orders if they had placed one, then an outer join would be required. This would allow all customers to be included along with any of their order dates. The OrderDate field would be Null for those customers who had not yet placed an order. Figure 2.5 shows the QBE grid for this query, based on the Northwind database.

Figure 2.5

An example of an outer join query.

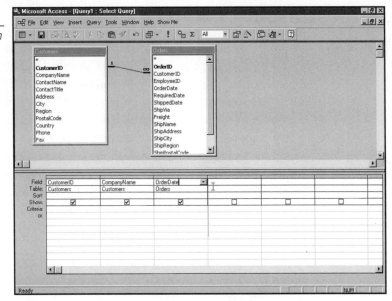

Right-Outer Joins versus Left-Outer Joins

If a dynaset includes all records in the first table and only those in the second where joined fields are equal it is considered a *left-outer join*. If it includes all records in the second table and only those in the first where joined fields are equal it is considered a *right-outer join*.

Referential Integrity

 Objective

When *referential integrity* is enforced in a relationship, data cannot be entered on the many side if a related record does not exist on the one side. The data for the foreign key cannot be entered until the data for the matching primary key has been entered. This prevents "orphaned" records.

If you try to enter data on the many side before the matching record is entered on the one side, then Access will not allow you to save the record. An error message will appear that says "Can't add or change record. Referential integrity rules require a related record in table "."""

Understanding Cascade Update

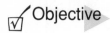 When establishing a relationship between tables in the Relationship window, there are options for Cascade Update and Cascade Delete. Checking *Cascade Update* means that if the data in the primary key (one side) changes, the related records will automatically change the data in the foreign key field. Perhaps you are using a customer's phone number as the primary key for the Customer table, for example. If you update the phone number in the Customer table (when the customer moves, for example) the phone number in any related tables (such as Orders) would automatically be updated. This enables you to use information that may change (such as a phone number) as a primary key.

If Cascade Update has been set, there is no warning that related records will be updated when the data is changed. It happens automatically and the user is not informed that related records will be changed.

Understanding Cascade Delete

Setting the *Cascade Delete* option causes all related records to be deleted when the one side is deleted. If Cascade Delete were set in the relationship between Orders and OrderDetails and the record containing OrderID 101 in the Orders table were deleted, all records in the OrderDetails table with an OrderID of 101 would be deleted. Access will warn you before it deletes a record on the one side of the relationship if it will cause related records to be deleted.

If Cascade Delete has not been set, Access will not allow a record to be deleted from the one side if there are matching records on the many side. For example, a salesperson could not be deleted from the Northwind database if there were related records in the orders table, because doing so would violate the rules of referential integrity.

Key Terms and Concepts

Table 2.1 identifies key terms from this chapter. Review the key terms and make sure that you understand each term for the exam.

Table 2.1

Key Terms: Database Design	
Term	Covered in Section...
Normalization	"Understanding the Concepts of Normalization"
Atomic	"First Normal Form"
Referential integrity	"Relationships"
Right-outer join	"Relationships"
Inner join	"Relationships"
Left-outer join	"Relationships"
Cascade Update	"Understanding Cascade Update"
Cascade Delete	"Understanding Cascade Delete"
Normal Forms	"Understanding the Concepts of Normalization"
Junction table	"First Normal Form"

Lab Exercise

This exercise gives you the opportunity to apply what you have learned about Database Design to a real-life situation. You are presented with an existing Access database (Manufacturing.mdb) that no longer fits the needs of the company. By applying the concepts learned in this chapter, you can provide a solution to the problem.

Exercise 2.1: Understanding Database Design

To demonstrate your understanding of the concepts of database design, evaluate a situation and modify an existing database to solve a problem. The original database used in this example is Manufacturing.mdb and can be found on the CD-ROM accompanying this book.

Objectives:

Make sure that tables are in First Normal Form and establish relationships between the tables (apply the basic concepts of normalization).

Use the Cascade Update and Cascade Delete options.

Time Estimate: 25 minutes

A small manufacturing company has suddenly won a large contract and as a result, they have expanded their workforce, and increased to three shifts a day. They have also purchased two new machines, and may have to purchase more in the future. Previously, when they ran only one shift per day, the shift manager entered all information into the PartsProduced Manufacturing database.

The company has asked you to modify their database to make it easier to track the new information. You have been given the following information: for each machine, they need to track the part number produced (PartNumber), hours ran, and total parts produced (TotalParts). One machine may produce several different parts in a shift. They need to be able to produce reports about each shift, and about each machine. In addition, the previous names of the machines need to be changed because they were given very useful names such as "By the Window" and "The Big Grey One." They do not want to refer to the machines by number alone, however; they always want to use a name, and they want the ability to change the name and still track the data.

Occasionally, a machine will be replaced by a new machine. Although the machine will be given a new ID number, the information tracked (in tblProduction) should be updated with the new number.

Shift information needed:

▶ Date

▶ Shift (1, 2, or 3)

▶ Manager

▶ Some way of identifying the shift (possibly an AutoNumber)

Information needed for each production run on a machine:

▶ ShiftInfo

▶ PartProduced

▶ [HoursRan]

▶ NumberPartsProduced

Remember, you may produce several different parts in one shift.

Steps:

1. Modify tblMachines so that the machine is no longer identified only by a name.

2. Add tblShift, which will track the information about each shift.

3. Add tblProduction which will track what each machine produced during each shift.

4. Establish relationships between all tables, using the Cascade Update and Cascade Delete options as appropriate.

Comments:

This exercise is a typical example of working with the concepts of database design. In an ideal world, we could design every database from scratch. In the real world, however, we usually have to work with what we are given and the challenge is to be able to modify it to fit our needs. This exercise helps you to prepare for the exam because it reinforces what you have learned about applying the rules of normalization.

Reading Reference:

Please see the section "Applying the Rules of Normalization" for more information.

Review Questions

1. You are setting up a database for a mail order catalog. A customer might order several products at a time. Therefore, you need to establish a many-to-many relationship between Orders and Products. The primary key of the Orders table is OrderID, and the primary key of the Product table is ProductID. How would you establish this relationship in Access?

   A. When setting the relationship between Orders and Products, choose many-to-many in the Relationship Type box in the Relationship window.

   B. Create a junction table named OrderDetails. The primary key of OrderDetails should contain OrderID and ProductID. Establish a one-to-many relationship between Orders and OrderDetails and a one-to-many relationship between Products and OrderDetails.

   C. There is no way to establish a many-to-many relationship in Access.

   D. Create a junction table named OrderDetails. The primary key of OrderDetails should be OrderDetailID. Establish a one-to-many relationship between Orders and OrderDetails and a one-to-one relationship between Products and OrderDetails.

2. The primary key of the Customer table is CustomerID, which is an AutoNumber field. The Orders table contains a Customer field, which is a Text field. Can you establish a relationship and enforce referential integrity between the Customer table and the Orders table based on these fields?

   A. No, you cannot establish a relationship between the Customer table and the Orders table, based on Customer and CustomerID. The fields must have the same name in order to establish a relationship between them and enforce referential integrity.

B. Yes, you can establish a relationship between the Customer table and the Orders table, based on Customer and CustomerID. The fields need not have the same name in order to establish a relationship between them.

C. Yes, you can establish a relationship between the Customer table and the Orders table, based on Customer and CustomerID. However, in order to enforce referential integrity, the fields must have the same name and be the same data type.

D. Yes, you can establish a relationship between the Customer table and the Orders table, based on Customer and CustomerID. However, in order to enforce referential integrity, the fields must be the same data type.

3. You have hired 15 new salespeople. Before each weekly sales meeting you generate a report in your Access database that shows each salesperson and the amount of revenue that they generated the previous week. The report is based on a query that contains the SalesForce table and the Revenue table. These tables are joined by the SalesPersonID key. This week you notice that two of the salespeople are not on the report. You know that they have been entered into the SalesForce table. Why would their names not appear on the report, and what is the best way to fix this problem?

A. They are not on the report because they have not generated any revenue. In order to make them appear on the report, enter a record in the Revenue table that uses their SalesPersonID but has $0 in the revenue line.

B. They are not on the report because they have not generated any revenue. There is no way to make their names appear on the report until they generate revenue.

C. They are not on the report because they have not generated any revenue. In order to make them appear on the report, change the relationship between the SalesForce table and the Revenue table. It should be a left-outer join in order to show all salespeople, whether or not they have generated any revenue.

D. They are not on the report because they have not generated any revenue. In order to make them appear on the report, change the relationship between the SalesForce table and the Revenue table. It should be a right-outer join in order to show all salespeople, whether or not they have generated any revenue.

4. You have created a database that tracks order information for each customer. There is a one-to-many relationship between customers and orders and referential integrity is enforced. A new customer calls to place an order. What would happen if you tried to enter the order before you had entered the customer into the Customer table?

A. You would receive an error message when you tried to save the record in the Orders table.

B. After entering the record in the Orders table, Access would save the record and prompt you to enter the customer information in the Customer table.

C. You would receive an error message as soon as you left the CustomerID field in the Orders table because there is no related CustomerID in the Customers table.

D. You would not receive any error messages. However, in order to prevent an orphaned record, you must remember to add a record to the Customer table with information about that customer.

5. Referential integrity has been enforced between Products and Orders. The manufacturer has discontinued product 345A and you can no longer sell it. What will happen if you try to delete product 345A from the Products table?

A. The record for Part 345A in the Parts table will not be deleted unless Referential Delete has been enforced.

B. The record for Part 345A in the Parts table will not be deleted unless Cascade Delete has been enforced.

C. The record for Part 345A in the Parts table will not be deleted unless All Cascades has been enforced.

D. The record for Part 345A in the Parts table will not be deleted unless Cascade Update has been enforced.

Answers to Review Questions

1. B is correct. Although you cannot create a many-to-many relationship in Access directly, you can create a junction table to accomplish this. The primary key of the junction table should be made up of the foreign keys from each of the tables that you are joining. You can learn about this concept in the section "Many-to-Many."

2. D is correct. In order to enforce referential integrity in a relationship, the joined fields must be the same data type. They do not have to have the same name. You can learn about this concept in the section "Relationships."

3. C is correct. A left-outer join between the SalesForce table and the Revenue table would include all employees, whether or not they had generated any revenue, and it would also include the revenue generated by each salesperson. You can learn about this concept in the section "Outer Joins."

4. A is correct. Referential integrity requires a record in the Customer table before entering a related record in the Orders table. The error would occur when Access saves the record in the Orders table (when the last field is exited, or when the user chooses Save Record, or when the user moves to a new record). You can learn about this concept in the section "Referential Integrity."

5. B is correct. If referential integrity has been enforced, Access will not allow you to delete a record from the primary table if related records exist in another table. If you enable Cascade Delete, then Access will delete the record in the primary table and all related records. You can learn about this concept in the section "Understanding Cascade Delete."

Answers to Test Yourself Questions at Beginning of Chapter...

1. The relationship between the Patient table and the Visits table should be a standard one-to-many relationship, using an inner join based on the PhoneNumber field. Checking the Cascade Update option will automatically update the phone number in the Visits table. You can learn about this concept in the section "Relationships."

2. A many-to-many relationship cannot be created directly. A junction table must be created to join them. You can learn about this concept in the section "First Normal Form."

Chapter 3

Microsoft Access SQL

By the end of this chapter, you will be able to execute the following test objectives:

 Objectives

- ▶ Refer to objects using Access SQL
- ▶ Use Access SQL to write common queries
- ▶ Use Union queries

Test Yourself! Before reading this chapter, test yourself to determine how much study time you will need to devote to this section.

1. You are writing a query in SQL based on the Customers, Orders, and Employees tables. Both the Customers and Employees tables have fields called Name. How would you select the Name field from the Employees table in the Select clause so that Access would be able to differentiate between the two?

2. The ProductID field of the Orders table uses five- or seven-digit numbers to identify products. By using SQL, how would you search for ProductIds that begin with 23 and are followed by 3 digits?

3. You are in charge of sending out this year's holiday greeting. You would like to create one recordset that combines information from the Employees table and the Customers table. The two tables are compatible, (for example, they each track name, address, and so on, but they have different field names). What type of SQL statement could you use to combine the data from the two tables?

Answers are located at the end of the chapter...

Structured Query Language (SQL) is the language used to communicate with the Microsoft Jet Database Engine. The *Query by Example grid (QBE)* allows a user to create a query without writing a SQL statement. When a query is created using the QBE grid, Access generates the SQL statement.

Certain types of queries, however, cannot be created using the QBE grid. Union, Pass-Through, and Data-Definition queries must be written directly in SQL.

For the exam, you should be familiar with the language and syntax of SQL statements. One way to become familiar with SQL statements is to view a query that you created in the QBE grid in SQL view. From the View menu in a query, select SQL. This enables you to view the SQL statement Access generated for the query. You should also be very familiar with Union queries.

Understanding the Types of Queries

This chapter discusses several types of queries that can be created in Access. We will begin with the most common type of query: Select. Select queries select rows of data from tables and return them as a dynaset recordset. (The results of a query are always referred to as a dynaset.) We will also discuss action queries that update data (Update, Delete, Insert Into, and Select Into) and action queries that define data (Create Table, Constraint, Create Index, Alter Table, and Drop). And finally, we will look at Union queries, which cannot be created in the QBE grid; they can only be created using Access SQL.

Referring to Objects by Using Access SQL

Objective

When writing SQL statements in Access, you always have to refer to fields, tables, and queries. If the name does not contain any spaces or illegal characters, you can simply use the actual name. However, if there are spaces or illegal characters in the field, table, or query name, you must enclose the name in square brackets. Note the following examples:

EmployeeID

[Employee#]

In addition, if the same field name is used in more than one table used in the query, you must precede the field name with the name of the table or query followed by a period. Following are two examples:

Customer.CustomerID

Order.CustomerID

This enables Access to differentiate between the two fields.

Using General SQL Statement Syntax

The syntax of the SQL statement follows:

```
SELECT [predicate] { * ¦ table.* ¦ [table.]field1 [AS alias1] [,
[table.]field2 [AS alias2] [, ...]]}
FROM tableexpression [, ...] [IN externaldatabase]
[WHERE... ]
[GROUP BY... ]
[HAVING... ]
[ORDER BY... ]
[WITH OWNERACCESS OPTION]
```

Any arguments in square brackets are optional. All other arguments are required.

Creating Common Queries

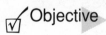

Although common queries can be created using the QBE grid, you must be familiar with the language and syntax of SQL statements. For the exam, you will probably have to be able to select the correct SQL statement from four choices, and/or determine the results of a particular SQL statement. In this section, we go over the keywords of SQL statements, and the syntax required with each one.

Tip
> If you are not familiar with SQL, you may want to view the SQL window for queries that you have created using the QBE grid. This enables you to see the SQL statement that Access has generated from the information entered in the QBE grid.

As mentioned earlier, Select queries are the most common type of query used in Access. A *Select query* is used to choose specific columns (fields) and rows (records) from a particular recordset and to choose what order to put the records in. All queries begin with the basic syntax of Select queries; therefore this is the most important thing to learn in SQL before learning about action queries or Union queries.

Select Clause

The Select statement is used to determine which fields and which rows of records from the underlying recordset will be included in the dynaset. The basic syntax of the Select statement is as follows:

```
SELECT [predicate] { * ¦ table.* ¦ [table.]field1 [AS alias1] [,
[table.]field2 [AS alias2] [, ...]]}
```

The Select clause and the From clause must be included in the Select statement. The Where and Order By clauses are optional.

The Select clause is used to specify which column should be included in the dynaset. This is the equivalent of adding the field name to the QBE grid.

To include more than one column in the output of the query, simply place a comma between each field. Note the following example:

```
SELECT[Customer #], LastName, FirstName
```

To include all fields from a particular table or query, use an asterisk (*):

```
SELECT *
```

Table 3.1 lists the arguments for the Select clause.

Table 3.1

Select Clause Arguments

Argument	Description
Predicate	The predicate is an optional argument used to restrict the number of records returned. The following keywords can be used as predicates: All, Distinct, DistinctRow, or Top. If no predicate is specified, the default is All. See the section "Using Predicates" for more information.
*	The asterisk specifies that all fields from the table or tables are selected. This is used in the same way that the asterisk is used in the QBE grid.
Table	This is a required argument, specifying the name of the table containing the fields from which records are selected. If the table name uses spaces or other illegal characters, you must enclose the name in square brackets.
Field1, Field2	These are the names of the fields to include in the dynaset. If the field name is included in more than one table, precede the field name with the table name and the dot (period) operator. If the field or table name contains any illegal characters, enclose the name in square brackets: [Customer Information].[First Name]
Alias1, Alias2	These are optional arguments that are used to rename the columns in the dynaset.
TableExpression	This is the name of the table or tables containing the data you want to retrieve.
ExternalDatabase	If the table or tables in the TableExpression are not contained in the current database, you must include the name of the database that contains the tables.

Remember, most of the above arguments are optional. The Select statement only has to contain the Select statement, the fields to include, and the table that contains those fields. Note the following example:

```
SELECT FirstName, LastName FROM Customers
```

Using Predicates

The *predicate* is an optional argument used to restrict the number of records returned. Four valid predicate arguments exist in Access SQL. Table 3.2 lists these arguments.

Table 3.2

Predicate Arguments

Predicate Argument	Description
All	This is the default predicate (assumed if no predicate is specified). The dynaset will include all rows that meet the specifications. This is the equivalent to setting both the UniqueValues and the UniqueRecords properties to No.
Distinct	This predicate causes Access to eliminate duplicates in the dynaset, based on the columns selected. In other words, no two rows that contain exactly the same data in the fields specified in the SQL statement are duplicated. This causes the dynaset to be read-only. This is the equivalent to setting the UniqueValues property to Yes in the QBE grid.
DistinctRow	This predicate corresponds to the UniqueRecords property in the QBE grid. DistinctRow tells Access to eliminate any duplicates in the dynaset, based on all columns in the source tables, not just the columns in the recordset. It has no effect on single-table queries, or on multiple-table queries, where there is at least one column from each table included in the dynaset. Although it is not necessary on these types of queries, it will not affect the performance of the query. In these situations, DistinctRow has the same result as Distinct, yet the recordset is updateable. In most instances, DistinctRow is preferable to Distinct.

continues

Table 3.2 Continued

Predicate Argument	Description
Top	Returns the top *n* rows, or top *n* percent from a recordset. The top predicate should be used only when the OrderBy clause is used. Otherwise, Access will simply return the first *n* records in the recordset. Because Nulls are considered the smallest value, they will be included in the dynaset. To eliminate Nulls from the resulting dynaset, be sure to use criteria to exclude them from the recordset. The Top predicate is unique to Access SQL. It is the equivalent of using the TopValues property in the QBE grid. Access processes this after all criteria and Order By clauses have been applied.

 Tip

The Distinct predicate is not necessary if you have included the primary keys of each table in a query. If the primary keys are included, the records will automatically be unique. Not only is Distinct unnecessary, this predicate will make your query less efficient. Only use the Distinct predicate when necessary.

The following examples show the results of queries based on the Products table and the OrderDetails table from the Northwind database. The query returns the names of products from orders in which the quantity was greater than 50. Each query is identical, except for the predicate used. Figure 3.1 uses the All predicate, figure 3.2 uses Distinct, figure 3.3 uses DistinctRow, and figure 3.4 uses Top. Notice that Distinct and DistinctRow each return 65 records (there are no duplicates). The dynaset resulting from the DistinctRow query is updatable, however, while the dynaset resulting from the Distinct query is not. Remember, you can always create these queries in the QBE grid and then view the SQL statement. This is an easy way to become more familiar with the syntax of SQL statements.

Predicate

Figure 3.1

Results of the Query Using the All predicate.

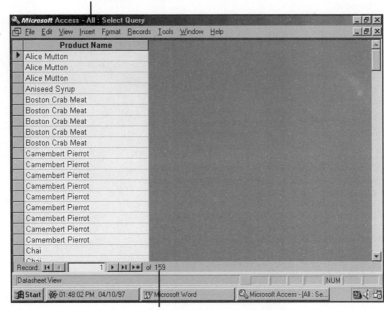

Number of records returned

Predicate

Figure 3.2

Results of the Query Using the Distinct predicate.

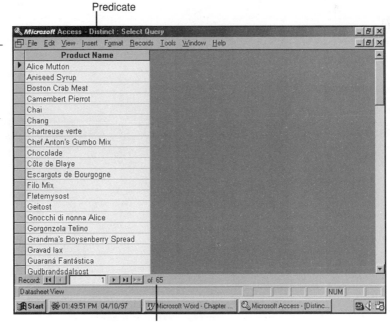

Number of records returned

Predicate

Figure 3.3

*Results of the
Query Using the
DistinctRow
predicate.*

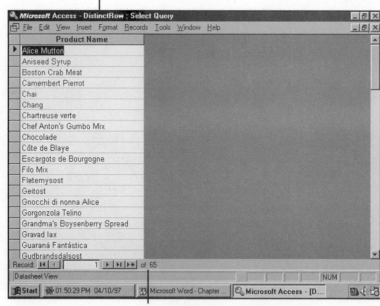

Number of records returned

Predicate

Figure 3.4

*Results of the
Query Using the
Top predicate.*

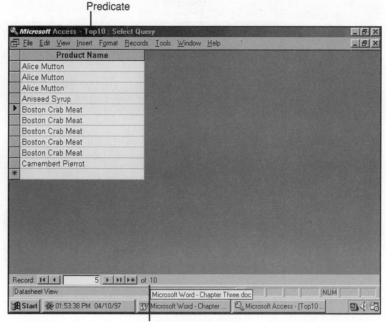

Number of records returned

From Clause

The From clause is used to specify which tables or queries you want to select records from. When more than one table or query is used, you must specify the tables that will be joined.

You can temporarily rename (alias) a table using the As keyword. Simply follow the name of the table with As *aliasname*. If the original table name is very long, an alias is sometimes created to make it easier to refer to the table in SQL. An alias must be created if you are using a self join.

Using Joins

Most queries are based on more than one table or query. In order to produce meaningful results in your dynaset, you must properly join the tables or queries by creating a relationship between them.

When using the QBE grid, any relationships that were established in the Relationship window will automatically be created when those tables are used in the query. However, when writing an SQL statement, you must join the tables in each query.

The join is created in the From clause. There are three join types: inner joins, outer joins, and self-joins.

Inner Joins

An inner join specifies that the query will return only records in which there is a match between both tables. If a customer is entered in the Customer table, for example, but has not yet placed an order (and therefore does not have an entry in the Order table), a query based on Customers and Orders using an inner join does not include that customer in its dynaset.

Outer Joins

An outer join is created when you need to include all records from one table, but from the related table need only those that include the matching record. For example, if a dynaset must include all customers (regardless of whether or not they have placed any orders) and the dates of any orders, an outer join is required. The outer join includes all customers and any order dates. The OrderDate field is Null for those customers who have not yet placed an order.

A left-outer join returns all records from the first (left) table, and only those from the second (right) table in which there is a match. In this case the left table is *preserved*, meaning that all of its records are returned.

Conversely, a right-outer join returns all records from the second (right) table and only those from the first (left) in which there is a match. In this case, the right table is preserved.

The following statement returns the name of all customers in the Northwind database, whether or not they have placed an order. If a customer has placed an order, the order date appears as well.

```
SELECT DISTINCTROW Customers.CompanyName, Orders.OrderDate
FROM Customers LEFT JOIN Orders ON Customers.CustomerID =
Orders.CustomerID;
```

Figure 3.5 shows the QBE grid view for the above Select statement.

Figure 3.5

This query uses a left-outer join to list all customers in the Northwind database, regardless of whether they have placed an order.

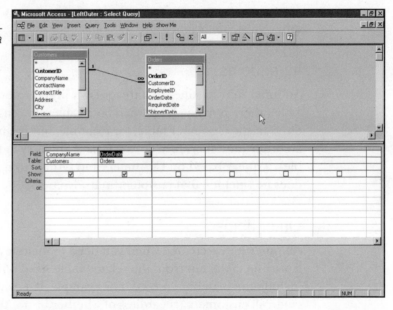

A table that has been preserved cannot be a part of another relationship in a query. This situation results in the error message "Query contains ambiguous outer joins." If you need to include more than two tables in your query and have an outer join, you must first create the query with the outer join, and then use that query as the basis for another query.

Self Joins

A table sometimes needs to be joined to itself. For example, suppose the Employees table contained the EmployeeID for an employee's supervisor. In order to show employees and their supervisors' names, a self join would be needed.

To create a self join you must create an alias of the table and then join the alias to the original table. To create an alias, use the keyword As after the table name in the join statement. In order to avoid confusion, it is usually a good idea to also create an alias for the field from the table alias that is used in the query.

The following SQL statement returns the first and last name of an employee and the last name of the employee's supervisor (Reports To field). An alias of the Employees table (Copy_of_Employees) is used. In addition, an alias (Manager) has been created for the Last Name field from the Copy_of_Employees table.

```
SELECT DISTINCTROW Employees.FirstName, Employees.LastName,
Employees_Alias.LastName AS [Reports To]
FROM Employees INNER JOIN Employees AS Employees_Alias ON
Employees.EmployeeID = Employees_Alias.ReportsTo;
```

Where Clause

The Where clause is an optional clause that is used to restrict the rows returned in the dynaset. This clause corresponds to the criteria row in the QBE grid. If a Where clause is not included, all records are returned. A field referred to in the Where clause does not need to be included in the dynaset. (Using the QBE grid, you would simply remove the check from the Show box.) The Where clause can contain up to 40 columns or expressions.

The syntax of the Where clause is as follows:

```
WHERE Expression1[And/Or Expression2{,...}]
```

When referring to a field name that includes spaces or punctuation characters, enclose the field name in brackets. When referring to dates, you must have a pound sign (#) at the beginning and end of the date, and the date must be in standard U.S. format. String expressions must be enclosed in quotation marks.

Using Like in Criteria

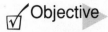 There most likely will be a question on the exam using Like and a wildcard in a Where expression. Be sure to understand the wildcard characters and the records that each returns.

Like is used to compare a string expression to a pattern in an SQL expression. Like is often used with wildcard characters in a Where expression. The wildcard character is used to replace certain parts of the expression. Table 3.3 lists the valid wildcard characters used in Access SQL.

Table 3.3

Wildcard Characters

Wildcard Character	Description
?	Any single character
*	Zero or more characters
#	Any single digit (0–9)
[charlist]	Any single character in charlist
[!charlist]	Any single character not in charlist

The [charlist] argument can contain a list of characters. For example Like "F[ia]t" would return Fit or Fat. The following statement will return all records that have data in the CompanyName field which begins with "S," followed by either "A" or "E," and then followed by any string:

```
SELECT DISTINCTROW Customers.CompanyName
FROM Customers
WHERE (((Customers.CompanyName) Like "S[ae]*"));
```

Figure 3.6 shows the dynaset returned by the query created in the above SQL statement.

Figure 3.6

A query that will return all records with data in the CompanyName field which begins with "S," followed by either "A" or "E," and then followed by any string.

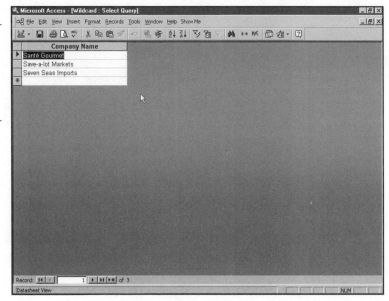

The following SQL statement returns all records in the Clients table that have data beginning with "S" in the CompanyName field.

```
SELECT DISTINCTROW Customers.CompanyName
FROM Customers
WHERE (((Customers.CompanyName) Like "S*"));
```

Figure 3.7 shows the dynaset returned by the query created in the above statement.

Order By Clause

The Order By clause is optional. It is used to sort the records in the dynaset by one or more columns. The keyword Asc (ascending) or Desc (descending) is used with this clause. The Order By clause corresponds to the Sort line in the QBE grid. The precedence in sorting is left to right, as it is in the QBE grid.

The field used in the Order By clause does not have to be included in the Select clause. This would be the equivalent of removing the check from the Show box in the QBE grid. You cannot use Memo or OLE-object type fields in an Order By clause.

Figure 3.7

A query that returns all records in the Clients table that have data beginning with "S" in the CompanyName field.

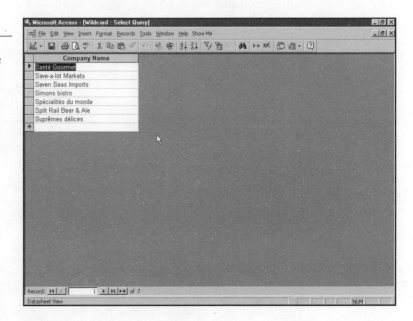

Aggregate Queries

Aggregate queries (sometimes referred to as *Totals* queries) are used when you need to perform a calculation on a group of records. If you need to determine the average price of a product in several categories, for example, an Aggregate query can be used.

Aggregate queries use two special arguments: Group By and Having. To create an Aggregate query in the QBE grid, choose Show Totals from the View menu. This adds a Total line to the grid. You then must enter an argument in the Total row for each field in the query.

Group By Clause

The Group By clause is an optional clause used in Aggregate queries. It is used to define the rows that should be grouped together in order to perform the Aggregate function. The expressions in the Group By clause can reference columns in a table, a calculated expression, or a constant.

The following SQL statement creates an Aggregate query in the Northwind database. This query determines the average price of products in each category.

```
SELECT DISTINCTROW Categories.CategoryName,
Avg(Products.UnitPrice) AS AvgOfUnitPrice
FROM Categories INNER JOIN Products ON Categories.CategoryID =
Products.CategoryID
GROUP BY Categories.CategoryName;
```

Figure 3.8 shows the results of the query created in the above SQL statement.

Figure 3.8

A query that determines the average price of products in each category.

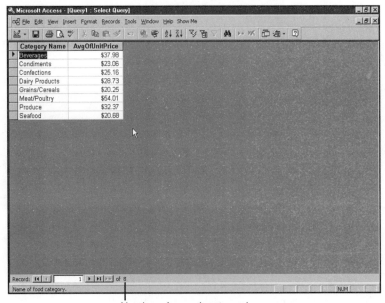

Number of records returned

You can use more than one field in the Group By expression. The groups are defined from left to right and are automatically placed in ascending order.

The following SQL statements create an Aggregate query, which uses two fields in the Group By clause. This is the same query created in the above example, with one more Group By field. This query shows the average price of products in each category, grouped by supplier.

```
SELECT DISTINCTROW Categories.CategoryName, Products.SupplierID,
Avg(Products.UnitPrice) AS AvgOfUnitPrice
FROM Categories INNER JOIN Products ON Categories.CategoryID =
Products.CategoryID
GROUP BY Categories.CategoryName, Products.SupplierID;
```

Figure 3.9 shows the results of the query created above. Notice that there are now 49 records, as opposed to eight records from the first query. Grouping by more than one field will increase the number of records returned in the dynaset.

Figure 3.9

A query that shows the average price of products in each category, grouped by supplier.

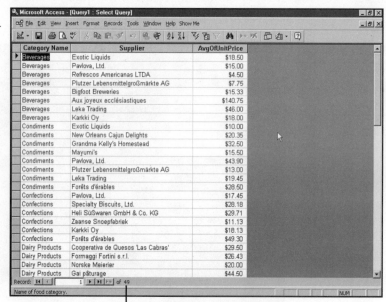

Number of records returned

Having Clause

The Having clause is an optional clause used in Aggregate queries. Like the Where clause, it is used to enter criteria that will restrict the records returned by the query. Criteria entered in the Where clause is applied before grouping the records. Criteria contained in the Having clause is applied after grouping the records. Therefore, the Having clause is used to filter records based on the aggregate calculation, rather than filtering individual records before applying the criteria.

When you use the QBE grid, any criteria placed in a field that uses Group By in the total row is translated into a Having clause in the SQL statement. Any criteria entered in a field that uses "Where" in the total row is translated into a Where clause in the SQL statement.

The following SQL statement creates a query that uses the Having clause. This query returns records whose order totals (sums of product totals) were over $100.00. There are 793 records in the dynaset.

```
SELECT DISTINCTROW Sum([UnitPrice]*[Quantity]) AS ItemTotal,
Orders.OrderID
FROM (Employees INNER JOIN Orders ON Employees.EmployeeID =
Orders.EmployeeID) INNER JOIN [Order Details] ON Orders.OrderID =
[Order Details].OrderID
GROUP BY Orders.OrderID
HAVING (((Sum([UnitPrice]*[Quantity]))>100));
```

Figure 3.10 shows the QBE view of the above statement.

Figure 3.10

A query that returns records whose order totals (sums of product totals) were over $100.00.

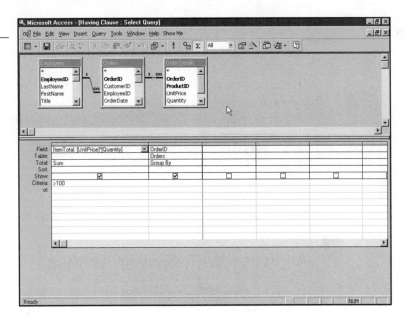

Figure 3.11 shows the QBE grid for a similar query. This query, however, applies the criteria before performing the Aggregate

calculation. In this case, only ProductTotals greater than $100.00 are included in the dynaset. This dynaset includes only 782 records.

Figure 3.11

Aggregate query that applies the criteria before performing aggregate function.

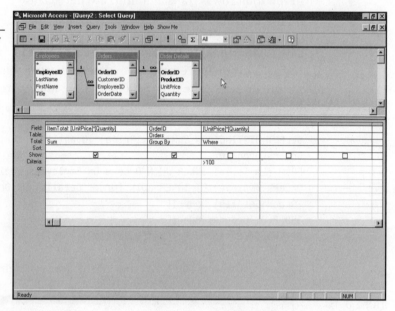

The following statement is the SQL statement for the above query.

```
SELECT DISTINCTROW Sum([UnitPrice]*[Quantity]) AS ItemTotal,
Orders.OrderID
FROM (Employees INNER JOIN Orders ON Employees.EmployeeID =
Orders.EmployeeID) INNER JOIN [Order Details] ON Orders.OrderID =
[Order Details].OrderID
WHERE ((([UnitPrice]*[Quantity])>100))
GROUP BY Orders.OrderID;
```

Notice the third column that is created in Figure 3.11.

Allowing With Owner Access

The With Owner Access Option declaration is an optional declaration used in a multi-user environment with secure workgroups. It can be used only with a saved query. It has no effect when used in a SQL statement in a form's RecordSource property.

With Owner Access Option enables the users of the query to inherit your security rights while running the query. If a user does not have the necessary security permission for one of the underlying tables, you must use this declaration so that the user can run the query.

This declaration is equivalent to setting the RunPermissions property to Owner's in the QBE grid. If you leave out this declaration, it is equivalent to setting this property to User's.

For more information about multi-user environments and security, please see Chapter 12, "Implementing Database Security."

Using Parameters in Queries

You can specify parameters in a SQL statement, just as you can in the QBE grid. Parameters are used to enable the user to enter criteria at runtime.

The Parameters declaration is used at the beginning of a query to specify a parameter in SQL. If more than one parameter is required, be sure to separate the parameters by commas. A semicolon is used to separate all of the parameters from the rest of the statement.

The syntax for a Parameters declaration follows:

```
PARAMETERS parameter1 datatype1 [,paramatr2 datatype2 [,...]]:
sqlstatement
```

The following statement enables the user to enter the order number and then returns the specified information from the Orders and Order Details tables.

```
PARAMETERS [Enter Order #] Long;
SELECT DISTINCTROW Orders.OrderID, Orders.CustomerID,
Orders.OrderDate, [Order Details].ProductID, [Order
Details].UnitPrice, [Order Details].Quantity
FROM Orders INNER JOIN [Order Details] ON Orders.OrderID = [Order
Details].OrderID
WHERE (((Orders.OrderID)=[Enter Order #]));
```

The preceding query prompts the user to "Enter the Order #" when the query is run.

Specifying parameters in queries allows the queries to be much more flexible. The criteria can be changed each time the query is run, without changing the structure of the query.

Creating Action Queries

Action queries begin like Select queries, in that they select particular columns (fields) and rows (records) from a table or tables. Action queries then add an additional step of performing some type of action on those records. There are two different types of Action queries: those that update data and those that define new data.

When you run Action queries, the records are immediately changed, but a result set is not generated. If you want to know which records will be changed, create and run a Select query, which uses the same criteria as the Update query.

Access SQL has four commands that allow you to update data. These commands can also be entered in the QBE grid by choosing them from the Query menu. Table 3.4 lists the four Update commands and their counterparts from the Query menu.

Table 3.4

Access SQL Update Data Commands	
SQL Statement	QBE Grid (Query Menu)
Update	Update
Delete	Delete
Insert Into	Append
Select Into	Make Table

The following sections cover each type of SQL statement command.

Update Statement

Update queries are used to change values in one or more columns in a table or query. If you are updating values in a query, the query must be updateable. The Update statement is used to create an Update query.

The syntax of the Update statement is as follows:

```
UPDATE table
SET newvalue
WHERE criteria;
```

Table 3.5 explains each argument of the Update statement.

Table 3.5

Arguments of the Update Statement

Part	Description
Table	The name of the table whose data you want to modify.
NewValue	Expression that determines the value to be inserted into a particular field in the updated records.
Criteria	Expression that determines which records will be updated. Only records that satisfy the expression are updated.

The following statement increases the prices of all products in the beverage category (CategoryID 1) by five percent:

```
UPDATE DISTINCTROW Categories INNER JOIN Products
ON Categories.CategoryID = Products.CategoryID
SET Products.UnitPrice = [UnitPrice]*([UnitPrice]*0.05)
WHERE (((Products.CategoryID)=1));
```

Delete Statement

The Delete statement is used to delete rows from tables. The syntax of the Delete statement is:

```
DELETE [table.*]
FROM table
WHERE criteria
```

Table 3.6 explains each argument of the Delete statement.

Table 3.6

Arguments of the Delete Statement	
Part	Description
Table.*	This argument is optional. The name of the table from which records are deleted.
Table	The name of the table from which records are deleted.
Criteria	An expression that determines which records to delete. Only records that meet the criteria will be deleted.

The following statement deletes from the Northwind database all customers who have never placed an order.

```
DELETE DISTINCTROW Customers.CustomerID, Orders.OrderID
FROM Customers
INNER JOIN Orders ON Customers.CustomerID = Orders.CustomerID
WHERE (((Orders.OrderID) Is Null));
```

Access does not allow you to delete records if doing so violates the rules of referential integrity. If you tried to delete a customer who had a related record in the Orders table, for example, you would receive an error message unless you had turned on Cascade Delete for these tables. (For more information about Cascade Updates and Deletes, please see Chapter 2, "Database Design.")

If there is more than one table used in the Select statement, you must use the asterisk (*) to select all of the fields that you would like to delete. Otherwise, Access will display the error message "Must Specify Tables to Delete From."

Insert Into Statement

 **Objective**

The Insert Into clause is used to copy rows from one table or query into another query. It can also be used to add a single row to a table using a list of values. The Insert Into clause is the equivalent of choosing Append from the Query menu in the QBE grid.

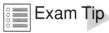 **Exam Tip**

> Because the Insert Into statement is considered to be one of the "Commonly Used Queries" it may well be included on the exam!

To use the Insert Into clause to add a single row to a table or query using a list of values, use the following syntax:

```
INSERT INTO target [(field1[, field2[, ...]])]
VALUES (value1[, value2[, ...])
```

If the column references are omitted in the Insert Into clause, you must include a value for each column in the target table, and they must be in the exact order that they appear in the table definition. If you do include column references, make sure that you include the primary key and any other required fields.

To use the Insert Into clause to add multiple rows to a table based on criteria, use the following syntax:

```
INSERT INTO target [IN externaldatabase] [(field1[, field2[, ...]])]
SELECT [source.]field1[, field2[, ...]
FROM tableexpression
```

Table 3.7 explains each argument used in the Insert Into statement.

Table 3.7

Arguments in the Insert Into Clause

Part	Description
Target	The name of the table or query to append records to.
ExternalDatabase	The path to an external database. For a description of the path, see the In clause.
Source	The name of the table or query to copy records from.
Field1, Field2	Names of the fields to append data to, if following a target argument, or the names of fields to obtain data from, if following a source argument.
TableExpression	The name of the table or tables from which records are inserted. This argument can be a single table name or a compound resulting from an inner join, left-outer join, or right-outer join operation, or a saved query.
Value1, Value2	The values to insert into the specific fields of the new record. Each value is inserted into the field that corresponds to the value's position in the list: value1 is inserted into field1 of the new record, value2 into field2, and so on. You must separate values with a comma, and enclose text fields in double quotation marks (" ").

Any Select statement that produces a recordset can be used with the Insert Into statement. This includes Group By clauses, joins, Union operators, and subqueries.

The following statement appends records from a table called MarketingList to the existing Customers table. Only those customers from the U.S. are added.

```
INSERT INTO Customers (CustomerID, CompanyName, Address, City,
Region, PostalCode, Country )
SELECT DISTINCTROW MarketingList.CustomerNumber,
MarketingList.Company, MarketingList.Address, MarketingList.City,
MarketingList.State, MarketingList.Zip, MarketingList.Country
FROM MarketingList
WHERE (((MarketingList.Country)="USA"));
```

Select Into Statement

The Select Into statement is very much like the Insert Into statement. The Select Into statement creates a new table and appends the data, rather than appending the data to an existing table. The syntax of the Select Into is as follows:

```
SELECT field1[, field2[, ...]] INTO newtable [IN
externaldatabase] FROM source
```

Table 3.8 lists the parts of the Select Into statement.

Table 3.8

Parts of the Select Into Statement

Part	Description
Field1, Field2	The names of the fields to be copied into the new table.
NewTable	The name of the table to be created. (Must follow standard naming conventions.) If NewTable is the same as the name of an existing table, a trappable error will result.
ExternalDatabase	The path to an external database.
Source	The name of the existing table from which records are selected. This can be a single or multiple tables or a query.

The fields in the new table inherit the data type and field size of the fields from the original table. However, no other field or table properties (such as default values, validation rules, and so on) are transferred.

Using Subqueries

Subqueries enable you to embed one Select statement into another. Subqueries can be nested into Select Into, Insert Into, Delete, or Update statements or inside another subquery. They are used to filter the query based on the values in another query. Subqueries are placed in the Where clause of an SQL Select statement. You may nest several subqueries into one Select statement. There is no documented limit to the number of subqueries that can be nested.

There are three forms of subqueries:

comparison [ANY I ALL I SOME] (sqlstatement)

expression [NOT] IN (sqlstatement)

[NOT] EXISTS (sqlstatement)

Table 3.9 explains each of the parts of a subquery.

Table 3.9

Parts of a Subquery

Part	Description
comparison	An expression and a comparison operator that compares the expression with the results of the subquery.
expression	An expression for which the result set of the subquery is searched.
sqlstatement	A Select statement that follows the same format and rules of any other Select statement. It must be enclosed in parentheses.

A subquery may be used instead of an expression in the field list of a Select statement or in a Where or Having clause. In a subquery, the Select statement provides a set of specific values to evaluate in the Where or Having clause.

To use a subquery in the QBE grid, place the Select statement in the Criteria or Field cell of a query.

The following statement finds all customers who have placed an order in January of 1995 in the Northwind database.

```
SELECT ContactName, CompanyName, ContactTitle, Phone
FROM Customers WHERE CustomerID IN (SELECT CustomerID FROM Orders
WHERE OrderDate BETWEEN #01/1/95# AND #01/31/95#);
```

Comparison Subqueries: Using ANY, ALL, SOME

A subquery can also be used to compare a value against rows in another query. This type of query also returns a single column. This form of the subquery simply uses another table or query in the WHERE clause. For example, the following SQL statements returns the ProductID of items from the Order Details table which are more expensive than Ikura in the products table.

```
SELECT * FROM Products
WHERE UnitPrice > ANY
(SELECT UnitPrice FROM [Order Details]
WHERE Quantity >= 50);
```

Expression Subqueries: Using IN and NOT IN

The In statement is used to retrieve only those records in the main query that have a match in the subquery. Using the In statements causes Access to check the value of a single column against the values in another table or query. This type of query only returns a single column. The following statement returns a list of all of the products that have been ordered in quantities of 40 or more.

```
SELECT Products.*, *
FROM Products
WHERE (((Products.ProductID) In (SELECT ProductID FROM [Order
Details]
WHERE Discount >= .15)));
```

Exists Subqueries: Using Exists and Not Exists

Using Exists and Not Exists in a subquery allows you to check for the existence of a particular value in another table or query. The following SQL statement returns any items from the Order Details table that have been discontinued.

```
SELECT DISTINCTROW Products.ProductID, Products.Discontinued
FROM Products
WHERE ((Not (Products.ProductID)=Exists (Select * from [Order
Details] Where ProductID = Products.ProductID)) AND
((Products.Discontinued)=Yes));
```

Creating Union Queries

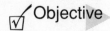 Objective

The Union operator is used to join together two or more queries that are compatible, but not necessarily related. If you wanted to send a Holiday letter to both employees and customers, for example, you could use a Union query to join these two tables into one recordset. Union queries can be created only in SQL; there is no equivalent in the QBE grid. The resulting recordset is always read-only.

When referring to an existing query in a Union query, you must enclose the name of the query in square brackets. The basic syntax of the Union query is as follows:

```
[TABLE] query1 UNION [ALL] [TABLE] query2 [UNION [ALL] [TABLE]
queryn [ ... ]]
```

query1 can represent a query or a table. If it represents a table, you must precede the name with Table.

The columns from each table or query are matched by their positions in the Select statement, not by their names. Therefore, all queries in a Union operation must request the same number of fields; however, the fields don't have to be of the same size or data type.

Using the All Predicate

Unless you specify the All predicate, no duplicate records are returned when you use a Union operation. Using the All predicate also makes the query run more quickly, even if there are no duplicates. This is because Access does not have to compare the recordsets to check for duplicates.

Using the TABLE Option

If you want to include all fields from a table or query you can use the TABLE option. This is the equivalent to using Select * From table-or-query. These statements can be used interchangeably. The basic syntax follows:

```
TABLE table-or-query
```

Sorting in Union Queries

The Order By clause can only be used in the last Select statement. Although each Select statement in a Union query can have an Order By clause, Access ignores all but the last one. If the column names differ, however (such as in EmployeeName and Customer-Name), you must reference the name assigned to the column in the first Select statement.

When you combine fields with different names, Access uses the column name from the first query. If the columns have different data types, Access converts the column to a single data type that is compatible with both columns. Text combined with a number produces a text column, and two number columns will always use the larger data type of the two. Memo and OLE fields cannot be used in Union queries.

The following statement is used to combine records from the Employees table and the Customers table. Because the Customer table uses ContactName, which includes the contact's first and last name, the FirstName and LastName fields of the Employees table are combined into the field name. Notice that in order to sort by the Name field, it must be included in the last Select statement, but it references the Name field, which is created in the first Select statement.

```
SELECT FirstName & " " & LastName as Name, Address, City, Region,
PostalCode, Country FROM Employees
UNION
SELECT ContactName,Address, City, Region, PostalCode, Country
FROM Customers
Order By Name
```

Figure 3.12 shows the dynaset that is created by the preceding Union query.

Figure 3.12

A Union query that combines records from the Employees table and the Customers table.

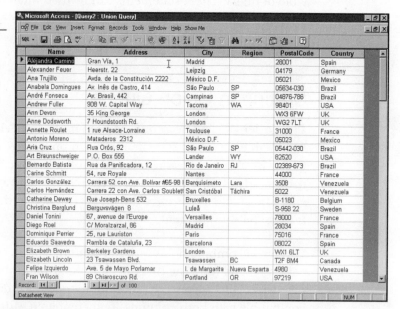

Key Terms and Concepts

Table 3.10 identifies key terms from this chapter. Review the key terms and make sure that you understand each term for the exam.

Table 3.10

Key Terms: Microsost Access SQL	
Term	Covered in Section...
Select Clause	"Creating Common Queries"
From Clause	"Creating Common Queries"
Where Clause	"Creating Common Queries"
Predicates	"Using Predicates"
Distinct	"Using Predicates"
DistinctRow	"Using Predicates"
Top	"Using Predicates"
Inner Join	"Using Joins"
Outer Join	"Using Joins"
Self Join	"Using Joins"
Like	"Using Like in Criteria"
Group By	"Aggregate Queries"
Having Clause	"Aggregate Queries"
With Owner Access	"Allowing With Owner Access"
Parameter	"Using Parameters in Queries"
Update	"Creating Action Queries"
Delete	"Creating Action Queries"
Insert Into	"Creating Action Queries"
Select Into	"Creating Action Queries"
Union Queries	"Creating Action Queries"

Lab Exercise

This exercise provides practice for you to create queries using SQL statements. To complete the exercise, you must be able to create queries using outer and self joins. In addition, you must be able to create a Union query.

Exercise 3.1:   Creating Queries Using SQL Statements

Objectives:

Create a query based on an outer join.

Create a query based on a self join.

Create a Union query.

Time Estimate: 30 minutes

Steps:

Using the LabThree.mdb, write SQL statements that will accomplish the following:

1. Create a dynaset that shows all customers (CustomerID) and the dates of the last orders they have placed. Make sure that you also include customers who have not yet placed an order.

2. Using a self join, create a dynaset that shows each employee's name and department, and the name of the person that each reports to. (ReportTo, not the ReportsTo #).

3. Create a Union query that joins the name and address information from the Employees and Customers tables.

Comments:

Although the first two queries can be created using the QBE grid, this will not give you any practice in creating SQL statements! Try to create these directly from a SQL statement.

Reading Reference:

For more information to help you complete these lab exercises, please refer to the sections "Creating Common Queries" and "Creating Union Queries."

Review Questions

1. Which of the following statements correctly include Customer# (from the Customers table) in the resulting dynaset? Choose all that apply.

    A. SELECT Customers.Customer# FROM Customers

    B. SELECT Customer# FROM Customers

    C. SELECT Customers.[Customer#] FROM Customers

    D. SELECT [Customer#] FROM Customers

2. Which of the following Select statements correctly creates an alias of Name for the ClientName field?

    A. SELECT Customers.ClientName ALIAS AS "NAME"

    B. SELECT Customers.ClientName ALIAS AS NAME

    C. SELECT Customers.ClientName AS Name

    D. SELECT ALIAS ClientName of Customers.ClientName

3. If no predicate is indicated in the Select statement, which predicate is returned?

    A. All

    B. Distinct

    C. DistinctRow

    D. End

4. Which of the following statements will return *all* customer numbers from the customer table, and the OrderIDs of those customers who have placed orders?

    A. SELECT DISTINCTROW Customers.CustomerID, Orders.OrderID Right JOIN Orders ON Customers.CustomerID = Orders.CustomerID;

    B. SELECT DISTINCTROW Customers.CustomerID, Orders.OrderID LEFT JOIN Orders ON Customers.CustomerID = Orders.CustomerID;

C. SELECT DISTINCTROW Customers.CustomerID, Orders.OrderID Right OUTER JOIN Orders ON Customers.CustomerID = Orders.CustomerID;

D. SELECT DISTINCTROW Customers.CustomerID, Orders.OrderID LEFT OUTER JOIN Orders ON Customers.CustomerID = Orders.CustomerID;

5. Which of the following statements creates a self join in the Employees table?

A. SELECT DISTINCTROW Employees.FirstName, Employees.LastName, Employees2.LastName AS [Reports To] FROM Employees SELF JOIN Employees AS Employees2 ON Employees.EmployeeID = Employees2.ReportsTo;

B. SELECT DISTINCTROW Employees.FirstName, Employees.LastName, ReportsTo SELF JOIN ReportsTo;

C. SELECT DISTINCTROW Employees.FirstName, Employees.LastName, ReportsTo INNER JOIN ReportsTo;

D. SELECT DISTINCTROW Employees.FirstName, Employees.LastName, Employees2.LastName AS [Reports To] FROM Employees INNER JOIN Employees AS Employees2 ON Employees.EmployeeID = Employees2.ReportsTo;

6. A query is created to find last names in the LastName column of the Customer table that match the following condition: S[ma]*y. Which of the following names would be included? Select all that apply.

A. Smith

B. Sandy

C. Smythe

D. Salamander

7. Which of the following statements will show the average price of products in each category?

   A. SELECT DISTINCTROW Categories.CategoryName, Avg(Products.UnitPrice) AS AvgOfUnitPrice FROM Categories INNER JOIN Products ON Categories.CategoryID = Products.CategoryID GROUP BY Categories.CategoryName;

   B. SELECT DISTINCTROW,GROUP BY Categories.CategoryName Categories.CategoryName, Avg(Products.UnitPrice) AS AvgOfUnitPrice FROM Categories INNER JOIN Products ON Categories.CategoryID = Products.CategoryID;

   C. SELECT DISTINCTROW Categories.CategoryName, Avg(Products.UnitPrice) AS AvgOfUnitPrice FROM Categories INNER JOIN GROUP BY Categories.CategoryName Products ON Categories.CategoryID = Products.CategoryID;

   D. SELECT DISTINCTROW,GROUP BY Categories.CategoryName Categories.CategoryName, Avg(Products.UnitPrice) AS AvgOfUnitPrice FROM Categories OUTER JOIN Products ON Categories.CategoryID = Products.CategoryID;

8. Assume that the field ProductTotal is a calculated expression based on [UnitPrice] * [Quantity]]. Which of the following statements will only include orders which have a total of over $500?

   A. SELECT DISTINCTROW Orders.OrderID, Sum([UnitPrice]*[Quantity]) AS ProductTotal FROM Orders INNER JOIN [Order Details] ON Orders.OrderID = [Order Details].OrderID WHERE (((([Order Details].UnitPrice)>500)) GROUP BY Orders.OrderID;

B. SELECT DISTINCTROW Orders.OrderID, Sum([UnitPrice]*[Quantity]) AS ProductTotal FROM Orders INNER JOIN [Order Details] ON Orders.OrderID = [Order Details].OrderID WHERE (((([Order Details].UnitPrice)>500)) GROUP BY Orders.ProductTotal;

C. SELECT DISTINCTROW Orders.OrderID, Sum([UnitPrice]*[Quantity]) AS ProductTotal FROM Orders INNER JOIN [Order Details] ON Orders.OrderID = [Order Details].OrderID GROUP BY Orders.ProductTotal HAVING (((Sum([UnitPrice]*[Quantity]))>500));

D. SELECT DISTINCTROW Orders.OrderID, Sum([UnitPrice]*[Quantity]) AS ProductTotal FROM Orders INNER JOIN [Order Details] ON Orders.OrderID = [Order Details].OrderID GROUP BY Orders.OrderID HAVING (((Sum([UnitPrice]*[Quantity]))>500));

9. The Order Information form is based on a query. When you open the form, you need to be able to find a specific order number by entering the criteria of OrderDate (Date/Time field) and CustomerID (text field). Which of the following SQL statements would enable the user to enter the CustomerID and the OrderDate?

A. PARAMETERS [Enter Customer ID]as Text, [Enter Order Date] as DateTime; SELECT DISTINCTROW Customers.CustomerID, Orders.OrderID, Orders.OrderDate, Orders.EmployeeID FROM Customers INNER JOIN Orders ON Customers.CustomerID = Orders.CustomerID WHERE ((((Customers.CustomerID)=[Enter Customer ID]) AND ((Orders.OrderDate)=[Enter Order Date]));

B. PARAMETERS [Enter Customer ID] Text, [Enter Order Date] DateTime; SELECT DISTINCTROW Customers.CustomerID, Orders.OrderID, Orders.OrderDate, Orders.EmployeeID FROM Customers INNER JOIN Orders ON Customers.CustomerID = Orders.CustomerID WHERE ((((Customers.CustomerID)=[Enter Customer ID]) AND ((Orders.OrderDate)=[Enter Order Date]));

C. SELECT DISTINCTROW Customers.CustomerID, Orders.OrderID, Orders.OrderDate, Orders.EmployeeID FROM Customers INNER JOIN Orders ON Customers.CustomerID = Orders.CustomerID WHERE ((((Customers.CustomerID)=[Enter Customer ID]) AND ((Orders.OrderDate)=[Enter Order Date])); PARAMETERS [Enter Customer ID] Text, [Enter Order Date] DateTime;

D. SELECT DISTINCTROW Customers.CustomerID, Orders.OrderID, Orders.OrderDate, Orders.EmployeeID FROM Customers INNER JOIN Orders ON Customers.CustomerID = Orders.CustomerID WHERE ((((Customers.CustomerID)=[Enter Customer ID]) AND ((Orders.OrderDate)=[Enter Order Date])); PARAMETERS [Enter Customer ID] as Text, [Enter Order Date] as DateTime;

10. Which of the following SQL statements would find all records that have the data "UK" in the country field and update that data to "United Kingdom"?

A. UPDATE DISTINCTROW Customers SET Customers.Country = "United Kingdom" WHERE ((((Customers.Country)="UK"));

    B. Select DISTINCTROW Customers WHERE
        (((Customers.Country)="UK")) UPDATE
        Customers.Country = "United Kingdom";

    C. UPDATE DISTINCTROW Customers.Country = "United
        Kingdom" WHERE (((Customers.Country)="UK"));

    D. UPDATE DISTINCTROW Customers ALTER
        Customers.Country = "United Kingdom" WHERE
        (((Customers.Country)="UK"));

11. Which of the following statements deletes those customers
who have not yet placed an order? (There is a one-to-many
relationship between customers and orders; Cascade Delete
has not been set.)

    A. DELETE DISTINCTROW Customers.*,
        Orders.OrderID FROM Customers INNER JOIN Or-
        ders ON Customers.CustomerID = Orders.CustomerID
        WHERE (((Orders.OrderID) Is Null));

    B. DELETE DISTINCTROW Customers.*,
        Orders.OrderID FROM Customers INNER JOIN Or-
        ders ON Customers.CustomerID <>
        Orders.CustomerID

    C. DELETE DISTINCTROW Customers.CustomerID,
        Orders.OrderID FROM Customers INNER JOIN Or-
        ders ON Customers.CustomerID = Orders.CustomerID
        WHERE (((Orders.OrderID) Is Null));

    D. DELETE DISTINCTROW Customers.*,
        Orders.OrderID FROM Customers LEFT JOIN Orders
        ON Customers.CustomerID = Orders.CustomerID
        WHERE (((Orders.OrderID) Is Null));

12. Which of the following SQL statements copies records of customers in the USA from Customers, creates a new table (Table1), and copies these records into Table1 without including the Country field in the new table?

    A. SELECT DISTINCTROW Customers.CustomerID, Customers.CompanyName, Customers.ContactTitle, Customers.Address, Customers.City, Customers.Region,Customers.Country INTO [Table 1] FROM Customers WHERE ((((Customers.Country)="USA"));

    B. SELECT DISTINCTROW Customers.CustomerID, Customers.CompanyName, Customers.ContactTitle, Customers.Address, Customers.City, Customers.Region MAKETABLE [Table 1] FROM Customers WHERE ((((Customers.Country)="USA"));

    C. SELECT DISTINCTROW Customers.CustomerID, Customers.CompanyName, Customers.ContactTitle, Customers.Address, Customers.City, Customers.Region INTO [Table 1] FROM Customers WHERE ((((Customers.Country)="USA"));

    D. SELECT DISTINCTROW Customers.CustomerID, Customers.CompanyName, Customers.ContactTitle, Customers.Address, Customers.City, Customers.Region, Customers.Country, MAKETABLE [Table 1] FROM Customers WHERE ((((Customers.Country)="USA"));

13. Which of the following SQL statements is used to select all records from Table1 and append them to Table2?

    A. INSERT INTO Table2 SELECT Table1.* FROM Table1;

    B. APPEND INTO Table2 SELECT Table1.* FROM Table1;

    C. INSERT INTO Table2 SELECT FROM Table1.* FROM Table1;

    D. UPDATE Table2 SELECT Table1.* FROM Table1;

14. You need to create a Union query that joins similar information from two different tables. The data should be sorted by LastName, and there should not be any duplicates. Which of the following SQL statements accomplishes this?

   A. SELECT FirstName & " "& LastName as Name, Address, City, Region, PostalCode, Country FROM Employees UNION SELECT ContactName,Address, City, Region, PostalCode, Country FROM Customers ORDER BY LastName;

   B. SELECT FirstName & " " & LastName as Name, Address, City, Region, PostalCode, Country FROM Employees ORDER BY LastName UNION SELECT ContactName,Address, City, Region, PostalCode, Country FROM Customers;

   C. SELECT FirstName & " " & LastName as Name, Address, City, Region, PostalCode, Country FROM Employees UNION JOIN SELECT ContactName,Address, City, Region, PostalCode, Country FROM Customers ORDER BY LastName;

   D. SELECT ALL FirstName & " " & LastName as Name, Address, City, Region, PostalCode, Country FROM Employees UNION SELECT ContactName,Address, City, Region, PostalCode, Country FROM Customers ORDER BY LastName;

Answers to Review Questions

1. C and D are correct. When a field name contains a space or other illegal characters (such as an asterisk) you must enclose it in brackets. The name of the table is optional in this statement. See the section "Referring to Objects by Using Access SQL" for more information.

2. C is correct. The keyword As is used to create an alias name. See the section "From Clause" for more information on this topic.

3. A is correct. ALL is the default predicate. For more information, see the section "Creating Common Queries."

4. B is correct. For more information, see the section "Using Joins."

5. D is correct. For more information, see the section "Self Joins."

6. B is correct. The first letter must be "S," followed by either an "m" or an "a," and the last letter must be a "y." See the section "Using Like in Criteria" for more information.

7. A is correct. The Group By clause is placed at the end of the Select statement. For more information see the section "Group By Clause."

8. D is correct. The Having clause applies the criteria after the aggregate function has been performed. See the section "Having Clause" for more information.

9. B is correct. The Parameters statement must come at the beginning of the SQL statement. The parameter is followed by the datatype; the word "as" is not used. For more information, see the section "Using Parameters in Queries."

10. A is correct. The words "update" and "set" must be used in an update query. For more information, see the section "Update Statement."

11. D is correct. For more information, see the section "Delete Statement."

12. C is correct. The Select Into statement is used to make a new table and copy records into it. For more information, see the section "Select Into Statement."

13. A is correct. The Insert Into statement is used to append records from one table into another. For more information, see the section "Insert Into Statement."

14. A is correct. Unless the All predicate is used, a Union query does not return duplicate records. For more information, see the section "Creating Union Queries."

Answers to Test Yourself Questions at Beginning of Chapter

1. You need to preface the field name with the name of the table.

   SELECT Employees.Name FROM Employees.

   For more information, see the section "Referring to Objects by Using Access SQL."

2. Enter the following criteria in the Where clause:

   Where ProductID Like "23????"

   For more information, see the section "Using Like in Criteria."

3. You must use a Union query to join these two recordsets together. For more information, see the section "Creating Union Queries."

Chapter

Programming with Objects

By the end of this chapter, you will be able to execute the following test objectives:

▶ Given a scenario, determine when to use Data Access Objects

▶ Differentiate between objects and collections

▶ Write statements that access and modify database objects

▶ Use Data Access Objects and Microsoft Access Objects

▶ Select appropriate methods and property settings for use with specified objects

Test Yourself! Before reading this chapter, test yourself to determine how much study time you will need to devote to this section.

1. What is the one property that all tables created by the Microsoft Jet Database Engine have?

2. You have a database that contains only one form. You need to write a line of code that will enable you to retrieve the name of the form. What would the syntax of that line be?

3. What type of collection can store instances of a Microsoft Access–specific object?

4. Write a code statement that opens the current database.

5. Of the two hierarchies (Application and Jet Engine), which one defines the objects (for example, the tables, queries, relationships, or indexes) that handle the data management tasks in a Microsoft Access database?

6. In working with objects, the New keyword enables you to create what?

7. When declaring object variables, what word should prefix the statement to associate the object variable with an existing object?

8. Objects have both properties and methods. Which one defines the object's characteristics? Which one performs a number of procedures that act on the object?

9. A Recordset object is a temporary set of records in memory from one or more tables. This distinguishes them from every other object in the hierarchy model. When do Recordset objects exist?

Answers are located at the end of the chapter...

This chapter covers the basics of Microsoft Access objects and database access objects (DAO)—in fact, the majority of this chapter is dedicated to DAO because of its power and flexibility.

This chapter also covers the basics of the two object hierarchies within Microsoft Access that are covered on the exam. These are the Application hierarchy (see fig. 4.1) and the Jet Engine hierarchy (see fig. 4.2).

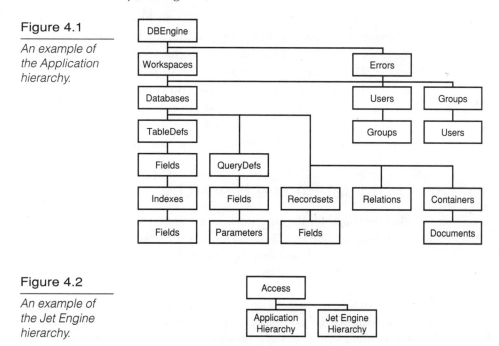

Figure 4.1

An example of the Application hierarchy.

Figure 4.2

An example of the Jet Engine hierarchy.

A good understanding of the object hierarchies is definitely necessary to pass the exam. This chapter also provides foundational knowledge needed for other topics that will be covered on the exam.

Understanding Object Hierarchy

This chapter introduces both object hierarchies (Application and Jet Engine) and provides information about the types of objects they contain.

Using Application Hierarchy

The *Application hierarchy* consists of the user interface objects that Access itself maintains. These objects include the forms, reports, controls, sections, and module objects that exist within Microsoft Access. This hierarchy also includes the Application, DoCmd, Screen, Err, and Debug objects. The Application hierarchy provides a method that enables the user to gather information about any open form or report, write to the Debug object, or retrieve information from the Screen object, for example.

Using Jet Engine Hierarchy

The Microsoft Jet Engine provides the actual *Engine hierarchy*. The Microsoft Jet Database Engine defines the objects (tables, queries, relationships, and indexes) that handle data-management tasks in a Microsoft Access database.

The structure of the Jet Engine was designed to conform to the requirements and recommendations of the Object Linking and Embedding (OLE) 2.1 specification. Because OLE Automation allows the sharing of components, any application that supports OLE can use the Jet Engine to work with objects in a database. This means that the Jet Engine works with a number of other software packages such as Microsoft Excel, Microsoft Word, and so on.

In other chapters you learn how to access data through the Access user interface. Data access objects (DAOs) provide a group of objects and collections that help a developer to create and manipulate database components programmatically. You can use the power of DAO to write procedures in your code to reference data and objects, or declare object variables that would represent them, for example. After an object is declared and assigned, it can be used as you would any declared variable within the system. You can change the value of a declared object variable.

The following code creates a table, Inventory, with a single field called ItemID:

```
Sub CreateTable ()
        'Declares variables
      Dim db As Database, tbl as TableDef, fld as Field
      'Assign the current database to a database variable
      Set db Ad CurrentDB()
      'Create a new table and field, and assign them to the
      'table and field variables.
      Set tbl = db.CreateTableDef("Inventory")
      Set fld = db.CreateField("ItemID", dbText)
      'Add the field to the table, then add the table to the
      'database.
      tbl.Fields.Append fld
      db.TableDefs.Append tbl
      db.TableDefs.Refresh
End Sub
```

Understanding Objects and Collections

Access organizes programmable objects into a hierarchical structure of classes of objects. Each object has a set of *properties* that defines its characteristics and one or more *methods* that you use to perform various operations on the object.

One member of the Microsoft Access Object mentioned briefly in the previous section is the Report object. You can use the class name in expressions as the identifier, for example:

```
Reports!ReportName!ControlName.PropertyName
```

In the example, Reports references the class name. The Report-Name references the name of the member of the object class.

Objects of a specific type are grouped together in what we call *collections*. Reports, in the preceding example, is the collection of open Report objects. Any object that is unopened does not appear in these collections. Collections are very similar to arrays, except that collections use references called *pointers* to member objects. Access arrays in Visual Basic for Applications consist of elements with assigned values. Collections, unlike arrays, can also appear or disappear without your intervention. The members of the Reports collection change as you open and close the Reports objects in your application, for example.

A thorough understanding regarding the concept of objects and collections is very important in working with objects. In a hierarchy most objects have collections that contain an object's class or a type's members.

 Tip

Remember, the Reports collection does not appear in the Jet Engine hierarchy figure (refer to fig. 4.2). The Reports collection, like the Forms, Scripts (macros), and modules collections, is not a DAO. As stated previously in the section "Understanding Object Hierarchy," the Forms and Reports collections are defined by Access, not by the Microsoft Jet Engine.

Referencing Objects

When making reference to an object in code, you should specify the hierarchical path that points to the object. A good rule for memory is to start with the DBEngine object and work your way through the object hierarchy, as shown in the following syntax:

```
DBEngine.ParentCollection.ChildCollection("Name of Object")
```

You can reference an object that is part of a collection in one of the three ways presented in table 4.1.

Table 4.1

Referencing Objects in Code	
Syntax	Use
identifier![ObjectName]	Directly name an object as a member of a collection. This syntax is required when referring to an object whose name contains a space or to an object whose name is a restricted Visual Basic identifier.

Syntax	Use
identifier("expression")	Directly name an object as a member of a collection or use a string variable to contain the object name.
identifier(index)	Refer to an object by its position in the collection. You can use this syntax to loop through all the members of a collection.

The following code shows these three different ways of referring to a form called frmMain. The last method makes the assumption that frmMain is the first form in the Forms collection:

```
Forms![frmMain]
Forms("frmMain")
Forms(0)
```

You can also make reference to properties of an object by using the syntax Object.property. For example, in Visual Basic you can set the Caption property of the form frmMain as follows:

```
Forms![frmMain].Caption = "Main Form"
```

Using the !(Bang) and .(Dot) Identifiers

These identifiers not only separate the objects in syntax but also help describe the relationships among the objects. They help reference that one object belongs to another.

The !(bang) identifier should be used when the object was created by the user and when the item to follow is a member of that collection. The .(dot) identifies an object created by the Microsoft Jet Engine.

Declaring Object Variables

An *object variable* is a variable that refers to a specific type of object. Object variables are different from regular variables in that object variables possess no intrinsic value, which is not true of regular variables, and they point to an object rather than a value. In other words, an object variable simply references an object's representation in memory. All object variables that are assigned to an object reference point to the same object.

There are a number of advantages to using object variables:

▶ You can write code that is easier to understand and maintain.

▶ You can avoid typing and maintaining long lines of code that reference objects. After your first reference to an object, you can continually refer to it instead of making repeated explicit references to the object through the DAO hierarchy.

▶ You can improve the performance of your application. Your code runs more quickly if you declare an object variable to reference the object instead.

Before you can use an object variable, the Set statement must be used to associate the object variable with an existing object. The Set syntax is as follows:

```
Set variablename = objectexpression
```

If you use the Set statement to associate more than one variable with a specific object type, you always refer to the same object. This means that if you change the property of one variable you will also change the properties of all variables of the same object type, as shown in the following syntax:

```
Dim frmMain1 As Form
Dim frmMain2 As Form
Set frmMain1 = Forms![frmMain]
Set frmMain2 = Forms![frmMain]
frmMain1.Caption = "Main Form"
```

When this code has been run, frmMain2.Caption is also set to "Main Form."

Creating an Instance of an Existing Object with the New Keyword

In one quick step you can create a new instance of an existing object by using the New keyword. When the new instance is created, it has its own set of properties. Here is an example of the use of the New keyword:

```
Sub AnotherForm()
        Dim frmMain As New Form_frmMain
        frmMain.Caption = "Main Form - 2"
        frmMain.Visible = True
End Sub
```

The preceding example uses the New keyword to create another form. It's interesting to note that setting the Caption property of a new instance of frmMain will not affect the Caption property of an existing form object.

The ability to use multiple instances of an object allows for great flexibility in an application.

Understanding Properties and Methods

Objects have properties and methods. Each object has a set of properties that defines the object's attributes and one or more of the methods that are used to perform various operations on the object.

The difference between properties and methods is easy to understand:

▶ Objects have properties that define their characteristics. The values retrieved from the properties represent the characteristics of the objects. These properties can be modified.

▶ Methods are procedures that can be applied to the object. Methods are very similar to procedures that you write in code; they differ, however, in that they are exclusively associated to a specific object.

The following example shows how several textbox properties can be set using the With…End With construct:

```
Sub NewForm()
      Dim frm As Form
      ' Create new form.
      Set frm = CreateForm
      ' Set form properties.
      With frm
            .Caption = "Main Form"
            .ScrollBars = 0
            .Visible = True
      End With
      ' Restore form.
      DoCmd.Restore
End Sub
```

Every object or collection has its own set of properties that help define it and its own set of methods that describe and manipulate the database components. Each object and collection forms a hierarchy or hierarchy model of the database, and its components can be dynamically controlled.

Working with DAO

Now that you have a basic understanding of objects, collections, properties, and methods, it's time to explore the various types of objects and collections that make up the DAO hierarchy.

DBEngine Object

The top object in the hierarchy model is the *DBEngine object*. It represents the Jet Database Engine. When referencing any object in the Microsoft Jet hierarchy, you start with the DBEngine object and work your way down. Remember that the DBEngine object contains and controls all other collections and objects in the DAO object hierarchy. There is only one instance of the DBEngine object in any given application (see table 4.2).

 Tip

The DBEngine object doesn't have an associated collection.

Table 4.2

Methods, Properties, and Collections of the DBEngine Object

Methods	Properties	Collections
Compact Database	Default Password	Errors
Create Workspace	Default User	Workspaces
Idle	IniPath	
RepairDatabase	Version	
RegisterDatabase	LoginTimeOut	
	SystemDB	

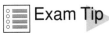 Exam Tip

> There are multiple ways to accomplish the same task in VBA. The exam may use properties of objects and methods with which you are not familiar to accomplish a specific task.
> To pass the exam, you must fully understand the Jet Engine hierarchy—not just a part of it.

Error Object

As you work with objects sometimes errors will occur. The Error objects receive all these errors and store them in the Errors collection. You can use the information contained in the Error objects to determine the cause of the error and to display the necessary messages for these errors in the application.

All previous error messages are removed from the Errors collection when a new error occurs. There can be more than one related Error object in the collection caused by a single operation (see table 4.3).

Table 4.3

Properties and Collections of the Error Object

Properties	Collections
Description	Properties
HelpContext	
HelpFile	
Number	
Source	

The following listing shows an error routine that scans through the Errors collection. This routine displays all errors that occurred from the data access object and the associated operation that caused the error.

```
Public Sub Display_Errors(ErrCd As Integer)
        Dim errErr As Error
        Dim txtErr As Control
        Dim I As Integer
        ' List the DAO errors collection
        Set the txtErr = txtErrors
        If (Errors.Count = 0) Or (Errors(0).Number <> ErrCd) Then
              txtErr.Value = "No information available."
        Else
              For I = 0 to Errors.Count - 1
                    Set errErr = Errors(I)
                    txtErr.Value = txtErr.Value &
                    ➥Str$(errErr.Number) & _
                    ": " & errErr.Description & Chr$(13) & Chr$(10)
              Next I
        End If
        txtErr.Locked = True
        Exit Sub
End Sub
        '
```

Workspace Object

Simply put, the *Workspace object* is used to define a session for the user. A Workspace object is available for every session of the Jet Database Engine. When a session is initiated, the Microsoft Jet Engine organizes the operations as determined by the user, the user's password, and the user's permissions.

Although the Workspaces collection contains all Workspace objects defined by the currently running instance of DAO, it maintains a separate object for each defined session. The Workspace object session maintains its transactions separate of other Workspace objects. This means that all transactions within a workspace are independent of other workspace transactions. This can be useful when managing multiple sets of transactions within an application.

When you start DAO, what happens with workspaces depends on whether or not security as been established for a user. If you don't have security established, DAO will automatically create the default Workspace object (see table 4.4).

Table 4.4

Methods, Properties, and Collections of the Workspace Object

Methods	Properties	Collections
Begin Trans	IsolateODBCTrans	Default Databases
Close	Name	Groups
CommitTrans	UserName	Properties
CreateDatabase		Users
CreateGroup		
CreateUser		
OpenDatabase		

Database Object

When working with DAOs, a currently opened database is signified by a database object. All database objects that are currently open in a Workspace object are contained within the Databases collection. Microsoft Access creates a default Workspace object when you open a database.

In VBA, no databases are open in a Workspace until you explicitly open them using the OpenDatabase method. As previously mentioned in the section "Referencing Objects," you can refer to the database according to its position in the Databases collection. If you open only one database, then you can refer to that database in any of the following ways:

```
DBEngine.Workspaces(0).Databases(0)
```

```
DBEngine.Workspaces(0)(0)
```

```
DBEngine(0)(0)
```

You can also use either the CurrentDb function or the DBEngine(0)(0) syntax to return a reference to the database that is currently open in Microsoft Access. The CurrentDb function differs from the DBEngine(0)(0) syntax in that the CurrentDb function creates another instance of the current database and returns a reference to that instance, and it refreshes all the collections in the current database. On the other hand, the DBEngine(0)(0) syntax doesn't refresh any collections, so it can perform faster.

If you switch from using the CurrentDb function to the DBEngine(0)(0) syntax, make sure your code doesn't depend on any collections being refreshed. If it does, you can refresh these individual collections separately (see table 4.5).

Table 4.5

Methods, Properties, and Collections of the Database Object

Methods	Properties	Collection
Close	CollatingOrder	Containers
CreateProperty	Connect	Properties
CreateQueryDef	Name	QueryDefs
CreateRelation	QueryTimeOut	Recordsets
CreateTableDef	RecordAffected	Relations
Execute	Transactions	Default TableDefs
MakeReplica	Updatable	
OpenRecordset	V1xNullBehavior	
Synchronize	Version	

User Object

The User object represents the user in session with the associated Workspace object. More than one user may be in session at a time, and they are contained in the Users collection (see table 4.6).

Table 4.6

Methods, Properties, and Collections of the User Object

Methods	Properties	Collection
CreateGroup	Name	Default Groups
NewPassword	Password	Properties
	PID	

Group Object

The Group object is very similar to the User object in that it represents groups that have been defined in the workgroup database. The Group object represents groups of users and their appropriate securities. Each user in a group is represented by a User object in the Users collection of the Group (see table 4.7).

Table 4.7

Methods, Properties, and Collections of the Groups Object

Methods	Properties	Collection
CreateUser	Name	Default Users
NewPassword	PID	Properties

QueryDef Object

The QueryDef object represents a saved query in the database. Its SQL property defines the SQL statement used to define the returned recordset. You primarily use QueryDef objects to work with saved queries or SQL pass-through queries (see table 4.8).

Table 4.8

Methods, Properties, and Collections of the QueryDef Object

Methods	Properties	Collection
CreateProperty	Connect	Fields
Execute	DateCreated	Default Parameters

continues

Table 4.8   Continued

Methods	Properties	Collection
OpenRecordset	LastUpdated	Properties
	LogMessages	
	Name	
	ODBCTimeout	
	RecordsAffected	
	ReturnRecords	
	SQL	
	Type	
	Updatable	

TableDef Object

The TableDef object represents table or stored table definitions in the current database. The table can be in the current database or in a linked table from an external database. With the TableDef object you can determine a table's validation rules or the number of records within it, or whether a table is attached or updatable (see table 4.9).

Table 4.9

Methods, Properties, and Collections of the TableDef Object

Methods	Properties	Collection
CreateField	Attributes	Default Fields
CreateIndex	ConflictTable	Indexes
CreateProperty	Connect	Properties
OpenRecordset	DateCreated	
RefreshLink	LastUpdated	
	Name	

Methods	Properties	Collection
	RecordCount	
	SourceTableName	
	Updatable	
	ValidationRule	
	ValidationText	

The following example uses the TableDef object's CreateIndex method to create and then name an index object. When the index has been created, you can define the field or fields from the TableDef on which the index is based. You can also set other index properties.

```
Dim dbs As Database
Dim tdf As TableDef
Dim ndx As Index
Dim fldField As Field

' Create new Index object
Set dbs = DBEngine.Workspaces(0).Databases(0)
Set tdf = dbs.CreateTableDef("DAO Objects")
Set ndx = tdf.CreateIndex("ObjName")
Set fldField = tdf.CreateField("Object Name")
ndx.Primary = True
ndx.Required = True
ndx.Fields.Append fldField
' Append it to Indexes collection
tdf.Fields.Indexes.Append ndx
'
```

Index Object

Indexes of a recordset or tabledef are represented by the *Index object*. Indexes specify an order to the records accessed in the table and provide for faster access to specific records when values for one or more fields in the index's Fields collection are either completely or partially specified.

Indexes on DAO collections are always *zero-based*. This means that the first element in the collection has an index number of 0. This is helpful information when you've worked with one-based indexes, where the first element has an index number of 1. You can retrieve the first element from a collection by subtracting 1 from the one-based index (see table 4.10).

Table 4.10

Methods, Properties, and Collections of the Index Object

Methods	Properties	Collection
CreateField	Clustered	Properties
CreateProperty	DistinctCount	Default Fields
	Foreign	
	IgnoreNulls	
	Name	
	Primary	
	Required	
	Unique	

Field Object

Fields are columns of a table that are visible in a table design. In a datasheet they are known as fields. The *Field object* defines the properties and methods that are applicable to a column. The Fields collection contains all Field objects in an associated table, query, recordset, relation, or index (see table 4.11).

Table 4.11

Methods, Properties, and Collections of the Field Object

Methods	Properties	Collection
AppendChunk	AllowZeroLength	Properties
CreateProperty	Attributes	
FieldSize	CollatingOrder	
GetChunk	DataUpdatable	

Methods	Properties	Collection
	DefaultValue	
	ForeignName	
	Name	
	OrdinalPosition	
	Required	
	Size	
	SourceField	
	SourceTable	
	Type	
	ValidateOnSet	
	ValidationRule	
	ValidationText	
	Value	

Recordset Object

Recordset objects are powerful robust data access objects that enable you to add, delete, edit, and view table fields, table rows, and tables. This isn't true only of the Microsoft Jet Engine tables but of other ODBC-supported databases such as Oracle, Informix, or SQL Server.

There are five types of Recordset objects:

▶ table-type Recordset objects

▶ dynaset-type Recordset objects

▶ snapshot-type Recordset objects

▶ forward-only-type Recordset objects

▶ dynamic-type Recordset objects.

A Recordset object is a temporary set of records in memory from one or more tables; it is the most powerful object in DAO because it offers programmatic access and manipulation to a number of different data sources. For example, Recordset objects can be based on queries that join multiple tables from two completely different databases, such as SQL Server and Informix.

The Recordsets collection contains all open Recordset objects in the current Database object. The Recordset object exists only while your code or application is running. For example, in Microsoft Access, when you are viewing a table through the user interface, this table isn't a Recordset object.

The following code starts at the first record, if any, and visits each record in the Recordset until the EOF property is True.

```
Dim db As database
  Dim rs As Recordset
Dim intTableCount As Integer

' Return Database object pointing to current database.
Set dbs = CurrentDb
' Create table-type Recordset object.
Set rs = dbs.OpenRecordset("DAO Objects", dbOpenTable)
Do While Not rs.EOF
        If rs![Object Type] = "TableDef" Then
             intTableCount = intTableCount + 1
        End If
      rs.MoveNext
Loop
rs.Close
db.Close
MsgBox "There are " & Str$(intTableCount) & " tables in DAO Objects"
```

To work through the table from the last record to the first, use the following code:

```
Dim db As database
  Dim rs As Recordset
Dim intTableCount As Integer
' Return Database object pointing to current database.
Set dbs = CurrentDb
' Create table-type Recordset object.
```

```
Set rs = dbs.OpenRecordset("DAO Objects", dbOpenTable)
rs.MoveLast
Do While Not rs.EOF
        If rs![Object Type] = "TableDef" Then
             intTableCount = intTableCount + 1
End If
      rs.MovePrevious
Loop
rs.Close
db.Close
MsgBox "There are " & Str$(intTableCount) & " tables in
➡DAO Objects"
End Sub
```

Relation Object

Relations can be established for a database that enable the Microsoft Jet Engine to enforce referential integrity. Relations define the relationship between fields in two or more tables. The associated Fields collection defines the actual fields involved in the relationship (see table 4.12).

Table 4.12

Methods, Properties, and Collections of the Relation Object

Methods	Properties	Collection
CreateField	Attributes	Default Fields
ForeignTable	Properties	
	Name	
	Table	

Parameter Object

With Microsoft Jet queries, you can define formal parameters. *Formal parameters* represent unknown values that must be supplied by the user running the query or by the program executing the query. A query's formal parameters are represented by *Parameter objects* in the Parameters collection of a QueryDef object. This collection is particularly useful when you execute a parameter query in code and have to supply values for the query parameters at runtime (see table 4.13).

Table 4.13

Properties and Collections of the Parameter Object	
Properties	Collection
Name	Properties
Type	

Container Object

The Container collection is created by an application so that it can store and organize its own objects in a database. The DBEngine object, as stated in the "DBEngine Object" section, is application-independent. This means that the engine isn't tied to any one particular application. The Containers collection is the manner in which the Microsoft Jet Engine gains its application independence. The *Container object* holds items like forms, reports, macros, modules, and databases.

Microsoft Access depends on the on Microsoft Jet Engine to store its own application-specific objects. The Microsoft Jet keeps track of these objects through the Containers collection. A good use of the Container object is setting security to the database object of a particular class by controlling Access (see table 4.14).

Table 4.14

Properties and Collections of the Container Object	
Properties	Collection
AllPermissions	Default Documents
Inherit	Properties
Name	
Owner	
Permissions	
UserName	

Document Object

As noted in the preceding section, Microsoft Access uses the Containers collection to organize its own objects such as forms, reports, macros, and modules. The *Document object* represents a specific individual application object in the Documents collection. For instance, when Microsoft Access creates a database, it also creates a Reports container that holds a Document object for each report in the database. Access creates containers for other objects like reports, macros, and modules, as well (see table 4.15).

Table 4.15

Properties and Collections of the Document Object

Properties	Collections
AllPermissions	Properties
Container	
DateCreated	
KeepLocal	
LastUpdated	
Name	
Owner	
Permissions	
Replicable	
UserName	

Property Object

Every data access object defined within an application has a Properties collection. The Properties collection holds all the properties associated with the object. A *Property object* contains information about the characteristics of a given property. The Properties collection provides some flexibility when working with the object; you can read property values to obtain information about an object's characteristics, for example, or write to a property to define an object's characteristics. You also have the flexibility to create your own properties and add them to an object's Properties collection (see table 4.16).

Table 4.16

Properties and Collections of the Property Object

Properties	Collection
Inherited	Properties
Name	
Type	
Value	

Working with Objects

Now that you've been introduced to a number of topics dealing with data access objects, take the time to review the following code. Please note that this code is for explanation purposes only and will not compile or work in Access.

```
Dim rs As Recordset
Set db = OpenDatabase(strdbPath)
Set rs = ds.OpenRecordset("Master", dbOpenTable)

With rs
     .Index = "MasterIndex"
     .Seek "=", strMaster
     If Not.NoMatch Then
            MsgBox "You have found the master."
     Else
            MsgBox "Cound not find " & strMaster" & "."
     End If
End With
rs.Close
db.Close
```

When the preceding code runs, the following steps take place:

1. Two object variables, db and rs, are declared. These variables are used to point to the actual database and recordset objects to be used in the example.

2. The Set statement and the OpenDatabase method return a reference to the database. The variable strDbPath contains

the name and location of the database. The variable strDb-Path is then assigned to the variable db. The variable db is representative of the database object.

3. The Set statement is used again to assign the rs object variable to the Master table. This is done by using the OpenRecordSet method of the Database object. This method instructs DAO to look in the database for the Master table.

4. The code tells DAO which index to use when searching the table. You can accomplish this by setting the Index property of the Recordset object to the value MasterIndex. This index exists on a field in the Master table.

5. The Recordset object's Seek method is called to find the specific record in which the value of the indexed field is equal to the value of strMaster.

6. The NoMatch property of the Recordset object is checked to see if a match has been found. If a match is found, the value of the Master field is displayed. If no match is found, an error message will be displayed.

7. The Close method at the end of the procedure closes the Recordset and Database objects.

The following list outlines a few concepts in the preceding example:

▶ DAO is a hierarchy of objects. The Master TableDef object is in the TableDefs collection of the Database object, and the MasterIndex object is in the Indexes collection of the Master TableDef object.

▶ Methods initiate actions on objects. The preceding example uses methods to open the database and table and then locate the specific record.

▶ Properties define characteristics of objects. In this example, the value of the Index property of the Recordset object is set to instruct DAO to specifically order the records that you want to search.

Creating Database Objects

You can use DAO to create objects, assign characteristics to objects by using properties, and interrogate the structure of existing objects.

The creation of a new object really requires two steps:

1. Creating the object and defining its characteristics.

2. Appending the object to its collection. The process of appending an object to a collection makes it a permanent or persistent part of the database.

Look ahead to exercise 4.1; it guides you through the creation of your first database.

Key Terms and Concepts

Table 4.17 identifies key terms from this chapter. Review the key terms and make sure that you understand each term for the exam.

Table 4.17

Key Terms: Programming with Objects	
Term	Covered in Section...
Container	"Container Object"
DAO	"Using Jet Engine Hierarchy"
Databases	"Database Object"
DBEngine	"DBEngine Object"
Document	"Document Object"
Error	"Error Object"
Field	"Field Object"
Index	"Index Object"
Parameter	"Parameter Object"

Term	Covered in Section...
Properties	"Property Object"
QueryDef	"QueryDef Object"
Recordset	"Recordset Object"
Relation	"Relation Object"
TableDef	"TableDefObject"
User	"User Object"
Workspaces	"Workspace Object"

Lab Exercises

These lab exercises enable you to practice a few of the objectives that were covered in this chapter regarding programming with objects. These exercises are simple in scope but provide you with some hands-on experience.

Exercise 4.1: Creating a Database

This exercise enables you to create a database, a table, and the resulting fields programmatically. This exercise enables you to implement the Jet Engine hierarchy to declare and use a database object, a tabledef object, and a field object. You use methods and properties of these objects in the exercise.

Objective:

▶ Use Data Access objects and Microsoft Access objects

Time Estimate: 20-25 minutes

Steps:

1. Open an Access database and go to the module.

2. Declare a database object for the database you want to create.

   ```
   Dim MyDb As Database
   ```

3. Use the CreateDatabase method of the Workspace object to create an empty database and database file.

   ```
   Set MyDb = Workspaces(0).CreateDatabase("MyDb")
   ```

4. Define each table in your new database. Obviously, if you were doing actual development you would already know which fields and indexes should go into this table.

5. Use the CreateTableDef method to create each table in the database.

   ```
   Dim tdf as TableDef

   Set tdf = MyDb.CreateTableDef("Employees"
   ```

6. Use the new TableDef object to create fields in the new table by using the CreateField method of the Field object. This example creates a number of different fields:

```
Dim fldField As Field
Set fldField As tdf.CreateField("Employee_ID", dbLong)
fldField.Attributes = dbAutoIncrField
tdf.Append fldField
Set fldField = tdf.CreateField("First_Name", dbText, 25)
fldField.Attributes = dbAutoIncrField
tdf.Append fldField
Set fldField = tdf.CreateField("Last_Name", dbText, 25)
fldField.Attributes = dbAutoIncrField
tdf.Append fldField
```

7. Now that the table is defined, append it to the database. This step actually creates the table in your database and appends it to the Database collection. You cannot make any changes to the appended fields after this point (you can, however, add and delete fields):

```
Mydb.Append tdf
```

8. At this point, you can create one or more indexes using the TableDef objects.

9. Use CreateIndex to create an Index object:

```
Set fldField = idx.CreateField("Employee_Id")
fldField.Primary = True
Set idx = tdf.CreateIndex("Employee")
```

10. Use the Create Field method of the Index object to create a field object for each indexed field in the Index object and append it to the Index object.

```
tdf.Indexes.Append idx
```

11. Now append each Index object to the Indexes collection of the TableDef objects using the Append method. Your table can have several indexes or no indexes.

continues

Comments:

Using the Access user interface is a much simpler way of creating a database and table but this is a very good learning exercise.

Reading Reference:

For more information about the concepts raised by the exercise, refer to the section "Working with DAO."

Exercise 4.2: Working with Objects and Properties in a Database

This exercise accesses the tables, queries, relations, and containers and prints the object name to the Debug window. This exercise also covers defining objects, and working with objects, methods, properties, and the Errors collection, which are all part of the Jet Engine hierarchy.

Objectives:

▶ Differentiate between objects and collections

▶ Write statements that access and modify database objects

Time Estimate: 5-10 minutes

Steps:

1. Open an Access database and go to a module.

2. Type the following in the module:

```
Dim db As Database
    Dim tf As TableDef
    Dim fd As Field
    Dim pr As Property
    Dim var As Variant

    ' Open the current database
    Set db = CurrentDb()
```

```
' Iterate through each table
For Each tf In db.TableDefs
    ' Print the table properties
    Debug.Print "Table: " & tf.Name
    For Each pr In tf.Properties
        Debug.Print RetrieveProperty(pr)
    Next pr
    Debug.Print

    ' Print fields and field properties
    For Each fd In tf.Fields
        Debug.Print "Field: " & fd.Name
        For Each pr In fd.Properties
            Debug.Print " " & RetrieveProperty(pr)
        Next pr
        Debug.Print
    Next fd
    Debug.Print
Next tf

End Function


Public Function RetrieveProperty(pr As Property) As String
    ' This procedure checks whether a property has a
    ' value.  It returns either the value or an
    ' appropriate error string.
    Dim var As Variant

    ' Enable error handling
    On Error GoTo ErrHandle
    ' Attempt to retrieve the property value.
    var = pr.Value
    RetrieveProperty = "Properties: " & pr.Name & vbTab &
    ➥vbTab & "Value: " & var
    Exit Function
ErrHandle:
    var = "Error: " & Err.Description
    Resume Next
End Function
```

Comments:

This exercise prints the properties of a TableDef object, the
names of its fields, the properties of each field object, and the

present values of those properties. Notice that the first procedure iterates through the Properties collection for the TableDef object and each Field object, then actually calls a RetrieveProperty procedure function for each Property object in each collection. The RetrieveProperty function returns a string containing the property's name and value. If an error is reported, the associated error message will be returned in the string.

Reading Reference:

For more information about the concepts raised by the exercise, refer to the sections "TableDef Object," "QueryDef Object," "Relation Object," and "Container Object."

Review Questions

1. Which of the following can be best accomplished by using DAOs?

   A. Establishing security within an application

   B. Providing the user the ability to modify fields, rows, and tables

   C. Declaring new datatypes within an application

   D. Providing the interface for SQL pass-through queries

2. Which statement best describes the New keyword?

   A. Creates an instances of a new object.

   B. Defines a user object.

   C. Creates a new instance of an existing object.

   D. Defines a new global variable.

3. Which of the following is true about the Workspace object?

   A. A Workspace object is created only when the CreateWorkspace method is initiated.

   B. Only one Database object per Workspace is allowed.

   C. A workspace object is available for every session of the Jet Database Engine.

4. Which of the following syntaxes would *not* open a database?

   A. Set db = CurrentDb()

   B. Set db = DBEngine.Workspaces(0).Databases(0)

   C. Set db = Workspaces(0)(0)

   D. Set db = DBEngine(0)(0)

5. Which of the statements are *not* true about the Recordset object?

   A. The Recordset object is an object that you explicitly open through code.

   B. Closing a Recordset object isn't a necessity.

   C. A table open in Microsoft Access is an example of a recordset.

   D. Recordset objects enable the manipulation of data at the record level.

6. Tom, who works for a medium size company, must develop an Access application to maintain personnel records for 200 employees. This program will be used on the network for all the employees to view their own data while enabling the managers to add, edit, or delete existing data. Tom will be utilizing DAO. What statements are true about DAO?

   A. Determines security based on user's permissions.

   B. Improves the performance of an application because of DAO's capability for one time referencing.

   C. Manages multiple transactions.

   D. Simplifies appearance and maintenance of code.

7. Which of the following refers to methods that can be applied to a Collection object?

   A. AddItem, RemoveItem

   B. AddItem, GetItem, RemoveItem

   C. Add, Item, Remove

   D. Add, Get, Remove

Answers to Review Questions

1. A and B are correct. Working with DAOs can be very power-ful. DAOs enable you to manipulate fields, rows, and tables. Utilizing the user and group objects within the Microsoft Jet Engine hierarchy enable you to provide security within an application. For more information, see the section "Working with DAO."

2. C is correct. The New keyword enables you to create an new instances of an existing object in one step. When the new instance is created, it has its own set of properties. For more information, see the section "Creating an Instance of an Existing Object with New Keyword."

3. C is correct. To define a session for the user, use the Work-space object. A Workspace object is available for every session of the Jet Database Engine; a session organizes a sequence of operations performed by Microsoft Jet. A session is initiated when a user logs on and ends when the user logs off. For more information, see the section "Workspace Object."

4. C is correct. When referring to a database, the DBEngine object is used. When using DAO from within Microsoft Ac-cess, the CurrentDB function can be used as a shortcut to refer to the DBEngine object for the current database. For example, the following code opens the current database:

```
Set dbCurrent = DBEngine.Workspaces(0).Databases(0)
Set dbCurrent = DBEngine.Workspaces(0)(0)
Set dbCurrent = DBEngine(0)(0)
Set dbCurrent = CurrentDB()
```

For more information, see the section "DBEngine Object."

5. B and C are correct. Recordset objects are used to manipu-late fields, rows, and tables. Because Recordset objects are opened through code, they are not visible until the applica-tion runs. Therefore, opening a table through the user inter-face is not an example of a Recordset object. You should also

close a Recordset object when you are finished using it, especially because it's a temporary object within memory. For more information, see the section "Recordset Object."

6. All choices are correct. This should make you aware of how powerful using the DAOs can be. For more information, see the section "Working with DAO."

7. C is correct. The Add method, the Item method, and the Remove method are available to both Jet Engine-defined and user-defined Collection objects. The Add method adds an item to a collection. The Item method is used to retrieve an item from a collection. The Remove method is used to remove an item from a collection. For more information, see the section "Understanding Objects and Collections."

Answers to Test Yourself Questions at Beginning of Chapter...

1. The Description property is the only property that is applicable to all created table objects. For more information, see the section "TableDef Object."

2. The code should appear as follows:

```
CurrentDB.Containers("Tables").Documents.Count
```

When you refer to objects in code, specify the hierarchical path that points to the object to which you want to refer. You should begin with the DBEngine object and work your way through the object hierarchy. For more information, see the section "Referencing Objects."

3. The Document object stores a specific instance of an application-specific object. For more information, see the section "Document Object."

4. When referring to a database, use the DBEngine object. When using DAO from within Microsoft Access, you can use the CurrentDB function as a shortcut to refer to the DBEngine object for the current database.

   For example, the following code opens the current database:

```
Set dbCurrent = DBEngine.Workspaces(0).Databases(0)

Set dbCurrent = DBEngine.Workspaces(0)(0)

Set dbCurrent = DBEngine(0)(0)

Set dbCurrent = CurrentDB()
```

For more information, see the section "DBEngine Object."

5. The Microsoft Jet Engine provides the actual Jet Engine hierarchy. The Microsoft Jet Database Engine defines the objects (tables, queries, relationships, and indexes) that handle data-management tasks in a Microsoft Access database. For more information, see the section "Understanding Object Hierarchy."

6. The New keyword enables you to create new instances of an existing object in one step. When a new instance is created, it has its own set of properties. For more information, see the section "Creating an Instance of an Existing Object with New Keyword."

7. Before you can use an object variable, you need the Set statement in order to associate the object variable with an existing object. The Set syntax is as follows:

```
Set variablename = objectexpression
```

For more information, see the section "Declaring Object Variables."

8. Objects have properties and methods. Each object has a set of properties that define its attributes and one or more methods that perform various operations on the object. For more information, see the section "Understanding Properties and Methods."

9. A Recordset object is a temporary set of records in memory from one or more tables. The Recordsets collection contains all open Recordset objects in the current Database object. The Recordset object only exists while your code or application is running. For more information, see the section "Recordset Object."

Debugging and Error Handling

By the end of this chapter, you will be able to execute the following test objectives:

 Objectives

▶ Use the Error collection and the Error object to trap errors

▶ Use debugging tools to suspend program execution, and to examine, step through, and reset execution of code

Test Yourself! Before reading this chapter, test yourself to determine how much study time you will need to devote to this section.

1. You are trying to force a Device Unavailable error to occur in your code. Why does the following code not work?

   ```
   Error.Raise (68)
   ```

2. You need to write code to handle a Data Access error in a form. Where would you write the code to respond to that error and how could you get more details about the error?

3. How do you direct Access to go to your error-handing code when an error is in your procedure?

4. What statement should you include in your procedure before your error-handling code to prevent the error handler from executing if no error occurs?

5. You have used Debug.Print in your code to print the name of your form and the current user to the Debug window. The procedure executed, yet you do not see the Debug window. Why not, and how can you view the Debug window?

6. While developing your application, you inadvertently created an endless loop. The loop should exit when X = 10, and you think that it should take only two loops for X to reach 10. How would you attempt to fix this problem?

7. You have a very lengthy procedure to debug. As you are stepping through the code, you want to skip an individual line because you know that it is error free. You choose Step Over, and yet Access executes the line and pauses at the next one. What should you have chosen instead of Step Over?

8. How can you use the Debug window to monitor the value of a variable when you have suspended execution of your code?

9. Your code is not executing properly because of a division by 0 error. The global variable that you are dividing by should have a value of 100. When you tested it in the first procedure, it had a value of 100. You have no idea why or at what point in your code, it is changing to 0. How would you solve this problem?

Answers are located at the end of the chapter...

This chapter discusses in detail the process of searching for errors in your code (debugging) and writing code to trap and handle potential errors (error handling). For the exam, you must be able to read code and determine what error will be generated and what a given error handler will do. You should be very familiar with stepping through code and setting break points, and you should know all of the options that are available in an error handler.

Using the Errors Collection and the Error Object to Trap Errors

 There are two collections that contain information about errors. The Errors collection, which contains Error objects, is used only for Data Access errors. Data Access errors occur when an Access form or report has the focus. The Err collection, which contains the Err object, contains information about runtime errors as well as Data Access errors. The Err collection is discussed in the section "Writing Error Handlers." The present section deals with trapping errors using the Errors collection and the Error object. Keep in mind that Err and Error cannot be used interchangeably. For the exam, you must know the differences between these objects.

Error Object versus Err Object

Whenever you use a form or report, Access is using the Jet engine for data access behind the scenes. When an error occurs, the OnError event is triggered. If the error occurred *while Access was manipulating the form or report*, an Error object is generated and placed in the Errors collection. When a runtime error occurs, the Err object is generated. Code that is placed in the OnError event is used to trap these errors. The Error object is a Data Access object and the Err object is not.

The Error Object and Errors Collections

An Error object is generated each time an operation involving Data Access objects occurs. The Error object and the Errors collection are Data Access objects. The Errors collection is a property of the DBEngine. To refer to the Errors collection, use the following syntax:

```
DBENgine.Errors()
```

The Errors collection contains all Error objects. Each time a Data Access object generates an error, it is placed in the Errors collection. Unlike most collections, the Errors collection does not append new Error objects. Instead, when a Data Access Object operation generates an error, the Errors collection is cleared and the new Error object is placed in the collection.

Although the Errors collection contains information about only one particular Data Access Object (DAO) error at any time, the Errors collection can contain many objects because each Data Access object operation may generate many different errors. The Errors collection contains all objects generated by one Data Access Object error. The first Error object is the lowest level error, the second is the next higher level, and so on.

To refer to a specific error in the collection, use its number. The first error in the collection is 0:

```
DBENgine.Errors(0)=Err.Number
```

In order to determine if the last data access error encountered is current and valid, you should compare the first error in the DAO Errors collection to the error number stored in Err.Number. Because the first error in the collection is always 0, you use the following code to compare the first error in the errors collection to Err.Number:

```
If DBEngine.Errors(0)=Err.Number
```

Properties and Methods of the Errors Collection

The Errors collection has one property Count. *Count* returns the number of objects currently in the collection. The Count property is never null; if there are no errors, the Count property returns 0.

The Errors collection has one method: Refresh. *Refresh* is used to update the objects in a collection.

Properties and Methods of the Error Object

The Error object has no methods. It has four properties, which are listed in table 5.1.

Table 5.1

Properties of the Error Object

Property	Description
Description	Returns a descriptive string associated with an error.
HelpContext	Returns a context ID, as a Long variable, for a topic in a Microsoft Windows Help file.
HelpFile	Returns a fully qualified path to the Help file.
Number	Returns a numeric value specifying an error. The Number property is the Error object's default property.
Source	Returns the name of the object or application that originally generated the error.

 Note
For a complete list of trappable Data Access errors, refer to "Trappable Data Access Errors" in the Access Jet Engine Error Help. The easiest way to find this entry is to go to Error object in the Help Index and choose "See Also, Trappable Data Access Error."

Trapping Errors Using the OnError Event

The Error event occurs when a runtime error is produced in Microsoft Access *when a form or report has the focus* (causing a Data Access error). This includes Microsoft Jet Database Engine errors, but not runtime errors in Visual Basic. To trap these errors, you must write code to respond to the form's OnError event.

To write code to respond to the OnError event, click the Build button on the OnError line of the property. When you go into the code builder for the OnError property, you see a shell that looks like this:

```
Private Sub Form_Error(DataErr As Integer, Response As Integer)

End Sub
```

DataErr is the value that would be returned by the Err.Number property, had the error occurred in code. You can substitute your own variable name instead of DataErr.

Response is an intrinsic constant that tells Access whether to report the error to the user. You can substitute your own variable name instead of Response. Table 5.2 shows the available constants and their meanings.

Table 5.2

Constants Used with the Response Variable	
Constant	Meaning
AcDataErrContinue	This tells Access to ignore the error and continue without displaying the default Microsoft Access error message. If you want, you can supply a custom error message in place of the default error message.
AcDataErrDisplay	This constant displays the default Microsoft Access error message. This is the default constant.

Writing Error Handlers

A *runtime error* occurs when Visual Basic for Applications (VBA) encounters a command that it cannot carry out, such as to divide by zero, or to create a table that already exists. When VBA encounters a runtime error, execution halts and a dialog box appears with a message that describes the error. You do not want the user to have to see the internal error messages and decide how to react. Instead, you should *trap* the error so that you can respond to it in your code.

An error handler is a section of code that is used to respond to (or handle) an error. Handling an error in Access requires three steps:

1. You must trap the error.

2. You must respond to the error.

3. You must exit the error handler.

You can examine in detail some of the responses that can be used, in the later section "Handling the Error."

Trapping the Error

The On Error statement is used to trap the error and invoke the error handler. Each procedure can have an unlimited number of On Error statements. Only the most recently executed On Error statement remains in force, however. If there are several areas in your code that might produce an error, you want to have a separate On Error statement for each one, which enables you to have a customized error handler for each event.

Note

For error trapping to work correctly, the Break On All Errors option in the Module tab (Tools, Options) must be clear.

On Error Resume Next

Occasionally, you do not need to write an error handler—you simply want Access to ignore the error. If you were to loop through all of the controls on a form and change the font size to 12, for example, an error would occur when Access reaches a control that does not have a font size property (such as a line). Because this error is not important and does not require any intervention, you want to continue through the code, without stopping for the error. If you want Access to ignore an error, you can use the On Error Resume Next statement. This instructs Access to execute the line immediately *after* the code that caused the error. There is no visible intervention from Access.

The following example uses the On Error Resume Next statement to ignore the error.

```
Sub ChangeFont(frm as Form)
    'Changes the FontSize of all controls to 12 pt
    Dim frm As Form
    Dim ctl As Control
    On Error Resume Next

    For Each ctl In frm.Controls
        ctl.FontSize = 12
    Next
End Sub
```

On Error GoTo Label

The On Error GoTo Label statement is used to cause Access to jump to a specific location in the code (marked with the label) when an error occurs. The error handling code that is marked by these labels is usually placed at the end of a procedure. The name of each error handler (the label) must be unique within the procedure.

You must include an Exit Sub line *before* the error handler label. Otherwise, the error handling code executes, even if no error has occurred.

 Tip

You should have only one way to exit the code. Therefore, it is a good idea to include a label with the Exit Sub statement, so that you can refer to it from other areas of the procedure.

The following example demonstrates the structure of a basic error handler:

```
Sub CodeWithErrorHandler()
    On Error GoTo CodeWithErrorHandlerErr
    'Code (which may cause error) goes here
CodeWithErrorHandlerDone:
```

```
        Exit Sub
CodeWithErrorHandlerErr:
    'Error Handling Code goes here
    Resume CodeWithErrorHandlerDone
```

On Error GoTo 0

Both the On Error GoTo Label and the On Error Resume Next statements remain in effect until the procedure is exited, another error handler is declared, or the error handler is canceled. The On Error GoTo 0 statement is used to cancel the error handler and reset the value of the Error object. This can be used if the error is irrelevant to the rest of your code, and you do not need to respond to the error or record the value of the error.

The Resume Statement

After your error handler has finished executing, you must use the Resume statement to return to the main part of your code. There are three choices with the Resume statement:

▶ Resume

▶ Resume Next

▶ Resume Label

Table 5.3 describes the three options that are available with the Resume statement.

Table 5.3

Resume Options

Option	Description
Resume	This option returns control to the statement that caused the error. This should be used only if the error handler actually fixed the problem that caused the error—otherwise, it causes an endless loop. Use this option with caution.

continues

Table 5.3   Continued

Option	Description
Resume Next	This is very similar to the On Error Resume Next statement. It returns control to the line immediately after the code that generated the error.
Resume Label	This option enables you to return to a specific line of code. This is often used when you want to exit the code. Rather than having two Exit Sub statements, you simply refer to the label associated with the Exit Sub statement. It is very similar to the GoTo statement, but Resume Label can be used only from within an error handler.

 Note

When an error-handling routine is running and an End Sub, End Function, or End Property statement is encountered before a Resume statement is encountered, an error occurs because a logic error is made. However, if an Exit Sub, Exit Function, or Exit Property statement is encountered while an error handler is active, no error occurs because the statement is considered a deliberate redirection of execution.

Handling the Error

The Err Object

Before you can decide what action to take to handle an error, you must determine what error occurred and what object or application generated the error. After you have this information, you can then determine how to respond to the error.

Beginning with Access 7.0 for Windows 95, Microsoft added a new method for dealing with errors, the Err object. The Err object is created each time a *runtime error* occurs in Access. You can read the properties of the Err object to get information about the error. This information then helps you decide what action to take in response to the error that was generated.

Properties of the Err Object

The Err object has several properties that give you information about the error. You can then use this information to determine how to handle the error. Table 5.4 lists the properties of the Err object.

Table 5.4

Err Object Properties

Option	Description
Description	Returns a string that describes the error. This is often used in a message box if you want to give the user information about the error.
HelpContext	Returns a Context ID for a topic in a Microsoft Windows Help file.
HelpFile	Returns the complete path to a Windows Help file.
LastDLLError	Returns a system error code produced by a call into a dynamic-link library (DLL). This occurs only on 32-bit Microsoft Windows operating systems. When a DLL call that requires a Declare statement is made, the called function usually returns a code indicating success or failure, and the LastDLLError property is filled. Whenever the failure code is returned, the Visual Basic application should immediately check the LastDLLError property. No exception is made when the LastDLLError property is set.
Number	Returns a numeric value that represents an error. This is the default property of the Err object.
Source	Returns the name of the object or application that generated the error.

Using a Select Case Statement in an Error Handler

After you have evaluated the Err object, you must decide how to respond to the error. The Select Case statement enables you to determine which action to take, based on the value of the Err.number. The following example shows the basic structure of a procedure that used On Error GoTo Label to trap the error and direct the code to the error handler. The error handler then uses the Select Case statement to determine what action to take.

```
Sub FileOpen()
On Error GoTo OpenFileErr

    'Code to open file goes here
OpenFileDone:
    Exit Sub
OpenFileErr:
    Select Case Err.Number
    Case 52      'Bad File Name
        MsgBox ("The file name is incorrect.
                Please try again"), , "Error Opening File"
    Case 55      'File Already Open
        MsgBox ("The file that you specified is
                already open!"), "Error Opening File"
    Case Else
        MsgBox ("An error occurred while trying to
                open the file.  Please contact your database
                administrator and give them the following
                information:  Err number: " & Err.Number &
                "Description: " & Err.Description)
    End Select
    Resume OpenFileDone
End Sub
```

 Tip

It is a good idea to use the Select Case statement, even if you have only one case to handle. If you need to add another case at a later date, it is very easy to add it to the code. You also always should include a Case Else statement for Err numbers that you did not anticipate.

Methods of the Err Object

The Err object has two methods: Clear and Raise. Clear is used to clear all property settings of the Err object (the settings are reset to zero-length strings). Clear is normally used at the end of an Error handler, to clear the Err collection. The syntax of the Clear method is:

```
Object.Clear
```

Object is always the Err object.

Visual Basic calls the Clear method when any of the following statements is executed:

▸ Any type of Resume statement

▸ Exit Sub, Exit Function, Exit Property

▸ Any On Error statement

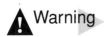Warning

The Err object could be cleared if you set up an error handler using On Error GoTo, and that handler calls another procedure. To retain values for later use, assign the values of Err properties to variables before calling another procedure or before executing Resume, On Error, Exit Sub, Exit Function, or Exit Property statements.

The Raise method is used to generate a specific runtime error. Occasionally, you need to raise an error within your error handler. The syntax of the Raise method is:

```
object.Raise(Number, Source, Description, HelpFile, HelpContext)
```

The Raise method of the Err object is similar to the Error object that was used in previous versions of Access and can be used instead of the Error statement. Although Error still works the same in existing code, Raise provides more information than Error. Because of this, Raise is more useful for generating errors when writing OLE Automation objects (even though both Error and Raise support OLE automation objects). For example, with the

Raise method, the original generator of the error can be specified in the Source property, Online Help for the error can be referenced, and so on.

Table 5.5 explains each of the arguments used in the Raise method.

Table 5.5

Arguments of the Raise Method	
Argument	Description
Object	The Object argument is always the Err object.
Number	This argument is required. It is a long integer that identifies the nature of the error.
Source	This argument is optional; it is a string expression naming the object or application that originally generated the error. When setting this property for an OLE Automation object, use the form project.class. If nothing is specified, use the programmatic ID of the current Visual Basic project.
Description	This optional argument is a string expression describing the error. If no description is specified, the number is examined. If the number can be mapped to a Visual Basic runtime error code, the string that is returned by the Error function is used as Description. If there is no Visual Basic error corresponding to Number, an Application-defined or Object-defined error is used.
HelpFile	This argument is optional; it is a fully qualified path to the Microsoft Windows Help file, in which help about this error can be found. If nothing is specified, Visual Basic uses the fully qualified drive, path, and filename of the Visual Basic Help file.
HelpContext	This optional argument is the context ID for identifying a topic within HelpFile to provide help for the error. If HelpContext is omitted, the Visual Basic Help file context ID for the error corresponding to the Number property is used, if the context ID exists.

Tip

Visual Basic errors (both Visual Basic-defined and user-defined errors) are in the range 0-65535. If you are setting the Number property to your own error code in an OLE automation object, you must add your number to the constant vbObjectError. For example, to generate the error number 1175, assign vbObjectError + 1175 to the Number property.

Hierarchy of Error Handlers

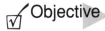 **Objective**

Use care when handling errors in a procedure that is called by another procedure. If procedure A calls procedure B and there is an error in procedure B, Access first checks procedure B for an error handler. If procedure B does not contain an error handler, Access looks for one in procedure A. Access then acts as if procedure A generated the error. If the Resume Next statement is used in the error handler, Access returns to the line of code immediately following the code that called procedure A rather than the line after the code in procedure B that actually caused the error.

The confusion increases if procedure A calls procedure B, which calls procedure C. If an error occurs in procedure C, and there are no error handers in procedures B or C, the error handler in procedure A is invoked. This can cause some unexpected results. It is a very good idea, therefore, to have an error handler in each procedure. Even though it is time-consuming to write an error handler for each procedure, this measure reduces unexpected results from your error handlers. For more information about tracing the calls from one procedure to another, see the "Using the Calls Dialog Box" section later in this chapter.

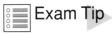 **Exam Tip**

For the exam, be prepared to read code that jumps from procedure to procedure and be able to determine what happens if an error occurs.

Debugging Code Samples

When you are testing your code, it often is convenient to be able to execute the code independent of the form, report, or module in which the code normally runs. The Debug window is designed for exactly this purpose. This tool enables you to execute your code in order to test it.

The Debug Window

The Debug window is a very useful tool for troubleshooting (debugging) your code. You can enter items directly into the Debug window or use the Print method of the Debug object.

To access the Debug window do one of the following:

- ▶ Click the Debug Window button on the toolbar.

- ▶ Select View, Debug Window.

- ▶ Press Ctrl + G.

The Debug window (formerly known as the Immediate window) has two sections. The top half is known as the Watch pane. This is visible only if you have set a watch expression. The bottom half of the window is known as the Immediate pane.

Entering Items in the Debug Window

You can do any of the following directly in the Debug window:

- ▶ Run a procedure.

- ▶ Display the return value of a function.

- ▶ Display the value of a variable.

- ▶ Execute a line of code.

Figure 5.1 shows the Debug window with a call to the IsOpen function. The Debug window enables you to test code directly, without having to use forms, macros, or any other method of running the code.

Figure 5.1

Calling a function in the Debug window.

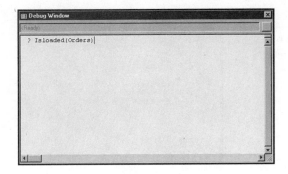

To run a procedure from the Debug window, simply type the name of the procedure in the Debug window and press Enter. To display the current value of a variable, simply type **Print** and the name of the variable and press Enter. The return value prints to the Debug window.

 Tip   Use a question mark (?) as a shortcut for Print to display the variable's current value.

To run a function from the Debug window, precede the name of the function or procedure with a ?. Take note of the following example:

```
? SampleFunction()
```

The preceding function executes the function (SampleFunction) and prints the return value of the function in the Debug window.

Figure 5.2 shows the Debug window after calling a function. Notice that a previous line is left in the Debug window, yet it does not affect the current code.

The Debug window displays the last 200 lines of output at all times. After 200 lines have been entered, the oldest lines begin to disappear from the window. If you want to re-execute code that has already been entered in the Debug window, place your cursor in that line and press Enter.

Figure 5.2

The Debug window after calling a function.

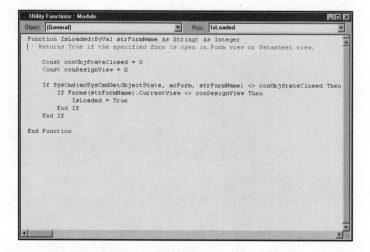

```
Utility Functions : Module                                                    _ □ ×
Object: [(General)]                          ▼     Proc: [IsLoaded]                     ▼
Function IsLoaded(ByVal strFormName As String) As Integer
  ' Returns True if the specified form is open in Form view or Datasheet view.

      Const conObjStateClosed = 0
      Const conDesignView = 0

      If SysCmd(acSysCmdGetObjectState, acForm, strFormName) <> conObjStateClosed Then
          If Forms(strFormName).CurrentView <> conDesignView Then
              IsLoaded = True
          End If
      End If

  End Function
```

To execute code directly from the Debug window, enter the line of code you need and then press Enter. You cannot enter a Dim, ReDim, Global, or Const statement in the Debug window, nor can you enter a multiple-line statement (such as a Select Case statement). To get around this restriction, you can use the colon (:) to separate multiple VBA statements in the same line. For example, you could execute the following code in the Debug window (assuming that you already declared the variable x in your code):

```
For x = 1 to 10: x=x+2:Next x
```

Using Debug.Print

The Debug window is technically known as the Debug object in Access. The Debug object has only one method: Print. The syntax is the Debug.Print command. The Print method of the Debug object instructs Access to print the value that follows the command. If you are in the Debug window, you do not have to specify the object because it is assumed to be the Debug object. You can simply use the Print command.

If you have a Debug.Print statement in your code, the Debug window does not automatically open. After the code runs, however, you can open the Debug window and view the output. This also means that you can distribute an application that has Debug.Print statements left in, because the user does not usually open the Debug window. However, it is a better idea to clean up your code before you distribute an application.

The following line was run during a procedure in order to determine the time of the last design change to a form. This line of code is placed in the OnOpen event of the form so that a programmer always knows when this form was last changed:

```
Debug.Print
CurrentDb.Containers!Forms.Documents!Orders.LastUpdated
```

 Tip

> Be careful not to confuse the LastUpdated and LastModified properties. LastUpdated is a property of the Document object, which shows the last time a design change was made to a given object. The LastModified property applies only to Recordset objects. LastModified returns a bookmark that points to the most recently changed or added record.

Debugging Tips

It is a good idea to develop a systematic method of debugging your code. Although debugging can be time-consuming, it is well worth the effort. It is much better for you to discover any mistakes before you distribute the code to your clients, when the mistakes are still relatively easy to fix.

Make sure that you fix only one piece of code at a time. After you find the code that you believe is causing the error, fix that particular line and test the code again. This may sound obvious, but it is all too easy to fall into the trap of altering several pieces of code before testing your code again. If you do this, you will not know which portion of code caused the error or which change fixed it.

Problems to Avoid When Debugging

Be aware of certain things when you are debugging your code. The simple fact that you have your Debug window open and your code halted causes certain parts of your program to act differently than they act were the code running under normal circumstances.

Certain properties and events may cause problems unique to debugging. Table 5.6 lists these problems and suggests how to avoid them.

Table 5.6

Events and Properties that Can Cause Problems When Debugging	
Potential Problem	Solutions
MouseDown	If you suspend execution during a MouseDown event, you can release the mouse button to perform your debugging tasks. However, when you resume execution, Access assumes that the mouse is still pressed down. You must press and release the mouse again to generate the MouseUp procedure.
KeyDown	You must take these same considerations after suspending execution during a KeyDown event. If you retain a breakpoint in a KeyDown event procedure, a KeyUp event might never occur.
GotFocus/LostFocus	Suspending execution during either of these procedures can cause inconsistent results. To avoid this problem, use the Debug.Print method to execute the code rather than suspending execution during the GotFocus or LostFocus event.
Screen.ActiveForm/ Screen.ActiveControl	Because the Debug window actually has the focus when you are working with your code in the Debug window, there is technically no active form or active control. Consequently, any attempt to use Screen.ActiveForm or Screen.ActiveControl when the Debug window has the focus results in an error. To avoid this problem, substitute the Me object for Screen in your procedures. No problem occurs when using Debug.Print.ActiveScreen or Debug.Print. ActiveForm in your code, as long as the Debug window does not have the focus when the code is running.

Note | Although the Me keyword is usually the same as ActiveForm or ActiveScreen, you must use care if code is running in a form that does not have the focus. If a timer event causes code to run in a form that does not have the focus, for example, Me refers to the form whose code is running, even though it does not have the focus. Just remember that Me always refers to the form whose code is currently executing.

Using Debugging Tools

You can use debugging tools to suspend program execution, examine code, step through, and reset execution of code. Access provides a rich assortment of debugging tools to help you track errors in your code. This section discusses the tools that enable you to detect any errors.

Setting Breakpoints

Breakpoints are used to temporarily halt execution of your code in order to determine which line is causing an error. A breakpoint enables you to stop executing the code at a particular spot, yet keep the system state in memory. All variables and function in the code are still in memory and can be examined in the code window.

You can set breakpoints on any line of executable code. They cannot, however, be set on any of the following lines of code:

▶ A blank line

▶ A comment line

▶ A variable declaration

▶ A dim statement

To set a breakpoint in a line of code, place your cursor anywhere in the line of code and do one of the following:

- ▶ Select Run, Toggle Breakpoint.

- ▶ Click the Breakpoint button on the toolbar.

- ▶ Press F9.

When you set a breakpoint on a line of code, that line has a dark bar around it to indicate that a breakpoint has been set. Figure 5.3 shows the code window with a line that has a breakpoint set.

Figure 5.3

A line of code with a breakpoint.

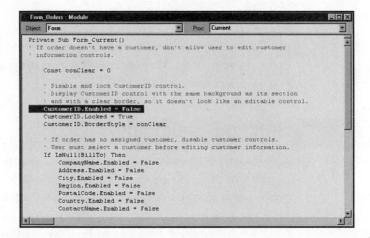

When the code is running, it suspends execution *before* it runs the line with the breakpoint. The code window immediately opens, and the line with the breakpoint now has a thin black border. Figure 5.4 shows the code window after the code halts at the breakpoint.

Stepping Through Code

After the code has been suspended, you have several options in the Run menu that enable you to move through the code. Table 5.7 lists the options for stepping through code. You can use any combination of these methods to step through your code while you are debugging.

Figure 5.4

*The code window
after halting at a
breakpoint.*

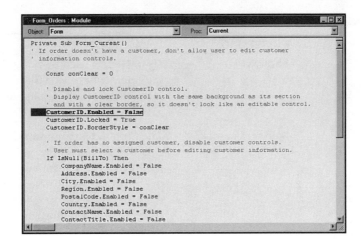

```
Form_Orders : Module                                          _ □ ×
Object: Form                        ▼    Proc: Current                ▼
Private Sub Form_Current()
' If order doesn't have a customer, don't allow user to edit customer
' information controls.

    Const conClear = 0

    ' Disable and lock CustomerID control.
    ' Display CustomerID control with the same background as its section
    ' and with a clear border, so it doesn't look like an editable control.
    CustomerID.Enabled = False
    CustomerID.Locked = True
    CustomerID.BorderStyle = conClear

    ' If order has no assigned customer, disable customer controls.
    ' User must select a customer before editing customer information.
    If IsNull(BillTo) Then
        CompanyName.Enabled = False
        Address.Enabled = False
        City.Enabled = False
        Region.Enabled = False
        PostalCode.Enabled = False
        Country.Enabled = False
        ContactName.Enabled = False
        ContactTitle.Enabled = False
```

Table 5.7

Stepping Through Code

Command	Explanation
Step Into	The Step Into command enables you to step through the code one line at a time. If the code contains a call to another procedure, it also steps through that procedure line by line. This feature can also be accessed by clicking the Step Into button on the Visual Basic toolbar or by pressing F8.
Step Over	This command also enables you to step through the code one line at a time. If the code contains a call to another procedure, however, it does not step through that procedure line by line. Instead, it executes that entire procedure and then returns to the procedure where the code was originally halted. This is very useful if you have already debugged the procedure that is being called. You can also access this feature by clicking the Step Over button on the Visual Basic toolbar or by pressing Shift + F8.
Set Next	Set Next enables you to place your cursor on any line in the code and begin running the code from that point. You are not able to skip to another procedure using Set Next, however.

continues

Table 5.7 Continued

Command	Explanation
Show Next	Show Next is used to bring you back to the statement where execution was paused. This is usually used when you have chosen Set Next and have several code windows open.
Step to Cursor	The Step to Cursor command enables you to run all the code between your breakpoint and the line that is selected when you choose Step to Cursor. Step to Cursor stops after it runs the line where you set Step to Cursor. You can select Step to Cursor from the Run menu or by pressing Ctrl + F8.

Using the Calls Dialog Box

When you are debugging code, it often is necessary to see a list of active procedures. The Calls dialog box enables you to see a list of procedures that have been started but not yet completed. If you are in Break mode, you can view the Calls dialog box. The Calls dialog box lists each active function, with the current function at the top of the list. This can be very useful when you are working with nested statements. To access the Calls dialog box, you do one of the following:

▶ Select Tools, Calls.

▶ Press Ctrl + L.

▶ Click Tools on the Visual Basic toolbar.

▶ Click the Build button in the Debug window.

Figure 5.5 shows the Calls dialog box.

While you are in the Calls dialog box, if you highlight one of the listed procedures, you can use the Show button to display that procedure and highlight the statement that executed last.

Figure 5.5

The Calls dialog box.

Removing Breakpoints and Resetting Code

Before you distribute your application, you must ensure that you have cleared all breakpoints. To clear a single breakpoint, you can select the line with the breakpoint and do any one of the following:

- ▶ Select Run, Toggle Breakpoint.

- ▶ Click the Breakpoint button on the toolbar.

- ▶ Press F9.

To clear all breakpoints in your code, you select Clear All Breakpoints from the Run menu. This resets all breakpoints in your entire application.

When you finish debugging one section, it is a good idea to reset the code. You can press Shit + F5 or choose Reset from the Run menu. This action halts the execution of all suspended code and reinitializes all variables. Resetting the code also clears the status of the code that is currently running, so that there is no current line of code.

Using the Debug Window to Monitor the Value of a Variable

When you are debugging code, you often need to determine what the value of a given variable is at a specific point in the code. For example, if you have an endless For...Next loop, you may need to monitor the value of X (the counter) as you step through the code.

Access offers several debugging tools that enable you to monitor the value of a variable. You can enter Debug.Print and the variable name in the Debug window, use the Instant Watch, and use the Watch Pane of the Debug window. (For more information about the Print method, please see the section "Using Debug.Print" earlier in this chapter.)

The Instant Watch

The Instant Watch is a dialog box that enables you to see the value of a variable or expression when you have halted execution of code. (In previous versions of Access, you had to use the print method to display the value in the Debug window.) To set an Instant Watch, place your cursor anywhere within the name of the variable and do one of the following:

▶ Press Shift + F9.

▶ Click the Instant Watch button.

While the Instant Watch dialog box is visible, you can also choose to add the watch to the Watch pane of the Debug window. To add the watch, click Add.

The Instant Watch dialog box displays the context of the variable or expression at the top of the window. This display shows the name of the database, form, report, or module in which the code is running and the name of the procedure. The Expression pane displays the variable or expression that you are evaluating, and Value displays the current value of the variable or expression. If the variable that you have selected has not been initialized yet (has no value), Expression displays "Out of Context." Figure 5.6 shows the Instant Watch dialog box with a variable that has not been initialized yet.

The Watch Pane

Although the Instant Watch dialog box is useful, you very often need to be able to watch the value of your variable or expression as you are stepping through the code. A feature such as this enables you to see how and when the value of your variable or expression changes (or doesn't change).

Figure 5.6

*The Instant Watch
dialog box.*

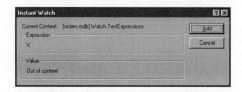

To add a watch to the Watch pane of the Debug window, choose Add Watch from the Tools menu. (You also can choose Instant Watch and then click the Add button on the Visual Basic toolbar.)

If an expression was selected in the Module window when you chose Add Watch, that expression automatically appears in the dialog box. If no expression was selected, you can enter the expression now. The expression can be a variable, a property, a function call, or any other valid expression.

Next, under Context, you must select the range for which you want the expression to be evaluated. It is usually most efficient to select the narrowest range for your expression.

Finally, you must choose how you want Access to respond to the watch. There are three types of watches that you can set:

▶ **Watch Expression.** This watch adds the variable or expression to the Watch pane of the Debug window and enables you to monitor the value as you step through your code.

▶ **Break When Expression Is True.** Access halts execution of code when this expression is true.

▶ **Break When Expression Changes.** Similar to Break When Expression Is True, this watch enables you to halt execution of code as soon as the value of your expression changes.

Figure 5.7 shows the Add Watch dialog box.

The following two Watch expressions were set:

X = 8   Break When Expression Is True

Y   Break When Expression Changes

Figure 5.7

The Add Watch dialog box.

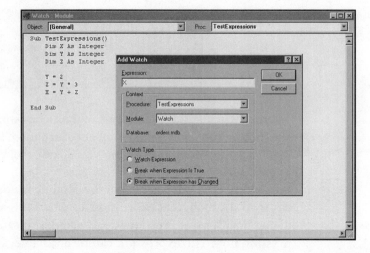

Because Y changed before X had a value of 8, the code was halted on the first line. Therefore, X = 8 has a value of False and Y has a value of 2.

Key Terms and Concepts

Table 5.8 identifies key terms from this chapter. Review the key terms and make sure that you understand each term for the exam.

Table 5.8

Key Terms: Debugging and Error Handling	
Term	Covered in Section...
Err	"Error Object versus Err Object"
Error	"Error Object versus Err Object"
OnError Statement	"Trapping the Error"
Resume	"Writing Error Handlers"
Resume Next	"Writing Error Handlers"
Select Case	"Handling the Error"
Debug Window	"Using Debugging Tools"
BreakPoint	"Using Debugging Tools"

Lab Exercises

These exercises give you the opportunity to work with debugging and error handling and apply the skills learned in this chapter. All lab exercises can be found on the CD-ROM included with this book.

Exercise 5.1:   Using the Debugging Tools

Objective:

Use debugging tools to suspend program execution, examine code and step through and reset execution of code, and monitor the value of a variable.

Time Estimate: 20 minutes

Steps:

1. Open LabFive.mdb found on the CD-ROM that accompanies this book.

2. Open frmExerciseOne and click the Command button.

3. Use the debugging tools to suspend execution of this code, and step through it line by line. Determine why it is not working properly.

4. After you discover the error, make the appropriate changes.

Reading Reference:

For more information about this topic, please see the section "Using Debugging Tools."

Exercise 5.2:   Writing Error Handlers and Using the Debugging Tools

Objective:

Use the debugging tools to determine why the current error handler does not work and then replace it with a more appropriate error handler.

Time Estimate: 20 minutes

Steps:

1. Open LabFive.mdb found on the CD-ROM that accompanies this book.

2. Open frmExerciseTwo and click the Command button. The Command button is used to output the Employees table as an Excel file.

3. You are prompted to choose a directory. However, nothing is actually output, and no error messages are generated.

4. Step through the code to determine the problem. Rewrite the error handler, so that it informs the user if there is an error.

Reading Reference:

For more information about this topic, please see the section "Writing Error Handlers."

Review Questions

1. Which event is fired if an error occurs while the Jet Engine is manipulating data in a form or report?

   A. No event is fired. An error message appears.

   B. No event is fired. The error-handling code is executed.

   C. The OnError event is fired.

   D. The DataError event is fired.

2. Which of the following lines of code verify that the current Error is valid?

   A. If DBEngine.Errors(0)=Err.Number

   B. If DBEngin.Errors.Count=Err.Number

   C. If Err.Number > 0 AND <256

   D. If Errors(0)=Err

3. Which of the following statements returns the fully qualified path to a valid Help file associated with an Error object?

   A. Error.Path(HelpFile)

   B. Err.Path(HelpFile)

   C. Error.HelpFile

   D. Err.HelpFile

4. Which of the following are valid Visual Basic constants used with the Response argument (in an OnError statement)? Choose all that apply.

   A. DataErrContinue

   B. acDataErrContinue

   C. DataErrorContinue

   D. acDisplay

5. Which of the following statements turns off error handling in a procedure? Choose all that apply.

    A. On Error GoTo 0

    B. On Error Ignore

    C. On Error Resume

    D. On Error acNoAction

6. You have written code that creates a table. If the table already exists, you do not want to display an error message, but you simply want to continue executing your code rather than creating a duplicate table. Which of the following statements would you place in your error-handling code to accomplish this?

    A. Resume

    B. Resume Next

    C. GoTo NextLine

    D. acDataErrContinue

7. Which of the following are properties of the Err object? Choose all that apply.

    A. LastDLLError

    B. Number

    C. Source

    D. HelpContext

8. What happens when the following procedure CanHandle is executed?

```
Sub CanHandle()
MsgBox "Hello World"
     On Error GoTo CanHandleErr
     NoCanHandle
CanHandleErr:
     MsgBox "There has been an error"
     Resume Next
End Sub
Sub NoCanHandle()
     Dim X as Integer
```

```
          Dim Y as Integer
          Y=/0
              MsgBox "GoodBye World"
     End Sub
```

   A. A message box (There has been an error) displays, followed by another message box (GoodBye World).

   B. A message box (There has been an error) displays, followed by another message box (Hello World).

   C. A message box (Error: Division by 0) appears and the procedure ends.

   D. A message box (Error: Division by 0) appears, followed by another message box ("Hello World").

9. Which of the following events calls the Clear method of the Err object? Choose all that apply.

   A. Resume

   B. Exit

   C. OnError

   D. Exit

10. Which of the following statements enables you to generate error number 240?

   A. Error.Raise (240)

   B. Error.Call (240)

   C. Err.Raise (240)

   D. Error.Raise (240)

11. Which of the following key combinations displays the Debug window? Choose all that apply.

   A. Ctrl + D

   B. Ctrl + G

   C. Ctrl + Shift + D

   D. Ctrl + Shift + G

12. Which of the following lines, when typed in the Debug window, displays the value of X?

    A. Print X

    B. ShowValue X

    C. ? X

    D. X

13. Which of the following lines, when typed in the Debug window, displays the return value of the function called MyFunction?

    A. MyFunction()

    B. MyFunction

    C. ? MyFunction()

    D. ? MyFunction

14. Which symbol can be used to separate multiple lines of code in the Debug window?

    A. :

    B. ;

    C. ,

    D. /

15. Which of the following lines of code prints the date of the last modification to the form in the Debug window?

    A. Debug.Print
       CurrentDb.Containers!Forms.Documents!Orders.LastUpdated

    B. Debug.Print
       CurrentDb.Containers!Forms.Documents!Orders.LastModified

    C. Debug.Print CurrentDb.Forms!Orders.LastUpdated

    D. Debug.Print CurrentDb.Forms!Orders.LastModified

16. Which of the following events can cause a problem when you are working in the Debug window? Choose all that apply.

    A. On Open

    B. MouseDown

    C. ActiveControl

    D. ActiveForm

17. Which of the following lines cannot have breakpoints on them? Choose all that apply.

    A. Dim X as Integer

    B. X = Y + Z

    C. "This is a comment"

    D. MsgBox "This is a Message."

18. Which of the following methods can be used to set a breakpoint? Choose all that apply.

    A. Shift F9

    B. F9

    C. Run, Toggle Breakpoint

    D. Run, Set Breakpoint

19. When a breakpoint is set, where does Access suspend execution of the code?

    A. Before it executes the line with the breakpoint.

    B. After it executes the line with the breakpoint.

    C. Before it executes the procedure containing the breakpoint.

    D. After it executes the procedure containing the breakpoint.

20. You are stepping through your code, and you know that the next two lines of code are error free. What can you do to move directly to the line after these error-free lines?

   A. Choose Step Over for each line that you know does not contain an error.

   B. Place your cursor on the line after the error-free lines and choose Step to Cursor.

   C. You cannot skip these lines—you must step through them.

   D. Place your cursor on the line after the error-free lines and press Enter.

Answers to Review Questions

1. C is correct. For more information, see the section "Using the Errors Collection and the Error Object to Trap Errors."

2. A is correct. For more information, see the section "Using the Errors Collection and the Error Object to Trap Errors."

3. C is correct. The HelpFile property of the Error object contains the fully qualified path statement to a valid Windows Help file. For more information, see table 5.1.

4. B and D are correct. acDataErrContinue and acDisplay are the only valid constants used with the Response argument. For more information, see table 5.2.

5. A is correct. Only On Error GoTo 0 turns off error handling in a procedure. For more information, see the section "On Error GoTo 0."

6. B is correct. Resume executes the line of code that caused the error and results in an endless loop. Resume Next causes the next line of code to execute. For more information, see the section "The Resume Statement."

7. A, B, C, and D are all correct. For more information, please see table 5.5.

8. B is correct. Because NoCanHandle does not have an error handler, the code moves back to CanHandle and execute its error handler. This causes the message box "There has been an error." to appear. The Resume Next line causes the code after the line that called the procedure with the error to execute. For more information, see the section "Hierarchy of Error Handlers."

9. A, B, and C are correct. For more information, see the section "Methods of the Err Object."

10. C is correct. The Raise method of the Err object enables you to generate a specific error. For more information, see the section "Methods of the Err Object."

11. B is correct. For more information, see the section "The Debug Window."

12. A and C are correct. The ? is a shortcut for the word **Print** in the debug window. For more information, please see the section "Entering Items in the Debug Window."

13. C is correct. To call a function from the Debug window, precede the function with the word **Print** or the ?. You must include the parentheses after the name of the function. For more information, please see the section "Entering Items in the Debug Window."

14. A is correct. The colon (:) is used to separate multiple lines of code in the Debug window. For more information, please see the section "Entering Items in the Debug Window."

15. A is correct. The LastUpdated property of a form contains the date of the last change made to the form. For more information, please see the section "Using Debug.Print."

16. B, C, and D are correct. For more information, see the section "Problems to Avoid When Debugging."

17. A and C are correct. You cannot set a breakpoint on a Dim statement or a comment line. For more information, see the section "Setting Breakpoints."

18. B and D are correct. For more information, see the section "Setting Breakpoints."

19. A is correct. Access suspends execution of the code before it executes the line with the breakpoint. For more information, see the section "Setting Breakpoints."

20. B is correct. Step Over is useful only if your code is calling another procedure. For more information, see the section "Stepping Through Code."

Answers to Test Yourself Questions at Beginning of Chapter...

1. This statement does not work because the Error object does not have any methods. Raise is a method of the Err object. For more information about this topic, see the section "Properties and Methods of the Error Object."

2. The code should be written in the On_Error event of the form. The properties of the Error object provide more information about the error (Number, Description, Source, and so on). For more information about this topic, see table 5.1.

3. Use the On Error GoTo LabelName statement, where LabelName is the name of the error-handling code. For more information about this topic, see the section "Writing Error Handlers."

4. You must have an Exit Sub or Exit Function statement before your error-handling code to prevent the error handler from executing. For more information about this topic, see the section "Writing Error Handlers."

5. The Debug window does not open automatically, even if something has printed to it. To open the Debug window, press Ctrl + G or select View, Debug Window. For more information about this topic, see the section "Debugging Code Samples."

6. First, you need to place a breakpoint somewhere within the loop (probably at the beginning). Next, you should put **X** in the watch pane so that you can monitor its value to see why it does not equal 10. Finally, you need to step through your code, line by line. For more information about this topic, see the section "Using the Debug Window to Monitor the Value of a Variable."

7. You should have placed your cursor on the next line that you wanted to step into and chosen Step to Cursor. Step Over is used when the procedure that you are debugging makes a call to another procedure, and you want to execute the entire procedure and then return to the procedure that called it to continue stepping through that code. For more information about this topic, see the section "Stepping Through Code."

8. In the Debug window, type **Print** (or **?**) and the name of the variable and then press Enter. Or, place your cursor on X and choose Tools, Instant Watch. For more information about this topic, see the section "Stepping Through Code."

9. Place the expression X = 0 in a Watch expression and choose Break When Expression Is True. This causes your code to halt when X = 0 so that you can determine what is causing it to change and at what point in your code it is equal to zero. Alternatively, place **X** in the expression and choose Break When Expression Has Changed so that you can monitor each change to the value of X. For more information about this topic, see the section "Setting Breakpoints."

C h a p t e r   6

Working with Sets of Records

By the end of this chapter, you will be able to execute the following test objectives:

 Objectives

- ▶ Identify and differentiate between the different Recordset object types

- ▶ Create Recordset objects

- ▶ Effectively use Recordset properties

- ▶ Use Recordsets to manipulate record locking

- ▶ Write procedures that manipulate data in a Recordset

- ▶ Create and manipulate QueryDef objects

- ▶ Alter an Access SQL statement that is set for an existing QueryDef object

- ▶ Create TableDef objects

- ▶ Implement transaction processing in a Workspace object

Test Yourself! Before reading this chapter, test yourself to determine how much study time you will need to devote to this section.

1. If you need to work in code with 1,000 records from an attached table, what type of Recordset should you choose?

2. Which of the following type-argument constants will create a read-only Recordset: dbOpenReadOnly, dbOpenStatic, or dbOpenSnapshot?

3. How do you create a Recordset based on a SQL string?

4. What Options argument constant do you use with the OpenRecordset method to create a forward-only scrolling Recordset?

5. When you set a Recordset's Sort property to a valid Sort string, is the Recordset immediately sorted?

6. If your Recordset's current record is the last record, what is the value of the Recordset's EOF property?

7. Analyze this situation: User1 issues the Edit method to change a record in a Recordset where LockEdits = False. User2 has changed and updated the same record. What happens when User1 issues the Update method?

8. Of the following method groups—Move, Find, and Seek—which can be used in table-type Recordsets? Which can be used with criteria? Which will cause an error when executed from an empty Recordset?

9. If you clone a Recordset and then make changes to the original, will the clone be affected? What happens to both Recordsets if the original is closed before the Update method is issued?

10. What Recordset method could you use to greatly speed processing on a Recordset, based on an ODBC source? Use local memory to store records instead of going to the ODBC source for each record.

11. Which processes faster: opening a Recordset using a SQL statement, or executing a QueryDef?

12. When changing a QueryDef's SQL property, what do you have to do to save the change?

13. Can you create a TableDef by using SQL?

14. What happens to changed data if you forget to use the CommitTrans method when modifying data through transactions?

Answers are located at the end of the chapter...

This chapter covers the concepts necessary to work with sets of records in code, including Recordset, QueryDef, and TableDef objects. They are described as follows:

▶ A *Recordset* object in code represents the records in a base table or the records returned when you run a query. You use Recordset objects to manipulate records in a database by reading and manipulating Recordset properties, and by executing Recordset methods.

▶ A *QueryDef* object in code represents a stored query definition in a database. You primarily use QueryDef objects to work with saved queries or SQL pass-through queries.

▶ A *TableDef* object in code represents a stored definition of a table—either a nonattached base table or an attached table.

Most of this chapter focuses on Recordset objects. You can do much more to manipulate and examine data with a Recordset than you can with a QueryDef or TableDef. Much of the information about these three objects overlaps, and instances in which a property or method can be used for multiple objects will be noted.

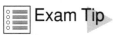 Exam Tip

> As you increase your knowledge of manipulating data through Recordsets, you will not only have a better chance of passing the exam, but you will also become a more powerful and flexible applications developer.

The purpose of a database is to store and manipulate data. Sometimes, you will want to develop an application that uses or manipulates data "behind the scenes" in code, which usually calls for programming with *DAO (Data Access Objects)*. Unless you are running a saved action query or deleting entire tables at a time, you will need to use Recordset objects to work with data in code.

Figure 6.1 illustrates the DAO hierarchy and the relative positions of the Recordsets, QueryDefs, and TableDefs collections.

Figure 6.1

The Recordsets collection is contained in the Databases collection, accessible through the DBEngine object.

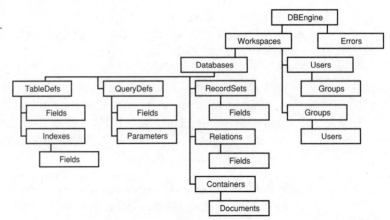

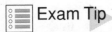 **Exam Tip**

"Working with Sets of Records" is a broad exam section that necessarily involves concepts from other exam sections, especially "Access SQL" and "Working with Visual Basic." Therefore, some of the concepts covered in this chapter may be covered in different contexts in other chapters.

You will definitely benefit by reinforcing your knowledge of Recordset concepts for two reasons:

▶ The majority of the questions on the exam will be about VBA (Visual Basic for Applications) and DAO (Data Access Objects), including questions about Recordsets.

▶ Recordset concepts are infinitely useful in the real world of developing applications with Access.

Choosing the Appropriate Recordset Type

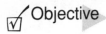 Objective

There are three types of Recordset objects: table-type, dynaset-type, and snapshot-type. As an overview, a *table-type* Recordset represents updatable records from one table in the database, a *dynaset-type* Recordset represents updatable records from a query, and a *snapshot-type* Recordset represents non-updatable records from a query.

Using a Table-Type Recordset

A table-type Recordset is a code representation of a *base table* (a nonattached table in a database). Table-type Recordsets are updatable, but include data from only one table at a time.

Some advantages to using a table-type Recordset are the abilities to work with the records in the order of one of the table's indexes and to use the Seek method. The Seek method is available only to table-type Recordsets. The Index property and Seek method are discussed in the section "Using the Seek Method," later in this chapter.

Another advantage to table-type Recordsets is that only one record is loaded into memory at a time. Also, table-type Recordsets are always updatable, so you can add, modify, or delete records from a table by using a table-type Recordset.

The primary disadvantages to using the table-type Recordset are that they cannot be created from attached or ODBC tables, and that they cannot contain information from more than one table at a time.

Using a Dynaset-Type Recordset

A dynaset-type Recordset object is an updatable representation of the result of a query. Like a table-type Recordset, a dynaset-type Recordset is updatable, so you can add, modify, or delete records by using a dynaset-type Recordset.

It is possible, however, to have a dynaset-type Recordset with only some fields updatable. This situation occurs when the Recordset is based on a query with calculated fields; calculated fields are not updatable.

Dynaset-type Recordsets differ from table-type Recordsets in a number of very important ways. First, because a dynaset-type Recordset is based on a query, it can contain information from multiple tables. It can also contain information from attached tables and ODBC sources.

Also, a dynaset-type Recordset does not actually contain records; instead, it contains a set of references to the records in the database. Although the Recordset object holds the unique key values for each selected record, the object does not hold the record itself. Because of this limitation, dynaset-type Recordsets only retrieve the actual data as needed, which can speed the retrieval process and lessen network traffic.

Using a Snapshot-Type Recordset

A snapshot-type Recordset is a non-updatable copy of the result of a query. Unlike a dynaset-type Recordset, which contains a set of references to data, a snapshot-type Recordset contains the entire data set in local memory. This could easily pose a problem when processing larger Recordsets on a machine with limited memory resources.

Like a dynaset-type Recordset, a snapshot-type Recordset can contain information from multiple tables. It also can contain information from attached tables and ODBC sources. Because the data in snapshot-type Recordsets are static data copies, they are often used to generate reports.

A forward-only scrolling snapshot-type Recordset is the fastest type of Recordset to process because only one pass through the data is allowed. For more information about making a snapshot-type Recordset scroll forward-only, see the section "Setting a Recordset to Scroll Forward-Only" later in this chapter.

Snapshot-type Recordsets cannot process sorts or work with indexes.

Choosing Between Recordset Types

The type of Recordset that you choose in a given situation depends on whether you want to modify data, and what you want to accomplish by creating the Recordset. Table 6.1 summarizes some differences between types to make your decision more clear.

Table 6.1

Determining the Types of Recordsets

Condition	Table	Dynaset	Snapshot
Can use the Seek method	Yes	—	—
Data is updatable	Yes	Yes	—
Stores bookmarks to data, rather than data itself, which allows for faster data retrieval and processing	—	Yes	Yes
Can include data from multiple tables	—	Yes	Yes
Can include data from attached tables	—	Yes	Yes
Can include data from ODBC tables	—	Yes	Yes
Can use the Sort property	—	Yes	Yes
Can be based on a query	—	Yes	Yes
Uses increased local memory resources	—	Yes	Yes
Fastest type to scan records	—	—	Yes
Fastest type to create reports	—	—	Yes
Can be made forward-only scrolling to increase processing speed	—	—	Yes

Given these facts, there are some situations that clearly require one type of Recordset over another. Anytime you create a Recordset that will be used only to check data or run a report, for example, the processing occurs much more quickly with a snapshot-type Recordset, especially for a smaller number of records (under 500). If you want to work with a table's indexes, on the other hand, you must use a table-type Recordset.

If you want to update an attached table or ODBC data, however, then you must use a dynaset-type Recordset. Also use a dynaset-type Recordset when you are dealing with a large number of records (more than 500) or when the recordset you're using contains Memo or OLE Object fields.

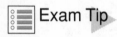 **Exam Tip**

> It is quite likely that one of the exam questions will ask either which type of Recordset is the default (table-type), or which Recordset type to choose in a given situation.

Specifying a Recordset Type in Code

Whether or not you have an exam question about choosing the appropriate Recordset type, you will almost certainly have questions about the Recordset type constants and the syntax of specifying a Recordset type in code.

Specify the Recordset type by using the Type argument of the OpenRecordset method (table-type is the default). The syntax of the OpenRecordset method is as follows:

```
Set variable = database.OpenRecordset (source [, type
➥[. options]])
```

The next section, "Creating Recordset Objects," covers the OpenRecordset method in more detail. Following are the type constants for the OpenRecordset method:

- ▶ **dbOpenTable.** Creates a table-type Recordset

- ▶ **dbOpenDynaset.** Creates a dynaset-type Recordset

- ▶ **dbOpenSnapshot.** Creates a snapshot-type Recordset

If you do not specify a type and it is impossible to create a table-type Recordset, the Jet Database Engine will attempt to create a dynaset-type Recordset, and then a snapshot-type Recordset object.

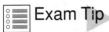

Exam Tip

An exam pitfall for many is a syntax question that offers a choice of statements, each one identical except for a non-existent constant. An example of a tricky exam question about Recordset types would be a choice between the following two lines of code:

```
Set rst = db.OpenRecordset ("Customer", dbOpenDynaset)

Set rst = db.OpenRecordset ("Customer", dbOpenReadWrite)
```

The constant dbOpenReadWrite does not exist, so your success on that question depends on your knowledge of the OpenRecordset type constants.

Creating Recordset Objects

Objective

To create a Recordset object, you must create a Recordset object variable, and then set the variable to some grouping of data by using the OpenRecordset method.

The OpenRecordset method can be used with a Database object, a TableDef object, or a QueryDef object. A Recordset can be based on a table, an existing query, a SQL string, or an existing Recordset.

This flexibility in the OpenRecordset method provides an almost infinite number of examples, and can cause some confusion. For the sake of simplicity, this section focuses on using the OpenRecordset method with a Database object, and bases the Recordset on an existing local table, except where otherwise noted. That way, each variation can be covered separately without crossing over into multiple variations.

The OpenRecordset method creates a new Recordset object and appends that object to the Recordsets collection. Once the Close method is used with a Recordset object

(RecordsetVariable.Close), the Recordset is automatically removed from the Recordsets collection.

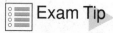 **Exam Tip**

> The questions about syntax for creating Recordsets can be among the most difficult on the exam because there are so many minor variations of the correct syntax that can be put in front of you.
>
> Don't forget that the only way to create a Recordset object, a QueryDef object, or a TableDef object is to use a Set statement and then perform the OpenRecordset, CreateQueryDef, and CreateTableDef methods, respectively.
>
> There is no CreateRecordset method, and the following line of code will not work because there is no Set statement:
>
> ```
> rst = db.OpenRecordset("Table")
> ```
>
> Don't panic, but don't underestimate how well you need to memorize the syntax for the OpenRecordset method, either!

The syntax for creating a Recordset from a Database object is as follows:

```
Set RecordsetVariable =
➥DatabaseOrDatabaseObject.OpenRecordset(source[, type[, options]])
```

Some detail about (and examples of) the different parts of the OpenRecordset method are offered here:

> **RecordsetVariable.** A variable that has been defined as a Recordset type object, either by a Dim statement or a Redim statement, such as the following:
>
> ```
> Dim rst As Recordset
> ```
>
> **DatabaseOrDatabaseObject.** A reference to either a database or a database object. Two examples follow:
>
> ```
> Set rst = DBEngine(0)(0).OpenRecordset(source[, type[,
> ➥options]])
> ```

```
Dim db As DATABASE
Set db = DBEngine(0)(0)
Set rst = db.OpenRecordset(source[, type[, options]])
```

Source. A string that represents the source of the data for the new Recordset. The Source string can be the name of a table, the name of a saved query, or a valid SQL string. In the following example, "Employee" is the name of an existing local table:

```
Set rst = db.OpenRecordset("Employee")
```

Type. One of the type-argument constants: dbOpenTable, dbOpenDynaset, or dbOpenSnapshot. The type argument is optional. If you do not specify a type, the Jet Engine first attempts to create a table-type Recordset. If that is not possible, it attempts to create a dynaset-type Recordset, and then a snapshot-type Recordset, if necessary. The following example creates a dynaset-type Recordset:

```
Set rst = db.OpenRecordset("Employee", dbOpenDynaset)
```

Options. One of several option-argument constants. The various options will be discussed at length in the later sections "Setting a Recordset to Scroll Forward-Only," and "Setting Other Recordset Options."

You can create as many Recordsets as you need, but it is important to keep in mind the memory requirements of different types of Recordsets. Table-type Recordset objects store only one record at a time in local memory. The entirety of dynaset- and snapshot-type Recordset objects are stored in local memory, although dynaset-type Recordset objects hold only references to data, not data itself, so these objects take up less memory than snapshot-type Recordset objects. If local memory does not have enough room to store the object, the Jet Engine saves additional data to a Temp disk space. After the Temp disk space is fully used, a trappable error occurs.

Basing a Recordset on a Linked Table

Access can link to other Access databases or to other types of databases using ODBC. There are only two differences between creating a Recordset based on a local table and creating one based on a linked table:

▶ The Source argument of the OpenRecordset method is the name of the attached Access table rather than the name of a local table.

▶ The Recordset created cannot be a table-type Recordset. Therefore, the Type argument must be dbOpenDynaset or dbOpenSnapshot. If you leave the Type argument blank, the Jet Engine will attempt to create a dynaset-type Recordset first. If it cannot, it will attempt to create a snapshot-type Recordset.

In the following example, the table "Customers" is a linked table:

```
Dim rst As Recordset
Set rst = CurrentDb().OpenRecordset("Customers", dbOpenDynaset)
```

See the later section "Setting Other Recordset Options" for detailed information about which options are available to attached tables. See Chapter 13, "Client/Server Application Development," for more information about linking to ODBC sources, and using SQL pass-through queries with ODBC tables.

Basing a Recordset on a Saved Query

There are only two differences between creating a Recordset based on a local table and creating a Recordset based on an attached Access table:

▶ The Source argument of the OpenRecordset method is the name of a saved query rather than the name of a local table.

▶ The Recordset created cannot be a table-type Recordset. Therefore, the Type argument must be dbOpenDynaset or dbOpenSnapshot. If you leave the Type argument blank, the

Jet Engine will attempt to create a dynaset-type Recordset first. If it cannot, it will attempt to create a snapshot-type Recordset.

In the following example, "qselNonUSCustomers" is a saved query that selects all customers outside the United States:

```
Dim rst As Recordset
Set rst = CurrentDb().OpenRecordset("qselNonUSCustomers",
dbOpenSnapshot)
```

The primary advantage to using a saved query is that saved queries remain compiled once they are saved and executed for the first time. Compiled queries yield better performance than SQL statements, which have to compile before they execute.

Basing a Recordset on SQL

There are only two differences between creating a Recordset based on a local table and creating a Recordset based on SQL (Structured Query Language):

▶ The Source argument of the OpenRecordset method is a valid SQL string rather than the name of a local table.

▶ The Recordset created cannot be a table-type Recordset. Therefore, the Type argument must be dbOpenDynaset or dbOpenSnapshot. If you leave the Type argument blank, the Jet Engine will attempt to create a dynaset-type Recordset first. If it cannot, it will attempt to create a snapshot-type Recordset.

What exactly constitutes "a valid SQL string" is covered in much greater detail in Chapter 3, "Microsoft Access SQL." This section focuses on the following examples:

▶ A simple SQL string

▶ A SQL string with a parameter passed to it from the function

▶ A SQL string that references a numeric control on a form

▶ A SQL string that references a text control on a form

These four examples highlight the most common Recordset SQL exam questions.

In all of the examples, the following are standard:

- ▶ Customers is a local Access table.

- ▶ CustomerID is the primary key field of the Customers table.

- ▶ CustomerState is a non-unique text field in the Customers table.

- ▶ frmCustomer is a loaded form that holds information from the Customers table.

- ▶ txtCustomerID is the text box on frmCustomer that is bound to the CustomerID field.

- ▶ cboCustomerState is the combo box on frmCustomer that is bound to the CustomerState field.

For the first SQL example, a dynaset-type Recordset is created from a simple SQL string:

```
Dim db As DATABASE, rst As Recordset
Set db = CurrentDb()
Set rst = db.OpenRecordset("SELECT * FROM Customers ORDER BY
➥CustomerID")
```

Sometimes, however, it is necessary to pass information to a SQL string. This second example passes information to the SQL string from the function parameter, and creates a dynaset-type Recordset:

```
Sub CustomersInState(strState As String)
  Dim db As DATABASE, strSQL As String,  rst As Recordset
  Set db = CurrentDb()
  StrSQL = "SELECT * FROM Customers WHERE CustomerState = '" &
  ➥strState & "'"
  Set rst = db.OpenRecordset(strSQL)
End Sub
```

This example does nothing with the Recordset; that information is covered in the section "Manipulating Data by Using Recordset Methods."

Key Concepts

> The correct syntax of quotation marks is a critical component of answering SQL exam questions correctly. Numbers do not need quotation marks around them, but text strings do require quotation marks. When you build a string, and the whole string is enclosed in double quotation marks (" "), you must use single quotation marks within the string (' '). Carefully study the examples and notice that text and numbers are handled differently.

At other times, you will want the SQL string to refer to information on a form's control. The quotation marks are slightly different when the string refers to a text form control and when it refers to a numeric form control. The third example refers to a text form control:

```
Dim db As DATABASE, strSQL As String,  rst As Recordset
Set db = CurrentDb()
StrSQL = "SELECT * FROM Customers WHERE CustomerState = '" &
         Forms!frmCustomer!cboCustomerState & "'"
Set rst = db.OpenRecordset(strSQL)
```

The fourth example refers to a numeric form control. Especially note the difference in quotation marks:

```
Dim db As DATABASE, strSQL As String,  rst As Recordset
Set db = CurrentDb()
StrSQL = "SELECT * FROM Customers WHERE CustomerID = " &
         Forms!frmCustomer!txtCustomerID
Set rst = db.OpenRecordset(strSQL)
```

The primary disadvantage to using a SQL source is that SQL strings must compile before they run, which can result in slower performance. Also, SQL can be more complicated to troubleshoot than a query in Design mode (the Query-By-Example grid).

A SQL source is more flexible than a saved query, however; you can pass parameters directly to the SQL string. A SQL string in code also takes up less storage space than a saved, compiled query.

Basing a Recordset on an Existing Recordset

There are situations in which you will want to create a Recordset based on an existing Recordset, especially to compare information or alter the Sort property of a Recordset, which is discussed in detail in the section "Using the Sort Property."

The syntax of using the OpenRecordset method on an existing Recordset is different than when using the OpenRecordset method on a database object; you do not need to use the source argument for an existing Recordset. The source *is* the existing Recordset. Therefore, the syntax of creating a Recordset based on another Recordset is as follows:

```
Set RecordsetVariable = RecordsetObject.OpenRecordset([type[,
→options]])
```

The RecordsetVariable, type, and options parts of the OpenRecordset method are the same as if the OpenRecordset method were being applied to a database object. The only difference is the RecordsetObject part of the OpenRecordset method, which is simply the Recordset variable that represents an existing Recordset.

The following example creates a dynaset-type Recordset object (rstB) based on an existing table-type Recordset object (rst), in which "Employees" is a local Access table:

```
Dim db As DATABASE, rst As Recordset, rstB  As Recordset
Set db = DBEngine(0)(0)
Set rst = db.OpenRecordset("Employees")
Set rstB = rst.OpenRecordset()
```

When the type argument is left blank, the Jet Engine attempts to create the second Recordset as the same type as the first Recordset. In the preceding example, rstB is a dynaset-type Recordset because the rstB could not be a table-type Recordset (because it is not directly based on a local table). If rst had been a snapshot-type Recordset, then rst2 would have been a snapshot-type Recordset as well.

Keep in mind the following restriction: you cannot base a Recordset on an existing forward-only scrolling Recordset; that would require another pass through the data, which is not possible with a forward-only scrolling Recordset.

Using the OpenRecordset Method with TableDefs and QueryDefs

The syntax for using the OpenRecordset method with TableDefs and QueryDefs is the same as the syntax for creating a Recordset based on an existing Recordset:

Set *RecordsetVariable* = *Object*.**OpenRecordset**([*type*[, *options*]])

Object is a TableDef or QueryDef object. No source argument is necessary because TableDefs are essentially table-type Recordsets and QueryDefs are essentially dynaset-type Recordsets. Therefore, the source is automatically specified when the OpenRecordset method is applied to a TableDef or QueryDef.

The following is an example of creating a snapshot-type Recordset based on a QueryDef:

```
Dim db As DATABASE, qdf As QueryDef, rst As Recordset
Set db = CurrentDb()
Set qdf = db.CreateQueryDef("qryEmployees")
Set rst = qdf.OpenRecordset(dbSnapshot)
```

The process to create a snapshot-type Recordset based on a TableDef is almost identical, as you can see in this example:

```
Dim db As DATABASE, tdf As TableDef, rst As Recordset
Set db = CurrentDb()
Set tdf = db.CreateTableDef("tblEmployees")
Set rst = tdf.OpenRecordset(dbSnapshot)
```

In conclusion, a Recordset based on a TableDef or QueryDef object cannot be a table-type Recordset, but it can be a dynaset-type Recordset or a snapshot-type Recordset.

Setting a Recordset to Scroll Forward-Only

The only type of Recordset that can be made *forward-only scrolling* is a snapshot-type Recordset. Data in such a Recordset is read only, records must be viewed one at a time in sequential order, and only one pass through the data is allowed. This greatly improves query performance, making a forward-only scrolling snapshot-type Recordset the most efficient way to process straightforward data.

One major drawback to a forward-only scrolling Recordset is that you cannot create another Recordset based on a forward-only scrolling Recordset. In addition, forward-only scrolling Recordsets will support only the MoveNext method, and cannot be cloned.

You create a forward-only scrolling snapshot-type Recordset by specifying the dbForwardOnly constant in the options argument of the OpenRecordset method, as shown in the following example:

```
Set rst = CurrentDb().OpenRecordset("qryEmployees",
➥dbOpenSnapshot, dbForwardOnly)
```

In some situations, it is strongly advisable to use a forward-only scrolling snapshot-type Recordset:

- ▶ When using Recordsets to process reports

- ▶ When making a single pass through a Recordset opened from an ODBC data source

- ▶ When performing simple processing, such as checking a Recordset for a certain value, or counting the number of records in a Recordset

Setting Other Recordset Options

In addition to dbForwardOnly, there are several other Recordset option argument constants that can be used with the OpenRecordset method. The following list describes the other options:

- ▶ **dbAppendOnly.** Enables the addition of new records to the Recordset, but prevents existing records from being read (dynaset-type only).

▶ **dbSQLPassThrough.** Sends an SQL statement to an ODBC database so that the processing is done on the ODBC database. A Recordset with this option is sometimes referred to as a *SQL pass-through Recordset.*

▶ **dbSeeChanges.** Generates a runtime error if another user changes Recordset data that you are editing.

▶ **dbDenyWrite.** Locks the Recordset so that other users cannot modify or add records.

▶ **dbDenyRead.** Locks the Recordset so that other users cannot view records (table-type only).

▶ **dbReadOnly.** Prevents updates to the Recordset and will not enable the addition of records.

▶ **dbInconsistent.** Allows inconsistent updates (dynaset-type Recordset only). An *inconsistent* update occurs when a multiple-table Recordset object updates all fields, even when tables do not have a one-to-one relationship. For example, in a Recordset created by joining two tables in a one-to-many join, you can update the ManyTable.OneTableID field so that it no longer matches the OneTable.OneTableID field.

▶ **dbConsistent.** Allows only consistent updates (dynaset-type only).

The dbConsistent and dbInconsistent constants cannot both be used on the same instance of OpenRecordset.

Setting Recordset Properties

Objective

A user's abilities to view and manipulate data in Recordsets can be modified through setting Recordset properties. The properties that are explained in the following sections are the most common Recordset properties.

Using the Sort Property

The Sort property can be used with dynaset- and snapshot-type Recordset objects to set the sort order for subsequent creations of the Recordset object. This process sounds a little confusing because it is. Logically, you may think that setting the Sort property of Recordset rst means that rst will be sorted right away. That is not true.

Instead, when you set the Sort property of Recordset rst, the information is stored for the next time a Recordset is created based on rst. The following example creates a Recordset based on the table "Employees," and sorts it by the EmployeeID field by creating a second Recordset:

```
Set db = CurrentDb()
Set rst = db.OpenRecordset("Employees", dbOpenDynaset)
rst.Sort = "EmployeeID"
Set rst2 = rst.OpenRecordset()
```

Notice that the initial Recordset, rst, must be created as a dynaset-type Recordset, because table-type Recordsets do not have a Sort property.

Using the Filter Property

The Filter property works in much the same way as the Sort property. The Filter property can be used with dynaset- and snapshot-type Recordset objects to set the filter criteria for subsequent creations of the Recordset object.

Setting the Filter property of Recordset rst does not mean that rst will be filtered right away. Instead, when you set the Filter property of Recordset rst, the filter information is stored for the next time a Recordset is created based on rst. The following example creates a Recordset based on the table "Employees," and filters it by the State field by creating a second Recordset:

```
Set db = CurrentDb()
Set rst = db.OpenRecordset("Employees", dbOpenDynaset)
rst.Filter = "[State] = 'TX'"
Set rst2 = rst.OpenRecordset()
```

Notice that the initial Recordset, rst, must be created as a dynaset-type Recordset, because table-type Recordsets do not have a Filter property.

Using the RecordCount Property

Common sense seems to dictate that the RecordCount property of a Recordset would return the number of records in a Recordset. In a table-type Recordset, this is true—a table-type Recordset has a stable RecordCount property that always returns the total number of records in the Recordset.

In dynaset- and snapshot-type Recordsets, however, the RecordCount property does not return the total number of records unless all records in the Recordset have been accessed. In dynaset- and snapshot-type Recordsets, the RecordCount property only returns the number of records that have currently been accessed.

If you create a dynaset-type Recordset that has 100 records, for example, and then use a Do Until...Loop statement to check for a certain value in one field, then after you find that value, the RecordCount property will return the number of records that have been accessed in the search, not 100. So if your Do Until...Loop reached only the seventh record, the RecordCount property returns 7.

To use the RecordCount property to find the total number of rows in a Recordset, you must first use the MoveLast method before checking the value of the RecordCount property.

Using the NoMatch Property

The NoMatch property of a Recordset is used in conjunction with either the Seek method or the Find method to indicate whether a particular record matches the criteria used in the Seek or Find method. The property returns either True (-1) or False (0). A True value indicates that no match has been found, and a False value indicates that a match has been found.

When the Recordset object is first opened or created, its NoMatch property is set to False.

If you plan to start the Seek or Find process from a certain record in the Recordset, and then to return to that record, be sure to retrieve that record's bookmark (or some other unique record value) before you execute the Seek or Find method. You need to "remember" the current record before Seeking or Finding because after the NoMatch property has been set to True, the record that was the current record is no longer the current record.

The NoMatch property is usually part of a Do...Loop or an If...Then test, where one set of actions happens if the record matches the criteria, and some other set of actions happens if the record does not. The following example uses the NoMatch property with an If...Then statement to prepare for the possibility of not discovering a match for the FindFirst method.

```
Dim rst As Recordset, strCriteria As String
Set rst = CurrentDb().OpenRecordset("Employees", dbOpenDynaset)
Criteria = "[State] = 'IA'"
rst.FindFirst Criteria
  If rst.NoMatch Then
    MsgBox "No Match available"
  Else
    MsgBox "First IA Employee is: " & rst![First Name] & " " &
rst![Last Name]
  End If
```

For more information about using the Seek and Find methods, see the sections "Using the Seek Method" and "Using the Find Methods" later in this chapter.

Using the Index Property

Only table-type Recordset objects have an Index property. The Index property sets or returns the name of the current Index object. Setting the Index property of a Recordset changes the order in which the records are returned.

Usually the Index property is set before using the Seek method, so that the records are returned in a predictable order. The only values that are valid for the Index property are Index objects that have already been defined.

The following example sets the Index property to the "FullName" Index of the "Employees" table, which is a multifield index by [Last Name] and then by [First Name], ascending:

```
Dim db As DATABASE, rst As Recordset
Set db = DBEngine(0)(0)
Set rst = db.OpenRecordset("Employees", dbOpenTable)
rst.Index = "FullName"
```

If a table has no indexes, then records are returned in no particular order.

Using the Bookmark Property

The *Bookmark* property of a Recordset returns a unique bookmark identifier for the Recordset's current record. The Bookmark property also is used to set the current Recordset record to a valid bookmark. Bookmarks are variants of byte data, and are usually used to set a variant type variable to a bookmark and then retrieve the value later without ever directly returning the bookmark value.

You can set as many bookmarks as you want, but bookmarks do not work in forward-only scrolling snapshot-type Recordsets.

In order to use the Bookmark property, the value of the Recordset's Bookmarkable property must be True. Any Recordset based on Microsoft Jet Engine Database tables will have a Bookmarkable value of True. Data that is gathered from other sources might not be able to use the Bookmark property.

```
Dim db As DATABASE, rst As Recordset, bmk as Variant
Set db = DBEngine(0)(0)
Set rst = db.OpenRecordset("Employees", dbOpenDynaset)
rst.Move 5   'move to record to bookmark
bmk = rst.Bookmark   'set bookmark
     'execute other code here to move off that record
     'then later, you to return to the bookmarked record:
rst.Move 0, bmk   'this moves 0 rows from bmk
```

An unusual use for the Bookmark property is to refresh a record's contents by setting the Recordset's Bookmark property to itself (for example, rst.Bookmark = rst.Bookmark). A potential negative side effect of this technique is that it cancels pending Edit and AddNew operations. A record's contents would need to be refreshed if you wanted to display them after a change.

Using the LastModified Property

The LastModified property returns a bookmark that indicates which record has most recently been added or changed. The most common use of the LastModified property is to move to a new record immediately after adding it (by using the AddNew method).

An example of code using the LastModified property can be found in the section "Using the AddNew Method."

Using the LastUpdated Property

The LastUpdated property returns the date and time of the most recent change made to the Recordset. If the Recordset is a table-type Recordset, then the LastUpdated property returns the date and time of the most recent change made to the base table.

Using the BOF and EOF Properties

The BOF and EOF properties return True (-1) or False (0) values that indicate whether the current position in the Recordset is before the first record (BOF True) or after the last record (EOF True).

The important thing to note is that if your current record position is the first record, then the BOF property will be False. The BOF property is true only when the current record is before the first record. And the converse is true of the EOF property—the EOF property is true only when the current record is after the last record.

It is as if there are invisible "padding" records before and after the Recordset, and those records are BOF and EOF.

BOF and EOF properties are commonly checked when executing Do...Loops, or when doing any kind of processing that involves processing every single record in a Recordset.

It is important to know when you have reached the end of the Recordset, because if EOF is True and you try to execute the MoveNext method, a trappable error occurs. It is safer and more efficient to trap the situation by testing for EOF than to set your error handlers to catch the error.

One possible area of confusion is how the Delete method affects the BOF and EOF properties—it doesn't. You may think that if you delete the last record in a Recordset, or if you delete all the records in a Recordset, then the EOF property would be set to True automatically, but that is not the case. The EOF property is not set to True until you execute a Move method on the Recordset.

If you open a Recordset that has no records, the RecordCount property value is 0, and both the BOF and EOF properties are set to True.

The following is an example of using the EOF property to halt a Do While...Loop after all records have been processed:

```
Dim db As DATABASE, rst As Recordset
Set db = CurrentDb()
Set rst = db.OpenRecordset("Employees")
  Do While Not rst.EOF
    Debug.Print rst![Last Name] & ", " & [First Name]
    rst.MoveNext
  Loop
rst.Close
```

Locking Records with Recordsets

From the Design mode in the user interface, you set locking properties with the RecordLocks property. You can also set or check locking settings in a Recordset, with the LockEdits property. The LockEdits property is available only to table- or dynaset-type Recordsets.

Whenever a Recordset updates data, the Jet Engine always locks the 2K page of memory where the affected record is located. You have a choice, however, about when the locking takes effect—for instance, whether the page locks when the Edit begins, or only when the Update method is performed.

When a page is locked, other users cannot edit any data on that page. Users can view records from locked pages, but cannot change the data.

The LockEdits property has a Boolean setting of True (-1) or False (0). When the LockEdits property is set to True, then *pessimistic* locking is in effect, meaning that the 2K page where the edited record is located locks when you use the Edit method. The page is unlocked again when you use the Update, Close, Find, Move, or Seek method.

When the LockEdits property is set to False, then *optimistic* locking is in effect, meaning that the 2K page where the edited record is located does not lock until you use the Update method. The syntax (see the following two examples) is simple:

```
Recordset.LockEdits = True
```

```
Recordset.LockEdits = False
```

If you set the LockEdits property to optimistic locking (False), and more than one user tries to change data on the same page at the same time, an error will be generated and the second user's changes could be lost. In contrast, if the LockEdits property is set to pessimistic locking, then when the second user attempts to perform the Edit method, an error occurs before the second user's changes are begun.

If your Recordset is based on an ODBC data source, the LockEdits property will always be False because the Jet Engine cannot control the locking abilities of other database engines.

Manipulating Data by Using Recordset Methods

 Objective

This section will focus on Recordset methods that manipulate data. There are other methods, but these are the most common, and the most commonly tested for on the exam.

 Tip

There are several valid syntaxes for referring to the value in a field because the default collection of a Recordset object is the Fields collection, and the default property of a Field object is the Value property. For example, all three of the following lines of code mean the same thing:

```
rst.Fields("ID").Value = 15

rst.("ID") = 15

rst!ID = 15
```

In the code in this section about manipulating data by using Recordsets, the ways of referring to the value of a field will vary to get you accustomed to seeing different valid syntax methods.

Navigating the Recordset

To successfully manipulate data by using a Recordset, you will need to know how to navigate. This section about the Move methods (Move, MoveFirst, MovePrevious, MoveNext, and MoveLast) and the next two sections about the Find methods and the Seek method will explain Recordset navigation.

The Move Method

The Move method changes the current record position of a Recordset object, by the number of rows specified, and from the starting point specified. The syntax is as follows:

```
Recordset.Move Rows[, Start]
```

The Rows argument of the Move method specifies the number of rows to move. Positive numbers (greater than 0) will move the current record forward in the Recordset, closer to the end of the Recordset. Negative numbers (less than 0) will move the current record backward in the Recordset, closer to the beginning of the Recordset.

The Start argument of the Move method stores a bookmark value and indicates with which record to begin the Move. If there is no Start value specified, then the Move starts with the current record.

The Move method sounds straightforward, and it is, but there are a few more details to keep in mind as you use that method:

► If you issue the Move method from a record where the BOF property is False (any record), and the move you specify moves the current record to a non-existent position before the first record, the current record position moves to the BOF position before the first record.

► Along the same lines, if you issue the Move method from a record where the EOF property is False (any record), and the move you specify moves the current record to a non-existent position after the last record, the current record position moves to the EOF position after the last record.

► If you issue the Move method from a record where either the BOF or EOF property is True (before the first record, after the last record, or in a Recordset with no records), and you attempt to move to a non-existent position, a trappable error occurs.

► If you issue the Move method from a Recordset that is based on a query, and the query has not yet populated fully (not all records have been accessed), the Move method forces the query to be run on the number of rows specified in the Rows argument.

► If you are working with a forward-only scrolling snapshot-type Recordset, you can use only a positive integer for the Rows argument. Also, you cannot choose a Start bookmark-position when working with a forward-only scrolling snapshot-type Recordset.

The following is an example of the Move method:

```
Dim db As Database, rst As Recordset
  Set db = CurrentDb()
  Set rst = db.OpenRecordset("SELECT * FROM Employees ORDER BY
[ZIP];")
  Debug.Print "1st record - Social Security #: " & rst![SSN]
  ' Move forward three rows.
    rst.Move 3
Debug.Print "4th record - Social Security #: " & rst![SSN]
```

The MoveFirst, MovePrevious, MoveNext, and MoveLast Methods

The MoveFirst, MovePrevious, MoveNext, and MoveLast methods change the current record position of a Recordset object by moving to the first, last, next, and previous rows of the Recordset. The syntaxes are as follows:

```
Recordset.MoveFirst   Recordset.MoveLast

Recordset.MoveNext   Recordset.MovePrevious
```

These four Move methods are straightforward, but there are a few details to remember as you use them:

▶ If you edit the current record of a Recordset, be sure to use the Update method to save your changes before you move to another record. Should you use any of the Move methods before updating, your changes will be lost without a warning error.

▶ If you use the MovePrevious method when the first record is current, the BOF property is set to True, and there is no current record.

▶ If you use the MoveNext method when the last record is current, the EOF property is set to True, and there is no current record.

▶ If you issue the MovePrevious method from a record where the BOF property is True (before the first record, or in a Recordset with no records), a trappable error occurs.

▶ If you issue the MoveNext method from a record where the EOF property is True (after the last record, or in a Recordset with no records), a trappable error occurs.

▶ If you issue the MoveFirst method when the first record is already current, or if you issue the MoveLast method when the last record is already current, the current record does not change.

▶ If the Recordset is based on a query, and you issue the MoveLast method, the query runs completely, and the Recordset is fully populated.

▶ Of the four Move methods, only MoveNext will function with a forward-only scrolling snapshot-type Recordset. (The MoveFirst, MoveLast, and MovePrevious methods will fail.)

The following is an example of the different Move methods:

```
Dim rst As Recordset
  Set rst = CurrentDb().OpenRecordset("qryEmployees")
    If rst.RecordCount > 0 Then
      rst.MoveLast
      Debug.Print rst![Name] & " is last."
      rst.MoveFirst
      Do While Not rst.EOF
        Debug.Print rst![Name]
        rst.MoveNext
      Loop
      Debug.Print "List completed."
    End If
  rst.Close
```

Using the Find Methods

Unlike in the Move method group, there is no independent Find method—there are only the FindFirst, FindPrevious, FindNext, and FindLast methods. The Find methods cannot be used on table-type Recordsets or forward-only scrolling snapshot-type Recordsets, but only on a dynaset-type or regular snapshot-type Recordset. The Find methods, respectively, change the current record to the first, previous, next, or last record in the Recordset that meets the search criteria. Four examples of syntax follow:

```
Recordset.FindFirst Criteria
```

```
Recordset.FindLast Criteria
```

```
Recordset.FindNext Criteria
```

```
Recordset.FindPrevious Criteria
```

The Criteria argument of a Find method is a string expression (like the Where clause in a SQL statement without the word Where) that specifies the criteria that a record must meet in order to become the current record.

If you issue a Find method and no record matches the specified criteria in the specified direction, then there is no current record and the NoMatch property is True.

The Find methods do not update impending changes to the current record, so if you edit the current record of a Recordset, be sure to use the Update method to save your changes before you use a Find method. Your changes otherwise will be lost without a warning error.

If the Recordset is based on a query, and you issue the FindLast method, the query runs completely, and the Recordset is fully populated.

Just for clarification, note the following details:

▶ The FindFirst method searches from the beginning of the Recordset to the end of the Recordset.

▶ The FindLast method searches from the end of the Recordset to the beginning of the Recordset.

▶ The FindNext method searches from the current record to the end of the Recordset.

▶ The FindPrevious method searches from the current record to the beginning of the Recordset.

Tip ▶ Always check the value of the NoMatch property to determine whether or not the Find operation has failed. If NoMatch is set to True, there is no current record, and you must make a valid record current.

The following is an example of a Find method:

```
Dim rst As Recordset, bmk As Variant
Set rst = CurrentDb().OpenRecordset("Employees")
bmk = rst.Bookmark
rst.FindFirst "Name = 'Peter Jones'"
   If rst.NoMatch Then        ' No record was found
      rst.Bookmark = bmk      ' Go back to  first record
                              ' Could also have used rst.MoveFirst
   Else                       ' Record found.
End If
```

The other Find methods work exactly the same way. The one major advantage to using Find methods is that they enable you to search a limited number of records at a time.

Using the Seek Method

The Seek method is used to change the current record to locate specific records in indexed table-type Recordsets. The criteria for the Seek search must be for the current index. The syntax is as follows:

TableRecordset.Seek *Comparison, Key1, Key2...*

The TableRecordset is the name of a table-type Recordset that has already had an index defined by the Recordset object's Index property. You must set a current index with the Index property before you use the Seek method.

The Comparison argument for the Seek method is one of the following string-expression logical operators: <, <=, =, >=, or >.

The key1, key2 arguments are one or more criteria values. The criteria values must correspond to fields in the Recordset's current index. In other words, you must specify values for all fields defined in the index. If you do not specify values for one or more of the fields, then the equal (=) operator is not valid because of possible Null values in those keys. The value for each key must be the same data type as the field to which it corresponds.

There are a few details to remember as you use the Seek method:

▶ If the Recordset's index determines that more than one record has a key that matches the criteria, Seek locates the first record that satisfies the criteria. That first matching record becomes the current record.

▶ If the Seek method does not locate any matching records, the NoMatch property is set to True, and there is no current record.

▶ If you are editing the current record, be sure to update the changes before you issue the Seek method. Your changes otherwise will be lost without a warning error.

▶ If the Seek method fails, the NoMatch property will be set to True, and there will be no current record. For this reason, after you use the Seek method, check the value of the NoMatch property setting to determine whether the Seek method succeeded.

The following is an example of the Seek method:

```
rst.Index = "DepartmentName"
rst.Seek "=", "Accounting"
If rst.NoMatch Then
   MsgBox "No Employees match the criteria!"
Else
   MsgBox "The First Accounting Employee is: " & rst![FullName]
End If
```

Just don't forget that you can use the Seek method only on indexed, table-type Recordsets. If you attempt to use the Seek method on another type of Recordset, it will cause an error.

Using the AddNew Method

The AddNew method creates a new record for an updatable (table- or dynaset-type) Recordset object. All the fields in the new record are initially set to their default values—if they have them—and Null in fields without default values.

After you create the new record using the AddNew method, you will need to edit the new record and then save the changes (study the Edit and Update methods, discussed in the following sections "Using the Edit Method" and "Using the Update Method"). If you move to another record before you save changes to the new record, the changes will be lost without a warning or an error. The AddNew method syntax follows:

Recordset.AddNew

The position of the newly created record depends on which type of Recordset you are using:

▶ In a dynaset-type Recordset, records are added to the end of the recordset, regardless of sorting or ordering rules that were in effect when the Recordset opened.

▶ In a table-type Recordset whose Index property has been set, records are returned according to the sort order, with the new record in its proper position in the sort order.

▶ In a table-type Recordset whose Index property has *not* been set, new records are added to the end of the recordset.

Note one peculiar thing about the AddNew method: the record that was current before you used AddNew remains current. Therefore, if you want to reposition the current record to your newly created record, you will need to use a Move method. You can locate the new record by setting the Bookmark property to the bookmark returned by the Recordset's LastModified property.

The following is an example of the AddNew method:

```
Dim db As DATABASE, rst As Recordset
Set db = CurrentDb()
Set rst = db.OpenRecordset("Employees")
With rst
  .AddNew
  ![LastName] = "Smith"
  ![FirstName] = "Sammy"
End With
rst.Update
rst.Move 0, rst.LastModified
```

There is one more peculiar thing about the AddNew method: when you use the AddNew method with a table-type Recordset, you cannot see the new record until you refresh the base table. You will need to use the Refresh method on the TableDef of the base table to refresh the base table.

Using the Edit Method

The Edit method enables you to make changes to the current record of an updatable Recordset (dynaset- or table-type Recordsets only) by copying the current record to the copy buffer for editing. The syntax is as follows:

```
Recordset.Edit
```

Since you are not making changes directly to the record, but rather to the copy buffer, you need to make sure to save the changes by issuing the Update method after all the changes are made. Modifications are handled this way so that all changes to a record are made at one time, locking time is reduced in optimistic locking, and you are assured that if any of your changes were successful, then all your changes were successful.

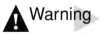 Warning

Be very cautious: ensure that every time you use the Edit method, you use the Update method to save all changes to the record. Otherwise, your changes will be lost without generating an error.

There must be a current record when you issue the Edit command, or an error will occur. After you use the Edit method, the current record remains current.

The Edit method will produce an error if any of the following is true:

▶ There is no current record in your Recordset.

▶ The Recordset is read only, or the database is read only.

▶ The record, in its entirety, is not updatable. (If any fields are updatable, the Edit method will succeed.)

▶ The database or Recordset is open exclusively by another user.

▶ Another user has locked the page containing your record.

The following is an example of the Edit method:

```
Dim rst As Recordset
Set rst = DBEngine(0)(0).OpenRecordset("Employees")
rst.MoveFirst
Do Until rst.EOF
  If rst![Department] = "Accounting" Then
    rst.Edit
    rst![Salary] = rst![Salary] + 3000
    rst.Update
    Exit Do
  End If
rst.MoveNext
Loop
rst.Close
```

Of course, the actions in that code sample could also be performed by an update query, but the demonstration of the Edit method remains valid.

Using the Update Method

The Update method enables you to save changes to the current record of an updatable Recordset (dynaset- or table-type Recordsets only) by saving the contents of the copy buffer to the current record. The syntax is as follows:

Recordset.Update

It is very important to use the Update method to save changes to the current record before moving off the current record. This is true no matter which method of moving off the record you choose—Find, Seek, Move, AddNew, Close, or by setting a Bookmark.

The following is an example of the Update method:

```
Dim rst as Recordset
Set rst = CurrentDb(). OpenRecordset("Employees")
Do Until rst.EOF
  If rst![Date Of Hire] <= #1/1/90# Then
    rst.Edit
    rst![Salary] = rst![Salary] + 2000
    rst.Update
  End If
rst.MoveNext
Loop
rst.Close
```

You must apply the Edit method to the Recordset before you can execute the Update method. If you have not used Edit first, you will cause an error when you issue the Update method.

Using the Delete Method

As you would probably expect, the Delete method deletes the current record in an updatable (table- or dynaset-type) Recordset. The syntax is as follows:

Recordset.Delete

Before you issue the Delete method, there must be a current record. If there is not a current record(BOF or EOF = True), then you will cause a trappable error. Once you have deleted the record, you must make another record current by issuing a Move, Find, or Seek method because the deleted record remains current directly after deletion. However, you cannot read from or write to any field in the record after it has been deleted.

You do not need to use the Update method to save a Delete action. The only way to undelete a record is if you have issued the Delete method in the midst of a transaction which is later rolled back. For more details about processing transaction, see the section "Using Workspace Transactions" later in this chapter.

The following is an example of the Delete method:

```
Dim rst As Recordset, strName As String
Set rst = CurrentDb().OpenRecordset("Employees")
rst.FindFirst "[Last Date Worked] <= #12/31/89#"
  If rst.NoMatch Then
    MsgBox "No outdated Employee Records to purge"
  Else
    strName = rst![First Name] & " " & rst![Last Name]
    rst.Delete
    MsgBox "Employee '" & strName & "' deleted"
  End If
```

Using the FillCache Method

Fills all or a part of a local cache for a Recordset that contains data from an ODBC data source. If the data is not from an ODBC data source, the FillCache Method will not work. The syntax follows:

```
Recordset.FillCache [Rows[, Start]]
```

The Rows argument is an Integer indicating the number of rows to fill in the cache. If you do not specify a value for this argument, the value is equal to the CacheSize property setting.

The Start argument is a valid bookmark value. When you use this argument, the cache fills in starting from the record indicated. If you do not specify a value for this argument, the cache fills starting from the record indicated by the CacheStart property.

Caching improves the performance of a Recordset that retrieves data from an ODBC source. You can retrieve data one record at a time from your local memory much more quickly than you can from an ODBC source, and when you issue the FillCache method, your local memory cache fills with records so you can access them even more quickly.

Using the Requery Method

The Requery method re-executes the query on which the object is based, thereby updating the data in the Recordset. Note the following example:

```
Recordset.Requery [NewQuerydef]
```

The NewQuerydef argument is a Querydef object, used to redefine the Recordset altogether. If you do not specify a NewQueryDef, then the Recordset is re-created from its original source.

Use the Requery method if you think there is a chance that some data in your Recordset has changed. The Requery method makes sure that your Recordset contains the most recent data.

Using the Clone Method

The Clone method creates a Recordset that is a duplicate of an original object. The syntax is as follows:

```
Set duplicate = original.Clone( )
```

Duplicate is a Recordset variable that will be an exact copy of another Recordset.

Original is the Recordset variable that you want to duplicate.

After you have issued the Clone method, you have two separate Recordsets, either of which can have its own current record. Using the Clone method, you can find a bookmark in one Recordset and find the corresponding record in the clone (and vice versa), because the bookmarks of a Recordset and its clone are identical and interchangeable.

Using the Clone method is faster and more efficient than creating a second Recordset by the OpenRecordset method, because the Clone method does not rerun any queries.

Note a peculiarity about a Clone Recordset: when you create a Recordset by using the Clone method, the Recordset initially does not have a current record. Therefore, the first action you must take with a new Clone is to set the Bookmark property, or use a Move, Find, or Seek method to set a current record.

You cannot use the Clone method with forward-only scrolling snapshot-type Recordsets.

Using the Close Method

The Close method closes a Recordset object and removes it from the Recordsets Collection. Any pending record edits or additions will not be saved if you use the Close method before updating the changes. The syntax follows:

```
Recordset.Close
```

Using the Close method on a clone does not affect the original Recordset in any way. Likewise, using the Close method on an original Recordset does not affect a clone of that Recordset.

Working with QueryDef Objects

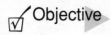Objective ▶

You can think of working with a QueryDef object as working with a permanently stored SQL statement. Working with a QueryDef is different than working with a Recordset because QueryDefs do not enable you to enumerate through the data, or to manipulate or edit data directly through the QueryDef object. You will modify data if you run a QueryDef that stores an action query, but you cannot use the Edit or Update methods with a QueryDef, and you cannot specify one certain record in the query. QueryDefs are used only to execute or modify existing queries. If you need to manipulate or edit data, you can always open a Recordset based on the saved query.

A QueryDef object is always compiled, so a QueryDef's SQL statement runs more quickly than a Recordset's SQL statement.

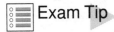 **Exam Tip**

> The role of the QueryDef on the exam is usually in the context of creating a QueryDef, changing a QueryDef's SQL property (covered in the later section "Working with the QueryDef SQL Property"), or using a QueryDef to run a pass-through query to an ODBC source (covered in Chapter 13, "Client/Server Application Development").
>
> In reality, you are probably more likely to create and change permanent queries through the query's Design mode, but there may be times when you will want to do that in code.
>
> One of the most useful qualities of a QueryDef in real-world applications is the capability to run a Query from code and pass in parameters, without prompting users for answers to parameters they may not know.

There are two ways to run a query from code:

```
DoCmd.OpenQuery(StringQueryName)
```

```
QueryDefObject.Execute
```

The second example uses the QueryDef's Execute method. The Execute method of a QueryDef is particularly helpful when you want to execute an action query.

If you want to create a Recordset based on a QueryDef, use the OpenRecordset method of the QueryDef. For more details, refer to the earlier section "Using the OpenRecordset Method with TableDefs and QueryDefs."

Using the CreateQueryDef Method

The CreateQueryDef method creates a new QueryDef object. You can use the CreateQueryDef method to create permanent, saved queries, or to create temporary queries. Temporary queries are especially useful when you want to run an action query that could be dangerous in the wrong hands—such as a Delete query that purges inactive Employee files.

Just as with Recordsets, you need to create a QueryDef-type variable in order to work with QueryDefs. The syntax is as follows:

```
Dim QueryDefObject As QueryDef
Set QuerydefObject = Database.CreateQueryDef([Name][, SQLString])
```

The Name argument is a string expression that sets the name of the new QueryDef. The name must be unique—it cannot be the name of a previously existing QueryDef.

The SQLString argument is a valid SQL statement string expression, which becomes the QueryDef's SQL property.

If you specify a name for the QueryDef, then QueryDef is automatically saved when you create or change it. You do not have to use a Save method or an Update method to save changes.

If you do not want to save the QueryDef, but instead you want to create a temporary QueryDef, just set the Name argument to a zero-length string (""). In the same way, if you change the Name property of an existing QueryDef to a zero-length string in code, that query will become temporary, and will be removed from the QueryDefs collection.

The following is an example of the CreateQueryDef method:

```
Dim db As Database, qdf As QueryDef, strSQL As String
  Set db = CurrentDb()
    strSQL = "SELECT * FROM Employees WHERE [HireDate] <= #1-1-
    ➡90#"
    Set qdf = db.CreateQueryDef("Due for Promotion Review",
    ➡strSQL)
    DoCmd.OpenQuery qdf.Name
```

The Close method works the same way on a QueryDef object as it does on a Recordset object; to close the QueryDef in the previous example, the next line of code would be as follows:

```
qdf.Close
```

Passing Parameters to a QueryDef

One of the most useful features of a QueryDef is its capability to pass in query parameters without prompting users. According to the definition of a query, anytime you designate a field name that is impossible for the query to locate (such as [Enter Start Date] in a query based on a table in which such a field does not exist), the Jet Engine treats the unknown field as a parameter and prompts the user for that data. The Message Box that appears is the name of the parameter (such as "Enter Start Date").

You refer to parameters the same way in which you refer to fields in a QueryDef. The following example is a query "qryEmployees," which has two parameters: [Enter Earliest Hire Date to Search] and [Enter Lowest Salary to Search]. Notice the two ways of referring to parameters:

```
Dim qdf As QueryDef
Set qdf = CurrentDb().QueryDefs("qryEmployees")
'refer to a parameter: Method 1
qdf("Enter Earliest Hire Date to Search") = #1/1/90#
'refer to a parameter: Method 2
qdf![Enter Lowest Salary to Search] = 18000
```

Working with the QueryDef SQL Property

 Objective

Working with the QueryDef SQL property is exactly like working with a Recordset's SQL property, as explained in the earlier section "Basing a Recordset on SQL."

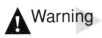 Warning

Exercise extreme caution when manipulating QueryDef SQL properties. When you change the SQL statement of a QueryDef object, the QueryDef is automatically saved with the new SQL property.

A QueryDef SQL property is a valid SQL string. What exactly constitutes "a valid SQL string" is covered in much greater detail in Chapter 3, "Microsoft Access SQL." For the purposes of this section, the following example shows only a simple SQL string; the saved "qryEmployees" query shows all Employees, sorted by Department. The example permanently changes the query to sort all Employees by Last Name.

```
Dim qdf As QueryDef, strSQL As String
strSQL = "SELECT * FROM EMPLOYEES ORDER BY [Last Name]"
Set qdf = DBEngine(0)(0).QueryDefs("qryEmployees")
qdf.SQL = strSQL
qdf.Close
```

If you just want to create a temporary set of records that is similar to an existing query, you can retrieve the SQL property of the existing query through the SQL property of its QueryDef object. Then you can modify the SQL statement as needed and open a Recordset based on that SQL string.

Working with TableDef Objects

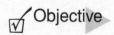 Objective

Working with TableDef Objects is similar to working with QueryDef objects, in that you are not working with a set of records, but rather with a saved database object. You can open a Recordset based on a TableDef by using the OpenRecordset method of a TableDef object, as explained in the earlier section "Using the OpenRecordset Method with TableDefs and QueryDefs."

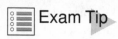 Exam Tip

There will probably be one or two questions about TableDefs and QueryDefs on the exam, and because working with them varies slightly from working with other Recordsets, you must be familiar with them.

From a TableDef object's properties, you can determine the TableDefs connection path (Connect property), name (Name property), record count (RecordCount property), whether or not the object is updatable (Updatable property), and other information. The only method covered in this section is the CreateTableDef method.

The CreateTableDef method creates a new TableDef object. This section will not go into great detail because usually you will be creating tables through the user interface, or through make-table queries.

Just as with Recordsets, you need to create a TableDef-type variable in order to work with TableDefs. The syntax is as follows:

```
Set TableDefObject = Database.CreateTableDef([Name[, Attributes[,
➥Source[, Connect]]]])
```

The Name argument is a string that uniquely names the new TableDef object.

The Attributes argument is a Long variable that indicates one or more characteristics of the new TableDef object. Refer to Access Help, and look up the Attributes property for more information.

The Source argument is a string that contains the name of an external table, if the new table is to be linked.

The Connect string contains information about the source of an external table, including ODBC information. Refer to Access Help, and look up the Connect property for more information on valid connection strings.

The following is an example of the CreateTableDef method:

```
Dim db As Database, tdf As TableDef
  Set db = CurrentDb()
  Set tdf = db.CreateTableDef("Zip Codes")
```

After you have executed the sample code, the TableDef object exists, but has no fields. You must define and append fields to the Fields collection of the TableDef object. For information about creating and appending objects, refer to Chapter 4, "Programming with Objects."

Once you have created a new TableDef object, you cannot close it; the Close method does not work with TableDef objects. Instead, the TableDef object becomes a permanent part of your database.

Using Workspace Transactions

 Objective ▶

Using workspace transactions is similar to using the Edit and Update methods to change data—the Update method saves all changes that have been made since the Edit method was issued. In the same way, the Workspace object's BeginTrans, CommitTrans, and Rollback methods enable you to save a group of changes at the same time.

The primary advantage to using workspace transactions is that they enable you to commit or cancel a group of changes simultaneously. These changes can be made to multiple records, multiple tables, or even to multiple Recordsets.

In some cases, the ability to change groups of records simultaneously would be essential. For example, if you were working on an accounting system in which every credit had to be balanced by a debit, then you would want to make sure that the credit change was always accompanied by a debit change, in that if either action fails, both should fail. Another example in which workspace transactions are necessary is when you process records in tables affected by referential integrity; if you add a record in a parent table and related records in a child table, you must add the records simultaneously.

The other tremendous benefit to using workspace transactions is that transactions are a considerably faster way to edit, update, and delete information. A transaction with multiple methods involved takes less time than individual methods executing one after another because during transactions the data about reads and writes is buffered, so the data occupies a readily available space in local memory.

The BeginTrans, CommitTrans, and Rollback methods of the Workspace object are used, respectively, to mark the beginning of a transaction, to save (commit) all changes that have been made since the BeginTrans method, and to cancel all changes that have been made since the BeginTrans method. The BeginTrans method must always begin a transaction—if you issue the CommitTrans or Rollback methods without having first issued the BeginTrans method, you will generate a trappable error.

Because the transaction methods are methods of the Workspace object, the CommitTrans or Rollback methods affect all transactions within the workspace that share the same ODBC connection. In other words, if User1 and User2 are somehow using the same workspace and ODBC connection (if applicable), then when User1 commits his transactions, User2's transactions will also be committed. The likelihood of such a situation occurring is nonexistent if each user has his own ODBC connection.

If you close a Workspace before issuing the CommitTrans method, then all changes made since the last BeginTrans in that workspace will be rolled back (cancelled).

The following code demonstrates the value of transactions:

```
Sub UpdateSalaries()
  Dim rst As Recordset, db As DATABASE, wrk As Workspace
  Set wrk =  DBEngine(0)
  Set db = wrk.Databases(0)
  Set rst = db.OpenRecordset("Employees")
    ' begin the transaction.
   wrk.BeginTrans
   rst.MoveFirst
   Do While Not rst.EOF
     rst.Salary = rst.Salary * 1.05
     rst.MoveNext
  Loop
  If MsgBox "Are you sure you want to raise salaries?", vbYesNo =
➥6 Then
    'commit all the transactions together
    'which will be much faster than one at a time
   wrk.CommitTrans
  Else
    'make no changes
    wrk.Rollback
  End If
rst.Close
End Sub
```

Transactions can include SQL pass-through queries, action queries, individual Recordset modifications, and so on. Basically, you can make any type of data change in the context of a transaction.

You need to make sure, however, if you are working with ODBC data, whether or not the ODBC server supports transactions.

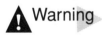 **Warning**

The Jet Engine assumes only single-level transaction support. In other words, you cannot nest transactions. If you attempt to nest transactions (for instance, issue two BeginTrans methods before issuing a Commit Trans method), only the very first BeginTrans and very last CommitTrans and Rollback methods are actually processed. Nested transaction methods will not cause errors, but they are silently ignored.

Key Terms and Concepts

Table 6.2 identifies key terms from this chapter. Review the key terms and make sure that you understand each term for the exam.

Table 6.2

Key Terms: Working with Sets of Records	
Term	Covered in Section...
Recordset	This chapter's introduction
QueryDef	This chapter's introduction
TableDef	This chapter's introduction
Table-type	"Choosing the Appropriate Recordset Type"
Dynaset-type	"Choosing the Appropriate Recordset Type"
Snapshot-type	"Choosing the Appropriate Recordset Type"
SQL	"Basing a Recordset on SQL"
Forward-only scrolling	"Setting a Recordset to Scroll Forward-Only"
Table index	"Using the Index Property"
Bookmark	"Using the Bookmark Property"
BOF, EOF	"Using the BOF and EOF Properties"
Record Locking	"Locking Records with Recordsets"
Query Parameter	"Passing Parameters to a QueryDef"
Transaction processing	"Using Workspace Transactions"

Lab Exercises

These exercises will provide practice for you to work hands-on with Recordsets. The operations will be fairly simple ones, with results being printed in the Debug window for the sake of simplicity. All three lab exercises will be run from databases that are included on the CD-ROM that accompanies this book.

Exercise 6.1: Working with a Table-Type Recordset

In this exercise, you will work with a table-type Recordset, using the Index property, the Seek method, the NoMatch property, and the AddNew Method.

Objectives:

Create a Recordset object.

Effectively use Recordset properties.

Write procedures that manipulate data in a Recordset.

Time Estimate: 5–10 minutes

Steps:

1. Open the Lab Exercise database 06-1.mdb. Go to the Modules tab, and click the New button.

2. Type in the following code:

```
Sub PracticeTable()
Dim db As DATABASE, rst As Recordset
Set db = CurrentDb()
Set rst = db.OpenRecordset("Employees")
  'set Index so you can use Seek method
  rst.Index = "Salary"
  rst.Seek ">", 60000
  If rst.NoMatch = True Then
    Debug.Print "No salaries are over $60,000"
    rst.Seek ">", 45000
    If rst.NoMatch = True Then
      Debug.Print "No salaries are over $45,000"
      rst.MoveFirst
```

```
         End If
      End If

      Debug.Print "Highest salary is: " & rst!LastName & ", " & _
         rst!FirstName & ": Salary is " & Format(rst!Salary,
         ➥"$##,###")

      'the following code could also use With...Wend
      rst.Edit
         rst.AddNew
         rst!LastName = "Piper"
         rst!FirstName = "JoAnna"
         rst!Title = "Departmental Assistant"
         rst!Salary = 20000
      rst.UPDATE

      'display records in alphabetical order by last name
      rst.Index = "LastName"
      rst.MoveFirst
      Do Until rst.EOF
         Debug.Print rst!LastName & ", " & rst!FirstName
         rst.MoveNext
      Loop
   End Sub
```

3. Open the Debug window and type **PracticeTable**, then press Enter.

4. Notice about the Index property that setting the Index to "Salary" makes it possible to quickly Seek only through the Indexed field [Salary]. When you change it to "LastName," it causes the list of Employees to print in alphabetical order by last name, with the newly created JoAnna Piper in the correct sort order.

5. Notice about the relationship between the Seek method and the NoMatch property that the first NoMatch is True because no one's salary is greater than $60,000. The second NoMatch is False because the Seek property succeeds. The Seek method can execute again even though there is not a current record after the NoMatch property is True, and after Seek is executed again, the NoMatch property resets to False.

6. Notice that the AddNew method succeeds because it is preceded by an Edit method and followed by an Update method. Without those two methods, it fails.

7. Close the database—you may save if you want to, but it is not necessary.

Comments:

This short exercise emphasizes the importance of detail in working with Recordset objects. Especially when updating or adding new data, the order of the methods is critical. Now that you've seen it work, you can try commenting out or moving a few lines (for example, comment out the Update method or Edit method) so you can be familiar with the error messages that occur.

Reading Reference:

For more information about the concepts raised by the exercise, refer to sections "Creating Recordset Objects," "Setting Recordset Properties," and "Manipulating Data by Using Recordset Methods."

Exercise 6.2: Working with Dynaset-Type Recordsets

In this exercise, you will work with a dynaset-type Recordset, creating it from a SQL statement and using the Sort and Filter properties, the Delete method, and the Transaction method.

Objectives:

Identify and differentiate between the different Recordset object types.

Create Recordset objects.

Write procedures that manipulate QueryDef objects.

Implement transaction processing in a Workspace object.

Time Estimate: 10–15 minutes

Steps:

1. Open the Lab Exercise database 06-2.mdb. Go to the Modules tab, and click New.

2. Type in the following code:

```
Sub PracticeSortFilter()
Dim db As DATABASE, rst As Recordset
Dim rstByHireDate, rstSalesReps As Recordset
  Set db = CurrentDb()
  Set rst = db.OpenRecordset("SELECT * FROM Employees")
    'Print all employees - in no particular order
    Do Until rst.EOF
      Debug.Print rst!LastName & ", " & rst!FirstName
      rst.MoveNext
    Loop
    Debug.Print
  'put in a message box so we can see what's happening
MsgBox "Employees have been printed - no order"

  'set Recordset's sort property, then create sorted
➥Recordset
rst.Sort = "HireDate"
Set rstByHireDate = rst.OpenRecordset()
  'Print all employees - by last name
  Do Until rstByHireDate.EOF
    Debug.Print rstByHireDate!LastName & ", " &
    ➥rstByHireDate!FirstName & _
      ": Hire Date is " & rstByHireDate!HireDate
    rstByHireDate.MoveNext
  Loop
  Debug.Print
  'put in a message box so we can see what's happening
MsgBox "Employees have been printed - By Hire Date"

  'set Recordset's Sort and Filter property, then create
➥filtered Recordset
rst.Sort = "LastName"
rst.Filter = "Title = 'Sales Representative'"
Set rstSalesReps = rst.OpenRecordset()
  'Print all employees - by last name
  Do Until rstSalesReps.EOF
    Debug.Print rstSalesReps!LastName & ", " &
    ➥rstSalesReps!FirstName & _
```

```
           ": Title is " & rstSalesReps!Title
        rstSalesReps.MoveNext
    Loop
    'put in a message box so we can see what's happening
    MsgBox "Sales Representatives have been printed - by last
    ➥name"
End Sub
```

3. Open the Debug window, and size it to where you can see about 25 lines at a time. Delete anything that is already in the Debug window. Type **PracticeSortFilter**, then press the Enter Key.

4. Notice that the new Recordsets reflected the sort and filter change from the original Recordset.

5. Now delete everything from your Debug window (not from the code window), and close it. Scroll down to the end of the code, and type in the following:

```
Sub PracticeTrans()
Dim db As DATABASE, rst As Recordset, tdf As TableDef
Dim wrk As Workspace
Set db = CurrentDb
Set wrk = DBEngine.Workspaces(0)

'check the number of records before processing
Set tdf = db.TableDefs("Orders")
  Debug.Print "The Orders table has " & tdf.RecordCount & _
    " number of records"
  Debug.Print

'open the recordset and begin a transaction
Set rst = db.OpenRecordset("SELECT * FROM Orders ORDER BY
➥ShippedDate")
wrk.BeginTrans
  rst.MoveFirst  'just in case
  Do Until rst.EOF
    If rst!ShippedDate <= #2/28/95# Then
      Debug.Print rst!ShippedDate & " - deleted"
      rst.Delete
    End If
    rst.MoveNext
  Loop
```

```
    wrk.CommitTrans

    'check the number of records again
    rst.Requery
    rst.MoveLast    'to get an accurate count
    Debug.Print "The Orders table NOW has " & rst.RecordCount & _
        " number of records"
    Debug.Print

    End Sub
```

6. Reopen the Debug window, and again delete anything that is already in it. Type **PracticeTrans**, then press Enter. Notice the number of records before and after you run the procedure.

7. Close the database—you may save if you want to, but it is not necessary.

Comments:

This exercise really demonstrates the exciting power and flexibility of Recordsets; you can create them from many different sources, and use them to accomplish many different tasks.

Reading Reference:

For more information about the concepts raised by the exercise, refer to the sections "Using the Sort Property," "Using the Filter Property," "Using the Delete Method," and "Using Workspace Transactions."

Exercise 6.3: Working with a Snapshot-Type Recordset

In this exercise, you will work with a snapshot-type Recordset that has been created from a QueryDef object, and use the Find method.

Objectives:

Create and manipulate QueryDef objects.

Alter an Access SQL statement that is set for an existing QueryDef object.

Time Estimate: 10-15 minutes

Steps:

1. Open the Lab Exercise database 06-3.mdb. Go to the Modules tab, and click New.

2. Type in the following code:

```
Sub PracticeSnapshot()
Dim db As DATABASE, qdf As QueryDef
Dim strSQL As String, rst As Recordset
Set db = CurrentDb
  'determine the current SQL of a query
  Set qdf = db.QueryDefs("Current Product List")
  Debug.Print qdf.SQL
  MsgBox "Read your SQL statement -" & _
    " ascending by Product Name. Click OK when ready"

  'change the SQL property
  strSQL = "SELECT ProductID, ProductName, UnitPrice " & _
    " FROM Products WHERE (((Discontinued) = No)) " & _
    " ORDER BY UnitPrice DESC;"
  qdf.SQL = strSQL

  'check it
  Debug.Print qdf.SQL
  MsgBox "Read your new SQL statement - & _
    " descending by Unit Price. Click OK when ready"

  'create a Recordset from this QueryDef
  Set rst = qdf.OpenRecordset(dbOpenSnapshot)

  'list all products priced under $10
  Do Until rst.EOF
    rst.FindNext "[UnitPrice] < 10"
    Debug.Print rst!ProductName & ": " & _
      Format(rst!UnitPrice, "$##.00")
    rst.MoveNext
  Loop
End Sub
```

3. Open the Debug window and size it to where you can see about 20 lines at a time. Delete anything that is already in the Debug window. Type **PracticeSnapshot**, then press Enter.

4. Notice that the records printed in the Debug window are ordered by UnitPrice, descending, even though the original query was sorted by ProductName, ascending.

5. Close the database—you may save if you want to, but it is not necessary.

Comments:

The capabilities of this exercise are limited by the fact that we cannot edit or add any information to snapshot-type recordsets.

Reading Reference:

For more information about the concepts raised by the exercise, refer to the sections "Using the Find Methods" and "Working with the QueryDef SQL Property."

Review Questions

The following questions will test your knowledge of the material in this chapter.

1. You need to search through data on a local table to return the total number of customers who live in a certain state. Which type of Recordset would yield the fastest possible results?

    A. Dynaset-type Recordset

    B. Forward-only scrolling snapshot-type Recordset

    C. Forward-only scrolling table-type Recordset

    D. Snapshot-type Recordset

2. Which OpenRecordset statement would be used to open a recordset to modify an ODBC table named "Employees"?

    A. Set db = DBEngine(0).OpenDatabase ("", False, False, "ODBC;")
       Set rst = db.OpenRecordset ("Employees", dbOpenTable)

    B. Set db = DBEngine(0).OpenDatabase ("", False, False, "ODBC;")
       Set rst = db.OpenRecordset ("Employees", dbOpenSnapshot)

    C. Set db = DBEngine(0).OpenDatabase ("", False, False, "ODBC;")
       Set rst = db.OpenRecordset ("Employees", dbOpenDynaset)

    D. Set db = DBEngine(0).OpenDatabase ("", False, False, "ODBC;")
       Set rst = db.OpenRecordset ("Employees", dbOpenODBC)

3. You have written the following code to create a recordset ("Locations" is a query based on multiple local tables, and includes some calculated fields):

```
Dim rst As Recordset
Set rst = DBEngine (0)(0).OpenRecordset("Locations")
```

Which type of Recordset has been created in rst?

A. Table-type

B. Dynaset-type, with some fields updatable

C. Dynaset-type, with all fields updatable

D. Snapshot-type

4. Your application contains the following code:

```
Dim db As DATABASE, rst As Recordset
Set db = CurrentDb()
```

You want to make rst an updatable Recordset that is based on a linked table named "Employees." Which of the following code fragments would successfully perform that task? (Choose as many as apply.)

A. Set rst = db.OpenRecordset("Employees", dbOpenDynaset)

B. rst.OpenRecordset("Employees")

C. Set rst = OpenRecordset("SELECT * FROM Employees")

D. Set rst = db.OpenRecordset("Employees")

5. A Recordset with the LockEdits property set to True is about to be updated. Which of the following statements are true?

A. Optimistic locking is in effect.

B. Executing the Update method will release the record lock.

C. Executing the Close method will release the record lock.

D. Executing the Seek method will release the record lock.

6. You are writing a procedure that will update an "Employees" table. The procedure will set the TimeForReview field to True for employees whose last review was more than 180 days ago.

```
1  Dim rst As Recordset
2  Set rst = CurrentDb.OpenRecordset("Employees")
3  Do Until rst.EOF
4    If rst![TimeForReview] < (Date() - 180) Then
5
6    End If
7  Loop
```

Which code fragment should you insert at line 5 to accomplish the changes?

  A. Set rst![TimeForReview] = True

  B. rst.Edit
    rst![TimeForReview] = True
    rst.Update

  C. rst![TimeForReview] = True

  D. rst.Edit
    rst![TimeForReview] = True
    rst.Requery

7. Which of the following code fragments would create a temporary QueryDef object?

  A. Set qdf = CurrentDb.CreateQueryDef(Empty, "SELECT * FROM Employees;")

  B. Set qdf = CurrentDb.CreateQueryDef(Null, "SELECT * FROM Employees;")

  C. Set qdf = CurrentDb.CreateQueryDef("Null", "SELECT * FROM Employees;")

  D. Set qdf = CurrentDb.CreateQueryDef("", "SELECT * FROM Employees;")

8. You want to change the SQL property of an existing QueryDef object. You have written the following code so far:

```
Dim qdf As QueryDef, strSQL As String
Set qdf = CurrentDb.QueryDefs("qryEmployees")
strSQL = "SELECT * FROM Employees WHERE Salary < 18000"
```

Which code fragment should be next?

A. qdf.SQL = strSQL
   qdf.Update
   qdf.Close

B. qdf.Execute strSQL
   qdf.Close

C. qdf.SQL = strSQL
   qdf.Close

D. qdf.Execute strSQL
   qdf.Update
   qdf.Close

9. Two users, User1 and User2, are using transaction processing in the same Workspace. Each user has her own ODBC connection. If both users have issued BeginTrans methods, what will happen when User1 issues a CommitTrans method?

A. User1's transaction will be committed; nothing will happen to User2's transaction.

B. User1's transaction will be committed; User2's transaction will also be committed, even though it is incomplete.

C. User1's transaction will not be committed and User1 will receive an error; nothing will happen to User2's transaction.

D. User1's transaction will not be committed and User1 will receive an error; User2's transaction will not be committed and User2 will also receive an error.

Answers to Review Questions

1. B is correct. A forward-only scrolling snapshot-type Recordset is the fastest way to check a set of data. You can only make a snapshot-type Recordset forward-only scrolling—not a table-type or a dynaset-type Recordset. For more information, refer to the section "Choosing the Appropriate Recordset Type."

2. C is correct. You would have to open a dynaset-type Recordset because you want to modify an external table, and the proper constant is db.OpenRecordset. For more information, refer to the section "Specifying a Recordset Type in Code."

3. B is correct. Because the Recordset is based on a query instead of on a single local table, it is dynaset-type by default. Only some fields are updatable because some of the fields in the query are calculated. For more information, refer to the section "Choosing the Appropriate Recordset Type."

4. A, C, and D are correct. All three will be updatable because they will be dynaset-type Recordsets, the default type of Recordset for linked tables. The Source argument for C is a valid SQL string. For more information, refer to the section "Creating Recordset Objects."

5. B, C, and D are correct. When the LockEdits property is set to True, then pessimistic locking is in effect, and issuing the Close, Update, or Seek methods will release the page lock. Of these methods, only the Update method will save the record changes. For more information, refer to the section "Locking Records with Recordsets."

6. B is correct. You must issue the Edit method to be able to change a Recordset record, and you must issue the Update method to save those changes. For more information, refer to the sections "Using the Edit Method" and "Using the Update Method."

7. D is correct. To create a temporary QueryDef object, set the Name argument to an empty string (""). For more information, refer to the section "Working with QueryDef Objects."

8. D is correct. To change an existing QueryDef's SQL property, you need only change it; you do not need to issue an Update method. For more information, refer to the section "Working with the QueryDef SQL Property."

9. A is correct. Because the two users had separate ODBC connections, the transactions are processed independently of each other. If the two users had been using the same ODBC connection, then choice B would have been correct. For more information, refer to the section "Using Workspace Transactions."

Answers to Test Yourself Questions at Beginning of Chapter...

1. You should choose to create a dynaset-type Recordset in that situation. You cannot choose a table-type Recordset because the data is from an attached table. When working with a large number of records (over 500), a dynaset-type recordset processes more rapidly than a snapshot-type recordset. For more information, refer to the section "Choosing the Appropriate Recordset Type."

2. The correct type-argument constant to use to create a read-only Recordset is dbOpenSnapshot. It is used with the OpenRecordset method of the database object, a TableDef object, or a QueryDef object. For more information, refer to the sections "Specifying a Recordset Type in Code" and "Creating Recordset Objects."

3. The minimum syntax for creating a Recordset based on a SQL string is as follows:

   ```
   Set RecordsetVariable = Database.OpenRecordset(SQLString)
   ```

   SQLString is a valid SQL Where clause. Optional arguments are type and options. For more information, refer to the section "Basing a Recordset on SQL."

4. The options argument constant of the OpenRecordset method used to create a forward-only scrolling Recordset is dbForwardOnly. For more information, refer to the section "Setting a Recordset to Scroll Forward-Only."

5. No; when you set a Recordset's Sort property, that Recordset is not immediately sorted. Instead, the next Recordset to be created from that Recordset will be sorted according to the Sort property. For more information, refer to the section "Using the Sort Property."

6. If your Recordset's current record is the last record, then the EOF property value is False. The EOF property is only True when the Recordset's current record is after the last record. For more information, refer to the section "Using the BOF and EOF Properties."

7. In that situation, User1 would receive a trappable error (3197) and not be able to update the record. For more information, refer to the section "Locking Records with Recordsets."

8. The Move and Seek methods can be used in table-type Recordsets. The Find and Seek methods can be used with criteria. All three types of methods will cause an error when executed from an empty Recordset. For more information, refer to the sections "The Move Method," "Using the Find Methods," and "Using the Seek Method."

9. If you clone a Recordset, and then make changes to the original, the clone will not be affected unless you specifically re-create it. If the original is closed before the Update method is issued, then the changes to the original Recordset will be lost, and nothing happens to the clone. For more information, refer to the sections "Using the Clone Method," and "Using the Update Method."

10. The FillCache method fills a local memory cache to hold records from an ODBC record source. This greatly improves viewing and processing time. For more information, refer to the section "Using the FillCache Method."

11. When the SQL properties of a QueryDef object and a Recordset object are identical, executing the QueryDef processes faster than opening a Recordset based on the SQL statement, because the QueryDef SQL is compiled and the Recordset SQL is not. For more information, refer to the section "Working with QueryDef Objects."

12. To save a change to a QueryDef's SQL property, all you have to do is change the property. There is no associated Save method or Update method. For more information, refer to the section "Working with the QueryDef SQL Property."

13. The only way to create a TableDef using a SQL statement is to run an action query, but you would not work directly with the TableDef in code in that case. You create a new TableDef by using the CreateTableDef method, and then by adding and appending fields. For more information, refer to "Working with TableDef objects."

14. If you forget to use the CommitTrans method when processing transaction modifications (meaning that you have used the BeginTrans method), then all your changes will be rolled back—none of them will be saved. For more information, refer to the section "Using Workspace Transactions."

C h a p t e r

Working with Forms and Reports

7

By the end of this chapter, you will be able to execute the following test objectives:

 Objectives

▶ Resolve sort order conflicts with underlying queries

▶ Choose which form-specific and report-specific properties to set

▶ Choose which control properties to set

▶ Use form methods

▶ Define and create form and report modules

▶ Assign event-handling procedures to controls in a form or report

▶ Identify when to use Me Property (Form) and when to use ActiveControl Property (Screen)

▶ Identify the order of form events

▶ Given sample code, identify the scope of a form or report module

▶ Open multiple instances of a form and refer to them

▶ Use the Property Get, Property Set, and Property Let statements to assign values to form properties

▶ Differentiate between forms and reports versus documents

Test Yourself! Before reading this chapter, test yourself to determine how much study time you will need to devote to this section.

1. Is it possible to change the sort order of a form to be a different sort order than the form's underlying query?

2. When is it possible for the Me keyword (used from a form) to refer to a different object than the Screen.ActiveForm object?

3. What occurs first, the Activate event of a form, or the GotFocus event of a form? When does the GotFocus event of a form occur?

4. To enumerate through all the *saved* forms in your application (as opposed to all the *open* forms), do you use the Documents collection or the Forms collection?

5. How do you create a non-default instance of a form?

6. What is the proper syntax to correctly refer to the DefaultValue property of a control (State) on a subform (AddressesSubform) of a form (Customers)?

7. What is the difference in function between a Property Get procedure and a Property Let procedure?

8. When you declare variables and constants in the Declarations section of a module, are they public or private by default? What about procedures?

9. What is the difference between issuing the Refresh method and the Requery method for a form?

10. What happens when you drag a form from the Database window and drop it on the Windows 95 desktop?

11. When is it possible to call a custom form or report procedure from a global module?

Answers are located at the end of the chapter...

As you read this chapter, you learn about each objective described previously. If you are reading this chapter only to study for the exam, this is not one of those chapters where some sections are more critical than others. Instead, you are equally likely to be tested on the information from any section in this chapter.

There are usually five to eight questions per exam on working with forms and reports (the official name of the test section is "Working with Forms," but it covers information about reports as well).

Resolving Sort Order Conflicts with Underlying Queries

Objective

There are many times when you are creating a form or report, and you already have a query that returns the correct information, with just one problem: it is sorted in the wrong order. Can you still use the query? YES. This section covers how to resolve sort order conflicts with underlying form and report queries.

Key Concepts

The most important thing to remember about resolving sort order conflicts with underlying queries is that *the form or report always wins*.

An example: you have a query that is sorted by ProductName. If you base a form or report on that query, but set the OrderBy property (form) or Sorting and Grouping (report) to sort by UnitPrice, the form or report will be sorted by unit price, not by product name.

Using the OrderBy Form Property

You can override the sort order of the query underlying a form by using the OrderBy property. (The OrderBy property also applies to queries, reports, and tables.)

The OrderBy property is a string expression made up of the name(s) of the field(s) on which you want to sort. When you want to sort by multiple fields, name the primary sort field first, then separate field names with a comma. If you want a field to sort in descending order, type **DESC** after that field name.

The following is an example: you already have a qryCustomers query that returns all pertinent customer information, sorted by the customer's Company Name. You want to base a form (frmCustomers) on qryCustomers, but you want the form to sort the customers by country, and then by the customer's company name. Therefore, you set the OrderBy property of the form to "Country, [Company Name]."

From the preceding example, if you want the countries to be sorted in descending order (although why you would want that particular thing, I'm not sure...), the OrderBy property of the form needs to be "Country DESC, [Company Name]."

You can set the property either by the property sheet or by using Visual Basic. The Visual Basic for the example in the preceding paragraph looks like this:

```
Forms!frmCustomers.OrderBy = "Country DESC, [Company Name]"
```

More information about referring to and setting form properties from code follows in the section "Setting Form and Report Properties."

Sorting and Grouping in Reports

You can override the sort order of the query underlying a report by changing the Sorting and Grouping settings for the report. The steps to changing Sorting and Grouping settings are as follows:

1. In the report's Design view, display the Sorting and Grouping box by clicking the Sorting and Grouping button (see fig. 7.1).

Figure 7.1

For reports, override a query's sort order by using Sorting and Grouping.

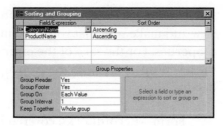

2. Set the Sorting and Grouping Field/Expression to the appropriate field(s) or expression(s), paying attention to whether the Sort Order is Ascending or Descending.

3. Set the Group Properties.

Explaining all the possible combinations of report group property settings goes beyond the scope of this chapter, but if you want more information, search Access Help for "Sorting and Grouping."

Setting Form and Report Properties

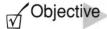 Objective

There are two ways to set the values of properties of a form or report: through the property box (available in the form or report's Design view) or through code. This section only briefly covers setting property values through Design view, because that is an interface you should already be familiar with.

To set a property for a form or report from Design view, first open the property sheet (choose Properties from the View menu). Then click the property you want to set, and choose or enter the value.

If an arrow appears in the property box, you can choose a value from a list by clicking the arrow and selecting a value. If a Build button appears next to the property box (...), click the Build button to display a builder (or choice of builders). Otherwise, just enter an appropriate value.

 Tip

You can always get help for any Access-defined property from online help by pressing F1. Help usually includes explanations of valid settings for the property and examples.

It is a good idea for you to open a form and a report in Design view and make sure that you are familiar with all the possible properties. For the sake of the exam, however, the following are the few property settings that you are likely to need to know in detail:

Form—RecordLocks: covered in detail in Chapter 6, "Working with Sets of Records"

Form—OrderBy: covered in the section "Resolving Sort Order Conflicts with Underlying Queries" earlier in this chapter

Form or Report—Caption: text string that displays as the title of the window when the form or report is open in Form view or Print Preview

Form or Report—The Event Properties: covered in the section "Creating Event Procedures" later in this chapter

To set a property for a form or report from Visual Basic, you need to know how to refer to the property and what settings are valid for the property. Because there are so many properties, this section focuses on referring to them, rather than explaining the function and valid settings of each possible property. For further information about any property, consult online Help (F1).

If you want to refer to a property of the current form or report, use the Me keyword, followed by the dot operator and the name of the property (more information about the Me keyword appears in the section "Choosing Me or Screen" later in this chapter). For example, you refer to the Visible property of the current form in this way:

```
Me.Visible
```

To assign a value to a property (and not just refer to its value), type the property reference, an equal sign, and then the value you want. For example, you set the Visible property of the current report in this way:

```
Me.Visible = False
```

If you want to refer to a property of a form or report that is not the current form or report, you must use the object's full identifier. For example, the following identifiers refer to the Visible properties of the Customers form and the Catalog report:

```
Forms![Customers].Visible = False
```

```
Reports![Catalog].Visible = False
```

You can refer to an object by enclosing its name in parentheses and quotation marks (" ") instead of using the ! operator. (This information is discussed in more detail in the Chapter 1, "Working with Visual Basic for Applications.") The following example is the functional equivalent to the example preceding this paragraph:

```
Reports("Catalog").Visible = False
```

To refer to or set properties of sections of a form or report, refer to the form or report, and then use the .(dot) operator, and then use the section name followed by the .(dot) operator, followed by the property name.

For example, the following code sets the background color for the page header of the Customers form to a pale neon green:

```
Forms!Customers.PageHeader.BackColor = 8454016
```

Key Concepts

As a general rule, use the . operator before the names of Access-defined objects, and the ! operator before the names of user-defined objects. Access-defined objects are property names, collections, and so on. User-defined objects are tables, queries, forms, reports, controls, and so on.

Therefore, you cannot use the ! operator before referring to a Form Section name because the section is an Access-defined object.

Sometimes you want to refer to or set a property in a subform or subreport, but because that involves referring to the subform or subreport controls, it will be covered in the next section, "Setting Control Properties."

Setting Control Properties

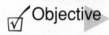 Objective

There are two ways to set the values of control properties on a form or report: through the property box in the form or report's Design view or through code. This section only briefly covers setting property values through Design view because that is an interface you should already be familiar with. If you are not familiar with the options of Design view, there is Help material available for each property of every object available in Design view.

To set a property for a form or report control from Design view, first open the property sheet (choose Properties from the View menu). Click the control whose property you want to set, click the property you want to set, and then choose or enter the value.

If an arrow appears in the property box, you can choose a value from a list by clicking the arrow and selecting a value. If a Build button appears next to the property box (...), click the Build button to display a builder (or choice of builders). Otherwise, just enter an appropriate value.

It is a good idea for you to open a form and a report in Design view, create different kinds of commonly created controls (especially text boxes, labels, list boxes, combo boxes, and subforms/subreports), and make sure that you are familiar with the possible properties. However, for the sake of the exam, there are only a few property settings that you are likely to need to know in detail:

> Form or Report—Text Box—ControlSource: if set to a field name, it binds the text box to a field. If set to an expression, it binds the text box to that expression. If not set, the Text Box is Unbound.

> Form—all data controls except option group objects, Auto-Number controls, or OLE controls—DefaultValue sets a value that is automatically entered in a field when a new record is created.

> Form or Report—Combo Box—BoundColumn: sets which column in a combo box is bound to the data in a field. Column numbers start at 1 and are numbered from left to right according to the order the columns appear in the combo box's underlying query.

Form or Report—Combo Box—ColumnWidths: sets the width of each column in a combo box, separated by semicolons (;). If you want to hide a column, set its column width to 0.

Form—most controls—Enabled: True or False, sets whether or not the value of the control can be changed. If a control's Enabled property is set to False, and you want to change the value in the control from Visual Basic, you have to first set the Enabled property to True and then set the value of the control.

Bound controls automatically inherit many properties from the fields to which they are bound. For example, if you create a form bound to the Customers table and create a text box bound to the CustomerState field, then that text box will inherit the Format, DecimalPlaces, InputMask, DefaultValue, ValidationRule, ValidationText, and StatusBarText (from Description) properties of the field. You are free to change these inherited values, and the value of the property in the form or report will override the field value for the purposes of that form or report.

To set a property for a form or report control from Visual Basic, you need to know how to refer to the control property, and which settings are valid for the property. Because there are so many properties, this section focuses on referring to them, rather than explaining the function and valid settings of each possible property. For further information about any property, consult online Help (F1).

You always begin referring to a form or report control property by referring to the form or control where the control resides, followed by the ! operator, then the name of the control followed by the . (dot) operator, then the name of the property. For example, the following statement assigns the value "TX" to the DefaultValue property of the CustomerState control on the current form:

```
Me![CustomerState].DefaultValue = "TX"
```

To decide between the Me keyword and the full identifier for the form or report, refer to the section "Choosing Me or Screen" later in this chapter.

To refer to or set a property of a control on a subform or subreport, several ways work. The following examples both set the background color of the CompanyName control on the Customer Subform subform of the Customers form to a pale sky blue, even though one identifier is more complex than the other:

```
Forms![Customers]![CustomerSubform]![CompanyName].BackColor =
⇥16777088

Forms![Customers]![CustomerSubform].Form![CompanyName].BackColor
⇥= 16777088
```

One interesting thing to keep in mind is that when you use the Expression Builder to refer to a control on a subform or subreport, the subform or subreport and its parent form or report must be open. Locate the parent object first, choose the name of the subform or subreport, and then choose the control.

Using Form Methods

 The following methods are available with forms:

▶ GoToPage moves the focus to the first control on a specified page in the active form.

▶ Recalc updates all calculated controls on a form.

▶ Refresh updates the records in the form's underlying record source to reflect changes made to the data since the data was first displayed or last refreshed. Equivalent to clicking Refresh on the Records menu.

▶ Repaint completes the form's pending screen updates and completes pending recalculations of the form's controls.

▶ Requery updates the form's underlying data by requerying the form's data source.

▶ SetFocus moves the focus to the specified form. Set focus can also be used to move the focus to a specified control on the active form, or a specified field on the active datasheet. The only difference in syntax is that the object is the control or field identifier rather than the form identifier.

If you need more specific details on the syntax and uses for each of these methods, refer to online Help. For the exam, however, the important thing to know is how to issue these methods from code. The proper syntax is to name the form, either by using the form's full identifier or the Me keyword (for more detailed information about that choice, refer to the section "Choosing Me or Screen" later in this chapter), followed by the . (dot) operator, then the form method, and then any arguments the method requires. Here are some examples:

```
Me.Requery
```

```
Forms!Customers.Refresh
```

```
Me!ctlCustomerState.SetFocus
```

The especially important things to remember for the exam are that methods are preceded by the . (dot) operator, and the difference between Recalc, Refresh, Repaint, and Requery.

Creating Form and Report Modules

 Objective

Creating a Form or Report Module is exactly the same as creating a regular module, except that the module is permanently attached to one form or to one report.

If you are working on a form or report with no code behind it, you can access the form or report's module from Design view by clicking the Code button or by choosing Code from the view menu. The resulting module looks and acts the same as a basic module created from the Database window with the following important distinctions:

▶ Variables and constants declared in the Declarations section of a form or report module are available only to procedures in that module, unless explicitly declared using the Public statement/keyword.

▶ Form and report modules store the event procedures for that form or report. For more information on event procedures, see the next section in this chapter, "Creating Event Procedures."

▶ Custom form and report procedures can be called only when the form or report is active in Form view or Print Preview. If the form or report is not loaded, its methods and procedures are not available, and attempting to call them results in an error.

▶ The syntax for calling a custom form or report procedure from another module is the form or report's full identifier, the . (dot) operator, and the procedure name, such as **Forms!Customers.TestProcedure** *Arguments*.

▶ The syntax for calling a custom form or report procedure from another procedure in the same module is just the procedure name, such as **TestProcedure** *Arguments*.

The event procedure in the next section, "Creating Event Procedures," is an example of custom form or report procedures.

Creating Event Procedures

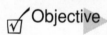

An event procedure is a form or report procedure that is triggered by a form or report event. The main difference in a form or report module between an event procedure and a non-event procedure is that event procedures are named according to a strict convention: *ObjectName_EventName*. Also, event procedures are private by default.

For example, the first line of the procedures for the Before Update, On Change, and On Lost Focus events for a form control named CustomerName would be as follows:

```
Private Sub CustomerName_BeforeUpdate(Cancel As Integer)
Private Sub CustomerName_Change()
Private Sub CustomerName_LostFocus()
```

The steps to creating a custom form or report event:

1. In Form Design or Report Design mode, select the form or report, section, or control for which you would like to create an event procedure.

2. View that object's property sheet by clicking the Properties tool on the toolbar or by choosing Properties from the View menu.

3. Choose the event from the property sheet and click the Build button (...) for that event.

4. Choose Code Builder from the Choose Builder dialog box. The form or report module opens with the procedure named properly.

5. Type in the statements that complete the procedure.

The following code listing is an example of an event procedure, which checks to make sure that the ContactName field of the Customers form is not null before updating.

```
Private Sub Form_BeforeUpdate(Cancel As Integer)
If IsNull(Me!ContactName) Then
    MsgBox "Please enter Contact's Name"
    Me!ContactName.SetFocus
    DoCmd.CancelEvent
  End If
End Sub
```

For more information about the Visual Basic possibilities for code, refer to Chapter 1.

Choosing Me or Screen

 Objective

When you are using Visual Basic to refer to forms or reports, you can use the Me keyword to refer to the form or report where code is currently executing. Use the ActiveForm or ActiveReport property of the Screen object to refer to the form or report that currently has the focus.

The only times you need to distinguish between Me and Screen.ActiveForm (or Screen.ActiveReport) is when the possibility exists of having multiple forms or reports loaded simultaneously. This could occur when you are executing code that works with another form or report, or when a Timer event occurs in an invisible loaded form.

If an invisible form has Timer event code that uses Screen.ActiveForm, all changes that refer to Screen.ActiveForm inadvertently change the active form instead of the invisible, inactive form. If the Timer event code uses the Me keyword, however, the code executes as expected.

As a general rule, use the Me keyword when you are working with procedures that operate on the current form. When using procedures that operate specifically with whatever form or report is active, then use the Screen.ActiveForm or Screen.ActiveReport property.

In addition to using the Screen.ActiveForm or Screen.ActiveReport properties, you can use the Screen.ActiveControl property to refer to the active control.

Understanding Form Event Order

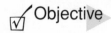 Objective

Some pieces of Access are straightforward and fairly intuitive, but event order is NOT one of those pieces. Event order is like anatomy—you just have to memorize the names of all those bones.

The good news is that exam questions tend to focus on the order of events for forms—and primarily for events that occur when the focus switches between forms. It is a good idea, however, to familiarize yourself with the other event orders as well.

Order of Form Events

Form events occur when you open a form, close a form, or change focus between forms. Events are affected by the presence of subforms, so this section also covers subform events.

Opening a Form, Closing a Form

In the following you see the order of events when you open a form with an active control:

> **Open** (form)→**Load** (form)→**Resize** (form)→**Activate** (form)→**Current**(form)→**Enter** (control)→**GotFocus** (control)

The confusing thing is that on forms where there are no active controls, the GotFocus event occurs for the form, not the control, and changes the events to occur in this way:

> **Open** (form)→**Load** (form)→**Resize** (form)→**Activate** (form)→**GotFocus** (form)→**Current** (form)

⟫ Key Concepts

> The two most important things to remember are as follows:
>
> 1. The form Activate event always occurs before the form GotFocus event.
>
> 2. The form GotFocus event does not occur unless the form has no controls, because GotFocus usually applies to the active control, not to the form.

When you close a form with an active control, no data changes:

> **Exit** (control)→**LostFocus** (control)→**Unload** (form)→**Deactivate** (form)→**Close**(form)

When you close a form with an active control, data changes:

> **BeforeUpdate** (control)→**AfterUpdate** (control)→**BeforeUpdate** (form)→**AfterUpdate** (form)→**Exit** (control)→**LostFocus** (control)→**Unload** (form)→**Deactivate** (form)→**Close**(form)

The confusing thing is that on forms where there are no active controls and no data changes, the LostFocus event occurs and changes the events to occur in this way:

> **Unload** (form)→**LostFocus** (form)→**Deactivate** (form)→**Close** (form)

Moving Between Forms

This is the order of events when you switch between two open Access forms:

> **Deactivate** (1st form)→**Activate** (2nd form)

Notice that the Activate (form) event occurs, not the GotFocus event, as you may expect. Some variations on the simple form switching follow:

▶ Deactivate (first form) also occurs when you switch from the form to another window in Microsoft Access (such as the Database window or a Module window).

▶ Deactivate (form) does not occur when you switch to a dialog box, to a PopUp form (a form whose PopUp property is set to Yes), or to another application.

▶ Open (form) does not occur if you move to a form that is already open, even if you moved to the form by carrying out an OpenForm action.

Working with Subforms

The main thing to remember when working with subforms is that the Activate and Deactivate events do not occur for subforms. Also, the subform loads *before* the main form and unloads *after* the main form. This may be counterintuitive for you, because it would seem that the main form should load first, but if the main form loads first, then it would have a tendency to activate before the subform was loaded, which would be counterproductive.

When you open a form with a subform, the order of events are as follows:

1. Events for the subform (such as Open and Load)

2. Events for the form (such as Open and Load)

3. Events for the subform's controls (such as Enter)

4. Events for the form's controls (such as Enter, including the subform control)

When you close a form with a subform, the order of events are as follows:

1. Events for the subform's controls (such as Exit and LostFocus)

2. Events for the form's controls (including the subform control)

3. Events for the form (such as Deactivate and Close)

4. Events for the subform

Order of Form Control Events

Although the previous sections briefly touched on the order of events for controls on forms, this section covers those events in greater detail.

Moving the Focus to a Control

This is the order of events when you move the focus from one control on a form to another control on the form:

> **Exit** (1st control)→**LostFocus** (1st control)→**Enter** (2nd control)→**GotFocus** (2nd control)

The GotFocus event always occurs when a control gains focus, even if the control gains focus from the form being opened.

The Enter event occurs only when the control first gets the focus— if the form loses focus and then regains focus, there will only be a GotFocus (control) event, and not an Enter (control) and GotFocus (control) event.

Changing and Updating Data in a Control

This is the order of events when you enter or change data in a control on a form and then move the focus to another control:

> **BeforeUpdate** (control)→**AfterUpdate** (control)→**Exit** (control)→**LostFocus** (control)

If you change text in a text box (or in the text box portion of a combo box), and then change focus, the Change and Key Press events occur in this order:

> **KeyDown** (control)→**KeyPress** (control)→
> **Change** (control)→**KeyUp** (control)→**BeforeUpdate**
> (control)→**AfterUpdate** (control)→**Exit**
> (control)→**LostFocus** (control)

Order of Form Record Events

Record events occur when you move the focus to a record (with and without data updates), delete an existing record or records, or create a new record.

Moving the Focus to a Record

The Current (form) event occurs whenever the form changes records. What other events occur when a form changes records depends on whether or not the record has been updated.

This is the order of events when the form changes records (no data changes):

> **Exit** (control on 1st record)→**LostFocus** (control on 1st record)→**Current** (form)→**Enter** (control on 2nd record)→**GotFocus** (control on 2nd record)

This is the order of events when the form changes records (with data changes):

> **BeforeUpdate** (control on 1st record)→**AfterUpdate** (control on 1st record)→**BeforeUpdate** (form)→**AfterUpdate** (form)→**Exit** (control on 1st record)→**LostFocus** (control on 1st record)→**Current** (form)→**Enter** (control on 2nd record)→**GotFocus** (control on 2nd record)

Deleting records

This is the order of events when you delete a record (Access displays a dialog box asking you to confirm the deletion):

> **Delete** (form)→**BeforeDelConfirm** (form)→**AfterDelConfirm** (form)

Creating a New Record

This is the order of events when you create a new record from a blank record:

> **Current** (form)→**Enter** (control)→**GotFocus** (control)→**BeforeInsert** (form)→**BeforeUpdate** (control)→**AfterUpdate** (control)→**AfterInsert** (form)

Choosing the Appropriate Scope

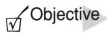 **Objective**
The scope of a procedure, variable, or constant refers to whether or not that procedure, variable, or constant can be used by another procedure. There are three levels possible: procedure-level scope, private module-level scope, and public module-level scope.

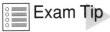 **Exam Tip**
The exam tests you on the differences between the scope levels and on the default scope level.

By default, all constants (declared by the Const statement) and variables (declared by the Dim statement) are private. By default, all procedures, including Sub procedures (declared by the Sub statement), Function procedures (declared by the Function statement), Property procedures (declared by a Property statement), and user-defined Type declarations (declared by the Type statement) are public. These defaults can be overridden by the Private and Public keywords.

Following is an example of the proper syntax for using the Public and Private keywords to override defaults for any of the preceding statements except Dim:

```
Public Const Pi = 3.14

Private Sub Test()
   statements
End Sub
```

You cannot use Private or Public in conjunction with the Dim statement—to explicitly declare Private or Public variables, use the words Private or Public instead of Dim, and rather than in conjunction with Dim. The following is an example:

```
Private MyForm As Form

Public MyInteger As Integer
```

The following sections explain more fully what it means to use Private or Public constants, variables, and procedures.

Procedure-Level Scope

By default, all variables and constants defined within procedures are private, which means they cannot be used outside that procedure—they will not be recognized by other procedures.

In the following example, the first procedure prints "The Local Integer = 25" in the Debug window. The second procedure causes an error, even when the two procedures are in the same module, because the variable strText and the constant intNumber are local to the first procedure.

```
Sub ProcedureLevelScope()
    Dim strText As String
    Const intNumber = 25
    strText = "The Local Integer = "
    Debug.Print strText & intNumber
End Sub

Sub OutsideOfScope()
    Debug.Print strText & intNumber
End Sub
```

The error generated by the second procedure is "Variable not defined."

Private Module-Level Scope

By default, all variables and constants defined within the Declarations section of a module are private, which means they cannot be used outside that module—they will not be recognized by procedures in other modules. Any procedures that use the Private keyword are also private.

In the following example, two private procedures are defined in the same module. The first procedure initializes the variable strText. The second procedure calls the first procedure to initialize the strText variable, and then prints "The Local Integer = 25" in the Debug window. Neither can be called from another module.

```
Dim strText As String
Const intNumber = 25

Private Sub FirstProcedure()
    strText = "The Local Integer = "
End Sub

Private Sub SecondProcedure()
    FirstProcedure
    Debug.Print strText & intNumber
End Sub
```

If you attempt to run this code from the Debug window, you need to remove the Private keyword from the second procedure, or else it will not run.

Public Module-Level Scope

By default, all procedures are public. Also public are all variables and constants defined with the Public keyword within the Declarations section of a module. Being of public scope, which means that they can be used outside that module, they will be recognized by procedures in other modules.

In the following example, two public procedures are defined in different modules. The first procedure initializes the variable strText. The second procedure calls the first procedure to initialize the strText variable, and then prints "The Local Integer = 25" in the Debug window (see fig. 7.2).

In Module1:

```
Public strText As String
Public Const intNumber = 25

Sub FirstProcedure()
    strText = "The Local Integer = "
End Sub
```

In Module2:

```
Sub SecondProcedure()
    FirstProcedure
    Debug.Print strText & intNumber
End Sub
```

Figure 7.2

*Public proce-
dures, variables,
and constants
can be called
from other mod-
ules in the same
application.*

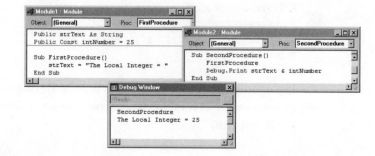

No errors will be generated if you attempt to run the second procedure from the Debug window.

Using Multiple Form Instances

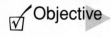 Objective

When you open only one instance of a form at a time, you are
opening the default instance of that form. Sometimes, however, you
want to create multiple instances of a form. An example would be if
you had an Employees form that related each employee to his manager. You could have a process to open another instance of the
Employees form with the manager's employee information, which
opens side-by-side with the subordinate's employee information.

The reason you are able to open multiple instances of a form in
Access for Windows 95 is because form modules (and report modules) are actually class modules, so they no longer act like standard modules (like they did in previous versions of Access).

Therefore, creating another instance of a form is actually creating
another instance of a class that is defined by that form.

To create a new, non-default instance of a form from code, you
need to declare a form module class variable and include the New

keyword in the variable declaration. In other words, the syntax is as follows:

```
Dim frm As New Form_FormName
```

FormName is the name of the form from which you would like to open a new, non-default instance. If you open a new instance of the Employees form, the code is as follows:

```
Dim frm As New Form_Employees
```

This non-default instance of the Employees form is *not* visible until you explicitly set its Visible property to true. Also, you cannot create another instance of a form open in Design mode.

To manipulate an instance of the form in code, you need to refer to the variable that refers to the instance. For example, to make the form instance created in the previous sample code, the code is as follows:

```
frm.Visible = True
```

You can also refer to a non-default instance of a form by referring to the instance's index number in the Forms collection. You cannot refer to the instance's name in the Forms collection because it does not have a name distinct from other instances of the form. Here is an example:

```
DoCmd.Close acForm, Forms(index).Name
```

Index is the index number of the form in the forms collection. As you can imagine, it can be confusing to refer to multiple instances of forms in this manner, because once one instance closes, all subsequent forms in the Forms collection have new index numbers. Also, you must know which index number belongs to which instance. It is much more straightforward to refer to instances by their variables.

When the procedure that has created an instance of a form finishes executing, the instance is destroyed, and no changes are saved to the form. The only exception is if you declare the variable representing the instance as a module-level variable. In that case, the instance exists until the variable is reset.

Property Get, Property Set, and Property Let

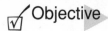

Objective

The Property statements—Property Get, Property Set, and Property Let—can be used together to create custom property procedures. Creating a custom property procedure enables you to create Runtime properties. Most Access programmers don't use the Property statements because Access has so many built-in properties, but for programmers with exposure to other development platforms, it is a welcome capability.

The Property statements can be confusing. You are highly unlikely to have more than one exam question about them, so if you just don't get it, don't worry—you can never understand how to create Runtime properties and still pass the exam.

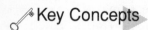

Key Concepts

> A *Custom property*, or a *Runtime property*, is a module-level variable that stores a value that is used by other procedures in the module. The Property procedures either read the value of that variable or change the value of that variable. So if you find it more helpful to mentally substitute the words *global variable* for *property* during this section, you can. The differences at this level of explanation are not so striking that you will become confused.

The most important things to learn in this section are the differences between Property statement types and what each Property statement type does. Here is a brief summarization:

- ▶ Property Get returns the value of a custom Runtime property. Used alone, a Property Get procedure reads and returns the value of a property (public or module-level variable), and thereby creates a Read-only property by returning the variable's value. After you have defined a Property Get procedure for a property, you can use the property in the right side of an expression, such as *ProcedureVariable = PropertyName()*.

- ▶ Property Set sets the value of a custom Runtime property to an object. Property Set procedures must have at least one argument—the object to which the property (public or module-level variable) needs to be set. After you have defined a Property Set procedure for a property, you can use the property in the left side of a Set expression, such as **Set FormName.PropertyName = AssignedObject.**

▶ Property Let assigns the value of a custom Runtime property. The difference between Property Set and Property Let is that Property Let does *not* have to set the value of the property (public or module-level variable) to an object—it can set the value of the property to any value accepted by the property. After you have defined a Property Let procedure for a property, you can use the property in the left side of a property assignment statement of a Let statement, such as ***PropertyName() = Value.***

In other words, you use Property Get and Property Let procedures together to create and modify a non-object-type Custom property. You use Property Get and Property Set procedures together to create and modify an object-type Custom property. You use a Property Get procedure alone to create a Read-only property.

The following code works with three properties: the FirstDay property (read-only), the Balance property (non-object-type), and the FromForm property (object-type). The last procedure, DisplayResults() uses all three properties.

```
Public blnFirstDay As Boolean
Public curBalance As Currency
Public objFromForm As Object


Property Get FirstDay() As Boolean
  FirstDay = blnFirstDay
End Property


Property Get Balance() As Currency
  Balance = curBalance
End Property


Property Let Balance(curTransaction As Currency)
  curBalance = curBalance + curTransaction
End Property
```

```
Property Get FromForm() As Object
  Set FromForm = objFromForm
End Property



Property Set FromForm(frmFormName As Form)
    Set objFromForm = frmFormName
End Property


Sub DisplayResults()
'initialize the blnFirstDay variable
 'which will be the same as the FirstDay property
 'FirstDay property = Is This The First Day of The Month?
    If DatePart("d", Date) = 1 Then
      blnFirstDay = True
    Else
      blnFirstDay = False
    End If
'Call Property Get FirstDay
    Debug.Print "FirstDay property = " & FirstDay()
'use Property Let to update Balance property
 'do two transactions (+$1,000 then -$50)
 '(the curBalance variable initialized as 0)
    Balance = 1000
    Balance = -50
'Call Property Get Balance
    Debug.Print "Balance Property = " & Balance()
'use Property Set to update FromForm property
 '(the objFromForm variable initialized as Nothing)
    Set FromForm = Forms!Customers
'Call Property Get FromFrom
    Debug.Print "FromForm Property = " & FromForm().Name
End Sub
```

That's quite a lot of code to sort through, but it's easiest if you analyze the code from looking at the DisplayResults procedure because the procedure spells out which Property procedures it is calling. Each time the comments in the DisplayResults procedure reference one of the Property procedures, look at that procedure.

If you decide to run this code, you need to have a form named Customers open when you type **DisplayResults** in the Debug window, or else you generate an error. After you run Display Results, the results in the Debug window are in figure 7.3.

Figure 7.3

*The results of
running the
DisplayResults
sample code.*

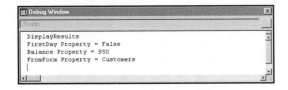

```
Debug Window                                              x
Ready

DisplayResults
FirstDay Property = False
Balance Property = 950
FromForm Property = Customers
```

Note

The FirstDay Property will be equal to True if you run the code
on the first day of the month.

Here is one last summarization, which is really the heart of what
you need to remember for the exam: Property Get is used to return the value of a property. Property Let and Property Set are
used to change the values of properties. The only difference between Property Let and Property Set is that Property Let changes
the value of non-object-type properties, and Property Set changes
the value of object-type properties.

Choosing Documents versus Forms or Reports

Objective

For the sake of simplicity in this section, the discussion centers
around Forms. The only adjustments that need to be made for
reports are that you refer to the Reports collection (same syntax,
different word—substitute Reports for Forms) and to the Documents of Containers("Reports") rather than to the Documents of
Containers("Forms").

There are times when you want to enumerate through all the
saved forms in your application, and other times when you want
to enumerate through all the open forms in your application. You
need to know which to use—the Documents collection or the
Forms collection—to refer to those different groupings of forms.

The Documents collection contains all the Document objects for
a specific type of object. Use the Documents collection when you
want to enumerate through all the saved forms in your application, such as the following code example, which prints all the
saved forms in the Debug window:

```
Dim db As DATABASE, cnt As Container
Dim doc As Document, x As Integer
Set db = CurrentDb
Set cnt = db.Containers("Forms")
For x = 0 To cnt.Documents.Count - 1
  Set doc = cnt.Documents(x)
  Debug.Print doc.Name
Next x
```

The Forms collection, on the other hand, contains all the forms that are currently open in the database. Use the Forms collection when you want to enumerate through all the open forms in your application, such as the following code example, which prints all the open forms in the Debug window:

```
Dim frm As Form
For Each frm In Forms
  Debug.Print frm.Name
Next frm
```

Lab Exercises

The following exercises all use sample databases included with the CD-ROM that accompanies this book.

Exercise 7.1:   Manipulating Reports

In this first exercise, you work with a simple report named Customers List by Country based on a table named Customers. This exercise assumes that you are able to create and position text boxes in the report's Design mode.

Objective:

To practice report skills, including Sorting and Grouping, changing report properties, and writing report event procedures.

Time Estimate: 10–15 minutes

Steps:

1. Open the database 07-1.mdb included with the CD-ROM.

2. Select the Customers List by Country report and click the Design button to open the report in Design view.

3. To view the report as it is before you change it, click the Report Preview button. Look through a few pages, and notice that the Customers are not grouped at all and are not sorted by country. Click the Close button to return to Design view.

4. Open the Sorting and Grouping property box by clicking the Sorting and Grouping button on the toolbar. In the first row, choose the Country field.

5. Change the group's properties so that Group Header = Yes, Group Footer = No, and Keep Together = "With first detail" (that setting prevents Access from putting a group header alone on the bottom of a page). See figure 7.4.

continues

Exercise 7.1: Continued

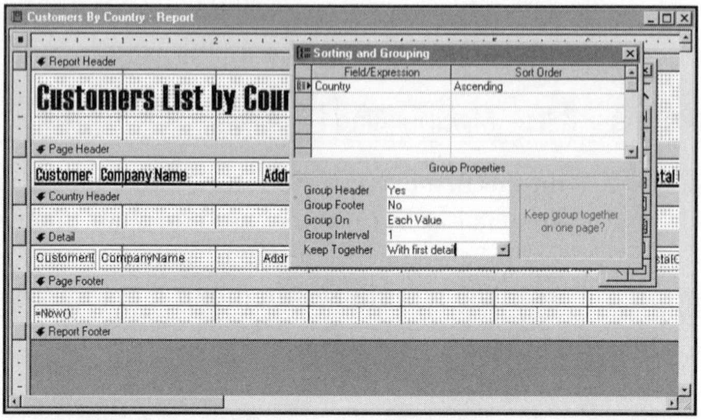

Figure 7.4

Change a report's Sorting and Grouping options.

6. In the second row of the Sorting and Grouping box, choose the CompanyName field, or else the companies will not be in alphabetical order. You do not need to change the properties for this sort. Close the Sorting and Grouping box.

7. Delete the Country label from the Page Header section. You may adjust the size of the Postal Code label to compensate for the gap if you want, but it is not necessary.

8. Drag the Country text box from the Detail section into the Country Header section. Align the Country text box with the left side of the section, and enlarge the font size to 18. Make the text box about 2.5 inches wide (see fig. 7.5).

Figure 7.5

Place the Country field in the Country Group header.

9. Preview the report by clicking the Preview Report button. Notice that the customers are now sorted by Country and then by Customer name, just as you specified. Return to Design Mode by clicking the Close button.

10. Make sure you have the Report selected (not a section or control) by choosing Select Report from the Edit menu. Open the report's property sheet by choosing Properties from the View menu.

11. Scroll down the property sheet and click in the On Open event property. Click the build (…) button to the right of the property. When the Choose Builder window appears, select Code Builder and click OK. The report's module opens with the procedure appropriately named for you (Report_Open).

12. Type the following lines of code:

```
DoCmd.Maximize
Reports![Customers By Country].Caption = "Customers by
Country - " & Date
```

13. Close the module window. Click in the On Close event property. Click the Build (…) button to the right of the property. When the Choose Builder window appears, select Code Builder and click OK. The report's module opens with the procedure appropriately named for you (Report_Close). Type the following line of code (see fig. 7.6):

```
DoCmd.Restore
```

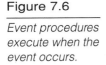

Figure 7.6

Event procedures execute when the event occurs.

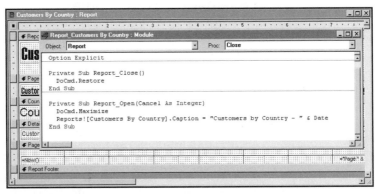

continues

14. Close the module window and save the report if you want. Preview the report and notice that it maximizes automatically. The caption should have today's date, and when you go back to Design mode by clicking the Close button, the report will no longer be maximized.

Comments

As you can see by the fact that you completely rewrote that report in fourteen steps, Access offers powerful functionality through Sorting and Grouping, report properties, and event procedures.

Reading Reference

For more information about the concepts raised by the exercise, refer to the sections "Sorting and Grouping in Reports," "Setting Form and Report Properties," and "Creating Event Procedures."

Exercise 7.2:   Manipulating Individual Forms

In this second exercise, you work with two simple forms named Customers and Add Country.

Objective:

To practice form skills, including event procedures, form methods, form properties, and control properties.

Time Estimate: 15–20 minutes

Steps:

1. Open the database 07-2.mdb included with the CD-ROM that accompanies this book.

2. Click the Tables tab and open the Countries table. It is a list of Countries available to other tables in the database, with an AutoNumber field as the first column.

3. Close the Countries table and open the Customers table. Notice that each country is a number. The values correspond to

the number of a country in the Countries table. Close the
Customers table.

4. Click the Forms tab and open the Add Country form. It is a
data entry form with two command buttons: Add This Country and Cancel. Close the form.

5. Open the Customers form. Notice that the Country field
combo box shows a numeric value—not too helpful from a
user's perspective. Click the drop-down arrow to view the
combo box's columns, and notice that the country is in the
second column. See figure 7.7.

Figure 7.7

*You need to hide
the first column in
the combo box.*

6. Now that you've patiently endured the tour, you can understand what you are going to do in this exercise: (1) you are
going to hide the number field in the County combo box on
the Customers form, and (2) you are going to enable a user
to add a new country to the Countries table from the Customers form by opening the Add Countries form from the
combo box's Not In List event.

7. Change to Design view by clicking the Design View button.
Notice that the form's Order By property is set to
Customers.CustomerID. Change the Order By property to
read Customers.ContactTitle.

8. Change to Form view and note that the Customer records
are now sorted by Contact Title, so the Accounting Managers
are first.

continues

9. Change back to Design view and return the Order By property to read Customers.CustomerID.

10. Select the Country combo box, click in the Column Widths property, and change the values to read 0;1—then save the form if you want and return to Form view. Notice that now the first column of the combo box is hidden, and the country name appears.

11. Return to Design view. Ensure that the combo box is still selected. Click in the On Not In List property. Click the build (...) button to the right of the property. When the Choose Builder window appears, select Code Builder and click OK. The form's module opens with the procedure appropriately named for you (Country_NotInList). Type in the following code:

```
Private Sub Country_NotInList(NewData As String, Response As Integer)
Dim ctl As Control
Set ctl = Me!Country
    'Prompt user to ask if they want to add to list
    If MsgBox(NewData & " is not on the Countries list. " & _
    " Adding it will save the current Customers record. Continue?", _
    vbOKCancel) = vbOK Then
        'This Response argument clears combo box & cancels errors.
        Response = acDataErrContinue
        'add to list by opening Add Country form & setting value
        DoCmd.OpenForm "Add Country"
        Screen.ActiveForm.Country = NewData
    Else
        'If user Cancels, clear combo box & cancel errors.
        Response = acDataErrContinue
        ctl.Undo
    End If
End Sub
```

12. Save the form, and exit the module and Customers form. Open the Add Country form in Design Mode. Feel free to resize it if you cannot see the entire form.

13. Select the Add This Country command button (cmdAddCountry). Click the On Click property, and then click the build (…) button to the right of the property. This opens the existing cmdAddCountry_Click procedure. You want to keep the two lines of code that exist for that procedure, and then add other code. When you finish typing, your procedure should look like this:

```
Sub cmdAddCountry_Click()
    'save country in Countries table & switch to Customers
    DoCmd.DoMenuItem acFormBar, acRecordsMenu, acSaveRecord,
    ➥, acMenuVer70
    Forms!Customers!Country.SetFocus
    'save Customer record & requery Country combo box
    DoCmd.DoMenuItem acFormBar, acRecordsMenu, acSaveRecord,
    ➥, acMenuVer70
    Screen.ActiveForm.Country.Requery
    'reset value of Country to invisible CountryID
    Forms!Customers!Country = Forms![Add Country].CountryID
    'requery again so that the country name displays (F9 =
    ➥requery)
    SendKeys "{F9}"
    'close Add Country
    DoCmd.Close acForm, "Add Country"
End Sub
```

14. Save and close the module, but keep the form open.

15. Select the Cancel command button (cmdCancel). Click in the On Click property, and then click the Build (…) button to the right of the property. This opens the existing cmdCancel_Click procedure. You want to keep the two lines of code that exist for that procedure, and then add one line between the others. When you finish typing, your procedure should look like this:

```
Sub cmdCancel_Click()
    DoCmd.DoMenuItem acFormBar, acEditMenu, acUndo, ,
    ➥acMenuVer70
    Forms!Customers!Country = Null
    DoCmd.Close
End Sub
```

continues

16. Save and close the module, and close the form. Open the Customers form. Add a new record, and have the customer's City be Athens, and the Country be Greece. You are prompted to add Greece to the list. Click OK.

17. The Add Country form opens with Greece already in the Country field. Click the Add This Country button, and Greece will be added and visible.

18. Close the Customer form and the database.

Reading Reference:

For more information about the concepts raised by the exercise, refer to the sections "Using the OrderBy Form Property," "Setting Control Properties," and "Creating Event Procedures."

Exercise 7.3: Working with Multiple Forms

In this third exercise, you work with a simple form named Customers, based on a table named Customers. This exercise assumes that you are able to create event procedures without quite as many step-by-step instructions as the previous exercises gave.

Objective:

To practice with multiple form instances, reinforce your awareness of event order, and demonstrate the distinction between the Forms collection and the Documents collection.

Time Estimate: 15–20 minutes

Steps:

1. Open the database 07-3.mdb included with the CD-ROM that accompanies this book.

2. Select the Customers form and click the Design button to open the form in Design view.

3. Open the form's module by clicking the Code button on the toolbar and type in the following code:

```
Public Sub ListForms()
Dim db As DATABASE, cnt As Container
Dim doc As Document, frm As Form
    Set db = CurrentDb
    Set cnt = db.Containers("Forms")
    'iterate through all saved forms
    Debug.Print
    Debug.Print "All Saved Forms:"
    For Each doc In cnt.Documents
        Debug.Print doc.Name
    Next doc

    Debug.Print
    'iterate through all loaded forms
    Debug.Print "All Loaded Forms:"
    For Each frm In Forms
        Debug.Print frm.Name
    Next frm
End Sub
```

4. Save the form if you want. In order to be able to run this code, the Customers form must be open in Form view. Therefore, open the Debug window, then change to Form view for the Customers form (you can choose Customers: Form from the Window menu, then click the Form View button. The Debug window remains on top.

5. In the Debug window, type **Forms!Customers.ListForms** and press Enter. The code prints saved forms, and then active forms. See figure 7.8.

continues

Exercise 7.3: Continued

Figure 7.8

*Public proce-
dures stored in
form modules are
called from other
modules by their
complete identi-
fier.*

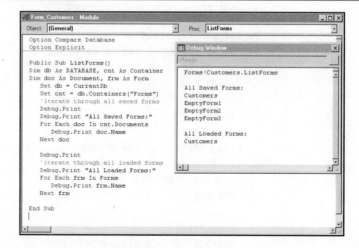

6. Close the Debug window and return to the Design view for the Customers form. Make sure the form is selected (Select Form from the Edit menu) and view the Form's property sheet.

7. Click in the On Activate event property. Click the build (...) button. Select Code Builder and click OK. In the Form_Activate procedure, type the following code:

```
MsgBox Me.Caption & " has been Activated"
```

8. Return to the form and click in the On Deactivate event property. Click the Build (...) button. Select Code Builder and click OK. In the Form_Deactivate procedure, type the following code:

```
MsgBox Me.Caption & " has been Deactivated"
```

9. Return to the form and click in the CustomerID text box. Then click in the On Got Focus event property for the control. Click the Build (...) button. Select Code Builder and click OK. In the CustomerID_GotFocus procedure, type the following code:

```
MsgBox Me.Caption & " CustomerID has received focus"
```

10. Return to the form and click in the On Lost Focus event property for the control. Click the Build (...) button. Select

Code Builder and click OK. In the CustomerID_LostFocus procedure, type the following code:

```
MsgBox Me.Caption & " CustomerID has lost focus"
```

11. In the module window, go to the Declarations section of the module and type in the following declaration:

```
Dim frm As Form
```

12. Now that frm is a module-level form variable, you can set frm to be a multiple instance of the customers form.

13. Return to the form and click the cmdMultiInstances command button. Then click the On Click event property for the control. Click the Build (…) button. Select Code Builder and click OK. In the cmdMultiInstances_Click procedure, type the following code:

```
Set frm = New Form_Customers
frm.Caption = Caption & " - Instance Two"
frm.Visible = True
```

14. Now you are ready to test these procedures. Feel free to save the form if you want. Close the module, and switch to Form view for the Customers form. Notice the order of the messages.

15. Now click the Multi Instances button. Notice that the caption of the new form being activated does not change to Customers, Instance Two until after the form is activated.

16. Experiment. Click one form and then the other. Move the focus to different controls, and to different records, until you can predict which event will occur next.

17. Close both instances of the Customers form and exit the database.

Reading Reference:

For more information about the concepts raised by this exercise, refer to the sections "Creating Event Procedures," "Understanding Form Event Order," and "Using Multiple Form Instances."

Review Questions

1. A form (frmProducts) is based on a query (qryProducts), and the query is sorted in ascending order by the [Product Name] field. Which of the following changes the sort order of the form to make it sort primarily by the [Unit Price] field in descending order (from most expensive to least), and secondarily by the [Product Name] field, in ascending order? Choose all that are correct.

   A. Type the following in the form's OrderBy property:

      [Unit Price] DESC, [Product Name] ASC

   B. Type the following in the form's OrderBy property:

      [Unit Price] DESC, [Product Name]

   C. Use the following bit of Visual Basic:

      ```
      Forms!frmProducts.OrderBy = "[Unit Price] DESC,
      ➥[Product Name] ASC"
      ```

   D. Use the following bit of Visual Basic:

      ```
      Forms!frmProducts.OrderBy = "[Unit Price] DESC,
      ➥[Product Name]"
      ```

2. Which statement changes the value of the active combo box, (cboProduct)—on a form that is currently active—to the number 1?

   A. Screen.ActiveControl = 1

   B. Screen.ActiveForm.ActiveControl = 1

   C. Me.cboProduct = 1

   D. Me!cboProduct = 1

3. You have just changed the text in a text box, and when you press the Tab key, it takes you to a combo box in another record. What is the order of events when you press the Tab key?

   A. **BeforeUpdate** (1st record text box)→**BeforeUpdate** (form)→**Exit** (1st record text box) →**LostFocus**

(1st record text box)→**AfterUpdate** (1st record text box)→**AfterUpdate** (form)→**Current** (form)→**Enter** (2nd record combo box)→**GotFocus** (2nd record combo box)

B. **BeforeUpdate** (1st record text box)→**AfterUpdate** (1st record text box)→**Exit** (1st record text box)→**LostFocus** (1st record text box)→**BeforeUpdate** (form)→**AfterUpdate** (form)→**Current** (form)→**Enter** (2nd record combo box)→**GotFocus** (2nd record combo box)

C. **BeforeUpdate** (1st record text box)→**AfterUpdate** (1st record text box)→**BeforeUpdate** (form)→**AfterUpdate** (form)→**Exit** (1st record text box)→**LostFocus** (1st record text box)→**Current** (form)→**Enter** (2nd record combo box)→**GotFocus** (2nd record combo box)

D. **Exit** (1st record text box)→**LostFocus** (1st record text box)→**BeforeUpdate** (1st record text box)→**AfterUpdate** (1st record text box)→**BeforeUpdate** (form)→**AfterUpdate** (form)→**Current** (form)→**Enter** (2nd record combo box)→**GotFocus** (2nd record combo box)

4. You write the following code in your application, which contains an Employees form:

```
Dim frm As New Form_Employees
Dim frmB As New Form_Employees
```

Which line of code makes the second instance of the form visible?

A. Form_Employees(1).Visible = True

B. frmB.Visible = True

C. Form_Employees(2).Visible = True

D. Forms("Employees").Visible = True

5. Your combo box query returns three columns: EmployeeID, LastName, and FirstName, in that order. You want the combo box to be bound to the EmployeeID column, but to display only the LastName and FirstName columns. To what values should the BoundColumn and ColumnWidths properties be set?

    A. BoundColumn: 0
       ColumnWidths: 1;1;1

    B. BoundColumn: 0
       ColumnWidths: 0;1;1

    C. BoundColumn: 1
       ColumnWidths: 1;1;1

    D. BoundColumn: 1
       ColumnWidths: 0;1;1

6. A control on a report is bound to a field with no format. What should you do to make that control display in all capital letters?

    A. On the report, set the control's Format property to >.

    B. In the report's underlying query, set the column's Format property to >.

    C. In the table underlying the report's underlying query, set the field's Format property to >.

    D. On the report, set the control's FontStyle property to CAPS.

7. If you have a custom property named Inverted that tracks whether or not an image on a form is inverted, what happens when you call the Property Let Inverted procedure?

    A. The value of the Inverted property is returned.

    B. The Inverted property is set.

    C. The image inverts.

    D. The image becomes non-inverted.

8. The following code is behind a form named Customers:

```
Private Sub HaltUpdateMsg()
    MsgBox "Update has been halted!"
End Sub
```

From where can you call this procedure?

    A. From code in referencing library

    B. From a macro on another form

    C. From procedures on Customers

    D. From any module in the database

9. You want to move the cursor to a specified control Customer-State on the active form. What line of code should you use?

    A. Me!CustomerState.SetFocus

    B. Me!Conrol!CustomerState.SetFocus

    C. Me!SetFocus

    D. Me!CustomerState!SetFocus

10. You have written a public subroutine TestSub behind a form named Customers. When the form is open in Form view, what syntax should you use to call the procedure from a global module?

    A. Forms_Customers!TestSub

    B. Forms!Customers!TestSub

    C. Forms!Customers.TestSub

    D. Forms_Customers.TestSub

11. Which of the following is an example of a valid first line of an event procedure for a text box named CustomerState? (Select all that apply.)

    A. Private Sub CustomerState_GotFocus()

    B. Private Sub CustomerState_OnGotFocus()

    C. Private Sub CustomerState_BeforeUpdate(Cancel As Integer)

    D. Private Sub CustomerState_OnBeforeUpdate(Cancel As Integer)

Answers to Review Questions

1. B and D are correct. For more information, refer to the section "Resolving Sort Order Conflicts with Underlying Queries."

2. A is correct. The Me keyword refers to the form that is executing the code, which may not necessarily be the same as the active form. For more information, refer to the section "Choosing Me or Screen."

3. C is correct. For more information, refer to the section "Understanding Form Event Order."

4. B is correct. The simplest way to refer to an instance of a form is to refer to the variable assigned to that instance. Forms(Employees) does not work because there is more than one form with the name Employees loaded. For more information, refer to the section "Using Multiple Form Instances."

5. D is correct. The bound column is the first column, which is BoundColumn 1, not 0. To hide a column, make its width equal to 0. For more information, refer to the section "Setting Control Properties."

6. A is correct. The property setting on a form or report control overrides the property setting for the field in the underlying table or query. There is no FontStyle property. For more information, refer to the section "Setting Control Properties."

7. B is correct. A Property Let procedure sets the value of a property. For more information, refer to the section "Property Get, Property Set, and Property Let."

8. C is correct. Private procedures can be called only from the module that contains them. For more information, refer to the section "Choosing the Appropriate Scope."

9. A is correct. Methods are preceded by the . (dot) operator, not the ! operator, and the SetFocus method needs the full identifier of the target control in order to function properly. Me.SetFocus sets focus to the first active control on the form. For more information, refer to the section "Using Form Methods."

10. C is correct. Call a form or report procedure by referring to the form's or report's full identifier (Forms!Customers), followed by the . (dot) operator, followed by the name of the procedure. For more information, refer to the section "Creating Form and Report Modules."

11. A and C are correct. The "On" portion of an event's designation in the property box is not included in the event procedure's name. For more information, refer to the section "Creating Event Procedures."

Answers to Test Yourself Questions at Beginning of Chapter...

1. Yes, it is possible to change the sort order of a form, so that there is a different sort order than the form's underlying query. For more information, refer to the section "Resolving Sort Order Conflicts with Underlying Queries."

2. The Me keyword refers to a different object than the Screen.ActiveForm property when the form which uses the Me keyword is not the active form. For more information, refer to the section "Choosing Me or Screen."

3. The Activate event of a form occurs before the GotFocus event. The GotFocus event of a form occurs only on forms with no active controls. For more information, refer to the section "Understanding Form Event Order."

4. To enumerate through all the saved forms in your application (as opposed to all the open forms), use the Documents collection. For more information, refer to the section "Choosing Documents versus Forms or Reports."

5. You create a non-default instance of a form by using the following syntax:

```
Dim Variable As New Form_FormName
```

For more information, refer to the section "Using Multiple Form Instances."

6. The proper syntax to correctly refer to the DefaultValue property of a control (State) on a subform (AddressesSubform) of a form (Customers) can be either of the following:

```
Forms!Customers!AddressesSubform!State.DefaultValue
```

```
Forms!Customers!AddressesSubform.Form!State.DefaultValue
```

For more information, refer to the section "Setting Control Properties."

7. A Property Get procedure returns the value of a property. A Property Let procedure changes the value of a property. For more information, refer to the section "Property Get, Property Set, and Property Let."

8. Variables and constants declared in the Declarations section of a module are private by default, so they can be used by any procedure in that module and by no procedures in other modules. Procedures, on the other hand, are public by default, so they can be called from any other module. For more information, refer to the section "Choosing the Appropriate Scope."

9. The Refresh method reflects changes made to existing records only since the data was last displayed—it does not reflect added or deleted records. The Requery method reflects all data changes since the data was last displayed—including added or deleted records. For more information, refer to the section "Using Form Methods."

10. When you drag a form from the Database window and drop it on the Windows 95 desktop, a shortcut is created that opens the database with the specified form. That information is not covered in the chapter, but may be covered on the exam as a random fact about Forms.

11. It is possible to call custom form or report procedures from a global module only when the form or report is open in Form view or Print Preview. For more information, refer to the section "Creating Form and Report Modules."

Chapter

OLE Automation

8

By the end of this chapter, you will be able to execute the following test objectives:

 Objectives

▶ Control other applications by using OLE automation

▶ Control Microsoft Access from other applications by using OLE automation

Test Yourself! Before reading this chapter, test yourself to determine how much study time you will need to devote to this section.

1. You would like to insert an Excel spreadsheet into your Access database, using Visual Basic for Applications code. However, you are not sure which properties and methods are available from Excel. How can you find out which properties and methods Excel exposes?

2. You need to print an Access report from Word. The users are very familiar with Word but have never used Access. Therefore, you do not want them to have to open Access or perform any actions in Access. How would you accomplish this?

Answers are located at the end of the chapter...

OLE automation is an industry-standard technology that applications use to expose their OLE objects to development tools, macro languages, and other applications that support OLE automation. Any application that supports OLE automation can expose its objects as OLE automation servers. Most applications can act as both *OLE automation servers* (by exposing their objects to other programs) and as *OLE automation clients* (by manipulating objects that another program has exposed).

For example, you may want to initiate a mail merge in Microsoft Word from your Access database. Because Word can expose its objects (OLE automation server) and Access can manipulate those object (OLE client), you can do just that.

In this chapter we will look at how you can control other applications such as Word, Excel, PowerPoint (or any application that is OLE-enabled) from Access. In addition, we will also look at how you can use OLE automation to control Access from other programs.

Controlling Other Applications by Using OLE Automation

Many times you need to manipulate data in another program, such as Word or Excel, from Access. When Access manipulates an object from another program, Access is acting as an OLE automation *controller.* The program that is allowing Access to manipulate its objects is acting as an OLE automation *server.* In this section, we will discuss how you can use other programs in Access.

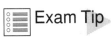 Exam Tip

Because you can use OLE automation to automate any program that is OLE-enabled, the exam will not ask questions specific to any one program. Rather, it will concentrate on the process of using OLE automation. Although it will be very useful to practice writing code to automate another program from Access, you do not have to concentrate on the specific properties or methods used by any one program. Instead, concentrate on how the process works, because the process of OLE automation is the same, regardless of the program that you are actually working with.

Using Object Type Libraries

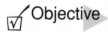

Objective

The first step that you must take in order to automate another program from Access is to set a reference to that program's Object Type Library. This will then allow you to see the objects, properties, and methods that the program exposes to you.

To set a reference to an object's library, complete the following steps:

1. From a module, open the Tools menu and choose References.

2. In the References box, select the name of the object that you would like to reference.

If you do not see the library that you need, click on the Browse button. Object libraries usually have a TLB or an OLB filename extension. Application (EXE) and dynamic-link library (DLL) files can also provide object libraries. To see the path statement for a library that is already visible in the References window, select the name of the library. The full path statement will be displayed at the bottom of the window. Figure 8.1 shows the References window.

Figure 8.1

The References window.

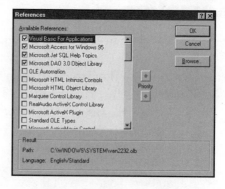

Note

If you are going to automate the program object from more than one database, you must set a reference in *each* database.

You can use the priority arrows to change the order in which Access resolves references. This is useful if, for example, two procedures from different libraries have the same name. You can increase the priority of the library that you want Access to use so that Access will resolve that reference first.

Using the Object Browser

The *Object Browser* enables you to view members of an application's type library. After you have set a reference to the object's Library, you can view the objects, properties, and methods available to you from that library in the Object Browser. To view the Object Browser, choose Object Browser from the View menu or press F2. Figure 8.2 shows the Object Browser.

Figure 8.2

The Object Browser.

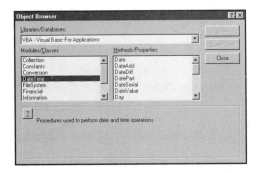

By default, the Object Browser will display the objects, properties, and methods in the current database. However, you can select the correct library from the Libraries/Databases drop-down list.

If you are not familiar with the objects, properties, and methods of a particular program, the Object Browser is a great way to learn more about them. In the Object Browser, objects (classes or modules) are listed on the right, and methods and properties are listed on the left.

Once you have selected the correct library or database, you must select the class or module that contains the procedure that you need. The object selected on the left determines which methods and properties will be displayed on the right. Figure 8.3 shows the Object Browser, open to the Excel library. The Worksheet class is selected; therefore the properties and methods of the Worksheet class are displayed on the right side of the screen.

Figure 8.3

The Object Browser open to the Excel library.

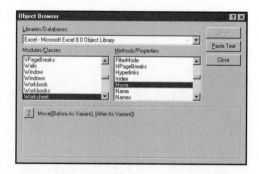

 Tip

If you need more information about a particular method or property, select the method or property and click on the question mark at the bottom of the Object Browser. This will display the Help topic for the selected method or property.

If you would like to use one of the methods in the current procedure, you can select the method and click on the Paste Text button.

OLE Automation Objects

Before you can use the objects, properties, or methods of an application, you must create an OLE automation object (a variable that points to an object of that application that you are controlling). Each application that supports OLE automation exposes at least one object; for example, Excel exposes the Application, Workbook, Worksheet, and Chart objects (among others). Usually, it is more efficient to assign the object to a variable and refer to the variable, rather than continually use the full syntax of the object. There are three ways to point a variable to an instance of an application: the CreateObject function, the GetObject function, and the New keyword. You must use the Set statement with one of these three options to assign the object to the variable.

Table 8.1 lists the objects available from some of the Microsoft Applications. (All applications in Office 97 use VBA and expose their objects.)

Table 8.1

Commonly Used Objects from Microsoft Applications

Application	OLE Automation Objects
Microsoft Word for Windows 95	Application
	Document
	WordBasic
Microsoft Excel for Windows 95	Application
	Chart
	Workbook
	Worksheet
Microsoft Project (version 4.0)	Application
Microsoft Access for Windows 95	Application

Applications behave slightly differently when they are opened by using OLE automation, so you must be very careful about how you start and exit the program when using OLE automation. Table 8.2 lists the programs in Microsoft Office 95 and shows how each acts when started using OLE Automation.

Table 8.2

Office 95 Products and OLE Automation

Application	Launches As	Has Visible Property?	Make Visible By	Application Terminates if Object Variable Destroyed?
Access	Icon with Visible property set to False	Yes	Visible by default	Yes, if it was launched using OLE

continues

Table 8.2   Continued

Office 95 Products and OLE Automation

Application	Launches As	Has Visible Property?	Make Visible By	Application Terminates if Object Variable Destroyed?
Excel	Hidden window with Visible property set to False	Yes	Visible by default	No
PowerPoint	Hidden window	No	Set visible property of AppWindow to True	No
Schedule +	Hidden window	No	Set schedule object's visible property to True	No
Word	Hidden window	No	Call the application object's AppShow method	Yes, if it was launched using OLE

Note For an application that is not destroyed when its corresponding object variable is set to nothing, you must first use Application. Quit to close the application.

Early versus Late Binding

When you declare a variable for an OLE automation object, you can declare it as a generic object data type, or you can declare it as a specific object, such as Excel.Application.

By declaring the variable with the generic Object data type, you are causing the program to use late binding for that variable. *Late binding* means that the reference cannot be resolved until the variable is set because the program does not know what type of object will be used.

On the other hand, by using a specific data type you are causing the program to use early binding for the objects, methods, and properties of the object. *Early binding* enables your code to run much more efficiently and allows for optimal use of memory. Whenever you know the type of object that is going to be used, you should declare the type rather than using the generic object data type.

Set Statement

Although the Dim, Private, Public, ReDim, and Static statements are used to declare a variable that refers to an object, they cannot be used to set the value of the variable. You must use the Set statement to actually make the variable point to a specific object.

The Set statement is used to assign an object reference to an object or variable, and is used with the CreateObject function, the GetObject function, or the New keyword to set the value of an object variable. The syntax of the Set Statement follows:

```
Set objectvar = {[New] objectexpression ¦ Nothing}
```

Table 8.3 lists the arguments of the Set statement.

Table 8.3

Arguments of the Set Statement

Argument	Description
ObjectVar	Name of the variable or property.
New	Keyword used to create a new instance of a Visual Basic object or an OLE automation object. The New keyword cannot be used to create new instances of any intrinsic data type or to create dependent OLE automation objects.
ObjectExpression	Expression consisting of the name of an object, another declared variable of the same object type, or a function or method that returns an object of the same object type. (See "CreateObject" and "GetObject" later in this chapter for more information.)
Nothing	Discontinues association of ObjectVar with any specific object. Assigning ObjectVar to Nothing releases all the system and memory resources associated with the previously referenced object when no other variable refers to it.

The Set statement simply creates a reference to the object; a copy of the object is not created for that variable. Consequently, more than one variable can refer to the same object. The variable is a reference to an object rather than a copy of that object. Any change in the object, therefore, is automatically reflected in all variables that refer to that object.

When you use the New keyword in the Set statement, however, you are actually creating an instance of the object. The new instance is not loaded until the first reference is made to it or one of the object's members.

CreateObject

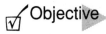 **Objective**

The CreateObject function is used to create a new OLE automation object. The syntax of the Create Object Statement is as follows:

```
CreateObject(class)
```

 Tip

Remember to use the Object Browser to see a complete list of objects available with each application.

The Class argument uses the syntax "appname.objecttype," in which appname is the name of the application providing the object and objecttype is the type or class of object to create. The appname and objecttype must be enclosed in quotation marks. For example, the following code declares an object variable (xlApp), creates a new Excel OLE automation object of Microsoft Excel, and assigns the new object to the variable:

```
Dim xlApp As Object
Set xlApp = CreateObject("Excel.Application")
```

When this code is executed, the application creating the object is started (Microsoft Excel in this example). If it is already running, a new instance of the application is started, and an object of the specified type (in this example, a workbook) is created. After you have created the object, simply use the variable to refer to the object.

 Note

Some objects (multiple-use servers) can have only a single instance (for example, the Word.Basic object in Microsoft Word 6.0). For these objects, only one instance of the object is created, no matter how many times CreateObject is executed. For more information, see "Single-Use versus Multiple-Use Servers" later in this chapter.

When you are finished working with an OLE automation object, you should release it from memory. To do this, you must set its value to Nothing (refer to table 8.1). Before setting the value of the variable to Nothing, you should also quit the application. For example, the following code closes (or quits) Microsoft Excel and releases the variable xlApp:

```
XlApp.Quit
Set xlApp = Nothing
```

If you have a function that requires an object as an argument, you can pass the CreateObject function as an argument, as seen in the following example:

```
Call MySub (CreateObject("Word.Basic"))
```

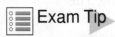 **Exam Tip**

For the exam, ensure that you understand the difference between CreateObject and GetObject. Know when to use which one, and what the results will be.

GetObject

 **Objective**

The GetObject function is used to retrieve an existing OLE automation object. The syntax of the GetObject statement follows:

```
GetObject([pathname][, class])
```

Table 8.4 lists the arguments used in the GetObject function.

Table 8.4

GetObject Function Arguments	
Part	Description
Pathname	The full path and name of the file containing the object to retrieve. If the pathname is omitted, a class is required.
Class	A string representing the class of the object.

Appname is the name of the application providing the object. Objecttype is the type or class of object to create.

Note
> Error 3011 (Couldn't Find Object) is generated when an object cannot be located within the specified pathname or if the name of the object is misspelled. Ensure that you indicate the correct path and that the name of the object is spelled correctly.

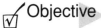**Objective**

If pathname is a zero-length string (""), GetObject returns a new object instance of the specified type. Consequently, using GetObject with a zero-length string has the same effect as using CreateObject. If the pathname argument is omitted entirely, GetObject returns a currently active object of the specified type. If there is no currently active object of the specified type, a new instance of that object is created. However, if no object of the specified type exists, error 429 (OLE Automation Server Can't Create Object) occurs.

When you are referring to a single-instance object, GetObject always returns the same instance when called with the zero-length string syntax (""), and it causes an error if the pathname argument is omitted. You cannot use GetObject to obtain a reference to a class created with Visual Basic.

Note
> Because the CreateObject function does not actually load the new instance until it is referred to, you can use the GetObject function with an empty string ("") to create the instance with the file already loaded.

Single-Use versus Multiple-Use Servers

A *multiple-use server* is a server that can only have one instance open at any given time. As we mentioned earlier, if you use the CreateObject method on a multiple-use server and there is already an instance running, the new variable will simply point to the existing instance.

A *single-use server* is a server that can have multiple instances open simultaneously.

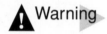

Warning

> You must be very careful about using CreateObject statements on single-use servers. You do not want to end up with five instances of a single-use server application, such as Excel, running.

Working with Custom OLE Controls

In addition to OLE automation objects, you can also use custom OLE controls in Access. Each custom control has properties, methods, and events that you can manipulate.

To see a list of custom controls that are currently available on your system, choose Custom Controls from the Tools menu. Figure 8.4 shows the Custom Controls dialog box.

Figure 8.4

The Custom Controls dialog box.

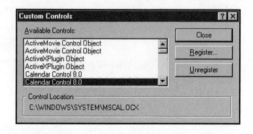

The custom controls that come with the Access Developer's Toolkit are automatically registered when you install the Toolkit. Other custom controls must be registered before they can be used. (Most will register themselves as part of their installation programs.) To manually register a custom control, click on the Register button in the Custom Controls dialog box and search for your file.

To insert a custom control in your form, choose Custom Control from the Insert menu, select the control, and click OK. To view the standard properties of the custom control (such as height, position, and so on) right-click the control and choose Properties.

Objective

To view the properties that are specific to that control, double-click the control itself. Figure 8.5 shows the Calendar control and its Property sheet.

Figure 8.5

*The property
sheet of a custom
control (Calen-
dar).*

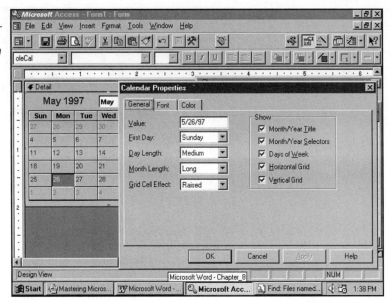

You can manipulate properties of custom controls by using VBA.
Simply refer to the control name followed by a dot (period) and
then the control's property name. For example, if you had a Calendar control called oleCal and you wanted to change the value
of the calendar to 1/1/98, the following code could be used:

```
oleCal.Value = "1/1/98"
```

You can also use the methods of any custom control. For example,
the Calendar control has a method called NextWeek, which incre-
ments the week and repaints the calendar. To use this method
with the oleCal object, use code similar to the following:

```
oleCal.NextWeek
```

To learn more about a particular control's properties and methods, look up the name of the control in the Help menu. Because
Access uses an integrated Help system, the Help files for the control are integrated into the Access Help file when the program is
registered. Figure 8.6 shows the Help menu for the Calendar control. Notice that you can choose to see a list of all of the properties, methods, or events associated with the control.

Figure 8.6

The Help menu for a custom control.

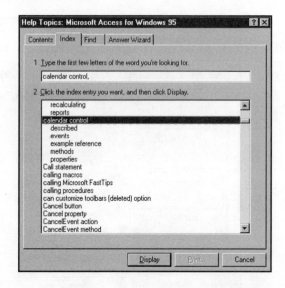

Some controls, such as the CommonDialog and ImageList, do not require direct user interaction. Consequently, they are visible only at design time. Other controls are visible at both design time and runtime because they require interaction from the user. Here is a list of the controls in the Access Developer's Toolkit that are available at both design time and runtime:

- ▶ Calendar

- ▶ DataOutline

- ▶ ListView

- ▶ ProgressBar

- ▶ RichText

- ▶ Slider

- ▶ SpinButton

- ▶ StatusBar

- ▶ TabStrip

- ▶ Toolbar

- ▶ TreeView

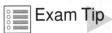 Exam Tip

> For the exam, you do not have to be familiar with the proper-
> ties or methods of a particular control. However, you do have
> to know how to register a control, insert it on a form, and ac-
> cess its properties and use its methods.

Determining Whether an Application Was Started by OLE

Occasionally, you need to be able to determine whether an object was created by the user or by OLE automation. For example, you might not want to close the application if it was originally started by the user rather than by OLE automation.

When an application object is created using OLE automation, two properties of the application object are set to False: Visible and UserControl. Therefore, by checking the values of these proper-ties you can determine how it was opened.

If a user opens an application, both the UserControl and Visible properties are set to True. When the UserControl property is set to True, the Visible property cannot be set to False.

When an application is started by OLE, however, the UserControl and Visible properties are both set to False. You can change the Visible property to True; however, the UserControl property is read only.

Table 8.5 lists the settings for the UserControl property.

Table 8.5

UserControl Property Settings	
Setting	Description
True (–1)	The current application was started by the user.
False (0)	The current application was started by another application using OLE automation.

The UserControl property is available only in Visual Basic.

Controlling Microsoft Access from Other Applications by Using OLE Automation

In the previous section, you learned how Access can manipulate objects from other applications by acting as an OLE controller. In this section you'll discover how Access can be an OLE server, allowing other programs to manipulate Access objects.

Any program that can act as an OLE controller can work with Access objects. Just as you might set a reference in Access to the *Object Type Library* of another application to be able to work with its objects, properties, and methods, you can set a reference to the *Access Type Library* in order to work with Access objects, properties, and methods. You can even use Microsoft Access as an OLE automation controller to manipulate another instance of Microsoft Access that is acting as an OLE automation server.

By including Access 95's type library (MSACCESS.TLB) as one of your references, you can declare object variables that map directly to the objects in Access. This action will also enable you to view context-sensitive help for a particular Access object.

Creating an Instance of Access

As with any OLE server, the first step is to create an instance of the program. Access only provides one object that can be created using OLE automation: the application object. This is referred to as Access.Application.

To create or refer to an instance of Access, use the CreateObject or GetObject function (see the previous sections "CreateObject" and "GetObject"). The following code, for example, declares an object variable (oleData), creates a new instance of Access, and assigns the object to the variable:

```
Dim oleData As Object
    Set oleData = CreateObject("Access.Application")
```

Opening Access Databases by Using OLE Automation

Once you have created an instance of Access, you must then open a database in order to manipulate the objects in that database. To open an Access database from another program, use either the OpenCurrentDatabase or NewCurrentDatabase functions.

OpenCurrentDatabase

This is a method of the Access.Application object that is used to open an existing database as the current database. The syntax of the OpenCurrentDatabase statement is as follows:

```
application.OpenCurrentDatabase dbname[, exclusive]
```

Table 8.6 lists the arguments used in the OpenCurrentDatabase method.

Table 8.6

Arguments Used in the OpenCurrentDatabase Method

Argument	Description
Application	The Application object.
Dbname	A string expression that is the name of an existing database file. This expression must include the path name and the filename extension. (If your network supports it, you can also specify a network path in the following form: \\Server\Share\ Directory\Filename.mdb)
Exclusive	Optional argument that specifies whether you want to open the database in exclusive mode. This argument requires an integer value (–1 for True). By default, the database opens in shared mode.

Note The OpenCurrentDatabase method is not the same as the data access OpenDatabase method. The OpenCurrentDatabase method actually opens a database in the Microsoft Access window. The OpenDatabase method simply returns a Database object variable that represents a database, but the database itself does not open in the Microsoft Access window. The application object does not support the OpenDatabase method.

**Warning** If the database identified by dbname does not exist, an error occurs.

NewCurrentDatabase

NewCurrentDatabase is another method of the Access.Application object. It is used to create a new database in Microsoft Access and make that the current database. The new database is opened under the Admin user account. The syntax of the NewCurrentDatabase method follows:

```
application.NewCurrentDatabase dbname
```

Table 8.7 lists the arguments used in the NewCurrentDatabase method.

Table 8.7

Arguments Used in the NewCurrentDatabase Method	
Argument	Description
Application	The application object
Dbname	\\Server\Share\Directory\Filename.mdb

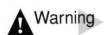**Warning** If the database identified by dbname already exists, an error occurs.

Working with Access

Once you have created an instance of Access and opened or created a database, you are ready to begin working with objects in Access. This process is basically the same as programming directly in Access; however, all code must be referenced through the application object. Use the Object Browser to see a complete list of the methods and properties of the application object. (Remember to first set a reference to the Access Type Library and select that library from the list.)

One of the most common reasons for using Access as an OLE server is to print reports. To print a report using an Access OLE server, you must use the DoCmd object of the Application object. The following code creates a new instance of Access, opens C:\Databases\Test.mdb, and opens the report MyReport in Print Preview:

```
Dim appAccess As Object
    Set appAccess = CreateObject("Access.Application")
    appAccess.OpenCurrentDatabase ("C:\Databases\Test.mdb")
    appAccess.DoCmd.OpenReport "MyReport", acPreview
```

The following code opens the same report.

```
Dim appAccess As Object
    Set appAccess = CreateObject("Access.Application")
    appAccess.OpenCurrentDatabase ("C:\Databases\Test.mdb")
    appAccess.DoCmd.OpenReport "MyReport"
    appAccess.DoCmd.Close acReport, "MyReport"
    Set appAccess = Nothing
```

However, the latter code hides Access and immediately prints the report, closes Access, and sets the variable to Nothing.

Closing Access Databases

When you set the object variable for an Access database to Nothing, the database will close if it was started using OLE automation. If it was not started using OLE automation (if GetObject was used to work with a current instance of Access, for example), you must close the database using VBA code. To close a Microsoft Access Database using OLE automation, you must use the CloseCurrentDatabase method of the Access.Application object. The syntax of the CloseCurrentDatabase method is as follows:

```
application.CloseCurrentDatabase
```

The application is the name of the application object.

 Note

Just as the OpenCurrentDatabase method of the Access.Application object is not the same as the OpenDatabase data access object, the CloseCurrentDatabase method of the Access.Application object is not the same as the data access Close method. The Close method closes a Database Object variable, causing it to go out of scope. It has no effect on the current database open in the Microsoft Access database window. The CloseCurrentDatabase method of the Access.Application object actually closes the database that is open in the Microsoft Access window.

OLE versus DDE

Access can be integrated with other applications using OLE automation or Dynamic Data Exchange (DDE). Just as Access can be an OLE server or an OLE automation client, Access can be both a DDE server and client. Some (mostly older) programs do not support OLE and you must use DDE to exchange data with these programs. In this section of the chapter, we will discuss the differences between using OLE and DDE.

Dynamic Data Exchange (DDE) is a set of services built into the Windows environment that enable applications to send and receive data with one another continually and automatically. There are several key differences between using OLE and DDE.

When using OLE, control can be shared between the client and server. With DDE, the client (the program that initiates the link) always maintains control. Therefore, if you want to be able to share control between the applications, you should use OLE rather than DDE.

When you insert an OLE object in your application, the object appears exactly as it does in the original (Server) application. DDE does not allow you to view the data as it appears in the Server application.

When you use an OLE object, the OLE server is started automatically. When using DDE, you must first check to see if the OLE server has been started. If it has not been started, you must start the OLE server before you can begin DDE.

With OLE, the entire object is brought into memory, which requires a large amount of system resources. DDE uses channels (active links between Windows applications through which data can be exchanged) for a "conversation" about a particular topic, which does not require many system resources.

As a DDE server, Microsoft Access supports the following topics:

▶ The System topic

▶ The name of a database (database topic)

▶ The name of a table (tablename topic)

▶ The name of a query (queryname topic)

▶ A Microsoft Access SQL string (sqlstring topic)

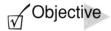 **Objective** Table 8.8 summarizes the differences between OLE and DDE.

Table 8.8

Differences Between OLE and DDE

OLE	DDE
Client and Server applications can share control.	Client application always maintains control of the object.
Can view data exactly as it appears in the Server application.	Cannot view data exactly as it appears in the Server application.

continues

Table 8.8   Continued

Differences Between OLE and DDE	
OLE	DDE
OLE server is automatically started.	Must check to see if the OLE server has already been started. If not, must start OLE server before beginning DDE.
Brings entire object into memory—uses many system resources.	Opens a conversation about one topic—does not require many resources.

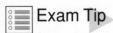 Exam Tip

For the exam, you do not have to discuss the specifics of starting DDE. However, you must be able to assess a situation and determine whether to use OLE or DDE.

Key Terms and Concepts

Table 8.9 identifies key terms from this chapter. Review the key terms and make sure that you understand each term for the exam.

Table 8.9

Key Terms: OLE Automation	
Term	Covered in Section…
Object Type Library	"Using Object Type Libraries"
Early Binding	"Early versus Late Binding"
Late Binding	"Early versus Late Binding"
Set Statement	"Early versus Late Binding"
CreateObject	"Early versus Late Binding"
GetObject	"Early versus Late Binding"
Single Use Server	"Single-Use versus Multiple-Use Servers"
Multiple Use Server	"Single-Use versus Multiple-Use Servers"

Term	Covered in Section...
UserControl	"Determining Whether an Application Was Started by OLE"
OpenCurrentDatabase	"Opening Access Databases by Using OLE Automation"
NewCurrentDatabase	"Opening Access Databases by Using OLE Automation"
CloseCurrentDatabase	"Opening Access Databases by Using OLE Automation"
DDE	"OLE versus DDE"

Lab Exercise

This lab exercise will provide practice for you in working with OLE objects. You will create an Excel object from within an Access database.

Exercise 8.1: Creating an OLE Automation Object

For this exercise, you will be creating an OLE automation object.

Objective:

Control Microsoft Access from other applications by using OLE automation

Time Estimate: 20 minutes

Steps:

1. Create a new database LabEight.

2. Create a subprocedure (CreateExcel) within a module (OLEAutomation).

3. Set a reference to Excel (Tools, References).

4. Declare an object variable (objExcel).

5. Use the CreateObject function to set objExcel to an Excel application object

6. Make objExcel visible.

7. Use the Add method to add a worksheet to objExcel.

8. Test the procedure by typing **CreateExcel** in the Debug window.

Reading Reference:

For more information about creating OLE automation objects, please see the section "OLE Automation Objects."

Review Questions

1. How do you set a reference to an Object Type Library?

    A. Use the SetReference command, supplying the name and location of the appropriate library as arguments.

    B. Choose References from the Insert menu.

    C. Use the SetNewReference command, supplying the name and location of the appropriate library as arguments.

    D. Choose References from the Tools menu.

2. Which of the following can be exposed by OLE servers? Choose all that apply.

    A. Properties

    B. Events

    C. Variables

    D. Methods

3. What is the shortcut key to display the Object Browser?

    A. Shift + F2

    B. F2

    C. Shift + F5

    D. F5

4. Which of the following statements create a new object variable for an Excel application? Choose all that apply.

    A. Set appExcel = CreateObject("Excel")

    B. Set appExcel = CreateObject(Excel.Application)

    C. Set appExcel = CreateObject ("Excel.Application")

    D. Set appExcel = GetObject ("","Excel.Application")

5. An OLE server named OLE_A has been started, but no instances of OLE_A are running. What will happen when the following code executes?

```
Set A = GetObject(,"OLE_A.SomeObject")
```

   A. A runtime error will occur.

   B. A syntax error will occur.

   C. A new instance of OLE_A will be started.

   D. The OLE_A server will be shut down.

6. You have opened a spreadsheet in Excel by using the CreateObject function. Which of the following actions would cause Excel to quit? Choose all that apply.

   A. Using the Close method on the Excel application object.

   B. Using the Quit method on the Excel application object.

   C. Setting the Excel application object to Nothing.

   D. Closing the OLE automation object within the server.

7. Microsoft Excel is currently running. The following code executes from Microsoft Access:

```
Dim appXL As Object
Set appXL = GetObject(, "Excel.Application")
appXL.Visible = True
appXL.Workbooks.Add
```

   What will happen when this code executes?

   A. A new workbook will be added in the current instance of Microsoft Excel.

   B. Error 429 (OLE Automation Server Can't Create Object) will occur.

   C. A syntax error will occur.

   D. A new instance of Excel will be started and a new workbook will be added.

8. Access 7.0 can serve as which of the following? (Choose all that apply.)

    A. An OLE Automation Client

    B. A DDE Client

    C. An OLE Server

    D. A DDE Server

9. You have purchased a custom OLE control from a vendor. You have copied the appropriate files to your machine (including Help files). However, you are unable to find the Help topic referring to the control, and the control does not appear in the custom controls list. What do you need to do to fix this?

    A. Register the control by choosing Register from the Insert menu.

    B. Call the company and ask for a new copy of the file because yours is corrupted.

    C. Register the control by choosing Custom Controls from the Insert menu and then clicking on the Register button.

    D. Register the control by choosing Custom Controls from the Tools menu and then clicking on the Register button.

10. How can you view the custom properties of an OLE custom control?

    A. Use the Object Browser.

    B. Double right-click the object.

    C. Double-click the object.

    D. Choose Custom Properties from the View menu (when the custom control is selected).

11. Before you quit Excel, you want to determine whether the instance of Excel to which the variable (appXL) is pointing was started by the User or by OLE automation. Which of the following property values would tell you that Excel was started by the User, not by OLE automation? Choose all that apply.

    A. appXl.UserControl = –1

    B. appXL.UserControl = 0

    C. appXL.Visible = False

    D. appXL.OLEControl = False

12. Which of the following objects does Access, as an OLE server, expose? Choose all that apply.

    A. Modules

    B. Forms

    C. Application

    D. Database

13. Microsoft Word is using Access as an OLE server to print a report. An object reference was created for the Access application. What method must be applied before using the DoCmd.OpenReport method?

    A. The Open method

    B. The OpenDatabase method

    C. The GetObject method

    D. The OpenCurrentDatabase method

14. If the following code is executed and there is no database name MyData.mdb, then what happens?

```
Dim appAccess as Object
Set appAccess = GetObject("Access.Application")
AppAccess.OpenCurrentDatabase("C:\Data\MyData.mdb")
```

    A. A syntax error occurs because the second argument was omitted.

    B. A runtime error occurs.

    C. Because the second argument was omitted, OpenCurrentDatabase acts like NewCurrentDatabase and MyData.mdb is created.

    D. An open dialog box appears, prompting the user to search for MyData.mdb.

15. Which of the following lines of code would cause an Access database that was started using OLE automation to close? The Access Application object is referred to by the object variable objAccess. Choose all that apply.

    A. Set objAccess = Nothing

    B. objAccess.Close

    C. objAccess.CloseCurrentDatabase

    D. Set objAccess = ""

16. Which of the following statements describe advantages of OLE over DDE? Choose all that apply.

    A. Fewer system resources are used.

    B. An object can be viewed exactly as it appears in its native application.

    C. The server will start automatically.

    D. The controller always maintains control of the object.

Answers to Review Questions

1. D is correct. For more information, see the section "Using Object Type Libraries."

2. A and D are correct. OLE servers expose their properties and methods. For more information, see the section "Using the Object Browser."

3. B is correct. F2 is the shortcut key that will display the Object Browser. For more information, see the section "Using the Object Browser."

4. C and D are correct. The CreateObject method requires a classname enclosed in quotes. When the first argument of the GetObject function is a zero-length string, it creates a new instance of the object. For more information, see the sections "CreateObject" and "GetObject."

5. C is correct. If OLE_A had not already been stated, a runtime error would have occurred. Because it was already started, this code simply creates a new instance of OLE_A and makes it the active object. For more information, see the section "GetObject."

6. B and D are correct. Setting the application object to Nothing does not terminate the application in Excel. There is no Close method of the Excel application object. For more information, please see table 8.

7. A is correct. If the first argument of the GetObject function (pathname) is omitted, then the currently active object is returned. appXl will now refer to the current instance of Excel. For more information, see the section "GetObject."

8. A, B, C, and D are correct. Access can serve as a server or client in both OLE and DDE. For more information, see the section "OLE versus DDE."

9. D is correct. To register a new control, choose Custom Controls from the Tools menu and click on the Register button to locate your file. For more information, see the section "Working with Custom OLE Controls."

10. C is correct. To see the properties of a custom control, double-click the control. For more information, see the section "Working with Custom OLE Controls."

11. A is correct. The UserControl property shows how the application was started. If it was started by OLE automation, the UserControl property has a value of 0. If the user started the application, UserControl has a value of –1. For more information, see the section "Determining Whether an Application Was Started by OLE."

12. C is correct. The only object that Access exposes as an OLE server is the Application object. For more information, see the section "Creating an Instance of Access."

13. D is correct. To open a Microsoft Access Database from another application, you must use the OpenCurrentDatabase method. The Application object does not support the Open-Database method. For more information, see the section "Opening Access Databases by Using OLE Automation."

14. B is correct. If the specified database does not exist, or if the path is incorrect, a runtime error would occur. For more information, see the section "Opening Access Databases by Using OLE Automation."

15. A and C are correct. Setting the object variable to Nothing causes the database and the instance of Access to close. The CloseCurrentDatabase is a valid method of the application object; the Close method is not. For more information, see the section "Closing Access Databases."

16. B and C are correct. For an overview of the differences between OLE and DDE, please see the section "OLE versus DDE."

Answers to Test Yourself Questions at Beginning of Chapter...

1. In order to see which properties and methods Excel will expose, you must first set a reference to Excel. After the reference has been set, you can view Excel's properties and methods in the Object Browser. For more information, please see the section "Using the Object Browser."

2. You need to use the CreateObject method to create an Access Application object. After that object has been created, use the OpenCurrentDatabase method of the Application object to open the appropriate database. Then, use the DoCmd.OpenReport method of the Application object to open the report. Use the DoCmd.Close method to close the report, and then set the object variable to Nothing, which will terminate Access. For more information, see the section "Controlling Microsoft Access from Other Applications by Using OLE Automation."

Chapter 9

Custom Controls

This chapter helps you prepare for the exam by covering the following objectives:

 Objectives

- ▶ Customize OLE controls

- ▶ Set properties for Custom Controls

Test Yourself! Before reading this chapter, test yourself to determine how much study time you will need to devote to this section.

1. What is the effect of setting the Locked property to Yes on an OLE control?

2. Custom Controls can be easily identified in a directory listing by their extension. What is the extension?

Answers are located at the end of the chapter...

As you read this chapter, you will learn about Custom Controls and the properties associated with them. Specifically, this chapter covers Custom Controls and the properties you must assign to them when designing them. Although you must understand the concepts of Custom Controls in order to answer the handful of questions about them on the exam, the topic is not usually covered extensively on the exam.

The material presented here is tremendously useful, however, in the real world. Understanding Custom Controls will allow you to create more robust databases.

Customizing OLE Controls

 Objective

To add Custom Controls to Access, go to the Tools menu and select Custom Controls, as shown in figure 9.1. If you chose the Microsoft OLE controls check box when the Access setup program was first run, then the Custom Controls included in Access were automatically registered and can be easily identified by the OCX extension. If you wish to register other controls, go to the Access Tools menu, select Custom Controls, and register them.

Before you can use a Custom Control, it must be registered. If it is not registered, choose the Register button shown in figure 9.2.

After choosing Register, you must enter the path to the control in the Add Custom Control dialog box that displays (see fig. 9.3). Following that, click OK and Close.

Adding OLE Controls to a Form or Report

Once registered, adding a Custom Control to a form or report is as simple as going to the form (or report) Design view, and clicking Custom Control on the Insert menu. Next, click the control you want in the list and choose where you would like it to be by clicking the appropriate place on the form or report.

After that, click the right mouse button to point it to the appropriate Object command and click Properties to open the Custom Control Property sheet.

Figure 9.1

Adding Custom Controls to Access.

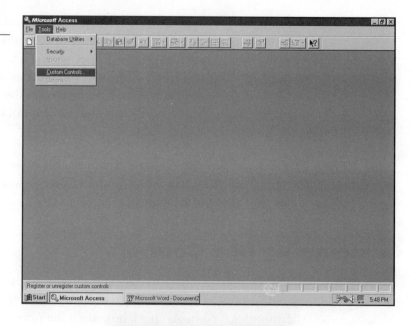

Figure 9.2

Registering a Custom Control.

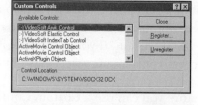

Figure 9.3

Entering the path to the Custom Control.

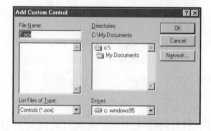

Toolkit Custom Controls

There are a number of Custom Controls that come with Access, as illustrated by figure 9.2. Several other Custom Controls are included in the Access Developer's Toolkit, including the following:

▶ Spinner

▶ TabStrip

▶ Rich Textbox controls

▶ Data Outline

▶ Common Dialog

The names of the Custom Controls, for the most part, are self-explanatory. Other Custom Controls can be located or created in versions of Visual Basic 4.0 or greater.

Setting Properties for Custom Controls

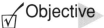 Objective ▶ The following properties and events apply to Custom Controls. For specific information on how these language elements work together, the Access Help Index contains an entry on Custom Controls that provides good information on Custom Control topics.

Using Properties

The following properties in Access apply to Custom Controls:

▶ BorderColor	▶ OLEClass
▶ BorderStyle	▶ OnEnter
▶ BorderWidth	▶ OnExit
▶ Class	▶ OnGotFocus
▶ ControlSource	▶ OnLostFocus
▶ ControlTipText	▶ OnUpdated
▶ DisplayWhen	▶ SpecialEffect
▶ Enabled	▶ TabIndex
▶ Height	▶ TabStop
▶ HelpContextId	▶ Tag
▶ Left	▶ Top

- ▶ Locked   ▶ Verb

- ▶ Name   ▶ Visible

- ▶ Object   ▶ Width

These properties are examined in the following sections.

BorderColor

The BorderColor property is used to specify the color of a control's border; it is a numeric expression that corresponds to the color you want to use for a control's border.

The border color is only visible when the SpecialEffect property is set to Shadowed or Flat; otherwise, setting the BorderColor property changes the SpecialEffect property setting to Flat.

BorderStyle

This property is used to specify the type of border and border elements (title bar, Control menu, Minimize and Maximize buttons) to use for the form. Different border styles are used for normal forms, pop-up forms, and custom dialog boxes.

BorderStyle properties used with controls, per Microsoft documentation, are as follows:

Setting	Description	Visual Basic
Transparent	(Default only for label, graph, and subreport) Transparent	0
Solid	(Default) Solid line	1
Dashes	Dashed line	2
Short Dashes	Dashed line with short dashes	3
Dots	Dotted line	4
Sparse Dots	Dotted line with dots spaced far apart	5

Setting	Description	Visual Basic
Dash Dot	Line with a dash-dot combination	6
Dash Dot Dot	Line with a dash-dot-dot combination	7

As with BorderColor, BorderStyle is only visible when the Special-Effect property is set to Shadowed or Flat; otherwise, the Border-Style property changes the SpecialEffect property setting to Flat.

BorderWidth

This property uses the following settings to specify the width of a control's border:

Setting	Description
Hairline	(Default) The narrowest border possible on your system
1 pt to 6 pt	The width as indicated in points

The SpecialEffect property must be set to Shadowed or Flat for BorderWidth to work properly, and BorderStyle must not be set to transparent.

Class

This property is used to specify (as a string expression) the class name of an embedded OLE object.

ControlSource

This property is used to specify which data appears in an option group control, and has the following settings, per Microsoft documentation:

Setting	Description
A field name	The control is bound to a field in a table, query, or SQL statement. Data from the field is displayed in the control. Changes to the data inside the control change the corresponding data in the field. (To make the control read-only, set the Locked property to Yes.)
An expression	The expression generates data for the control. This data is read-only and is not saved in the database.

ControlTipText

This property is used to specify the text (up to 255 characters) that appears in a screen tip when the mouse pointer is over a control.

DisplayWhen

This property uses the following settings, per Microsoft documentation, to specify which of a form's sections or controls you want displayed on screen and in print:

Setting	Description
Always	(Default) The object appears in Form view and when printed.
Print Only	The object is hidden in Form view but appears when printed.
Screen Only	The object appears in Form view but not when printed.

Enabled

This property uses the following settings, per Microsoft documentation, to specify whether a control can or cannot have the focus when in Form view:

Setting	Description
Yes	(Default for all controls except unbound object frames) The control can have the focus. If the control is an unbound object frame, double-clicking the control executes the control's primary verb. For example, an unbound object frame could play an embedded sound object.
No	(Default for unbound object frames) The control can't have the focus and appears dimmed. If the control is an option group, neither the option group nor the controls inside the option group can have the focus.

TabStop can be combined with Enabled to stop the use of the Tab key to select a command button, while at the same time allowing use of the button by clicking on it.

Height

This property is used in conjunction with Width to size an object to desired dimensions. The default for controls is set using the default control style.

HelpContextID

This property specifies the context ID (in the form of a long integer between 0 and 2,147,483,647—default is 0) for a topic in the custom Help file. The custom Help file is specified by the Help-File property setting.

Left

This property works in conjunction with Top to specify an object's location on a form or report in terms of distance measured from the left border to the left edge of the section containing the control.

Locked

The Locked property specifies whether you can or cannot edit data in a control in Form view, and it uses the following settings, per Microsoft documentation:

Setting	Description
Yes	(Default for unbound object frames) The control functions normally but doesn't enable editing, adding, or deleting data.
No	(Default for all controls except unbound object frames) The control functions normally and enables editing, adding, and deleting data.

Locked can protect data in a field by making the data read-only. Locked can also be combined with Enabled to produce the following results, per Microsoft documentation:

Enabled	Locked	Effect
Yes	Yes	The control can have the focus. Data is displayed normally and can be copied but not edited.
Yes	No	The control can have the focus. Data is displayed normally and can be copied and edited.
No	Yes	The control can't have the focus. Data is displayed normally but can't be copied or edited.
No	No	The control can't have the focus. Control and data are disabled (gray).

Name

This property is used to specify a string expression (up to 255 characters) that identifies the name of the control.

Object

This property is used to specify a linked or embedded OLE Automation object in a control.

OLEClass

This property is used to obtain a description of the kind of OLE object contained in a chart or an unbound object frame.

On

The properties beginning with "On" are considered event properties—this causes the control to take action upon the occurrence of an event. That event is signified by the rest of the name of the property—enter, exit, and so on.

SpecialEffect

This property is used to specify whether special formatting will apply to a section or control using the following settings, per Microsoft Help documentation:

Setting	Description
Flat	The object appears flat and has the system's default colors or custom colors that were set in Design view.
Raised	The object has a highlight on the top and left and a shadow on the bottom and right.
Sunken	The object has a shadow on the top and left and a highlight on the bottom and right.
Etched	The object has a sunken line surrounding the control.
Shadow	The object has a shadow below and to the right of the control.
Chiseled	The object has a sunken line below the control.

This property affects related properties for BorderStyle, BorderColor, and BorderWidth.

TabIndex

This property is used to specify a control's place in the tab order on a form as an integer representing the position of the control (anywhere from 0 to the total number of controls minus 1).

TabStop

The TabStop property is used to specify whether a control can receive the focus in Form view. TabStop does not apply to check boxes, option buttons, or toggle button controls, and it uses the following settings, per Microsoft documentation:

Setting	Description
Yes	(Default) You can move the focus to the control by pressing the Tab key.
No	You can't move the focus to the control by pressing the Tab key.

Tag

This property is used to store any extra information (in the form of a string expression up to 2,048 characters long) about a control needed by your application.

Top

The Top property works in conjunction with Left to specify an object's location on a form or report as distance measured from the top border to the top edge of the section containing the control.

Verb

This property is used to specify the operation to perform when an OLE object is activated, which is permitted when the control's Action property is set to acOLEActivate.

Visible

This property is used to show or hide a control, and uses the following settings, per Microsoft documentation:

Setting	Description
Yes	(Default) The object is visible.
No	The object is not visible.

Width

This property is used in conjunction with Height to size an object to specific dimensions.

Using Events

The following events in Access apply to Custom Controls:

▶ Enter

▶ Exit

▶ GotFocus

▶ LostFocus

▶ Updated

These are described in the following sections.

Enter

This event occurs prior to a control receiving the focus from another control on the same form, and is not applicable to check boxes, option buttons, or toggle buttons.

Enter events occur prior to focus, and thus can be useful in displaying instructions to users prior to their performing any actions.

Exit

This event occurs before a control surrenders focus to another control on the same form, and is not applicable to check boxes, option buttons, or toggle buttons.

GotFocus

GotFocus occurs after Enter, when a control receives the focus. To use it, the control must be both visible and enabled.

GotFocus occurs every time a control receives focus, whereas with Enter, it is only on the first occurrence.

LostFocus

This event occurs when a control (which must be visible and enabled) loses the focus.

LostFocus occurs every time a control loses the focus, whereas Exit occurs only before a control loses the focus to another control on the same form. In logical order, LostFocus occurs after Exit.

Looking at the four events as they relate to one another, the logical operating order is as follows:

1. Enter

2. GotFocus

3. Exit

4. LostFocus

Updated

This event occurs when the data for an OLE object has been modified and applies only to controls on a form, not controls on a report.

Key Terms and Concepts

Table 9.1 identifies key terms from this chapter. Review the key terms and make sure that you understand each term for the exam.

Table 9.1

Key Terms: Custom Controls

Term	Covered in Section…
Custom Controls	"Customizing OLE Controls"
Registering	"Customizing OLE Controls"
Properties	"Setting Properties for Custom Controls"

Review Questions

1. Custom Controls are added to Access via which menu?

   A. File

   B. Tools

   C. Controls

   D. Help

2. Which of the following properties specifies that a control should appear as a dotted line?

   A. BorderColor

   B. BorderStyle

   C. BorderWidth

   D. Class

3. Which event occurs first for a control when first accessing it?

   A. Enter

   B. Exit

   C. GotFocus

   D. Updated

4. Which property is a string expression identifying the control itself?

   A. Class

   B. Object

   C. Name

   D. Tag

5. Which property is a string expression containing extra information about the control?

A. Class

B. Object

C. Name

D. Tag

Answers to Review Questions

1. B is correct. To add Custom Controls to Access, go to the Tools menu and select Custom Controls. For more information, refer to the section "Customizing OLE Controls."

2. B is correct. BorderStyle properties define the type of border placed around the control. For more information, refer to the section "Setting Properties for Custom Controls."

3. A is correct. The Enter event takes precedence over all others. For more information, refer to the section "Setting Properties for Custom Controls."

4. C is correct. The Name property identifies the control. For more information, refer to the section "Setting Properties for Custom Controls."

5. D is correct. The Tag property is used to hold additional information about a control. For more information, refer to the section "Setting Properties for Custom Controls."

Answers to Test Yourself Questions at Beginning of Chapter...

1. The Locked property keeps the control from being updated. For more information, refer to the section "Customizing OLE Controls."

2. Custom Controls have an extension of OCX. For more information, refer to the section "Setting Properties for Custom Controls."

C h a p t e r 10

Using Windows DLLs

By the end of this chapter, you will be able to perform the following test objectives:

 Objectives

▶ Properly declare Windows API functions

▶ Use the ByVal and ByRef keywords

Test Yourself! Before reading this chapter, test yourself to determine how much study time you will need to devote to this section.

1. If you need to use a DLL throughout your entire program, should you specify the Declare statement as Public or Private?

2. Which option argument in the Declare statement enables the user to call the function in the VBA code by another name?

3. If the location path is not included in the Declare Statement, which order will Windows use to search for the DLL: the current directory, the Windows System directory (Windows\System), the directory from which the application is loaded, or the Windows directory (Windows\)?

4. If a DLL is returning a value, should the Declare Function or Declare Sub format be used?

5. There are two ways to pass arguments to a DLL: by value or by reference. Which one copies the actual value of what is being passed onto the memory stack?

6. The sub or function name in the Declare statement is referred to as what?

7. Windows has two ways of storing strings: BSTR and LPSTR. Except for the calls that deal with OLE, which one does Windows API use?

Answers are located at the end of the chapter...

This chapter discusses how to properly use Dynamic Link Libraries (DLLs) from VBA procedures. DLLs are powerful functions and procedures used to manipulate Windows. These functions are collectively called the *Windows API.*

> The *Application Programming Interface* (API) provides a method by which a program can access or modify the Windows operating system. In 32-bit Windows there are about 1,000 functions provided by DLLs. Programmers call them *hooks.*

Calling a DLL from a procedure enables you to perform tasks that are otherwise extremely difficult, if not impossible, with VBA alone. For example, VBA has no internal function that can determine the amount of system resources available; however, this can easily be done with the Windows API.

This chapter helps you understand the procedures in DLLs and the arguments to each of those procedures. In order to make a call to the Windows API, you need to understand the documentation for the DLL. Because DLLs were originally designed to be called from C or C++, most of the documentation is written in terms of calling functions from C or C++. In addition, you need to learn how to translate the terminology from the C environment into the VBA environment. This can take some time, but it is well worth it. Learning how to properly construct and use DLLs will help you develop more power and flexibility with Access. It will also help you prepare for this topic in the certification exam.

Remember, there have been entire books written that cover the DLL topics. This chapter gives you a solid foundation on which to take the exam.

Declaring Windows API Functions

Before calling a function in a DLL, you must provide a Declare statement in the General Declarations section of a module. This tells VBA where to find the function and how to call it.

Following are two examples of a Declare statement:

```
Public Declare Function WinHelp Lib "User32" Alias "WinHelpA" _
(ByVal hwnd As Long, ByVal lpszHelp As String, _
ByVal uCommand As Integer, dwData As Any) As Long

Private Declare Function GetWindowText Lib "User32"
(ByVal hwnd As Long, ByVal lpString As String
ByVal cch As Long) As Long
```

Note When creating a DLL, you can use a file called a *type library*. A type library describes the procedures within the DLL and is registered with the OLE component of Windows. A type library file can be identified because it has the extension .OLB or .TLB. Once a type library is registered within the Windows Registry, there is no need to use Declare Statements. The type library includes all the functionality of the Declare statement. However, the Windows API does not have a type library. You *must* use Declare statements to call the Windows API.

When you first start calling the DLLs, you won't need to construct the Declare statements. Fortunately, these statements have been constructed for you. You can get them from some source, such as the WIN32API.TXT. This file, which Access provides, has all the Declare statements and the definitions of certain constants and user-defined type declarations.

Tip The Microsoft Access Developer's Toolkit comes with a tool named the API Text Viewer. It provides the Declare statements and other definitions you need. This tool searches the WIN32API.TXT and finds the proper Declare statement for the function that you want to use.

Six pieces of information should be included about the procedure contained within the Declare statement:

▶ The scope of the declaration

▶ The name of the procedure that you define your code to call

▶ The name and path containing the DLL

▶ The name of the procedure as it exists within the DLL

▶ The number and data types of the arguments necessary for the procedure

▶ If the procedure is a function, the data type of the return value of the function

When VBA has this information, it is able to find the function on the hard disk and organize the arguments on the stack so that they are acceptable to the DLL. Programs use the *stack*, which is simply a segment of memory, to store temporary data. When a DLL function is called, VBA manipulates the arguments, and then places those argument onto the stack. When processing has completed, the return value is then placed back onto the stack to be returned to your program.

Before you start defining a Declare statement, it must exist at the module level. You should also be aware that defining a VBA Declare statement is similar to that of any other sub or function, except that there is no body to the procedure. The body of procedures exists in the DLL. Once the Declare statement has been specified, you can use the procedure as though it were an intrinsic part of VBA.

The Declare statement determines what the DLL function arguments mean and defines the sizes of those arguments. It is extremely important that appropriate information is given to the DLL function. If incorrect arguments are given to the DLL a General Protection (GP) fault can occur. If a GP fault occurs, Access crashes without allowing object saving.

The following examples show the two types of Declare statements. One Declare statement doesn't return a value:

```
[Public ¦ Private] Declare Sub subname Lib "libname"
[Alias "aliasname"] [([argumentlist])]
```

The second example does return a value:

```
[Public ¦ Private] Declare Function functionname Lib "libname"
[Alias "aliasname"] [([argumentlist])] [As type]
```

Tip

> If a function returns a value, you should use the Declare Function format. If the function does not return a value or the return type isn't necessary, you should use the Declare Sub format of the Declare statement.

Specifying Public or Private

The first clause of the Declare statement is the scope at which other procedures can call the DLL. The rules are as follows:

- ▶ If you prefix the Declare statement with the word Private, you can call only the procedure within the same form or module.

- ▶ If the Declare statement is prefixed with the word Public, you can call a DLL function from any form or module.

- ▶ If you declare a DLL procedure in a standard module without using either Public or Private, it is Public by default and can be called anywhere in your application.

- ▶ A Declare statement in a module can have either Public or Private scope.

- ▶ A Declare statement in the General Declarations section of a form can have only the Private scope.

Specifying the Procedure Name

The sub or function name in the Declare statement is the name used when you call it in your VBA code. The procedure name must follow the same Microsoft naming rules that apply to any VBA procedure name. The Microsoft naming rules are as follows:

- ▶ It must begin with a letter.

- ▶ The other characters must be in the sets A-Z, a-z, 0-9, or an underscore character.

- ▶ It must be unique within the same scope.

▶ It cannot be longer than 255 characters.

▶ It cannot be a VBA keyword.

 Note The name of the procedure in your application must match the name of the function in the DLL if an Alias clause isn't specified. If the name in your VBA code doesn't match the name specified in your declaration, a run-time error will occur.

Specifying the Lib

The third clause of the Declare statement is the Lib section. The Lib section tells VBA the DLL's name. The Lib section can also instruct VBA as to the actual location of the DLL, if specified. The Lib name of the DLL must be enclosed in quotes and is not case-sensitive. If you are declaring one of the functions of the main Windows DLL, you do not have to include the .DLL extension. For instance, you can use "User32," "GDI32," or "Kernel32." VBA appends the .DLL extension to these names. For other DLLs, however, you must include the DLL name and extension.

Windows searches in the following order for the DLL if the location is not included in the Lib section:

1. The directory from which the application loaded (for Access, that's the directory from which Access is loaded, not the directory where your MDB is stored)

2. The current directory

3. Windows NT only: the 32-bit Windows system directory (Windows\System32)

4. The Windows system directory (Windows\System)

5. The Windows directory (Windows)

6. The directories that are listed in the PATH environment variable

Specifying the Alias

The Alias clause enables you to change the name of the function in VBA from how it was originally specified in the DLL. An Alias clause may or may not be included when you declare a procedure. There are several reasons why you might include an Alias clause in the Declare statement.

▶ **Reason 1: To change the procedure name in the DLL to one VBA permits.** The power of using DLLs is that it enables you to use DLLs written in the C programming language. However, the C language allows for function names that can be different from those that VBA allows. VBA functions must begin with a letter and consist of alphanumeric or underscore characters. C function names usually begin with an underscore. An alias should be used when a Declare statement doesn't contain a valid VBA function or follow the standard VBA naming conventions.

You should also use an alias if the name in the Declare statement conflicts with a reserved word in VBA or conflicts with a declared global variable or function.

The following example shows an alias being implemented, since VBA does not allow function names to begin with a leading underscore:

```
Declare Function lread Lib "kernel32" Alias "_lread"
(ByVal hFile As Long, lpBuffer As Any,
ByVal wBytes As Long) As Long
```

▶ **Reason 2: To change the case sensitivity of the DLL function.** When working with Declare statements, you need to remember that the name of the procedure is case-sensitive. This means that when we reference the DLL in our code it must exactly match the case of the procedure name as defined in the Declare statement. You can use an Alias clause in the Declare statement, however, if you want the procedure name in your code to use a different capitalization than that in the DLL.

This wasn't the case in 16-bit Windows, and is something you should be aware of if you are working with Declare statements in old 16-bit code. It is also important if you want to convert this old code.

To support the changes in a 32-bit Windows environment, there are four things to remember when converting 16-bit to 32-bit Windows in the Declare statement.

▶ Calls may simply need to reference the Windows32 libraries instead of the Windows16 libraries.

▶ Calls may not be supported under Windows32.

▶ Calls may have a new extended version or functionality. (For example, GetWindowExt has a new extended version, GetWindowExtEx.)

▶ **Reason 3: To set the procedure name exposed by ordinal.** A DLL may or may not contain a number of different functions. A unique number called an *ordinal* is assigned to every function in a DLL.

Functions within a DLL can expose their names. Whether or not the procedures that exist within the DLL can be called from code existing outside the DLL is determined by how the code was written. If a function can be called outside, it is said to be *exposed.* A DLL is not required to expose every function.

To call a function by its ordinal, you must know the ordinal number for the function. If any documentation exists for the DLL, you can add this information there or in the .DEF file for the DLL. There are also tools available that can examine the DLL and report the ordinal. To call a DLL by its ordinal, specify the #ordinalnumber for the alias name. You must include the pound sign followed by the decimal number of the ordinal. For example, the same lread declaration presented earlier in the chapter might be declared as follows:

```
Declare Function lread Lib "kernel32" Alias "#25" _
(ByVal hFile As Long, lpBuffer As Any,
ByVal wBytes As Long) As Long
```

Because later versions of the DLL may not use the same ordinal for the function but most likely will keep the same name, calling the function by its name is recommended.

▶ **Reason 4: Renaming of functions.** As discussed previously, the alias can be used to do any renaming of functions. This is commonly used to rename the ANSI Windows API calls that have a trailing "A" to the same name, simply without the "A."

▶ **Reason 5: To have a unique Access library procedure name.** It is important to remember that each declared function at any defined level of scope in VBA must have a unique name. If this isn't the case, problems will occur.

Here's an example. Let's say your library calls the GetUser-Name() Windows API call. If you declare the function in the library with a Public scope but do not use an alias, VBA uses the name GetUserName(). If a user then decides to use Get-UserName() in their own code and declares it as Public, the name conflicts with the name in your library. For this reason alone, Public declarations in a library should always use an alias.

This problem usually isn't relative since it's highly unusual for a programmer to give two different functions the same name or declare the same function twice in the code. If you are developing a library database that will be distributed on different systems and that library calls functions in a DLL, however, this becomes a very important issue.

As stated at the beginning of this section, the Alias clause can be used for a number of reasons so that a declared DLL function can be called from VBA code by another name.

Passing Arguments to the DLL Using ByVal and ByRef

Correctly declaring arguments is the trickiest part of using DLLs from VBA. The are two ways to pass arguments on the stack to the DLL: by value or by reference.

As stated in the section titled "Declaring Windows API Functions," you pass arguments to a DLL on the stack. The DLL expects those arguments to have a certain size on the stack and be placed in a particular order. VBA looks to the Declare statement for direction on how to place the arguments on the stack.

The DLL places the arguments on stack. The arguments on the stack appear as a series of bytes. The DLL takes the arguments and groups them. It also decodes those bytes to be used in the specified parameters for these DLL call. If a conflict exists between the VBA Declare statement and the DLL on exactly what those bytes mean, incorrect data appears in the parameters for the DLL call. When a DLL tries to use these parameters, it retrieves the wrong information. Worse yet, if your program doesn't place enough data on the memory stack, the DLL reads the information left over from the previous stack. As you can see, this can cause quite a problem, and as previously mentioned, the dreaded GP faults.

By value means that a copy of the actual value of what is being passed is pushed onto the stack. *By reference* means that the address of what is being passed is pushed onto the stack. The semantic difference between passing by value and by reference is as follows:

▶ When you pass by value, a copy of the value is placed on the memory stack. Any changes to the value inside the DLL affects only the copy and do not change the value for the calling code.

▶ When you pass by reference, the address of the original value is placed on the stack. If the DLL makes changes to the value, the calling code is able to see those changes.

VBA passes all arguments by reference unless indicated otherwise. However, most of the DLLs are written in C, and C passes all arguments by value, unless you tell the DLL to pass its arguments by reference by passing an address.

One thing to remember for the exam is that when working with DLLs, passing a 0% to a DLL procedure by value passes a Null pointer value. An ampersand character after the 0 indicates that the value is of the long type.

With the preceding section taken into consideration, you can see that the VBA Declaration must be set up correctly. All arguments must be defined properly and in the appropriate order to pass the arguments correctly.

Processing Strings Returned from DLLs

The last topic covered in this chapter is returning strings from a DLL.

Using BSTR and LPSTR

Windows has two ways of storing strings: BSTR and LPSTR. All the Windows API calls (except those that deal with OLE) utilize LP-STRs, not BSTRs. A DLL cannot change the size of the LPSTR string, which causes problems when needing to return a value from a string.

Since the DLL cannot change the size of the LPSTR that is passed to it, the string must be large enough to accept the data to be returned before passing it to the DLL. To do this you must fill the string with enough characters to create a buffer for the DLL to fill in. This can be accomplished with the Space$() function. The DLL must not write past the end of the string, since this could result in a GP fault. To protect against this happening, a DLL function that returns a string normally has another argument that specifies how much space should be allocated for the string.

The GetWindowText() function is an example of a Windows function that returns a string. It is passed a handle to a window, then it returns the text associated with the window into a buffer.

The following is a Declare statement for GetWindowText():

```
Declare Function GetWindowText _
Lib "user32" Alias "GetWindowTextA" _
(ByVal hwnd As Long, ByVal lpString As String, _
ByVal cch As Long) As Long
```

When calling GetWindowText(), control is passed into the Windows USER32.DLL. The GetWindowText() function inside the DLL looks up the handle in Windows internal data environment. The API then fills in the lpString parameter with the text associated for the appropriate window. The GetWindowText() is called as follows:

```
Dim strReturnedString As String
Dim intRet As Integer

' Allocate enough space for the return value.
strReturnedString = Space$(255)

' Call the GetWindowsText function
intRet = GetWindowText(Me.hwnd, strReturnedString, _
Len(strReturnedString) + 1)

' Truncate the string down to the proper size
strReturnedString = Left$(strReturnedString, intRet)
```

In this example the Space$() function returns a string of 255 spaces, which is then followed by a Null character. A Null character has the ANSI value 0 and is used in LPSTRs to terminate (end) a string. This enables the user to utilize window captions up to 255 characters.

The code then calls the GetWindowText() function. There are two effects to this call:

- ▶ The contents of strReturnedString is changed to be the caption of the window indicated by the hwnd argument, then followed by a Null character.

- ▶ It returns the length of the string placed into strReturned-String, without counting the terminating Null character.

The string is still 255 characters long. The length recorded in the header information of the VBA string hasn't changed, and memory has not been de-allocated. Since the DLL cannot make the string shorter, you must truncate the string before using strReturnedString, prior to the Null character that GetWindowText() function will tell exactly how many characters should appear in the final string. The Left$() function is then used to truncate the string. If an invalid value for the hwnd argument is passed, Windows returns a value indicating that the API call failed.

If the DLL function you are calling doesn't return a value telling you how many characters are in the string, search for the Null character to determine how long the string should be. The Instr() function is in combination with the Left$() function to accomplish this:

```
strReturnedString = Left$(strReturnedString, _
Instr(1, strReturnedString, Chr$(0)) - 1)
```

You have probably discovered that the GetTextString() example is optional. The same information could be retrieved by using the form's Caption property. The example, GetTextString(), however, does work with any windows in the entire operating system, not just windows in the Access forms.

Using the vbNullString Constant

Sometimes the documentation for a DLL function indicates that a string needs to pass, and sometimes a Null needs to pass. A Null is a 4-byte zero placed directly on the memory stack. The main thing to remember is that passing the vbNullstring constant to a Null can be used.

For example, a Windows API function named SetVolumeLabel() sets the volume label of a file system volume. The following is the Declare statement for the function:

```
Declare Function SetVolumeLabel _
Lib "kernel32" Alias "SetVolumeLabelA" _
(ByVal lpRootPathName As String, _
ByVal lpVolumeName As String) As Long
```

There are two arguments to SetVolumeLabel:

- ▶ LpRootPathName—Points to a Null-terminated string specifying the root directory of a file system volume. This is the volume the function will label. If this parameter is Null, the root of the current directory is used.

- ▶ LpVolumeName—Points to a string specifying a name for the volume. If this parameter is Null, the function deletes the name of the specified volume.

To set the volume label on the C drive to DRIVE_C, execute the following code:

```
fRet = SetVolumeLabel("C:\", "DRIVE_C")
```

To delete the volume label using the method documented on the C drive, you need to pass a Null as the second argument. To do so, execute the following code:

```
fRet = SetVolumeLabel("C:\:, vbNullString)
```

You cannot pass an empty string to the DLL function because it would then pass a pointer to an empty string, which would result in an error on the memory stack.

Key Terms and Concepts

Table 10.1 identifies key terms from this chapter. Review the key terms and make sure you understand each term for the exam.

Table 10.1

Key Terms: Using Windows DLLs	
Term	Covered in Section...
Alias	"Specifying the Alias"
API	"Declaring Windows API Functions"
ByVal	"Passing Arguments to the DLL Using ByVal and ByRef"
ByRef	"Passing Arguments to the DLL Using ByVal and ByRef"
Declare statement	"Declaring Windows API Functions"
DLL	"Declaring Windows API Functions"
Lib	"Specifying the Lib"
Private	"Specifying Public or Private"
Public	"Specifying Public or Private"

Lab Exercises

These Lab Exercises enable you to work with the two objectives covered in the this chapter. These exercises are simple in scope but provide you with some hands-on experience.

Exercise 10.1:   Declaring a Function Using User32.dll to Return a String

This exercise enables you to declare a function that returns a string using the User32.DLL. Please note that this exercise was discussed in detail in the "Processing Strings Returned from DLLs" section.

Objectives:

Properly declare Windows API functions

Use the ByVal and ByRef keywords

Time Estimate: 10 minutes

Steps:

1. With Access running, create a new form.

2. When the new form is opened, select the Code menu option under the View menu.

3. Type the following code in the General Declaration section of the form:

```
Option Compare Database
Option Explicit
Private Declare Function GetWindowText Lib "user32i" _
Alias "GetWindowTextA" (ByVal hwnd As Long, _
➥ByVal lpString As String, ByVal cch As Long) As Long
```

4. Close the form module.

5. Make sure the Form object is selected. Under the View menu, select the Property menu option.

continues

---

6. Type **Test Window** in the Caption property.

7. Close the Properties window.

8. Add a Command button to the form.

9. You now need to add VBA code to the Click event of the Command button. Type the following:

```
Private Sub Command1_Click()
    Dim strReturnedString As String
    Dim intRet As Integer

    ' Allocate enough space for the return value.
    strReturnedString = Space$(255)

    ' Call the GetWindowsText function
    intRet = GetWindowText(Me.hwnd, strReturnedString, _
    Len(strReturnedString) + 1)

    ' Truncate the string down to the to the proper size
    strReturnedString = Left$(strReturnedString, intRet)

    MsgBox strReturnedString
End Sub
```

The screen should look like figure 10.1.

Figure 10.1

API Declaring Test Window.

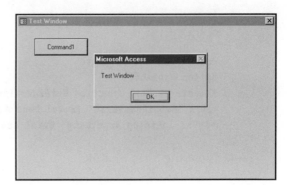

Comments:

The GetWindowText() function is an example of a Windows function that returns a string. You pass it a handle to a window, and it returns the text associated with window into a buffer.

Reading Reference:

For more information about the concepts in the exercise, refer to the sections titled "Processing Strings Returned from DLLs" and "Passing Arguments to the DLL Using ByVal and ByRef."

Exercise 10.2:   Using the Windows API to Perform Clipboard Functions

This exercise demonstrates using the Windows API to perform two Clipboard functions. The first is putting the text on the Windows clipboard, and the second is getting the text from the Windows clipboard.

Objectives:

Properly declare Windows API functions

Time Estimate: 25 minutes

Steps:

1. With Access running, create a new form.

2. When the new form is opened, Select the Code menu option under the View menu.

Type the following code in the General Declaration section of the form:

```
Option Compare Database
Option Explicit

Private Declare Function glr_apiIsClipboardFormatAvailable _
    Lib "user32i" Alias "IsClipboardFormatAvailable" _
    ByVal uFormat As Integer) As Integer

Private Declare Function glr_apiIsClipboardFormatAvailable _
    Lib "user32" Alias "IsClipboardFormatAvailable" _
    (ByVal uFormat As Integer) As Integer

Private Declare Function glr_apiOpenClipboard _
    Lib "user32" Alias "OpenClipboard" _
    (ByVal Hwnd As Long) As Integer
```

continues

```
Private Declare Function glr_apiGetClipboardData _
    Lib "user32" Alias "GetClipboardData" _
    (ByVal uFormat As Integer) As Long

Private Declare Function glr_apiGlobalSize _
    Lib "kernel32" Alias "GlobalSize" _
    (ByVal hMem As Long) As Integer

Private Declare Function glr_apiGlobalLock _
    Lib "kernel32" Alias "GlobalLock" _
    (ByVal hMem As Long) As Long

Private Declare Sub glr_apiMoveMemory _
    Lib "kernel32" Alias "RtlMoveMemory" _
    (ByVal strDest As Any, _
    ByVal lpSource As Any, _
    ByVal Length As Long)

Private Declare Function glr_apiGlobalUnlock _
    Lib "kernel32" Alias "GlobalUnlock" _
    (ByVal hMem As Long) As Integer

Private Declare Function glr_apiCloseClipboard _
    Lib "user32" Alias "CloseClipboard" () As Integer

Private Declare Function glr_apiGlobalAlloc _
    Lib "kernel32" Alias "GlobalAlloc" _
    (ByVal uFlags As Integer, ByVal dwBytes As Long) As Long

Private Declare Function glr_apiEmptyClipboard _
    Lib "user32" Alias "EmptyClipboard" () As Integer

Private Declare Function glr_apiSetClipboardData _
    Lib "user32" Alias "SetClipboardData" _
    (ByVal uFormat As Integer, ByVal hData As Long) As Long

Private Declare Function glr_apiGlobalFree _
    Lib "kernel32" Alias "GlobalFree" _
    (ByVal hMem As Long) As Long

Private Const GMEM_MOVABLE = &H2&
Private Const GMEM_DDESHARE = &H2000&
Private Const CF_TEXT = 1
```

```
'Error return codes from Clipboard2Text
Public Const CLIPBOARDFORMATNOTAVAILABLE = 1
Public Const CANNOTOPENCLIPBOARD = 2
Public Const CANNOTGETCLIPBOARDDATA = 3
Public Const ANNOTGLOBALLOCK = 4
Public Const CANNOTCLOSECLIPBOARD = 5
Public Const CANNOTGLOBALALLOC = 6
Public Const CANNOTEMPTYCLIPBOARD = 7
Public Const CANNOTSETCLIPBOARDDATA = 8
Public Const CANNOTGLOBALFREE = 9
```

3. The ClipboardSetText does the following:

   ▶ It uses the Windows GlobalAlloc() function.

   ▶ It moves the passed-in string into it.

   ▶ It opens the Clipboard.

   ▶ It empties the current contents of the Clipboard.

   ▶ It writes the data onto the Clipboard.

   ▶ It closes the Clipboard.

```
Function ClipboardSetText(strText As String) As Variant
    ' Puts some text on the Windows clipboard

    Dim varRet As Variant
    Dim fSetClipboardData As Boolean
    Dim hMemory As Long
    Dim lpMemory As Long
    Dim lngSize As Long

    varRet = False
    fSetClipboardData = False

    ' Get the length, including one extra for a CHR$(0)
    ' at the end.
    lngSize = Len(strText) + 1
    hMemory = glr_apiGlobalAlloc(GMEM_MOVABLE Or _
        GMEM_DDESHARE, lngSize)
    If Not CBool(hMemory) Then
        varRet = CVErr(CANNOTGLOBALALLOC)
        GoTo ClipboardSetTextDone
    End If
```

continues

```
' Lock the object into memory
lpMemory = glr_apiGlobalLock(hMemory)
If Not CBool(lpMemory) Then
    varRet = CVErr(CANNOTGLOBALLOCK)
    GoTo ClipboardSetTextGlobalFree
End If

' Move the string into the memory we locked
Call glr_apiMoveMemory(lpMemory, strText, lngSize)

' Don't send clipboard locked memory.
Call glr_apiGlobalUnlock(hMemory)

' Open the clipboard
If Not CBool(glr_apiOpenClipboard(0&)) Then
    varRet = CVErr(CANNOTOPENCLIPBOARD)
    GoTo ClipboardSetTextGlobalFree
End If

' Remove the current contents of the clipboard
If Not CBool(glr_apiEmptyClipboard()) Then
    varRet = CVErr(CANNOTEMPTYCLIPBOARD)
    GoTo ClipboardSetTextCloseClipboard
End If

' Add our string to the clipboard as text
If Not CBool(glr_apiSetClipboardData(CF_TEXT, _
    hMemory)) Then
    varRet = CVErr(CANNOTSETCLIPBOARDDATA)
    GoTo ClipboardSetTextCloseClipboard
Else
    fSetClipboardData = True
End If

ClipboardSetTextCloseClipboard:
    ' Close the clipboard
    If Not CBool(glr_apiCloseClipboard()) Then
        varRet = CVErr(CANNOTCLOSECLIPBOARD)
    End If

ClipboardSetTextGlobalFree:
    If Not fSetClipboardData Then
        'If we have set the clipboard data, we no longer own
        ' the object—Windows does, so don't free it.
```

```
            If CBool(glr_apiGlobalFree(hMemory)) Then
                varRet = CVErr(CANNOTGLOBALFREE)
            End If
        End If

ClipboardSetTextDone:
    ClipboardSetText = varRet
End Function
```

4. The ClipboardGetText does the following:

   ▶ Validates that there is some text on the Clipboard that can be read.

   ▶ If text exists, it opens the Clipboard.

   ▶ Retrieves the current contents of the Clipboard.

   ▶ It copies the current contents into a string.

   ▶ It truncates the string to the correct size.

   ▶ It closes the Clipboard.

```
Public Function ClipboardGetText() As Variant
    ' Gets some text on the Windows clipboard
    '

    Dim hMemory As Long
    Dim lpMemory As Long
    Dim strText As String
    Dim lngSize As Long
    Dim varRet As Variant

    varRet = ""

    ' Is there any text on the clipboard? If not, produce error.
    If Not CBool(glr_apiIsClipboardFormatAvailable _
        (CF_TEXT)) Then
        varRet = CVErr(CLIPBOARDFORMATNOTAVAILABLE)
        GoTo ClipboardGetTextDone
    End If

    ' Open the clipboard
    If Not CBool(glr_apiOpenClipboard(0&)) Then
```

continues

```
            varRet = CVErr(CANNOTOPENCLIPBOARD)
            GoTo ClipboardGetTextDone
        End If

        ' Get the handle to the clipboard data
        hMemory = glr_apiGetClipboardData(CF_TEXT)
        If Not CBool(hMemory) Then
            varRet = CVErr(CANNOTGETCLIPBOARDDATA)
            GoTo ClipboardGetTextCloseClipboard
        End If

        ' Find out how big it is and allocate enough space
        ' in a string
        lngSize = glr_apiGlobalSize(hMemory)
        strText = Space$(lngSize)

        ' Lock the handle so we can use it
        lpMemory = glr_apiGlobalLock(hMemory)
        If Not CBool(lpMemory) Then
            varRet = CVErr(CANNOTGLOBALLOCK)
            GoTo ClipboardGetTextCloseClipboard
        End If

        ' Move the information from the clipboard memory
        ' into our string
        Call glr_apiMoveMemory(strText, lpMemory, lngSize)

        ' Truncate it at the first Null character because
        ' the value reported by lngSize is erroneously large
        strText = Left$(strText, InStr(1, strText, Chr$(0)) - 1)

        ' Free the lock
        Call glr_apiGlobalUnlock(hMemory)

ClipboardGetTextCloseClipboard:
        ' Close the clipboard
        If Not CBool(glr_apiCloseClipboard()) Then
            varRet = CVErr(CANNOTCLOSECLIPBOARD)
        End If

ClipboardGetTextDone:
        If Not IsError(varRet) Then
            ClipboardGetText = strText
```

```
    Else
        ClipboardGetText = varRet
    End If
End Function
```

5. Close the form module.

6. Make sure the Form object is selected.

7. Add a text field and call it "txtText."

8. Add the following code (the Lost_Focus and After_update events for txtText field):

```
If Not IsNull(txtText.Text) Then
txtString = txtText.Text
End If
```

9. Add another field to the form below the txtText field and call it "txtPaste."

10. Add a button on the form to the right of the txtText field and call it cmdCopy.

11. You now need to add VBA code to the Click event of the cmdCopy Command button. Type the following:

```
Call ClipboardSetText(txtString)
```

12. Add another Command button to the right of the txtPaste field and call it "cmdPaste."

13. You now need to add VBA code to the Click event of the cmdPaste Command button. Type the following:

```
Dim txtGetPaste As String
    txtGetPaste = ClipboardGetText
    txtPaste.SetFocus
    txtPaste.Text = txtGetPaste
```

14. The screen should look like figure 10.2.

continues

Exercise 10.2: Continued

Figure 10.2

*The Clipboard
API Window.*

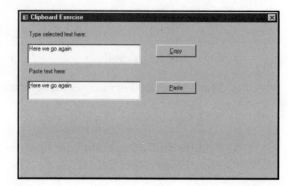

Comments:

The preceding exercise demonstrates the functionality of two
DLL functions. You enter some text in the top text box, txtText.
When you click the Copy button, the text is copied to the Windows Clipboard. When you click the Paste button, the text is then
copied to the txtPaste field.

Reading Reference:

For more information about the concepts in the exercise, refer to
the section titled "Processing Strings Returned from DLLs."

Review Questions

1. What precaution should a programmer take before issuing a call to a Windows DLL procedure that returns a Null-terminated string?

   A. Make sure the string is initialized as empty.

   B. Make sure the string does not already contain the Null character.

   C. Make sure the string is declared as a fixed-length string.

   D. Make sure the string length is 255.

2. Which of the following passes a Null pointer to a C-based DLL procedure?

   A. ByVal Null

   B. By Val ""

   C. ByVal 0&

   D. Dim NullPntr As Inter

      NullPntr = Null

      - - -

      ByVal NullPntr

3. Why would you implement the Alias keyword when declaring a DLL procedure?

   A. If DLL Procedure does not conform the VBA naming conventions

   B. If an undeclared variable is passed to the DLL procedure

   C. If an Object variable is passed to the DLL procedure

   D. If the DLL procedure's name is already being used by another DLL procedure

4. Which statement about passing a string to a DLL procedure written in C is true?

   A. Only a pointer to string is passed to a C-based DLL procedure.

   B. The actual value of a string is passed to a C-based DLL procedure.

   C. A string passed to a DLL procedure cannot be modified by a procedure.

   D. Using the ByVal argument causes the actual string value to be passed.

Answers to Review Questions

1. C is correct. A DLL procedure may write past the end of a string declared in Access. This may corrupt other areas of memory in an Access application. To ensure that a string passed back from a DLL procedure does not exceed its length, it is good idea to declare the returned string with a fixed length (up to 255 characters). To extract the actual data from the string, the Mid function combined with the Len function could be used. For more information, please refer to the section titled "Processing Strings Returned from DLLs."

2. C is correct. Passing a 0% to a DLL procedure by value passes a Null pointer value. The ampersand character after the 0 indicates that the value is of the long type. For more information, please refer to the section titled "Passing Arguments to the DLL Using ByVal and ByRef."

3. D is correct. If a DLL procedure has a non-unique name, it must be declared using the Alias keyword. The DLL procedure then is declared by the alias procedure name instead of its original procedure name. For more information, please refer to the section titled "Specifying the Alias."

4. A is correct. Using the ByVal keyword when passing a string argument specifies that VB should automatically convert the argument to a Null-terminated string. For more information, please refer to the section titled "Passing Arguments to the DLL Using ByVal and ByRef."

Answers to Test Yourself Questions at Beginning of Chapter

1. If you prefix the Declare statement with the word Private, you can call only the procedure within the same form or module. If the Declare statement is prefixed with the word Public, you can call a DLL function from any form or module. For more information, please refer to the section titled "Specifying Public or Private."

2. The Alias clause enables you to change the name of the function in VBA from how it was originally specified in the DLL. You can then call the function by the alias name. For more information, please refer to the section titled "Specifying the Alias."

3. If the path is not included on the DLL name, Windows uses the following order to search for the DLL:

   ▶ The directory from which the application loaded (for Access, that's the directory from which Access is loaded, not the directory where your MDB is stored)
   ▶ The current directory
   ▶ Windows NT only: the 32-bit Windows system directory (Windows\System32)
   ▶ The Windows system directory (Windows\System)
   ▶ The Windows directory (Windows)
   ▶ The directories listed in the PATH environment variable

   For more information, please refer to the section titled "Specifying the Lib."

4. If a function returns a value, use the Declare Function format. If the function does not return a value or the return type isn't necessary, use the Declare Sub format of the Declare statement. For more information, please refer to the section titled "Declaring Windows API Functions."

5. By value means that a copy of the actual value of what is being passed is pushed onto the stack. By reference means that the address of what is being passed is pushed onto the stack. VBA passes all arguments by reference unless it is told otherwise. For more information, please refer to the section titled "Passing Arguments to the DLL Using ByVal and ByRef."

6. The sub or function name in the Declare statement is the procedure name used when you call it in your VBA code. It is the name of the DLL you are accessing through the Windows API. For more information, please refer to the section titled "Specifying the Procedure Name."

7. Windows has two ways of storing strings: BSTR and LPSTR. All the Windows API calls (except those that deal with OLE) utilize LPSTRs, not BSTRs. A DLL cannot change the size of the LPSTR string, which causes problems when needing to return a value from a string. For more information, please refer to the section titled "Using BSTR and LPSTR."

Chapter 11

Database Replication

By the end of this chapter, you will be able to execute the following test objectives:

 Objectives

- ▶ Identify the advantages of using replication for synchronization

- ▶ Use Visual Basic for Applications, Microsoft Access, Briefcase, or Replication Manager to make a database replicable

- ▶ Understand how to keep objects local

- ▶ Understand the different synchronization topologies

- ▶ Use Replication Manager to manage a synchronization schedule

- ▶ Identify the changes that the Microsoft Jet database engine makes when it converts a nonreplicable database into a replicable database

- ▶ Explain the purpose of the ReplicationID

- ▶ Explain how Replication Manager resolves synchronization conflicts, synchronization errors, and design errors

Test Yourself! Before reading this chapter, test yourself to determine how much study time you will need to devote to this section.

1. What are some advantages to using replication to synchronize databases, as opposed to using file synchronization or to writing custom code to update database changes?

2. What are the four different ways you can make a database replicable?

3. You're responsible for designing a replicable Access application for a group of salespeople who are wonderful salespeople but not terribly advanced computer users. Which replication method should you use?

4. How can you schedule synchronization?

5. What noticeable changes does Access make to a database when it becomes replicable?

6. How does Access make sure that it updates the correct record?

7. What is the difference between a synchronization conflict and a synchronization error?

8. What is the simplest way to resolve synchronization conflicts?

Answers are located at the end of the chapter...

Database replication involves the Windows 95 Briefcase and the Replication Manager from the Access Developer's Toolkit (ADT).

 Warning

> If you don't have the Windows 95 Briefcase installed, or if you don't have a copy of the ADT, or if you are not on a computer configured to share network files, you cannot complete the exercises at the end of the chapter.

This chapter attempts to thoroughly demonstrate the use and interface of the Windows 95 Briefcase and the Replication Manager, but if you have never experienced these tools first-hand, it is more difficult for you to answer replication questions at the time of the Exam.

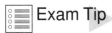 **Exam Tip**

> As you read this chapter, you learn about each Database Replication Exam objective. If you are reading this chapter only to study for the exam (and not to teach yourself to actually *do* database replication), the reading is more important than the exercises.
>
> Exam questions about replication (usually 2–3 per exam) tend to be factual rather than conceptual. In other words, the exam questions most likely ask you facts about types of application that make good candidates for replication, changes made to a replicable database, replication methods, or synchronization conflict resolution. Most likely, the exam will not give you a situation and ask you to choose the best replication solution.

Making the Most of Synchronization

 **Objective**

In many situations database replication is the best choice for keeping databases in multiple locations synchronized with one another. The most obvious and prevalent example of the need for database replication and synchronization occurs in companies with mobile sales forces, where people in many locations need to access the same data. Other examples include reservations systems, stock market or warehouse inventory updates, and trade-show order-entry systems.

Rather than using automated replication you can also use code to synchronize databases, with which you can check for changes between databases. Writing such code, however, is a very time-consuming process, and any object that is not thoroughly checked can cause a non-synchronized database. Another alternative to replication is *file synchronization*, which you usually do manually to save automation costs, where the system compares two files with the same name, and the file that has been changed most recently entirely overwrites the other file. File synchronization is not a sophisticated or flexible process because it cannot recognize or handle simultaneous modifications to multiple copies of the same file. Whichever file was modified last becomes the existing copy, and you lose all changes in the other file.

Synchronization is the process of keeping two or more databases up-to-date with each other, so their data and design are the same. (Exceptions with Local Objects are discussed in the section "Keeping Objects Local.")

Database replication is a technology that enables you to make multiple copies of a database and ensure that changes in data and changes in design are synchronized throughout all copies. This chapter focuses on database replication through Microsoft Access and the Replication Manager included in the Access Developer's Toolkit (ADT).

Access performs replication by making one database the *Design Master*. Each additional copy of the database is called a *replica*. Together, the Design Master and all the replicas are called the *Replica Set*, so changes are replicated across the Replica Set.

Replication is a very good solution for many situations, but sometimes it is not advisable. The following few sections of this chapter address system needs, so you can recognize whether or not replication is recommended for each situation.

Sharing Data Among Locations

Any company with multiple satellite offices in other locations faces the challenge of sharing data among locations—sometimes hundreds or thousands of miles away from one another. The ideal solution is to install a wide-area network (WAN) that is constantly available and never crashes when you connect the various offices. However, redundant, fault-tolerant WANs are an expensive proposition. In many cases, the affordable choice is to have a copy of the company database at each location. Users can then access data on local-area networks (LANs).

You can use database replication to create the database copies (replicas) for each company location. A common example is the names, addresses, and primary contacts of customers; each location has local contacts as well as company-wide contacts. In this example, each remote office needs to update data in their replicas (company-wide contacts in their region whose information changes). The updated data can be synchronized with the replica at the main data center. Because local contacts do not need to be replicated company-wide, however, each office's replica can have local tables with information that is not synchronized company-wide.

Sharing Data Among Dispersed Users

Many companies have remote locations, and many companies also have "Road Warriors"—employees dispersed over a wide area; many of whom travel frequently; all of whom need up-to-date data on their machines. These Road Warriors cannot always remain connected to the company's main network. Once again, the most affordable solution is to provide each mobile employee with a replica of the database for her laptop.

Database replication enables mobile users to update and add data to any replica of the database from any location. Then the replica can be synchronized with data at the company's data center anytime the mobile employees establish an electronic connection with the company's network. Depending on the number of changes that occur each day, a company policy can stipulate that mobile employees dial into the network at the beginning or end of each day to synchronize their replicas. That way, the employees always have a current version of the data.

Synchronizing Data for Single Users

Users can easily have both an office computer and a home computer—or a laptop and a desktop computer—and want to keep information current between the two computers. The databases in such a situation need to be synchronized, and replication is a very straightforward solution for such a limited number of users and changes.

Reducing Server Load for Faster Data Access

Traditionally, many companies used large, centralized mainframe databases to manage their data resources. To ensure security control and data integrity, the mainframe solution limited access to different segments of the mainframe. Today, however, with the cost of local-area servers decreasing, and the computer expertise of an average employee growing, many companies are decentralizing both their data and their information services staffing resources. Therefore, the demand is growing to share more data across more locations and departments.

Having a second or third server with separate replicas of company data relieves the demand on any individual server, and the plan also improves the user's processing time to access data by reducing the server's response time. The challenge in such a situation is keeping multiple copies of the database synchronized. Although database replication is not ideal for all situations, database replication can be a cost-effective solution to evenly distribute network traffic across servers. Then groups of users can connect to separate replicas. For example, salespeople can use one server to access contact information, and the accounting department can use another server to process invoices and payments.

The ideal situation for using replication to balance traffic across multiple servers is in databases in which the data is mostly stable, such as pricing information that changes occasionally, or data on customer history that never changes. You don't need to update such databases in real time, but you do need to update the data on a regular basis. You can appropriately adjust the synchronization schedule for replicas.

Distributing Updates to Applications

Although the primary justification for database replication is to inexpensively synchronize data among end users, database replication is also an inexpensive and powerful way to distribute updates to an Access application. When two databases synchronize, the database automatically synchronizes both the data and also the application objects, routines, and modules. Because design changes can be made only in the Design Master of a Replica Set, the database administrators must keep the Design Master under their control. This gives the administrators the ability to make any changes to the design of the database and then during the next synchronization, the changes transmit. Administrators no longer have to distribute entirely new versions of the software.

Backing Up Data

Database replication is not the same as merely copying a database. The difference is that the replica does not have to be replaced with a whole new file whenever the database changes—instead the replica needs to synchronize with the original at regular intervals. You can, of course, use the replica as a backup database if the original database is destroyed, and the data and design are valid since the last synchronization. Another advantage to using replication for backing up data is that users at any replica can access the database during the backup process.

Situations in Which Not to Use Replication

Although database replication is the best solution for many problems in distributed data processing, data replication is not the best solution in several situations. Applications that process a large number of transactions per record or that require instantaneous data consistency probably need a centralized database.

Synchronizing Large Numbers of Updates at Many Replicas

Synchronization conflicts occur when users make two or more changes to a single record from separate replicas. Any application that constantly updates existing records from multiple replicas is likely to cause a large number of conflicts. Because you need to manually resolve conflicts, they require a lot of resources and time. On the other hand, an application that mostly adds new records to a database is much less likely to cause conflicts. An example of data changing from separate replicas is a team project management system where team members constantly revise target dates, percent complete, and budget details.

The more likely that two changes will be made to the same record from different replicas (even if the changes are to different fields within the record), the more likely that synchronization will result in record conflicts and will require more time to resolve.

Immediately Synchronize Critical Data

Applications that update critical, rapidly changing data usually use a transaction method to update data. Some examples of up-to-the-minute data are airline reservations and banking transactions. Access does not support transactions across replicas, which means that Access processes a transaction only one replica at a time. If the transaction caused a conflict with any other replicas, Access may take two passes through the entire synchronization process to ensure that any one transaction has been replicated to all other replicas in the Replica Set.

Choosing the Appropriate Replication Method

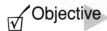 Objective

Microsoft provides programmers and users four ways to replicate and manage a database: Access Replication, Briefcase Replication, ADT Replication Manager, and DAO programming. The first three replication tools provide an easy-to-use visual interface, while the last enables programmers to build replication into their application without requiring any special skills or extra knowledge from end users.

Replication can be used on a variety of computer networks, including Windows 95 peer-to-peer networks, Windows NT (3.51 and later), and Novell® NetWare® (3.x and later) servers.

No matter which tool you choose, four activities need to take place:

▶ Converting a database into a replicable database

▶ Making additional replicas

▶ Synchronizing replicas

▶ Resolving synchronization conflicts

Some tools offer additional functionality as well, as you will discover in the upcoming sections.

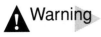 Warning

The Jet Engine does not enable you to password-protect a replicable database. Therefore, before you attempt to convert any database into replicable form, make sure you remove password protection from the database. User-level security, where individual users from a workgroup have different assigned permissions, is still permitted, and the security does not interfere with replica synchronization.

Microsoft Access Replication

Microsoft Access for Windows 95 provides a user-friendly interface for replication. From the Tools menu, you choose Replication and have a choice of the following options:

▶ **Synchronize Now.** Synchronizes the open replica or Design Master with another member of the Replica Set.

▶ **Create Replica.** Creates a replica of the open database at a designated location.

▶ **Resolve Conflicts.** Starts the Conflict Resolver, which displays records that were in conflict during previous synchronizations.

▶ **Recover Design Master.** Makes the open replica the Design Master for the Replica Set.

After you have a database open, the only Replication menu choice available is Create Replica. After you create a replica (just answer the questions from the wizard), you have a Design Master. With the new Design Master open, you can choose Create Replica again to create another replica in the Replica Set. Synchronize Now and Resolve Conflicts are also self-explanatory step-by-step processes.

If you have a replica open (not the Design Master) and choose Recover Design Master, the open replica becomes the Design Master. You should never have a Replica Set with more than one Design Master, or synchronization cannot succeed throughout the Replica Set. You need only to Recover Design Master if the Design Master becomes irreparably corrupted or damaged in some other way.

Windows 95 Briefcase Replication

Windows 95 includes the Briefcase, a tool that you can use for Access database replication. To use Briefcase replication, drag the database file from the Windows 95 Explorer to the My Briefcase icon. For example, if you work on a laptop PC that is connected to your desktop PC, open Windows Explorer, find the database file from the desktop PC, and drag the file to the Briefcase icon on the laptop. Then you can disconnect the two computers and work on the laptop database (open it by double-clicking the Briefcase and then double-clicking the database file in the Briefcase window). When you reconnect to your desktop PC, go to your laptop's Briefcase and click Update All on the Briefcase menu. Update All automatically takes the updates from your laptop Briefcase files and merges the changes to the files on your desktop computer.

This is the simplest form of making a database replicable and includes very little user involvement. The Briefcase does not directly support making additional replicas, but if more than one user drags an original database into their separate Briefcases, all replicas can still synchronize with the original. You need to manage synchronization conflicts from the Resolve Conflicts menu choice inside the Access user interface (choose Replication from the Tools menu and then choose Resolve Conflicts), but in applications with a limited number of users, Briefcase replication may be the best solution.

When you drag your database file with the .mdb extension into Briefcase, the system calls the Briefcase reconciler code to convert the database into a replicable form. First, before the conversion, the reconciler asks whether you want to make a backup copy of the original database file. The backup copy has the same file name as the original, except that it has a .bak file name extension instead of an .mdb file name extension. The copy is in the same folder as the original database file.

The reconciler then converts the database into a replicable form, leaves the Design Master at the source, and places a replica in the Briefcase. The reconciler also gives you the option of putting the Design Master into your Briefcase and leaving a replica on the desktop.

Unlike the Replication Manager utility, Briefcase replication does not enable you to schedule synchronization. Instead, synchronization occurs only when you click the Update command.

Also, replication occurs only between the Briefcase replica and whichever replica you chose at the replication. If you want to synchronize the replica with other members of the Replica Set, you have to manually specify the other replica.

Microsoft Replication Manager Utility (ADT)

The Microsoft Access Developer's Toolkit (ADT) provides Microsoft *Replication Manager,* which is a visual interface for converting databases (from non-replicated to replicated), making additional replicas, viewing the relationships between replicas, and setting the properties on replicas. For simpler replication problems, replication through the Access interface or the Briefcase are powerful enough solutions. However, the Replication Manager is the tool to choose in any of the following situations:

- ▶ **Manage a large number of replicas.** It is much easier to schedule synchronization with multiple members of a Replica Set through the Replication Manager than through the user interface or through the Briefcase.

- ▶ **Support laptop users who connect and synchronize sporadically.** Replication Manager enables such users to specify a network file location where synchronization information is deposited for later processing. The process greatly reduces synchronization time and valuable long-distance connection time.

- ▶ **Create replicas of more than one database.** For example, if you have a code database that connects to a data database, you want to use the Replication Manager to ensure that both .mdb files get synchronized.

- ▶ **Schedule synchronization.** Microsoft Replication Manager provides a graphical user interface for scheduling synchronizations between replicas, as well as enabling on-demand synchronization using a single menu command.

▶ **Customize synchronizations.** Replication Manager enables you to choose whether you want to only send data, only receive data, or to both send and receive data.

▶ **Use additional tools for troubleshooting errors.** Replication Manager provides a wider range of troubleshooting than Access or Briefcase alone. The specific tools are not covered on the exam.

The Replication Manager uses a special tool called the Transporter to monitor changes to a replica and handle synchronization. Each replica is assigned to a Transporter, and usually one Transporter is on each computer that has a replica and a copy of Replication Manager.

The advantage of Transporter synchronization is that the Transporter can perform either direct or indirect synchronizations between two members of a Replica Set. *Direct synchronization* is the type of synchronization that normally occurs when both replicas open simultaneously and synchronize. *Indirect synchronization* occurs when direct synchronization is not possible because one Replica Set member is not available. During indirect synchronization, the Transporter for the first replica leaves messages for the Transporter of the second replica. While the target replica is unavailable, the messages are left in a shared network folder, which stores the messages sent by all other Transporters in the Replica Set. After the target replica becomes available, its Transporter synchronizes with the messages in the shared folder.

To run the Replication Manager Wizard, which converts a regular database to a replicated database, simply launch Replication Manager and choose Convert Database to Design Master from the File menu. From there, wizards take you step-by-step through the process. For more detail on using Replication Manager to schedule synchronizations, refer to the section "Scheduling Synchronization" later in this chapter.

To make additional replicas from the Design Master within Replication Manager, choose the Design Master you want to replicate and then click the Create Replica toolbar button, or choose Create Replica from the File menu. The wizard asks in which folder you want to place the new replica and what you want to name the replica.

You cannot resolve synchronization conflicts from the Replication Manager, but the Transporter Log in the Replication Manager indicates whether a synchronization failed. Therefore, you must regularly check the Transporter Log if you use the Replication Manager.

DAO Replication

DAO (Data Access Objects) programming enables you to directly access the Microsoft Jet Engine. The following Replication tasks are possible through DAO:

▶ Converting a database into replicable format

▶ Making additional replicas

▶ Synchronizing replicas

▶ Keeping objects local

▶ Resolving synchronization conflicts

This section covers the first three functions. For more information about manipulating replication properties, refer to the section "Keeping Objects Local." For more about resolving synchronization conflicts through DAO, refer to the section "Resolving Synchronization Conflicts Through DAO."

Checking the Replicable Status of a Database Programmatically

The process of converting an Access database to replicable form involves changing the Replicable property of the database to "T." The hitch is that databases don't automatically have a Replicable property—usually they do not have a Replicable property until you convert them to a replicable form. When you convert a database through the Access interface, the Briefcase, or the Replication Manager, the tools create the Replicable property and set it to T. However, if you are replicating a database strictly through code, you need to check for (or create) the Replicable property.

The following code returns a value of True if you set the Replicable property of the database to T. The function returns a value of False if the Replicable property does not exist, or if you set the property to F.

```
Function ReplicableIsT(strDBChecking As String) As Integer
  Dim intFound As Integer, dbChecking As Database, X As Integer
  Dim Wrk As Workspace

  On Error GoTo ReplicableIsT_Error
  Set Wrk = DBEngine(0)
  Set dbChecking = Wrk.OpenDatabase(strDBChecking, False)
  'If Replicable property doesn't exist, return False.
  For X = 0 To dbChecking.Properties.Count - 1
    If dbChecking.Properties(X).Name = "Replicable" Then intFound
    ➥= True
  Next X

  If intFound = True Then
    If dbChecking.Properties("Replicable") = "T" Then
      ReplicableIsT = True
      GoTo ReplicableIsT_Exit
    End If
  End If

ReplicableIsT = False
GoTo ReplicableIsT_Exit

ReplicableIsT_Error:
  MsgBox "ERROR " & Err & ": " & Error
    IsReplicable = Err
    GoTo ReplicableIsT_Exit

ReplicableIsT_Exit:
End Function
```

The next section covers how to create and set the Replicable property.

Replicating a Database Programmatically

As noted earlier in the chapter, an Access database is not replicable until the Replicable property is set to T. Most databases, however, do not have a Replicable property at all, so to programmatically replicate a database, you must create and append the Replicable property to the Database object.

Also, just because the database is replicable does not automatically make it a Design Master. Every Replica Set needs to have one and only one Design Master—the first replica created. If you convert a database to replicable form through the Access interface, the Briefcase, or the Replication Manager, the tools automatically set and appropriately recognize the Design Master status. When you replicate through DAO, however, you must make sure to set the DesignMasterID property equal to the ReplicaID property. Then your database is converted and made into the Design Master.

The process of creating the Replicable property is very similar to the process of creating any user-defined property. The following code example creates and appends the Replicable property (if it had not existed), sets the Replicable property to T, and then makes the database into the Design Master:

```
Function MakeReplicable(strDBConvert As String) As Integer
  Dim prpReplicable As Property, dbConverted As DATABASE
  Dim dbOriginal As DATABASE, Wrk As Workspace

  On Error GoTo MakeReplicable_Error
  Set Wrk = DBEngine(0)
  Set dbConverted = Wrk.OpenDatabase(strDBConvert, True)

  'Create - Append - Set Replicable property
  Set prpReplicable = dbConverted.CreateProperty("Replicable",
➥dbText, "T")
    dbConverted.Properties.Append prpReplicable
    dbConverted.Properties("Replicable") = "T"
      'Set DesignMasterID
```

```
      dbConverted.DesignMasterID = dbConverted.ReplicaID
    MakeReplicable = True
    MsgBox "Replication successful!"

    GoTo MakeReplicable_Exit

MakeReplicable_Error:
    MsgBox "ERROR " & Err & ": " & Error
      MakeReplicable = Err
      GoTo MakeReplicable_Exit

MakeReplicable_Exit:
End Function
```

Remember that your database retains all its property settings during the conversion process (all properties other than Replicable).

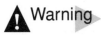

Warning

> Always remember to make a backup copy of your database before replicating it. Usually, nothing goes wrong, but why take that chance?

Making Additional Replicas Programmatically

After you convert your database by using any replication tool, you have a Replica Set with only one member—the Design Master. You can make all subsequent replicas from any other replica, but all members of the Replica Set must have the same Design-MasterID. You create another replica through DAO by using the MakeReplica method. For example:

```
Sub MakeAnotherReplica(strDBReplicateFrom, strNewReplica)
  Dim db As Database, Wrk As Workspace
  Set Wrk = DBEngine(0)
  Set db = Wrk.OpenDatabase(strDBReplicateFrom)
    db.MakeReplica strNewReplica, "Replica of" &
    ➥strDBReplicateFrom
    db.Close
End Sub
```

The MakeReplica method also enables you to make the replica read-only, if you do not want replica users to make any changes to any replicated object, including data. If you want to make the replica read-only, the MakeReplica line of code looks like the following:

```
db.MakeReplica strNewReplica, "Replica of" & strDBReplicateFrom,
dbRepMakeReadOnly
```

But for all other applications where the replica users need the ability to modify data, you don't use the dbRepMakeReadOnly constant.

Synchronizing Replicas Programmatically

You will want to synchronize replicas through DAO in a case in which your application's users are less sophisticated, for instance, because you do not want them to venture into menus or the Replication Manager. You use the Synchronize method and specify the target database file name. The method enables you to synchronize one user's replica with the same replica or with a variety of replicas by changing the target database file name.

You can also customize which replica sends and receives updates, depending on the constant. Exchanges made with the dbRepExportChangesSend constant only send changes from the current database to the target database. Exchanges made with the dbRepImportChangesReceive constant only receive changes from the target database and do not send any changes. Exchanges made with the dbRepImpExpChanges (Default) constant are bi-directional exchanges, because both databases send and receive updates.

The following is an example of a bi-directional exchange:

```
Sub SynchDBs(strDBCurrent, strDBTarget)
  Dim db As Database, Wrk As Workspace
  Set Wrk = DBEngine(0)
  Set db = Wrk.OpenDatabase(strDBCurrent)
    db.Synchronize strDBTarget, dbRepImpExpChanges
  db.Close
End Sub
```

If you choose to synchronize through DAO, chances are good that you will choose to resolve synchronization conflicts through DAO as well. The topic is covered in the section "Resolving Synchronization Conflicts through DAO."

Choosing Microsoft Replication Manager or DAO Replication

The choice between Replication Manager and DAO depends on your needs. Replication Manager is the quickest way to create an entire Replication Set without programming—including scheduling synchronization changes. In many cases, you can do all the replication through Replication Manager, and you do not want end users to be able to create new additional replicas at all.

However, some situations require DAO programming—specifically, when you need event-driven synchronization or when you have less sophisticated users. For example, in a contact management application that records when a salesperson sends a fax, you may want to synchronize any time an urgent fax is sent, so the rest of the sales force knows that the customer has already been contacted. Replication Manager does not support event-driven replication, so you need to use DAO in this case.

If Replication Manager, and perhaps the Briefcase, are beyond the abilities of your users, you must build a "push-button" system, in which any user can do any task from within an Access form. In this case, you need to design a simple replication interface with DAO programs running behind the forms.

Keeping Objects Local

 Objective

By default, every single object in a database is replicated when the database is replicated. However, you choose whether to make any object Local, which means that the object is not replicated or synchronized. Objects have two properties involved in the process of making the object local: the KeepLocal property and the Replicable property.

The KeepLocal Property

When you first convert a database to a replicable form, all its objects become replicable objects—except for objects that have their KeepLocal properties set to "T." Therefore, before you begin the replication process, you must decide whether you don't want to replicate some objects to the entire set. After the database is replicable, you have a more difficult time making the object local.

For each object that you want to keep local before you replicate a database, you need to append and set the KeepLocal property to "T." The KeepLocal property does not exist unless you append it. For example, if your application has a separate table with confidential data, information on strictly local customers, or a listing of local exchange rates, you may want to keep that information only at your replica. You can set the table's KeepLocal property to "T" to keep it local while all other objects are replicated when the database is replicated.

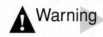 **Warning**

> The fact that you cannot set the KeepLocal property of a table while a relationship exists between that table and another can create complications. Therefore, before you set the KeepLocal property for a table with a relationship to another table, you need to remove the relationship between the tables. Then after you have set the KeepLocal property, you need to add the relationship to the tables and continue converting the database to replicable form.

The following code shows how to check a table to discover whether it already has the KeepLocal property set to "T":

```
Function IsLocal(strTbl As String, strDBCurrent As String) As
➥Integer
  Dim intFound As Integer, TblDef As TableDef, db As Database
  Dim X As Integer, Wrk As Workspace

  On Error GoTo IsLocal_Error
    Set Wrk = DBEngine(0)
    Set db = Wrk.OpenDatabase(strDBCurrent, False)
    Set TblDef = db.TableDefs(strTbl)
```

```
'Check for the existence of the KeepLocal property
For X = 0 To TblDef.Properties.Count - 1
  If TblDef.Properties(X).Name = "KeepLocal" Then intFound =
  ➥True
    Debug.Print TblDef.Properties(X).Name
Next X

If intFound = True Then
  If TblDef.Properties("KeepLocal") = "T" Then
    IsLocal = True
    GoTo IsLocal_Exit
  End If
End If

IsLocal = False
GoTo IsLocal_Exit

IsLocal_Error:
  MsgBox "ERROR " & Err & ": " & Error
    IsLocal = Err
    GoTo IsLocal_Exit

IsLocal_Exit:
End Function
```

For TableDef and QueryDef objects, the KeepLocal property is created and appended to the object's Properties collection. However, on non-data-storing objects (forms, reports, macros, and modules), the KeepLocal property is created and appended to the Properties collection of the Document object representing the object.

For example, the following code sets the KeepLocal property for a form that is located in the Properties collection of the form's Document object:

```
Sub KeepLocalT(db As Database)
  Dim Doc As Document, Prp As Property, Cont As Container

  Set Doc = db.Containers!Forms.Documents![Local Pricing Changes]
  Set Prp = Doc.CreateProperty("KeepLocal", dbText, "T")
  Doc.Properties.Append Prp
End Sub
```

Remember, if you attempt to set the KeepLocal property before it has been appended or inherited, you will generate an error. Even if an object has inherited the KeepLocal property, you must set the property for each object separately.

Here is an example of smart code, which includes an error handler in case the KeepLocal property has not been created and appended. The error handler appends and sets KeepLocal, without sending any message to the user.

```
Sub SmartKeepLocalT(objLocal As Object)
  Const errPropNotFound = 3270
  On Error GoTo SmartKeepLocalT_Error
  objLocal.Properties("KeepLocal").Value = "T"
  GoTo SmartKeepLocalT_Exit

SmartKeepLocalT_Error:
  If (Err = errPropNotFound) Then
    objLocal.Properties.Append objLocal.CreateProperty("KeepLocal",
    ➥dbText, "T")
  End If
  Resume Next
  'Other custom error handling

SmartKeepLocalT_Exit:
End Sub
```

After an object has been made replicable, you cannot apply the KeepLocal property to it. You also must watch the relationships between tables—if two tables have a relationship, either both of them must have KeepLocal = "T" or neither of them can have KeepLocal = "T." If the KeepLocal properties for the two tables are different, the database will not successfully convert to a replicable format.

The Replicable Property

The KeepLocal property applies to objects before you convert the database to replicable form, but the Replicable property applies to objects after the database has been converted. After a database is replicable, all new objects—whether they are created in the Design Master or in another replica—are local objects.

If you have an object in a replicable database that you want to change from local to replicable, you first need to make sure that the object is in the Design Master. If you created the object in another replica that is not the Design Master, you need to export the object to the Design Master and then delete the object from all other replicas—if the object is in another replica, the synchronization fails.

After the object is in the Design Master, set the object's Replicable property to "T." The Replicable property is found in the same place as the KeepLocal property: for TableDef and QueryDef objects, the Replicable property is created and appended to the object's Properties collection. However, on non-data-storing objects (forms, reports, macros, and modules), the Replicable property is created and appended to the Properties collection of the Document object representing the object.

The following code appends the Replicable property for a report—so the property must be appended to the Properties collection for the report's Document object:

```
Sub SetReplicable(db As Database)
   Dim Doc As Document, Prp As Property
   Set Doc = db.Containers!Reports.Documents![Local Pricing
   ➥Report]
   Set Prp = Doc.CreateProperty("Replicable", dbText, "T")
   Doc.Properties.Append Prp
End Sub
```

Also, as with the KeepLocal property, if you attempt to set the Replicable property before it has been appended or inherited, you will generate an error. Even if an object has inherited the Replicable property, you must set the property for each object separately.

Here is an example of smart code, which includes an error handler in case the Replicable property has not been created and appended. The error handler appends and sets Replicable, without sending any message to the user.

```
Sub SmartReplicableT(objLocal As Object)
   Const errPropNotFound = 3270
```

```
On Error GoTo SmartKeepReplicableT_Error
objLocal.Properties("Replicable").Value = "T"
GoTo SmartKeepReplicableT_Exit

SmartKeepReplicableT_Error:
  If (Err = errPropNotFound) Then
    objLocal.Properties.Append objLocal.CreateProperty("Replicable",
    ➥dbText, "T")
  End If
  Resume Next
  'Other custom error handling

SmartKeepReplicableT_Exit:
End Sub
```

After you have set the Replicable property to "T," the next synchronization will cause the object to replicate throughout the Replica Set.

Conversely, if you want to change a replicable object into a local object, set its Replicable property to "F." After an object has a Replicable property, you can also change the value of the property from the object's property sheet in the Access user interface.

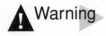 Warning

> When the status of an object changes to local from replicable, the object is deleted from all replicas in the Replica Set except the Design Master. Even if you localize a replicable table temporarily at the Design Master and immediately make it replicable again, the table will still be deleted and re-created from every replica during the next synchronization. You will lose all data entered and updated from all other replicas since the last synchronization. Therefore, it is very important to synchronize all replicas before you make any kind of design change that affects the Replicable property of any object.

When using the Replicable property of a database, after you've converted a database into replicable form, you cannot directly convert it back to a nonreplicable database. The only way to use the database in a nonreplicable form is to create a new, nonreplicable database and export all the objects and data from your replicated database into the new database. The tricky thing is to make sure that you do not export any of the additional system fields, tables, or properties that were added during replication.

Choosing the Appropriate Synchronization Topology

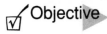 Objective

You must plan the synchronization topology to appropriately update data and design changes throughout the Replica Set. A *topology* is the definition of the relationship between the replicas in the Replica Set, and the definition of the synchronization plan throughout the Replica Set.

Keep in mind when planning a replication topology that the first database you convert becomes the Design Master for your Replica Set, and each Replica Set can have only one Design Master. All design changes, whether a change to the database design or to the design of any replicable object (table, query, form, report, macro, or module) can be done only in the Design Master. This keeps synchronization conflicts to a minimum, and protects the design of a Replica Set from being accidentally altered by someone without proper authorization. Therefore, the Design Master should always be available to the primary database administrator. This also means that while the administrator is working on design changes, she should disable all scheduled or event-driven synchronization until the design changes are complete.

If you use Replication Manager for replication, you create the topology for the Replica Set as you graphically link the replicas in the Replication Manager window. Therefore, it is important to think through the implications of the timing of synchronizations. For example, if Bob's database and Nancy's database synchronize before Nancy's database and Dan's database synchronize, you have a decision to make about whether the next synchronization will be between Bob's database and Dan's database (which have not synchronized directly), or between Bob's database and Nancy's database (which have synchronized directly already). The decision will probably be made dependent on whether or not

Nancy needs more up-to-date information than Bob and Dan, or if all three have the same information demands.

The diagrams in Figure 11.1 show the most common replication topologies.

Figure 11.1

Five common replication topologies.

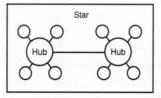 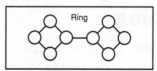
 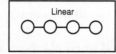 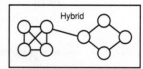

The star topology is the most common, the simplest to implement, and usually the most effective, especially for replicas located on separate servers. As you can see from the hybrid topology, however, any topology can be combined with any other topology, depending upon the needs of the particular system.

Key Concepts

> The replica that initiates and controls synchronization is called the *controlling replica.* Some topologies have multiple controlling replicas; others have only one. The controlling replica can synchronize itself with another replica, or can synchronize two other replicas with one another by using the DAO Synchronize method.

As you plan your synchronization topology, you will need to plan a backup measure in case the controlling replica fails to initiate replication. One common backup measure is to periodically have other replicas check, through the OpenDatabase method, to see if the controlling replica is available. If it is not, the replica that checked can take over as the controlling replica temporarily. Other backup plans include having more than one controlling replica in a Replica Set, or having the controlling replica create a replicated log, which other replicas check periodically.

Star Topology

The *star topology* is a Replica Set in which one hub periodically synchronizes with each of the replicas in its satellite grouping. All data is shared among replicas through a centralized database. The star topology is efficient because it reduces the amount of synchronizations needed to replicate data throughout the Replica Set. With only two rounds of synchronization around the set, you are guaranteed that any given data has updated within every other member of the set. The star topology is especially effective when the volume of changed data to replicate is small.

However, because the hub is involved with every synchronization, the star topology requires that the hub be capable of handling a much greater load than any of the satellite replicas. If you find the load on one hub becoming greater than it can handle, you can create additional stars and have their hubs synchronize with each other, which reduces the load on each individual hub.

The star topology is weakened by the fact that it has a single point of failure—the hub. Therefore, it is critical in a star topology system to create backup measures to reassign the controlling replica through code.

When using the star topology, the Design Master should be at a satellite computer, not at the hub. All design changes must come through the Design Master, and having the Design Master at a satellite allows for greater control over modifications. You will need to test modifications before replicating them, which you would not be able to if the Design Master were also the hub. Also, having the Design Master at a satellite protects it from users at other satellites who have permission to modify the design of database objects.

Ring Topology

In a ring topology with four members, 1 synchronizes with 2, 2 synchronizes with 3, 3 synchronizes with 4, and then 4 synchronizes with 1. The primary advantage of the ring is that each replica's load is approximately equal. Its disadvantage is that data requires more synchronizations to replicate throughout the Replica Set than with the star topology. If it is critical that data be replicated quickly, the ring topology will not be the appropriate choice.

Fail-safe measures need to be implemented in each replica of a ring topology Replica Set because if any of the replicas is unavailable, data will not replicate throughout the Replica Set. This must be handled in code by routing information around the failed replica instead of through it.

Fully Connected Topology

The *fully connected topology* is a Replica Set in which each replica synchronizes with each other replica. One of the primary benefits of a fully connected topology is that data changes replicate quickly throughout the Replica Set. There is no indirect synchronization needed (as is necessary when a replica receives data modifications from a replica that did not initiate the changes) because data updates are sent directly to all replicas. Another advantage to this topology is its high degree of redundancy and reliability. Because each replica is a controlling replica, the impact of computer or replica failure is minimized.

A fully connected topology can be inefficient, however, because it involves a higher number of synchronizations. If network traffic is a precious commodity, you should choose another topology. In a fully connected topology Replica Set, with x number of replicas, there needs to be x times x number of synchronizations—20 replicas would involve 400 separate synchronizations, for example. You definitely should consider staggering replication schedules to reduce the number of simultaneous synchronizations.

Linear Topology

The linear topology is identical to the ring topology, except that the loop is not completed—the first and last replicas do not synchronize with each other. While simple to implement, linear topology requires a high number of synchronizations to ensure that data has been updated throughout the Replica Set.

For example, in a linear topology Replica Set with four members, if a change is made to data in replica 4, it would take six synchronizations, starting at 1, before all other replicas have 4's updates: 1-2, 2-3, 3-4, 1-2, 2-3, 1-2. As a ring topology, in contrast, 1 and 4 would be directly synchronized; it would take only four synchronizations for 4's changes to be fully dispersed: 1-2, 2-3, 3-4, 4-1.

Hybrid Topology

A *hybrid topology* combines elements from at least two topologies to better accommodate the particular situation at hand. A system shared between two departments, such as Human Resources and Order Processing, in which one department needs to share data rapidly and the other needs only infrequent updates is one example. The HR group could be on a ring topology with infrequent synchronizations. Order Processing could be on a star topology with more frequent synchronizations, and the two would connect through the star hub.

Scheduling Synchronization

 When your replication topology has more than one controlling replica, it is a wise choice to stagger synchronization schedules. When two members of a Replica Set both attempt to synchronize with a third member at approximately the same time, one of the synchronizations will succeed and the other will fail. The replica that failed to synchronize will continue to attempt the synchronization. This creates a large amount of network traffic. By using a staggered synchronization schedule, you can greatly reduce the number of times in which the target replica is busy when synchronization is initiated.

Microsoft Replication Manager provides the ability to schedule synchronizations ahead of time so they occur at specific times and can be completed unattended. Replication Manager gives you the greatest control over the order and timetable for synchronization of any Microsoft Jet Database Engine tool. To schedule synchronization, complete the following steps:

1. Launch Microsoft Replication Manager.

2. Select a Replica Set transporter to schedule, and right-click the icon for that transporter. Select Edit Locally Managed Replica Schedule.

3. Edit the Replication Schedule (darkened time slots are chosen for synchronization) by clicking on time slots to toggle between Selected and Not Selected for synchronization. Here is an example of a customized synchronization schedule: the databases in this Replica Set can be set to synchronize Mon-Fri at 6:00 a.m., then again on M-W-F at 10:00 a.m. and T-Th at 11:00 a.m.

4. Click OK.

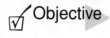 **Tip**

When you schedule synchronizations through the Replication Manager, it is a good idea to make sure that the Transporter is in your StartUp folder. If it is not, you can add the Transporter to your StartUp folder by adding a shortcut to the file MSJTTR.EXE, which is probably located in your Replication Manager shared files, usually at C:\Program Files\Common Files\Microsoft Shared\Replication Manager\MSJTTR.EXE.

Replication Manager's flexibility makes it the right tool to use when you want to reduce network traffic and ensure that all replicas are synchronized within a certain timeframe.

Understanding Replicated Databases

 Objective

When you convert a nonreplicable database into a replicable database, Microsoft Jet makes several significant changes to increase the size of your database by adding fields to each table and adding tables and properties to the database. Jet also changes the way AutoNumber fields function.

Additional Fields in Each Table

In order for Access and the Jet Engine to keep track of updates and changes to data in a replicated database, each table needs a few additional fields: a unique identifier, a generation indicator, and a lineage indicator. All three fields are added as system fields, so they are not normally visible to the user, unless the user has specified not to hide system objects.

Unique Identifier

Each record of each table needs to have a unique identifier that is the same across all replicas of the Replica Set. The field size for this new field, called the s_Guid field, is a 16-byte ReplicationID AutoNumber. The specifics of how the ReplicationID is generated can be found in the section "Understanding the ReplicationID" later in this chapter.

Generation Identifier

Another field that the Jet Engine adds to each table in the database during conversion is called s_Generation. The s_Generation field enables synchronization tools to distinguish records that have been updated since the last synchronization from records that have not been updated since the last synchronization. This speeds the synchronization process by enabling the sending replica to avoid sending records that have not been updated since the last synchronization.

When a record is modified for the first time after it is created or made replicable, its generation is set to 0. Any record with generation 0 is sent during synchronization. Once a generation 0 record has been sent, its generation is incremented to one more than the last generation (which would be 1), which now becomes the new highest generation. The next time it synchronizes, it will send only that record if the generation is higher than 1.

The sending replica knows the last generation sent to that specific receiving replica, and sends only records with generation 0 and generations higher than the previous generations.

In some cases, there is more than one generation field per record. Whenever a record has Memo or OLE Object fields (also called BLOBs, or Binary Large OBjects), more generation fields are added to the record, one for each BLOB. When the BLOB is updated, the generation field associated it is set to 0 so that the BLOB is sent during the next synchronization. If fields other than BLOB are updated, the BLOB generation is not set to 0 and the BLOB is not sent.

BLOB generation fields are named Gen_*xxxx*, where *xxxx* is the first four characters of the BLOB's field name. If this name already exists, the characters are changed one character at a time, until a unique name is found. The ColGeneration property is then added to the BLOB field to identify the name of the BLOB's associated generation field.

Lineage Identifier

The Jet Engine also adds a field named s_Lineage to each table. The s_Lineage field is a binary field that holds a list of nicknames for all the replicas that have updated the record. It also holds the last version created by each of those replicas. Because it is a binary field, it is indecipherable to most users.

Additional System Tables

In order for Access and the Jet Engine to keep track of updates and changes to data in a replicated database, the database needs a few additional tables. Just like the additional system fields, the additional tables are *system* tables, which are not normally visible to users. They also cannot be manipulated by DAO. The following list briefly describes the major tables:

▶ **MsysRepInfo.** Stores Replica Set information, including the ReplicationID of the Design Master. There is only one record in this table, and it is identical for all members of the Replica Set.

▶ **MsysReplicas.** Stores Replica Set information about the individual Replica Set members. This table is identical for all members of the Replica Set.

▶ **MsysTableGuids.** Stores the *Global Unique Identifier (GUID)* associated with table names, which speeds the process of renaming tables. This table also tracks the level number used to order tables to speed updates processing. This table is changed only by the Design Master, because it is concerned with replicable design changes. It is replicated to all other members of the Replica Set.

▶ **MsysSchemaProb.** Stores information about design synchronization errors. This table is local, is not replicated, and does not exist unless a design conflict has occurred between the local replica and another member of the Replica Set.

▶ **MsysErrors.** Stores information about data synchronization errors. This table is replicated through all Replica Set replicas.

▶ **MsysExchangeLog.** Stores information about synchronizations that have occurred between this replica and other replicas in the Replica Set. This is a local table, so it is not replicated.

▶ **MsysSideTables.** Stores the identification of conflict tables, which contain conflicting records, and the tables that experienced the synchronization conflict. This table is local, is not replicated, and does not exist unless a conflict occurs between the local replica and another member of the Replica Set.

▶ **MsysSchChange.** Stores information about design changes. The data in this table is deleted periodically to minimize the size of the table.

▶ **MsysTombstone.** Stores information on deleted records, and enables deletes to be replicated. This table is replicated throughout the Replica Set.

▶ **MsysTranspAddress.** Stores addressing information for all transporters associated with the Replica Set. This table is replicated throughout the Replica Set.

▶ **MsysSchedule.** Stores synchronization scheduling information. The transporter associated with the local replica uses this table to determine when the next synchronization should take place, and whether the exchange will be send only, receive only, or bidirectional.

▶ **MsysGenHistory.** Stores a generation history. This table contains one record for each generation that a replica has come in contact with, either by generating the generation, or by receiving the generation during synchronizaiton. This table is replicated throughout the Replica Set.

▶ **MsysOthersHistory.** Stores a generation history of generations received from other replicas. It contains one generation from every message received from other replicas.

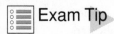 Exam Tip

There is no need to memorize these tables for the exam, but it is a good idea to be vaguely familiar with them. You will need to know about only a few of these tables if you synchronize through DAO. If you synchronize through a synchronization tool, you will never need to access any of the system tables at all.

Additional Database Properties

In order for Access and the Jet Engine to keep track of updates and changes to data in a replicated database, the database needs a few additional properties: Replicable, ReplicaID, and DesignMasterID. Unlike the additional system fields and tables, the additional properties are not system properties: they can be viewed and manipulated.

When the *Replicable* property of a database is set to "T," it is converted to a replicable database. Once that has happened, the Replicable property cannot be changed without causing an error. The *ReplicaID* is a 16-byte value that provides each member of the Replica Set with a unique identification. The *DesignMasterID* property is equal to the ReplicaID of the Design Master for the Replica Set.

It is possible to change this property, making the current replica a Design Master, but be very cautious. No Replica Set can have two Design Masters—this potentially can corrupt your data and partition your Replica Set into two separate, irreconcilable sets. If you absolutely need to reset the DesignMasterID, first synchronize the replica with all other replicas in the Replica Set.

Implications of the Increased Size of Your Database

Because the Jet Engine adds new fields to every table, the limit for the maximum size of a record changes. In a nonreplicable database, the limit is 2,048 bytes, not counting Memo or OLE Object fields. When a database is made replicable, it adds 28 bytes to each record that does not contain Memo or OLE Object fields. For each Memo and OLE Object field, the Jet Engine adds another 4 bytes. This reduces the maximum size allowed per record.

Also, normally there is a limit of 255 fields in a table, and when a database becomes replicable, that number decreases by three for tables without Memo or OLE Object fields. For tables with Memo or OLE Object fields, the maximum number of fields becomes 255 – 3 – 1 for each Memo field – 1 for each OLE Object field.

Perhaps a more common concern is that Microsoft Jet replication limits the number of nested transactions allowed. In a nonreplicable database, you are allowed a limit of seven nested transactions, but a replicated database loses the ability to nest seven transactions—it can nest only six.

Changes to the Behavior of AutoNumber Fields

When a database becomes replicable, all the AutoNumber fields change from incremental to random. AutoNumber fields remain long integers, and all records that were created before the database became replicable retain their values, but new records will have random numbers. This greatly reduces the chances—to the point of eliminating the chances—that two replicas of a Replica Set will both add a record to the same table and generate the same AutoNumber, which would result in a synchronization conflict.

Any time records are sorted by the random AutoNumber field (such as when a table has a random AutoNumber primary key), the records appear in the order of ascending random numbers, not in chronological order. If this causes a problem, you may want to add a date/time field to stamp each record with the date/time it was added.

Understanding the ReplicationID

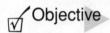 Objective

The ReplicationID occurs in two places: there is one generated for each replica—actually called the ReplicaID—and one ReplicationID AutoNumber generated for each record in the database. The important thing to remember is that the ReplicationID is a 16-byte GUID (sometimes referred to as a UUID, or Universal Unique Identifier), which is *extremely* unlikely to be accidentally reproduced by any other record or replica. The following is an example of a ReplicationID:

{579E172A-C858-11D0-A342-444553540000}

Hyphens and braces are used only for readability, and are not a part of the GUID. A GUID is created from the network NodeID, a time value, a clock sequence value, and a version value. There is absolutely no need to go into each of those elements of the GUID, but if you really want to delve, each element is explained in the Replication white paper—MSJTWTPR.doc—that is installed with the Replication Manager.

Resolving Synchronization Issues

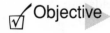 Objective

Three things can go awry when synchronizing replicas: synchronization conflicts, synchronization errors, and design errors.

Synchronization conflicts occur when the same record is modified by two different members of the Replica Set. When the Jet Engine synchronizes the two versions, the overall synchronization succeeds, but the changes are not updated at both replicas. Instead, the changes are updated at one replica, and the other replica stores the conflict to be resolved.

Synchronization errors occur when a data change at one Replica Set member cannot be updated in another replica due to a referential integrity rule or some other table validation or uniqueness rule. The overall synchronization succeeds, but the data remains different at the two replicas, which is more significant than a synchronization conflict.

Finally, *design errors* occur when a design change at the Design Master conflicts with a design change at a replica. The overall synchronization fails, which is more significant than either a synchronization conflict or a synchronization error.

Synchronization Conflicts

When one record has been updated at more than one replica between synchronizations, you experience a synchronization conflict, even if the updates made at one replica are in a different field than the updates made at the other replica. The Jet Engine does not attempt to permanently resolve the conflict, but rather provides a temporary solution. One of the record versions is chosen to be the official version.

The Microsoft Jet Engine chooses which record to accept as the official version by first comparing the version numbers (from the s_Lineage field) of the records from the two replicas. The record with the higher version number is chosen, because it has been altered more times. If the version numbers are identical, the record from the replica with the lowest ReplicaID wins.

The version that lost (the one not chosen to be the official version) is written into a conflict table in the replica that generated the losing record, named table_Conflict, where table is the original table name. The conflict then needs to be resolved by the Access user interface or DAO, which is discussed in the sections "Resolving Synchronization Conflicts Through the Access Interface" and "Resolving Synchronization Conflicts Through DAO."

Resolving Synchronization Conflicts Through the Access Interface

When you synchronize through the Microsoft Access user interface, Access automatically notifies you of synchronization conflicts. The notification occurs each time you open a database with conflicts, including when you open the database directly after synchronization. Access ships with a conflict resolver interface that allows for user-friendly conflict resolution. It automatically displays a list of all tables with synchronization conflicts, and enables the user to choose whether to keep the official version, or to apply the data from the conflict table.

When asked if you want assistance resolving the conflicts, you run the conflict resolver by clicking Yes. You also can run the conflict resolver by starting from the database window, choosing Replication on the Access Tools menu and clicking Resolve Conflicts.

If you don't want to use the default conflict resolver, you can replace it with a custom function instead. You do this by creating a ReplicationConflictFunction property and setting the value to the text string name of the custom function. The custom function must reside in a replicable Design Master module. You cannot replace the default conflict resolver with a function stored in a separate dynamic-link library. The specific steps to replace the Microsoft Access conflict resolver are as follows:

1. Open Access without a database open. From the File menu, choose Open Database.

2. Select the database that has the conflicts you want to resolve using the custom conflict resolver function. Click OK.

3. From the File menu, choose Database Properties.

4. Click the Custom tab.

5. In the Name field, enter **ReplicationConflictFunction** (make certain you do not put spaces between the words).

6. In the Value field, enter the name of the custom function (see fig. 11.2).

Figure 11.2

Set the Database Properties to handle synchronization through DAO.

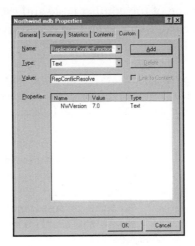

7. Click OK to exit the dialog box.

8. From the Tools menu, choose Replication, and then click Resolve Conflicts. This will start your custom function.

To return to using the default conflict resolver, set the ReplicationConflictFunction property's value to "" (an empty string).

Resolving Synchronization Conflicts Through DAO

If you do not want your users to use the Access interface to resolve synchronization conflicts, you can use DAO. After two replicas synchronize, you will need to review each conflict to determine that the correct information was applied to the database.

You can check to see whether conflicts have occurred for a specific table by checking the ConflictTable property of the table in question, which stores the name of the conflict table containing records that conflicted with the table during synchronization.

Because the default conflict resolver is adequate for almost any situation, it is impossible to generalize why different people use DAO to resolve synchronization conflicts. For that reason, the following example does not actually choose a criteria by which to automatically resolve the conflict. Instead, it simply finds the name of the conflict table and cycles through each conflict record, which would be necessary components of any custom conflict resolver.

```
Sub FincConflicts(db As Database)
  Dim Tdf As TableDef, Rst As Recordset
  For Each Tdf In db.TableDefs
    If (Tdf.ConflictTable <> "") Then
      Set Rst = db.OpenRecordset(Tdf.ConflictTable)
      ' Cycle through each record
      Rst.MoveFirst
      While Not rstConflict.EOF
          ' Put code to specifically handle each conflict here
          ' Delete the conflicting record when finished resolving
          Rst.Delete
          Rst.MoveNext
      Wend
      Rst.Close
    End If
  Next Tdf
End Sub
```

If there is no conflict table, or if the database is nonreplicable, the ConflictTable property returns a zero-length string.

Synchronization Errors

Synchronization errors occur when the synchronization requires some processing function that would violate database or table rules. The following are examples of four sources of synchronization errors:

▶ Table-level validation (TLV) rules

▶ Duplicate unique indexes

▶ Referential integrity

▶ Record locks

Synchronization errors are recorded in the MSysErrors table and replicated to all members of the Replica Set.

When a synchronization error occurs, the two replicas that were attempting to synchronize are no longer in synchronization. This is a dangerous condition, and needs to be addressed as quickly as possible.

Just as Microsoft Access for Windows 95 automatically notifies you of a synchronization conflict each time you open a database with conflicts, it also notifies you of any synchronization errors. The default conflict resolver enables you to review each error and take the appropriate action to correct it.

Table-Level Validation Rules

Each table can have table-level validation (TLV) rules. An example would be a contacts database in which two fields, SourceType and SourceDetail, store information about how that customer found out about your company. You could make a table-level validation rule that says if SourceType = "Other," then SourceDetail cannot be Null. A user would then be forced to enter SourceDetail information whenever SourceType is "Other."

In this example, a TLV conflict could occur if you added the TLV rule after the database became replicable. You would need to change the Design Master to add the TLV rule, and test existing data to ensure that it meets the rule. Then the rule needs to be replicated throughout the set. If someone at another replica in the Replica Set has added or updated records so that those records do not satisfy the new rule, however, when you attempt to synchronize, you will experience a synchronization error.

Synchronization errors are written to the MSysErrors table at the receiving replica. You must correct the invalid data at the replica that does not yet have the TLV rule and then retry synchronization.

Duplicate Unique Indexes

Duplicate unique indexes occur two ways. Users at different replicas might add the same new record with the same values in fields that are indexed uniquely. An example would be if your Employee table had a unique index (primary key or separately created index) that consisted of FirstName, MiddleInitial, and LastName. A synchronization error would occur if two HR users at two replicas both attempted to enter a new record for the same new employee with the same combination of FirstName, MiddleInitial, and Last-Name.

A synchronization error from duplicate Unique Index might also occur if two users change existing records, and both happen to use the same value. In either case, when the replicas are synchronized, the overall synchronization succeeds, but the Jet Engine writes a duplicate key error to the MSysErrors table for each duplicate unique index conflict.

The only way to correct a duplicate unique index error is to change the value of one of the keys or delete a duplicate record.

Referential Integrity

When you enforce referential integrity in your database, you are protecting the relationship between tables when adding or deleting records. An example would be between Employees and Departments: each employee belongs to only one department, each department contains one or more employees, and a department must exist in the Department table before an employee can be assigned to it.

Enforced referential integrity can possibly result in synchronization errors. Using the example above, if a department has not had anyone assigned to it for a while, a user at one replica may decide to delete the department. At the same time, someone else at another replica could decide to assign an employee to that department. This would cause two referential integrity synchronize errors, because the department cannot be deleted from one replica while an employee is assigned at the other. To correct the two errors, you must unassign the employee, temporarily delete the department, synchronize, and then re-create the department and reassign the employee.

Record Locks

If a record is locked when the Jet Engine attempts to synchronize it, Jet retries the update several times. If the record remains locked after repeated attempts, the synchronization fails and an error is recorded in the MSysErrors system table.

This type of error is quite rare, but might occur in certain multiuser applications. There is no need to take action on the error, because it will be handled the next time the two databases synchronize. It is unlikely that the same record will be locked during the next synchronization; at that point, the record updates and the error is removed from the MSysError table.

Design Errors

Ideally, a design error will never occur, because these errors can be time-consuming to resolve. The best way to ensure that they never occur is never to make any changes to the database. Barring that possibility, another option is to enable only the user who controls the Design Master to create any local objects. The Design Master is the only member of a Replica Set that can propagate design changes to existing replicable objects. A design error could occur, however, if the person at the Design Master creates new objects that have the same names as existing local objects at other replicas.

For example, you create a table named EmployeePref that lists the dining preferences of each employee (vegetarian, chicken, and so on) You create this table at the request of Human Resources. Without your knowledge, however, one forward-thinking person in HR has already created a table named EmployeePref, and has started storing information in it. When the design change of a new table EmployeePref attempts to synchronize, the entire synchronization will fail.

The way to resolve this conflict is to delete the local EmployeePref from the replica and retry the synchronization.

Design errors are recorded in the MSysSchemaProb system table. Conflict records in the MsysSchemaProb table are deleted when the synchronization succeeds after the problem is resolved.

Key Terms and Concepts

Table 11.1 identifies key terms from this chapter. Review the key terms and make sure that you understand each term for the exam.

Table 11.1

Key Terms: Database Replication	
Term	Covered in Section...
Synchronization	"Making the Most of Synchronization"
Database replication	"Making the Most of Synchronization"
Design Master	"Making the Most of Synchronization"
Replica	"Making the Most of Synchronization"
Replica Set	"Making the Most of Synchronization"
Local object	"Keeping Objects Local"
Replicable	"DAO Replication"
Topology	"Choosing the Appropriate Synchronization Topology"
ReplicationID	"Understanding the ReplicationID"
Synchronization conflict	"Resolving Synchronization Issues"

Lab Exercises

The exercises for this chapter will be a bit unusual because of the nature of experiencing hands-on practice with replication. There will be four exercises, and each exercise accomplishes almost the exact same tasks, but they do so through different interfaces. In each exercise, you accomplish one or more of the following tasks, depending on which interface you are practicing:

▶ Create a Design Master from a nonreplicable database, leaving some objects local while replicating others.

▶ Create another replica from the Design Master.

▶ Make data changes in both the Design Master and the replica and then synchronize the two databases.

▶ Resolve synchronization conflicts.

▶ Schedule future synchronizations.

The four databases you will be working with, Address1–4, are identical databases, created from the New Database Wizard, because this will not be an exercise in database design.

Exercise 11.1: Implementing Database Replication Through the Microsoft Access Interface

In Exercise 1, you practice implementing database replication through the Microsoft Access interface. It is not possible to schedule future synchronizations through the Access interface.

Objectives:

Create a Design Master from a nonreplicable database.

Create another replica from the Design Master.

Make data changes in both the Design Master and the replica and then synchronize the two databases.

Resolve synchronization conflicts.

continues

Time Estimate: 15–20 minutes

Steps:

1. Open the Address1.mdb database included on the CD accompanying this book.

2. Choose Replication from the Tools menu and then click Create Replica.

3. A message box pops up asking whether you want to close the database. Click Yes.

4. After a pause, another message box pops up asking whether you want to create a backup of the database, which will be named Address1.bak. Click Yes.

5. A status bar dialog box informs you that it is converting the database to the Design Master. Let it run its course until a dialog box appears asking you to choose the location of the new replica. Navigate to the directory where Address1.mdb is located, and accept the default name (so it will be "Replica of Address1.mdb" in the same directory in which the original was located). Click OK.

6. Another status bar dialog box informs you that it is creating the replica. Let it run its course until a dialog box appears announcing that the original database has been converted to the Design Master and a new replica has been created. Click OK.

7. Click the Enter/View Addresses button on the Switchboard.

8. Change the Address on the first record (Steven Buchanan) from "14 Garrett Hill" to "14 Garrett Hill, 2nd floor."

9. Add a new record by clicking the Add New Record button. Enter yourself into the database, with as much or as little detail as you like. (None of the fields are required, so if you want to add only your name, that's fine.)

10. Close the Addresses form and click Exit this Database.

11. Open the replica you just created, named "Replica of Address1.mdb." Click the Enter/View Addresses button on the Switchboard.

12. Notice that Steven's address is still "14 Garrett Hill," even though you changed the value in the Design Master. In this replica, instead of changing the address, change Steven's work phone from (712)555-5858 to (712)555-1111.

13. Notice that there are only five records—your record has not yet been added to this replica. Close the Addresses form.

14. From the Tools menu, choose Replication and click Synchronize Now to synchronize the two databases. A dialog box appears asking if you want to close all objects. Click Yes.

15. The next dialog box gives you a choice of which replica in the Replica Set to synchronize with. In this case, there is only one other member of the set, so just click OK.

16. A status bar dialog box informs you that it is synchronizing replicas. Let it run its course until a dialog box appears stating that synchronization has been successfully completed, and asking if you want Access to close and reopen the database. Click Yes.

17. Once the database is open, a dialog box appears warning that this member of the Replica Set has conflicts, and asks if you want to resolve conflicts now. Click Yes.

18. A dialog box appears listing the tables with synchronization conflicts. In this case, there is only one. Click Resolve Conflicts.

19. The default conflict resolver opens, which shows you the two records in conflict. Notice that even though the changes were made to different fields, the fact that changes occurred in the same record in two replicas caused a synchronization conflict.

continues

Exercise 11.1: Continued

20. Change the WorkPhone field of the Existing Record to be (712)555-1111 so that it matches the Conflict Record. Then click the Keep Existing Record button. Click Yes in the warning dialog box and then click OK in the dialog box that informs you that you have successfully resolved conflicts. Click Close on the Resolve Replication Conflicts dialog box.

21. Click Enter/View Addresses on the Switchboard. Notice that the changes have been recorded, both the updates to Steven Buchanan's record and the addition of your record (they're in alphabetical order by last name, so your name may not be the last record). Close the database.

Reading Reference:

For more information about the concepts raised by the exercise, refer to the sections "Microsoft Access Replication" and "Resolving Synchronization Conflicts Through the Access Interface."

Exercise 11.2: Implementing Database Replication Through the Microsoft Windows 95 Briefcase

In Exercise 2, you practice implementing database replication through the Microsoft Windows 95 Briefcase.

 Note To successfully complete this exercise, you must have the Windows 95 Briefcase installed. You also must have installed the Briefcase Replication component of Access when you installed Access. If this exercise fails, you will need to run either Windows 95 Setup to install the Briefcase, or Office 95 Setup to install the Briefcase Replication component of Access.

Objectives:

Create a Design Master from a nonreplicable database, and another replica in the Windows 95 Briefcase.

Make data changes in both the Design Master and the replica and then synchronize the two databases.

Resolve synchronization conflicts.

Time Estimate: 15–20 minutes

Steps:

1. Open the Windows Explorer. Make sure that the size of the Explorer is not maximized, but that you can see the Windows 95 Briefcase on the desktop to the side of the Explorer. If your Explorer is maximized, click the Restore button, which is the button between the Minimize (dash) button and the Close (X) button at the top right of the Explorer window.

2. Navigate to the folder where the Address2.mdb database is located.

3. Drag the Address2.mdb file from the Explorer to the Briefcase (see fig. 11.3)

Figure 11.3

Create a Design Master and replica by dragging a database file into the Windows 95 Briefcase.

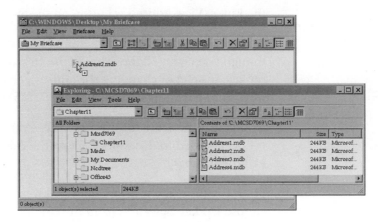

4. A message box pops up asking if you want to make the database replicable. Click Yes. Another message box then asks if you want to create a backup of the database, which will be named Address2.bak. Click Yes again.

continues

5. After some processing, another message box asks you which database should enable design changes. The default is the original copy. Leave that as the default and click OK.

6. Open the Address2.mdb file in Access. (You will make the same changes in this exercise as you made in Exercise 1.) Click the Enter/View Addresses button on the Switchboard.

7. Change the Address on the first record (Steven Buchanan) from "14 Garrett Hill" to "14 Garrett Hill, 2nd floor."

8. Add a new record by clicking the Add New Record button. Enter yourself into the database, with as much or as little detail as you like. (None of the fields are required, so if you want to add only your name, that's fine.)

9. Close the Addresses form and then click Exit this Database.

10. Open the replica from inside the Briefcase by double-clicking on the Address2.mdb file inside the Briefcase window. Click the Enter/View Addresses button on the Switchboard.

11. Notice that Steven's address is still "14 Garrett Hill," even though you changed the value in the Design Master. In this replica, instead of changing the address, change Steven's work phone from (712)555-5858 to (712)555-1111.

12. Notice that there are only five records—your record has not yet been added to this replica. Close the Addresses form, and exit the database.

13. From the Briefcase window, select Address2.mdb and then choose Update Selection from the Briefcase menu. A message box appears informing you that the original file needs to be merged (synchronized) with the Briefcase file (see fig. 11.4). Click Update. The status bar runs, and then two replicas synchronize.

14. Open the Briefcase replica again. Once the database is open, a dialog box appears warning that this member of the Replica Set has conflicts, and asks if you want to resolve conflicts now. Click Yes.

Figure 11.4

*When changes
have been made
at both replicas,
Briefcase merges
(synchronizes)
the two files.*

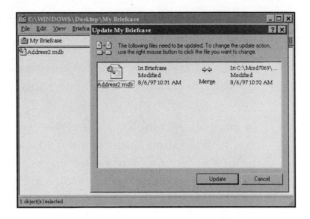

15. A dialog box appears listing the tables with synchronization conflicts. In this case, there is only one. Click Resolve Conflicts.

16. The default conflict resolver opens, which shows you the two records in conflict. Notice that even though the changes were made to different fields, the fact that changes occurred in the same record in two replicas has caused a synchronization conflict.

17. Change the WorkPhone field of the Existing Record to be (712)555-1111 so that it matches the Conflict Record. Then click the Keep Existing Record button. Click Yes to the warning dialog box and then click OK in the dialog box that informs you that you have successfully resolved conflicts. Click Close on the Resolve Replication Conflicts dialog box.

18. Click Enter/View Addresses on the Switchboard. Notice that the changes have been recorded, both the updates for Steven Buchanan's record and the addition of your record (they're in alphabetical order by last name, so your name may not be the last record). Close the database.

Reading Reference:

For more information about the concepts raised by the exercise, refer to the section "Windows 95 Briefcase Replication."

Exercise 11.3: Implementing Database Replication Through the Microsoft Replication Manager

In Exercise 3, you practice implementing database replication through the Microsoft Replication Manager.

To successfully complete this exercise, you must have the Microsoft Replication Manager installed and configured. In order for the Replication Manager to run properly, you must be on a computer with shared network folders. Even if any of these conditions do not exist on your computer, you can read through the exercise and note the interface from the figures.

Objectives

Create a Design Master from a nonreplicable database, leaving some objects local while replicating others.

Create another replica from the Design Master.

Make data changes in both the Design Master and the replica, and then synchronize the two databases.

Resolve synchronization conflicts.

Schedule future synchronizations.

Time Estimate: 15–20 minutes

Steps:

1. Open the Replication Manager. From the File menu, click the Convert Database to Design Master button on the toolbar. This will launch the Convert Database to Design Master Wizard.

2. A dialog box opens up asking for the location of the database to convert to the Design Master. Navigate to the directory where the Address3.mdb resides, and select Address3.mdb. Click Open.

3. The Convert Database to Design Master Wizard opens. The default name for the Replica Set, Address3, is fine. Click Next.

4. The next step of the wizard opens, asking for the folder in which to place the new Design Master. Choose the default folder that was first set up when you configured Replication Manager, usually c:\Program Files\Common Files\Microsoft Shared\Replication Manager\Replicas. Notice the choice of whether to create a backup. In this case, leave the check box checked. Click Next.

5. The next step of the wizard opens, asking if you want to enable read-write capabilities for the replicas. Leave the first button selected, indicating that you would rather have read-write replicas, rather than read-only replicas. Click Next.

6. The next step of the wizard opens, asking if you want to replicate all objects, or keep some local. Click the radio button for Make Some Objects Available to the Entire Replica Set. This will take you into the Select Replicated Objects dialog box. Change to the Reports tab. See figure 11.5.

Figure 11.5

Choose which objects to replicate, and which to leave local, through the Replication Manager.

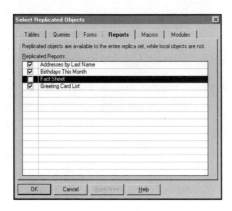

7. Click the check box in front of Fact Sheet to keep that report local. Click OK and then click Next.

continues

Exercise 11.3: Continued

8. Accept the default name Design Master of Address 3 and click Finish. Let the various processes run their courses and then click OK in the dialog box that informs you that the conversion has been successful. You are left with an icon of your computer, which represents the transporter on your computer (see fig. 11.6). Notice that the Replicas drop-down list box has only member: "Design Master of Address 3."

Figure 11.6

The transporter in the Replication Manager interface.

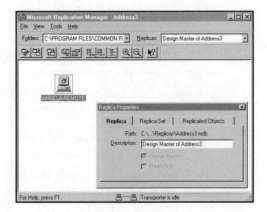

9. With the transporter selected, click Create Replica from the File menu.

10. Choose the Address3.mdb file, and click Open.

11. A wizard opens, asking if you want this replica to have read-write capabilities, or if you want it to be read-only. Accept the default (I Want to be Able to Make Changes in this Replica) and click Next.

12. Choose the default Replication Manager\Replicas folder, and click Next. Accept the default description, which consists of your computer's network name and the database name. Click Finish. Let the processes run their course, and click OK when the dialog box appears informing you that the operation has completed successfully.

13. Notice that there is not a graphical representation of the two separate databases. The only time you will see two separate

icons is when you are setting up synchronization to occur between two separate transporters on two separate computers.

14. Notice that now you have a choice of two databases in the Replicas drop-down list. Choose the Design Master. See figure 11.7.

Figure 11.7

Change between Replica Set members in the Replication Manager.

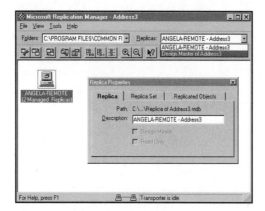

15. From the Tools menu, click Edit Database in Microsoft Access. This opens the Design Master in Access. (The following changes in this exercise are identical to the changes made in the database in Exercise 1.)

16. Click the Enter/View Addresses button on the Switchboard.

17. Change the Address on the first record (Steven Buchanan) from "14 Garrett Hill" to "14 Garrett Hill, 2nd floor."

18. Add a new record by clicking the Add New Record button. Enter yourself into the database, with as much or as little detail as you like. (None of the fields are required, so if you want to add only your name, that's fine.)

19. Close the Addresses form and then click Exit this Database.

20. Go back to the Replication Manager, and choose the replica from the Replicas drop-down box (as opposed to the Design Master). This changes the Replication Manager's focus to that replica. Then from the Tools menu, click Edit Database in Microsoft Access. This opens the Replica in Access.

continues

21. Click the Enter/View Addresses button on the Switchboard.

22. Notice that Steven's address is still "14 Garrett Hill," even though you changed the value in the Design Master. In this replica, instead of changing the address, change Steven's work phone from (712)555-5858 to (712)555-1111.

23. Notice that there are only five records—your record has not yet been added to this replica. Close the Addresses form, click the Preview Reports button, and then click the Preview the Fact Sheet Report button. There will be an error: the report was not replicated to this replica because we designated it as local. Click OK to the error dialog box, then exit the database.

24. Return to the Replication Manager. From the Tools menu, click Synchronize Now. The Synchronize Now dialog box appears with various options (see fig. 11.8). Accept the default values and click OK.

Figure 11.8

You can change synchronization options when synchronizing through the Replication Manager.

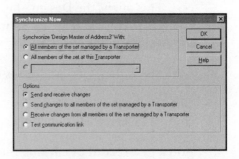

25. The transporter synchronizes the two databases. The only indication that the process is occurring is the appearance of the icon of the two computers at the bottom of the Replication Manager. This icon changes from a straight line and a message "Transporter is idle" to a jagged line and a message with the path and file name of the other replica involved in the synchronization. There is no dialog box that notifies when the synchronization is complete.

26. Open the replica "Replica of Address1.mdb" in Access. Once the database is open, a dialog box appears warning that this member of the Replica Set has conflicts, and asks if you want to resolve conflicts now. Click Yes.

27. A dialog box appears listing the tables with synchronization conflicts. In this case, there is only one. Click Resolve Conflicts.

28. The default conflict resolver opens, which shows you the two records in conflict. Notice that even though the changes were made to different fields, the fact that changes occurred in the same record in two replicas caused a synchronization conflict.

29. Change the WorkPhone field of the Existing Record to be (712)555-1111 so that it matches the Conflict Record. Then click the Keep Existing Record button. Click Yes to the warning dialog box and then click OK in the dialog box that informs you that you have successfully resolved conflicts. Click Close on the Resolve Replication Conflicts dialog box.

30. Click Enter/View Addresses on the Switchboard. Notice that the changes have been recorded, both the updates to Steven Buchanan's record and the addition of your record (they're in alphabetical order by last name, so your name may not be the last record). Close the database.

31. Return to the Replication Manager. Right-click the Transporter icon and then select Edit Locally Managed Replica Schedule.

32. Edit the Replication Schedule (darkened time slots are chosen for synchronization) by clicking on time slots to toggle between Selected and Not Selected for synchronization. It does not matter how you edit the schedule, although you will probably want to start by clearing all scheduled times. The Replica Set is currently scheduled to synchronize once every hour, seven days a week.

33. When you have established a reasonable schedule, click OK.

continues

Exercise 11.3: Continued

Comments:

Because this exercise assumes that you have only one computer at your disposal, the example given demonstrated only one Transporter. To experience replication between multiple Transporters, you would need to create replicas of the Replica Set from different computers' Replication Managers.

Reading Reference:

For more information about the concepts raised by the exercise, refer to the sections "Microsoft Replication Manager Utility (ADT)" and "Scheduling Synchronization."

Exercise 11.4: Implementing Database Replication Through DAO Programming

In Exercise 4, you practice implementing database replication through DAO programming.

Objectives:

Create a Design Master from a nonreplicable database, leaving some objects local while replicating others.

Create another replica from the Design Master.

Make data changes in both the Design Master and the replica and then synchronize the two databases.

Resolve synchronization conflicts.

Time Estimate: 15–20 minutes

Steps:

1. Open the Address4.mdb database included on the CD that came with this book.

2. Restore the database window by double-clicking the window that is minimized in the lower-left corner of the Access window. Go to the Modules tab, and click New. Type the following code to mark an object to keep it local:

```
Sub SmartKeepLocalT(objLocal As Object)
  Const errPropNotFound = 3270
  On Error GoTo SmartKeepLocalT_Error
  objLocal.Properties("KeepLocal").Value = "T"
  msgBox "Object Kept Local"
  GoTo SmartKeepLocalT_Exit

SmartKeepLocalT_Error:
  If (Err = errPropNotFound) Then
    objLocal.Properties.Append
objLocal.CreateProperty("KeepLocal", dbText, "T")
    MsgBox "Object Kept Local"
  End If
  'Resume Next
  'Other custom error handling

SmartKeepLocalT_Exit:
End Sub
```

3. Compile the module and then save the module as basReplicate.

4. Open the Debug window and type:

```
SmartKeepLocalT(DBEngine(0)(0).Containers!Reports.Documents![Fact
Sheet])
```

5. Press Enter to execute the code. The Fact Sheet Report is not replicated. Close the module and the database.

6. Create a new, blank database in Access by choosing New Database from the File menu and then double-clicking the Blank Database.mdb icon. Name it db1.mdb and locate it in the same directory in which the chapter exercise files are located. Click Create.

7. Go to the Modules tab in db1.mdb and click New. Type in the following code to convert the Address4.mdb to a new Design Master:

```
Function MakeReplicable(strDBConvert As String) As Integer
  Dim prpReplicable As Property, dbConverted As DATABASE
  Dim dbOriginal As DATABASE, Wrk As Workspace
```

continues

Exercise 11.4: Continued

```
On Error GoTo MakeReplicable_Error
Set Wrk = DBEngine(0)
Set dbConverted = Wrk.OpenDatabase(strDBConvert, True)

'Create - Append - Set Replicable property
Set prpReplicable =
dbConverted.CreateProperty("Replicable", dbText, "T")
    dbConverted.Properties.Append prpReplicable
    dbConverted.Properties("Replicable") = "T"
      'Set DesignMasterID
      dbConverted.DesignMasterID = dbConverted.ReplicaID
  MakeReplicable = True
  MsgBox "Replication successful!"

  GoTo MakeReplicable_Exit

MakeReplicable_Error:
  MsgBox "ERROR " & Err & ": " & Error
    MakeReplicable = Err
    GoTo MakeReplicable_Exit

MakeReplicable_Exit:
End Function
```

8. Compile the module and then save the module as basDesign-Master.

Note

Normally, you would make a backup of a file before you convert it to replicable format, but because you already have three other backups of the same file on your system, it is unnecessary in this case.

9. Open the Debug window and type the following code:

```
MakeReplicable("path&Address4.mdb"),
```

path&Address4.mdb is the path and file name of Address4.mdb. For example, note the following:

```
MakeReplicable("c:\Program Files\Acc70-69\Chap11\Address4.mdb")
```

10. When the message box appears saying that the replication has been successful, click OK.

11. Close db1.mdb and open the Address4.mdb database. Restore the database window by double-clicking the window that is minimized in the lower-left corner of the Access window. Go to the Reports tab, right-click on Fact Sheet, and choose Properties. Notice that the Replicated check box is not checked. You could change the property from here because this is the Design Master, but we will set the property from DAO instead. Close the Property sheet.

12. Go to the Modules tab, and open basReplicate. Scroll down past the end of the existing code and type the following code to create another replica from this Design Master:

```
Sub MakeAnotherReplica(strDBReplicateFrom, strNewReplica)
  Dim db As Database, Wrk As Workspace
  Set Wrk = DBEngine(0)
  Set db = Wrk.OpenDatabase(strDBReplicateFrom)
    db.MakeReplica strNewReplica, "Replica of" &
    ➥strDBReplicateFrom
    db.Close
  MsgBox "Replica created!"
End Sub
```

13. Open the Debug window, and type in the following to run the code:

```
MakeAnotherReplica("path&Address4.mdb", "path&Replica of
Address4.mdb")
```

path is equal to the path of the two files. For example, note the following code:

```
MakeAnotherReplica("c:\Program Files\Acc70-69\Chap11\
➥Address4.mdb")
```

14. Click OK when the message box appears. Close the Design Master, Address4.mdb, and open the replica, Replica of Address4.mdb. Click the Preview Reports button and then click the Preview the Fact Sheet Report button. There will be an error because the report was not replicated to this replica; we designated it as local. Click OK in the error dialog box.

continues

15. Click the Enter/View Addresses button on the Switchboard.

16. Change the Address on the first record (Steven Buchanan) from "14 Garrett Hill" to "14 Garrett Hill, 2nd floor."

17. Add a new record by clicking the Add New Record button. Enter yourself into the database, with as much or as little detail as you like (none of the fields are required, so if you want to add only your name, that's fine).

18. Close the Addresses form and then click Exit this Database.

19. Open the Design Master, Address4.mdb. Click the Enter/View Addresses button on the Switchboard.

20. Notice that Steven's address is still "14 Garrett Hill," even though you changed the value in the Design Master. In this replica, instead of changing the address, change Steven's work phone from (712)555-5858 to (712)555-1111.

21. Notice that there are only five records—your record has not yet been added to this replica. Close the Addresses form.

22. Restore the database window by double-clicking the window that is minimized in the lower-left corner of the Access window. Open the basReplicate module.

23. Scroll down past the end of all code, and type the following to make the Fact Sheet replicable during the next synchronization:

```
Sub SmartReplicableT(objLocal As Object)
  Const errPropNotFound = 3270
  On Error GoTo SmartKeepReplicableT_Error
  objLocal.Properties("Replicable").Value = "T"
  GoTo SmartKeepReplicableT_Exit
  MsgBox "Object Made Replicable"

SmartKeepReplicableT_Error:
  If (Err = errPropNotFound) Then
```

```
objLocal.Properties.Append objLocal.CreateProperty("Replicable",
➥dbText, "T")
  End If
  Resume Next

SmartKeepReplicableT_Exit:
➥End Sub
```

24. Open the Debug window, type the following and then press Enter:

```
smartReplicableT(DBEngine(0)(0).Containers!Reports.Documents!
[Fact Sheet])
```

25. After the code executes, click OK. Close the module and save it. Go to the Reports tab on the Database window, and right-click Fact Sheet, and then choose Properties. Notice that the Replicated check box is now checked. Close the property sheet by clicking OK.

26. Reopen the module basReplicate. Scroll to the end of the code and type the following code to synchronize the two databases:

```
Sub SynchDBs(strDBCurrent, strDBTarget)
  Dim db As DATABASE, Wrk As Workspace
  Set Wrk = DBEngine(0)
  Set db = Wrk.OpenDatabase(strDBCurrent)
    db.Synchronize strDBTarget, dbRepImpExpChanges
  db.Close
  MsgBox "Synchronization completed"
End Sub
```

27. Open the Debug window, and type in the following to run the code:

```
SynchDBs "path&Address4.mdb", "path&Replica of Address4.mdb"
```

path is equal to the path of the two files. For example, note the following:

```
SynchDBs "c:\Program Files\Acc70-69\Chap11\Address4.mdb",
➥"c:\Program Files\Acc70-69\Chap11\Replica of Address4.mdb"
```

continues

28. Click OK when the message box appears.

29. Close the module and the database. Open the Replica of Address 4.mdb database. A dialog box appears warning that this member of the Replica Set has conflicts, and asks if you want to resolve conflicts now. Click Yes.

30. A dialog box appears listing the tables with synchronization conflicts. In this case, there is only one. Click Resolve Conflicts.

31. The default conflict resolver opens, which shows you the two records in conflict. Notice that even though the changes were made to different fields, the fact that changes occurred in the same record in two replicas caused a synchronization conflict.

32. Change the WorkPhone field of the Conflict Record to be (712) 555-1111 so that it matches the Conflict Record. Then click the Keep Conflict Record button. Click Yes to the warning dialog box and then click OK in the dialog box that informs you that you have successfully resolved conflicts. Click Close in the Resolve Replication Conflicts dialog box.

33. Click Enter/View Addresses on the Switchboard. Notice that the changes have been recorded, both the updates to Steven Buchanan's record and the addition of your record (they're in alphabetical order by last name, so your name may not be the last record). Close the database.

Reading Reference:

For more information about the concepts raised by the exercise, refer to the sections "DAO Replication" and "Keeping Objects Local."

Review Questions

1. Which of the following applications are well served by using replication?

   A. An application that takes real-time traffic information and relays it to the local media

   B. A credit card transaction-processing application that handles 1,000,000 transactions a week

   C. A remote order-entry application in which salespeople on the road can track contact information and add 10-50 orders per day

   D. A production database for a company that makes custom dolls, in which the workers in one building constantly update and access a centralized database

2. Which of the following actions produce a Design Master for a new Replica Set? (Select all that apply.)

   A. Setting the Replicable property of the database to "T" using DAO

   B. Dragging the database from Windows Explorer to the Windows 95 Briefcase

   C. From the Tools menu, choosing Replication and then Create Replica

   D. From the Replication Manager, selecting a replica from an existing Replica Set and then Recover Design Master from the Tools menu

3. Which of the following does *not* occur when a database is made replicable?

    A. Additional queries are added to the database.

    B. Additional tables are added to the database.

    C. Additional system fields are added to each table.

    D. Additional properties are added to the database.

4. A database that has been in existence for a while is converted to replicable form. The primary key in the Employees table is an AutoNumber field. Now that the database is replicable, what is the value of the AutoNumber field when a new employee is added?

    A. The next number in the sequence

    B. A random long integer

    C. 0

    D. A random 16-byte GUID

5. When does a database have the same value for the ReplicaID and the DesignMasterID? (Select all that apply.)

    A. When the database is in the process of synchronizing with the Design Master

    B. When the database has been created from the Design Master in the Replication Manager

    C. When the database was made replicable by setting its Replicable property to "T" through DAO

    D. When the database is the Design Master for its Replica Set

6. Which of the following examples could be a valid ReplicationID?

   A. CD2351FA

   B. CD2351FA-C85A

   C. CD2351FA-C85A-11D0-A342

   D. CD2351FA-C85A-11D0-A342-444553540000

7. Two users at two separate replicas have both updated the same record since they last synchronized; one user updated the record once and the other user updated the record twice. What criteria determines which record is accepted as the official record goes to the conflict table?

   A. The ReplicationID of the records

   B. The version number of the records

   C. The contents of the records

   D. The ReplicaID of the databases

8. You have a replicable database in which the Employee table has been replicated. You need to change the table to be non-replicable because you want to start storing salary information in the table. What is the best way to accomplish this?

   A. Set the Replicable property of the table to "F."

   B. Set the KeepLocal property of the table to "T."

   C. Delete the table from the Design Master synchronizing throughout the Replica Set and then re-create the Employee table with the new information as a local object.

   D. It is not possible.

Answers to Review Questions

1. C is correct. Replication is ideal for applications with geographically scattered users and relatively low data processing volume. The traffic application needs too much real-time data, the credit card application processes too many transactions per day, and the dolls application does not need replication due to the availability of a centralized database. For more information, see the section "Making the Most of Synchronization."

2. A, B, and C are correct. D is incorrect because it would take a replica and turn it into a second Design Master for its current Replica Set, which could result in data loss and failed synchronizations. For more information, see the section "Microsoft Replication Manager Utility (ADT)."

3. A is correct. No new queries are added to the database when it is converted to a replicable form. For more information, see the section "Understanding Replicated Databases."

4. B is correct. When a database is converted to a replicable form, all AutoNumber fields are converted to random long integer fields. For more information, see the section "Changes to the Behavior of AutoNumber Fields."

5. C and D are correct. Setting a database's Replicable property to "T" through DAO converts the database to replicable form, which makes it the Design Master of a new Replica Set. The Design Master's DesignMasterID and ReplicaID are always identical. For more information, see the section "Replicating a Database Programmatically."

6. D is correct. A ReplicationID is a 16-byte GUID. For more information, see the section "Understanding the ReplicationID."

7. B is correct. The first criteria to determine which record is selected as the official record is the version number of the records, so the record which had been updated twice would

win. If the version numbers had been identical, the record from the database with the lowest ReplicaID would have won. For more information, see the section "Synchronization Conflicts."

8. B is correct. Once an object is replicable, you can change it to local by setting the KeepLocal property to "T." For more information, see the section "Keeping Objects Local."

Answers to Test Yourself Questions at Beginning of Chapter...

1. Replication is more flexible and powerful than file synchronization because two databases can update each other bi-directionally. And it is much simpler to use existing replication methods than to attempt to re-create the process of replication through code. For more information, see the section "Making the Most of Synchronization."

2. The four ways to make a database replicable are through the Microsoft Access user interface, through the Windows 95 Briefcase, by using the Microsoft Replication Manager, or programmatically through DAO. For more information, see the section "Choosing the Appropriate Replication Method."

3. When designing a replicable application for people who are not comfortable learning advanced skills, you would be well served to program synchronization through DAO. DAO enables you to write synchronization methods behind command buttons on forms; this method of synchronization is less intimidating for users than venturing into the Briefcase or the Replication Manager. For more information, see the section "Choosing the Appropriate Replication Method."

4. You can schedule synchronization through the Replication Manager. For more information, see the section "Scheduling Synchronization."

5. The only two noticeable changes made to your database when it becomes replicable are that its overall size increases, and the AutoNumber fields become random instead of incremental. The overall size increase is due to the less noticeable changes of additional system fields, tables, and properties. For more information, see the section "Understanding Replicated Databases."

6. Access ensures that it is updating the correct record in replicable databases by assigning each record a ReplicationID, which is a 16-bit GUID, which makes it extremely unlikely that the same ID would be accidentally generated twice within one Replica Set. For more information, see the section "Understanding the ReplicationID."

7. A synchronization *conflict* occurs every time one record is modified by both replicas between synchronizations. A synchronization *error* occurs when some synchronization action cannot finish processing because of table-level validation conflicts, duplicate unique indexes, referential integrity, or record locks. For more information, see the section "Resolving Synchronization Issues."

8. The simplest way to resolve synchronization conflicts is through the default conflict resolver that ships with Microsoft Access. For more information, see the section "Resolving Synchronization Conflicts Through the Access Interface."

Chapter

Implementing Database Security

12

By the end of this chapter, you will be able to execute the following test objectives:

Objectives

▶ Analyze a scenario and recommend an appropriate type of security

▶ Explain the steps for implementing security

▶ Identify and differentiate between different types of permissions

▶ Write code to implement security options

▶ Analyze code to ensure that the code sets security options

▶ Encrypt a database

Test Yourself! Before reading this chapter, test yourself to determine how much study time you will need to devote to this section.

1. If you're implementing security for a database that will be replicated, which type of security do you choose?

2. What is the first step you need to take in order to successfully implement user-level security?

3. In which database are permissions for individual objects (tables, forms) stored—the database you use or the workgroup database?

4. Which user automatically has all permissions for an object?

5. In order to implement security in an Access database, are end-users necessarily required to remember a password?

6. When referring in code to security groups and users, which collection contains the other—groups or users?

7. What does the Security Wizard do?

8. What does encrypting a database do?

Answers are located at the end of the chapter...

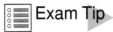Exam Tip

As you read this chapter, you will learn about each Security test objective described earlier in the chapter. If you're learning only Security for the exam, concentrate your study on the sections "Setting Security Through Code" and "Analyzing Security Code" (although one test question will probably come from "Implementing Basic User-Level Security"...). On the other hand, if you're honestly interested in the issue of implementing security in your databases, concentrate on all the sections in this chapter. Why? In most real-world situations, you can thoroughly accomplish your security goals for a database without using code at all.

Choosing the Appropriate Level of Security

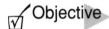Objective

Access provides two methods of securing a database:

▶ Setting a database password, which restricts all the objects in a database at one level of all-or-nothing security, is the first method. The database password is sometimes called share-level security. *Share-level security* is security defined by the object not by the user—so each object has its own password.

▶ Establishing *user-level security*, which enables different individuals to have different levels of permissions within the database, is the second method.

The difference between a database password and user-level security is similar to the difference between a skeleton key and an apartment building key: a skeleton key (database password) unlocks every door in the building with one key, whereas an apartment building key (user-level security) might let you only in the front door and the laundry room—depending on how tightly the building security is organized.

Setting a Database Password

Assigning a database password is the most straightforward way to secure a database, yet the setting provides no options. When a user tries to open a database with an assigned password, a dialog box appears requesting the password. After the user enters the correct (case-sensitive) password, the user opens the database with full permissions, including rights to modify design, to administer the database, and even to remove the password.

A database password is a perfectly acceptable method of security if the data is not extremely sensitive, if not many people use the database, and if the database will never be replicated or linked. However, if you need to hide some information (salary information, for example) from users, or if you want to prevent users from accidentally changing design or code, you need to implement user-level security (see the section "Implementing Basic User-Level Security" later in the chapter).

You cannot replicate databases with passwords. Well, that's not exactly true. You can replicate them, but you can't synchronize them. You can have many copies of one database that don't match one another—but why would you want to have the copies? If you need replication, you must choose user-level security. For more information, refer to Chapter 11, "Database Replication."

You also should seriously consider user-level security if the information from your database will link to other databases. When you link a table from a database with a password, Access asks for the password and saves the password along with other information about the link (path, table name, and so on). If the password on the linked database changes, Access prompts the user for the new password. The prompt can be very disconcerting to an unsuspecting user in a multiuser environment and can easily wreak havoc on your code.

To assign a password to a database, complete the following steps:

1. Make sure you have the database open exclusively before you begin. You cannot set or remove a password on a database

unless you have it open exclusively (to open a database exclusively, open it from the Open dialog box and check Exclusive). If someone else is using the database, you cannot open it exclusively, so you have to either assign a password during off-hours when nobody uses the database, or ask everyone who has the database open to close it while you perform the task.

 Tip

If you are on a Microsoft NT network, you can use the Server Manager to see whether anyone else has an open session and is connected to the database. In that case, you can immediately disconnect other users by turning off the sharing permissions of the database folders.

A strong disadvantage to the preceding method is that the users have no warning that you are disconnecting them, so they may be in the middle of changing a record or running a query. Interrupting record-locking processes can cause database corruption.

2. With the database open to the Database Window, choose Tools, Security, Set Database Password from the menu (see fig. 12.1).

3. Type the case-sensitive password twice to verify it and click OK.

The next time anyone attempts to open the database, the program prompts the user for the database password.

To remove the password, have the database open to the Database Window, choose Tools, Security, Unset Database Password from the menu.

Establishing User-Level Security

User-level security takes more time and concentration than assigning a database password, but provides immeasurably greater flexibility. Instead of assigning a password to a database, user-level security assigns a password to a database *user*. You can then assign the user to a group with other users. You can assign to the whole group permissions for each object in the database.

Figure 12.1

Assign a password to the database.

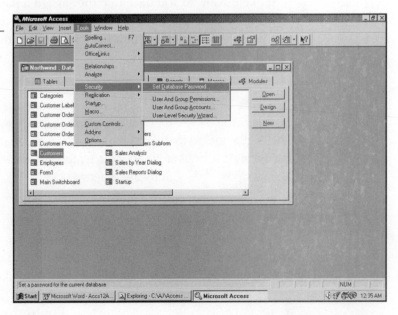

For example, if you want the Accounting and Sales groups to view commissions but not change them, the Management group to view and change commissions, and nobody but you to change the design of the database, user-level security is the ideal solution.

Some other advantages to user-level security over database passwords include the following:

▶ Because you can separately add and delete users, you don't have to change and redistribute the database password each time the user-group changes; you must change only that user.

▶ Users can administer their own passwords.

▶ You can keep users from accidentally altering design and code.

▶ You can prevent everyone from intentionally tampering with your intellectual property—your design and code.

When you begin the process of implementing user-level security, understanding the Microsoft Jet security model helps you, whether you implement security through code or through the Access interface. The Jet security model is composed of several pieces— each of which you need to configure properly in order to provide an effective security solution.

This section explains what user-level security is, and a later section, "Implementing Basic User-Level Security," discusses the process of how you assign user-level security.

Users and Groups

A *user* is anyone who uses your database. When you create a user, you must provide a User Name and a *Personal ID (PID)*—both may include spaces. The Personal ID is *not* the user's password; it is a piece of information used to uniquely identify the user. The PID enables you to re-create the exact same set of users if the workgroup database is destroyed or becomes corrupted. The Jet Engine takes the User Name and PID, encrypts them, and produces a *Secure ID (SID)*. The Secure ID is stored in the workgroup database.

Access predefines one default user named *Admin*. Whether you're aware of it or not, you log on as Admin to every Access database that you open without a password. Admin is quietly assigned ownership of every database, table, query, form, report, macro, and module that you create. If Admin has a password, everyone in that workgroup must enter a password. If Admin does not have a password, Access prompts nobody for a password. The section "Redefining Administrative Accounts" discusses the details of different ways to use the Admin user.

A *group* is a logical association of users who need the same permissions to the same objects. When you create a group, you provide a Group Name and PID that work together to make a SID for the group, just like the User Name and PID work together to make a user's SID.

Access predefines two groups: Admins and Users. You can never delete these groups, but you can certainly reassign their permissions. Every new user, by default, is assigned to the Users group. When you assign permissions, you should assign the most restrictions to the Users group because every single user in the workgroup has all the Users group's permissions.

This system of users and groups enables you to easily manage permissions for a large number of users. You still have to create each user separately, but you can simultaneously assign permissions to an entire group of users without having to reassign permissions to each user. If you find that five people need a special set of permissions, you can easily create a new group, assign the five users to the new group, and then assign permissions to the new group—you don't have to assign the exact same permissions to *each* user.

Workgroup Database

The workgroup database holds the information about users, groups, and passwords. Access starts with a default workgroup database, system.mdw (in previous Access versions, system databases were .mda files). The database contains the user Admin and the Admins and Users groups. Any user can join any workgroup database as a member of its Users group, but the right to administer individual permissions resides in the user database, not the workgroup database. Anyone can open the workgroup database, but neither Admins nor Users can directly manipulate the workgroup database because all objects are read-only.

User Database

The user database is the database that users use. Each database contains objects (tables, reports, and so on), and each object has permissions assigned to it.

It is important to understand the difference between accounts and permissions. *Accounts* (users and groups) are stored in the workgroup database, and *permissions* are stored in the user database.

For example, when a user logs in to Access with the password FrootFly747, the workgroup database validates the information. The user database caches the SID and information about the user's group assignments. When the user tries to look at the design of the Customers form, Access checks the SID against the permissions in a hidden system table in the user database, and Access allows or denies permission to the user.

 Tip

> The best Access passwords—as with all passwords—are combinations of alpha and numeric characters. The preceding example of FrootFly747 combines capital letters, lowercase letters, numbers, and a misspelled word, making it an excellent example. Favorite uncommon dictionary words, such as Maudlin16 or Traipse70 also make easy-to-remember, difficult-to-crack passwords. Avoid your address, birthday, children's names, and mother's maiden name because those items are relatively simple codes to crack.

In order for a security system to work, each user must log onto Access from the workgroup .mdw file that has the user account information.

Jet Engine

The Jet Engine is responsible for processing security transactions. In other words, when a user logs in, the Jet Engine queries the workgroup database to verify user and password information and then to make the user's SID available to each user database that opens during that user's Access session.

Similarly, when a user requests access to an object in the user database, the Jet Engine checks permissions in the hidden system table and allows or denies permission.

The role of the Jet Engine in Access security is invisible if you implement security through the Access interface. However, if you implement security through code, you need to access the Jet Engine through DAO (Data Access objects) to process security transactions.

Implementing Basic User-Level Security

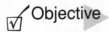 Objective

The basic process of implementing user-level security is multi-step, and the order of the steps is very important. If you create a database before you create a workgroup information file and user/ group accounts, you have considerably more work to do in securing your database than if you had completed the steps in the recommended order (recommended by Access Online Help and other documentation).

The steps listed in this section are general and work in any situation. You do not have to practice the steps as you read them, because the exercises at the end of the chapter provide practice.

Creating or Joining a Secure Workgroup

The workgroup database file holds all the information about users and groups. The only way to make sure your database is secure is to use a workgroup file other than the default workgroup (system.mdw). In the new workgroup file, you create an entirely different set of permissions than someone could re-create by using the default workgroup. Therefore, if you implement security at a site for the first time, the critical first step is always to create a new workgroup, so that nobody can copy your database, re-create groups and permissions, or break security.

The Jet Engine uses several pieces of information to make sure each workgroup is unique: the Name, Organization, and Workgroup ID. Just as the User Name and PID are combined to create a unique SID, the workgroup Name, Organization, and Workgroup ID are combined to create a unique identifier for each workgroup.

Write down and keep in a safe place exactly what you enter for the Name, Organization, and Workgroup ID when you create a workgroup because in order to re-create the workgroup database, you must enter the exact same information (case-sensitive). Permissions to your database depend on the user and group information stored in your workgroup database, and you can completely lose permissions to your database if you lose your workgroup database and cannot re-create it. An intelligent developer does not take chances, so keep your workgroup database information in a safe place.

To create a new secure workgroup, complete the following steps:

1. Make sure that no copies of Access are running. You cannot have Access open and successfully change to a different workgroup.

2. Start the Workgroup Administrator by navigating to the folder where Access is installed (by using My Computer or Windows Explorer) and double-clicking Wrkgadm.exe.

3. Click Create. Then fill in your Name, Organization, and a Workgroup ID. The Workgroup ID makes sure the workgroup database is completely unique. Without a Workgroup ID, you cannot be completely sure that your database is safe. Someone else can theoretically create an identical workgroup and identical users and gain permissions that they should not have (see fig. 12.2).

Figure 12.2

Create a new secure workgroup.

4. Choose a path and name for the new workgroup database and then click OK. The name must have an .mdw extension. If you want other people on your network to use this workgroup file, you must store the file in a shared network folder.

5. Click Exit to leave the Workgroup Administrator.

To join an existing workgroup, complete the following steps:

1. Make sure that no copies of Access are running. You cannot have Access open and successfully join a different workgroup.

2. Start the Workgroup Administrator by navigating to the folder where Access is installed (by using My Computer or Windows Explorer) and double-clicking Wrkgadm.exe.

3. Click Join and then Browse. A typical file-selection dialog box opens. Navigate to the workgroup database file (.mdw extension) that you want to join. After you select the correct file, click Open and then click OK. You see a confirmation OK dialog box.

4. Click Exit to leave the Workgroup Administrator.

In either case, whether you create a new workgroup database or join an existing one, the workgroup database you choose is active the next time you start Access. As long as you don't explicitly change the workgroup, all the user and group changes that you make save in that workgroup database.

 Tip

> If you are developing in a Microsoft NT environment, it is very important to distinguish between MS Office security and MS BackOffice security. BackOffice is integrated, so each BackOffice application utilizes NT security already in place. However, BackOffice does not integrate with NT, so you must create groups and users for Access, even if the groups and users already exist in NT.

Redefining Administrative Accounts

This section discusses the tasks involved in redefining who administers your database, and then a numbered list explains how to accomplish these tasks.

In a newly created workgroup database, one user (Admin) and two groups (Admins and Users) are in the database. Admin, as the default user, has no password and all rights. You want to assign a password to Admin, which forces everyone who starts Access under this workgroup to log on with a password.

After you set an Admin password, you create a new Administrator. Then remove Admin, the default user, from the Admins group, so you can assign Admin the most restrictive permissions. Last, log back on as the new Administrator and assign yourself a password.

The following are detailed instructions on redefining who is assigned to the Admins group:

1. Open Access with or without a database open. You are making changes only to the workgroup database file not to the user database, so you can have a database open.

2. Assign a password to Admin. From the Tools menu, choose Security, User and Group Accounts, and then go to the Change Logon Password tab. Notice that you're logged on as Admin. The old password does not exist, so type a new password in the New Password and Verify boxes (see fig. 12.3). Click Apply.

Figure 12.3

*Change the
Admin password.*

3. Create a new Administrator. Change to the Users tab on the User and Group Accounts dialog box and then click New. Type a new User Name and a Personal ID. Both names and PIDs can have spaces in them. Make sure you write down and keep in a safe place *exactly* what you type in these boxes in case you must re-create the account. Click OK.

4. Make the new user an Administrator. With the new user selected in the User Name box, select Admins in the Available Groups list box and then click Add. You must make the new user an Administrator before you remove Admin from the Admins group because at least one user must be in the Admins group (or else nobody has permission to administer any databases).

5. Remove Admin from the Admins group. Choose Admin from the User Name combo box. Select Admins in the Member Of list box, click Remove, and then click OK to close the dialog box.

6. Log in as the new Administrator. Close and restart Access. The program prompts you for a user name and password. Change the user name from Admin to your new user name and leave the password box blank. Click OK.

7. Give the new Administrator a password. You don't have to open a database, so click Cancel when Access prompts you to open or to create a database. From the Tools menu, choose Security, User and Group Accounts. Click the Change Logon Password tab. Notice that you're logged on as your new user. The old password does not exist, so type a new password in the New Password and Verify boxes. Click Apply.

Notice that next to the New button is the Delete button. If you make a mistake, you, as the administrator, can always delete a user and start over. Make sure that your records and PIDs are accurate.

Now that you have redefined who is assigned to the Admins group, you can create all your other users and groups and assign appropriate permissions. Remember to always log on as the new administrator.

Creating Groups and Users

The following instructions for creating a new group are almost identical to creating a new user:

1. From the Tools menu, choose Security, User and Group Accounts. Click the Groups tab.

2. Click New. Type the Group Name and Personal ID—make sure to write them down exactly as you type them—and click OK (see fig. 12.4).

Again, if you need to delete a group, the Delete button is next to the New button.

Figure 12.4

Create a new group.

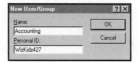

After you create appropriate user groups for the workgroup, you can assign users to the correct groups by selecting the user name, selecting the correct group, and clicking Add. You can assign each user to as many groups as you want.

Running the Security Wizard (Optional)

The Security Wizard is a simple way to secure a database that was created from an unsecured workgroup. If you use a secure workgroup before you create a new database, you may not need to run the Security Wizard because as you develop, you can choose who owns the database and all its objects.

The most important reason to run the Security Wizard is that the wizard reassigns ownership of every single object in the database to whatever user is logged on when the Wizard runs. In other words, if you're logged on as John when you run the Security Wizard, the new, secured database and all its objects belong to John. Therefore, pay attention to how you log on to Access when you run the Security Wizard.

When you run the Security Wizard on an existing database, the wizard creates a new, encrypted database that is owned by the user who runs the Wizard (for further information about encrypting, see the section "Encrypting a Database" later in this chapter). Then the Security Wizard exports all the objects in the database to the new, secure database and re-creates table relationships. Next, the wizard revokes all permissions for all selected objects (the wizard enables you to choose which objects to secure). The only users with any permission to those secured objects are the user who now owns the secure database, and all users assigned to the Admins group.

The Security Wizard does not change the original database—the database from which you run the wizard—in any way. Instead, the wizard creates a whole new database.

To run the Security Wizard, complete the following steps:

1. Make sure you're logged on as the user you want to own the new, secure database. If you're not, you need to restart Access and log on as the correct user.

2. Open the database you want to secure.

3. From the Tools menu, choose Security, User-Level Security Wizard. Follow the directions in the dialog boxes and pay special attention to which objects you choose to secure.

When you choose the objects to secure in the Security Wizard, keep in mind that all objects you choose to secure are not available, not even on a read-only basis, to anyone other than the new owner and any users in the Admins group.

Assigning Permissions to Appropriate Groups

After you set up your users and groups, you can assign appropriate permissions to the groups. You can also assign permissions to individual users, but by doing so, you miss out on the power and ease of assigning group permissions.

The two most important things to keep in mind as you're assigning permissions are the following:

▶ Owners always have total rights to an object.

▶ Users have the permissions of the most permissive groups to which they belong.

The following is an example of ownership. User John is only in the Users group, which has read-only permission to all tables. John is the *owner* of the Customers table, which means that John can modify and administer the Customer table any way he wants to change it. Also, if John is the owner of the database, John can do anything to any object in the database, regardless of group permissions. For more information on changing ownership of an object, see "Changing Ownership" in the following section.

The following is an example of group permissions. User John is in the Users group, which has read-only permission to all tables. Then John is assigned to the Managers group, which has update and delete permissions to the Employee table. John is now able to modify and delete information in the Employee table because permissions are assigned according to the *most* permissive assigned group.

To assign permissions to a user or group, complete the following steps:

1. Open the database you want to secure in Access.

2. From the Tools menu, choose Security, User and Group Permissions. Click the Permissions tab.

3. Choose the user or group name for which you want to change permissions (you can change the view between users and groups by clicking the List: Users or Groups option buttons).

4. Choose the object(s) for which you want to change permissions (the Ctrl and Shift keys enable you to select multiple objects simultaneously). You can change Object Types through the Object Type combo box. Notice that you can select objects only from one Object Type at a time, so you must assign permissions separately for your tables, queries, forms, reports, macros, and modules.

5. Choose the permissions for the selected objects. If you choose Read Data for a table or query, the Read Design permission automatically appears. The two are permanently linked; you cannot have one without the other. However, you may separately assign Modify Design. Other permissions are logically linked as well, such as the Administer permission and all the other permissions. If you can administer an object, you can do anything else to the object (see fig. 12.5).

Figure 12.5

Assign permissions to database objects.

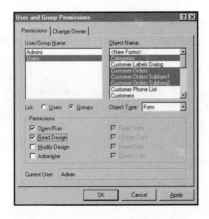

6. Click Apply. If you try to move off these objects or users, the program prompts you to save the changes you made.

7. Don't forget to assign permissions for the database object type, and the <New [Object Type]> category at the top of every Object Name list. Assume that your database may grow, and you want to keep control over the database.

Assigning permissions is the heart of your user-level security system. Take your time and check the results. If you find that one user unexpectedly has total permissions to an object, see the section "Changing Ownership" to learn how to correct the problem.

Choosing the Appropriate Permission Strategy

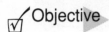
Objective ▶

The incredible flexibility afforded by the Jet Engine user-level security model available in Access means you can use many possible strategies for securing your database. This section discusses some possibilities, when you should use them, and the relative advantages and disadvantages to each strategy.

Changing Ownership

Whatever user has ownership of an object automatically has all permissions for that object. All permissions means the right to read, modify, and administer (the right to *administer* an object means the right to assign permissions to the object).

Therefore, whatever user has ownership of the database automatically has all permissions for every single object in the database. To make sure your database is secure, then, you always must change ownership of all objects that are owned by the default Admin user. A user logged onto another workgroup as the default Admin user can export any object owned by the default Admin user from your secure database in a secure workgroup into an unsecure database in a unsecure workgroup. That would be bad.

Sometimes you want different users to own different objects. For example, if you have a database that is being distributed to several different sites, and you want the local Administrator to have full permissions for the table that stores their site-specific information, it is probably appropriate to assign ownership of each site-specific table to the local Administrator and distribute your custom workgroup database file with your database. Then those local Administrators can modify and administer those objects as they choose.

Remember that reassigning ownership of a table deletes all the relationships for that table. You must re-create all the table's relationships in the Relationships window after you reassign ownership of it.

If you want to reassign the ownership for a database and every object in the database, you can either run the Security Wizard (logged on as the new owner), or you can log on as the new owner and create a new database and import all the objects from the old database (owned by whomever) into the new database (owned by the new owner).

To change ownership, complete the following steps:

1. Open the database you want to secure in Access. Make sure you're logged on as a user with the right to administer the objects for which you want to change ownership.

2. From the Tools menu, choose Security, User and Group Permissions. Click the Change Owner tab.

3. Choose the object(s) for which you want to change ownership and then change the owner from the New Owner combo box. Notice that you can change ownership only for one Object Type at a time.

4. Click Change Owner. If you click just OK, ownership does not change.

5. Notice that you cannot change the owner of the database through this interface. To change ownership of the database, you must either run the Security Wizard while logged on as the new owner, or create a new database as the new owner and import all the objects from the old database into the new database.

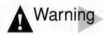

Warning

When you reassign ownership of tables, do not forget to re-create table relationships as the new owner. If you run the Security Wizard to reassign ownership of an entire database, the Wizard re-creates table relationships for you. If you reassign ownership of a database by creating a new database as the new owner and importing all the objects, however, you need to re-create all the table relationships.

Assigning Owner Permissions for Queries

Each query has a Run Permissions property. By default, the property is set to User's, meaning that users who run the query have their own permissions. However, by changing the Run Permissions property to Owner's, the Jet Engine checks the owner's level of permission to run the query and not the current user's level of permission.

One consequence of running a query with owner permissions is that only the owner (not any of the Admins) can save changes to the query.

A good time to use this strategy is when you have public and sensitive data in the same table, such as an Employee table with phone extensions (public knowledge) and salary information (sensitive data). You can set highly restrictive permissions for the table and then write a query that returns only public information. Make the query run with owner permissions and then base your forms and reports off the query rather than the table.

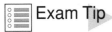 Exam Tip

> A good bet for a tough question on the exam involves an example of a table with both public and sensitive data. The question asks whether you should split a table into two tables, public and private information, or whether you should run owner's permission queries off the public data. The correct answer is to run owner's permission queries off the public data because splitting the table violates principles of good database design.

To change the Run Permissions property of a query, complete the following steps:

1. Open a query in Design mode. From the View menu, choose Properties. Make sure that the property sheet that opens is the property sheet for the whole query (titled Query Properties) and not for any one field. If it is not, click the background next to one of the tables in the top portion of the query design, and the sheet changes to Query Properties).

2. Change the Run Permissions property to Owner's.

3. Save the query.

Now any user can run the query and view all its data. Also, if the query is updateable, and the owner has permission to update data from the query, any user can also update data from this query.

Using Invisible Admin Security

Access asks users for a logon password only if a password is on the default Admin account. If Admin does not have a password, all users log on as Admin by default with no password prompt, even if other users in the workgroup have passwords. You can use the setup to your advantage to create *"invisible" security*, with which users don't have to log on or remember a password.

You need to develop the database in a secure workgroup by logging on as the user who owns all the objects. Assign appropriate permissions to the Admin user. Then remove the Admin user's password. You have invisible security that works no matter which workgroup a user joins—even the default system.mdw.

Of course, invisible security raises the following question. If Access does not prompt you for a logon, how do you log on to that database as any user other than Admin? You can either access the database as the owner from a different secured workgroup that requires a logon, or use the /user and /pwd command-line options when starting Access.

Setting Security Through Code

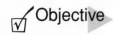 Objective

Sometimes, especially in distributed Access applications, you want to set security through code, so you need to use the DAO interface (the Jet Engine manages all security, so DAO manages all security programming).

DAO Permissions

Because of the complexity of security information, security objects are a bit convoluted in the DAO hierarchy. Permissions within containers and documents is the easiest collection with which to begin. Remember that permissions to specific objects are stored in each object's document (see fig. 12.6).

As you can see in figure 12.6, *Documents* are a part of the Containers collection. *Containers* are groups of objects that have documents, such as tables or forms. *Permissions* are stored in the Permissions and AllPermissions properties of Document objects.

Figure 12.6

The position of the Containers and Documents collections in the DAO hierarchy.

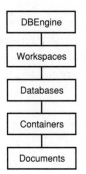

After you set the UserName property of a Container or Document object, the AllPermissions property of a Document object returns all the permissions that apply to that UserName. AllPermissions includes permissions that a user has from being a member of a group, as well as permissions that are specifically assigned to the user.

On the other hand, the Permissions property returns only the permissions that you have specifically assigned to the user. Permissions does not include any additional permissions that the user has as a group member.

The following example shows how to access the Customer table's document to stop user John Doe from deleting data:

```
Dim db as Database, Doc as Document, Usr, Tbl as String
Usr = "John Doe"
Tbl = "Customer"
    Set db = dbEngine(0)(0)

    'choose object's document
    Set Doc = db.Containers!Tables.Documents(Tbl)

    'choose user or group
    Doc.UserName = Usr

    'set permissions
    Doc.Permissions = Doc.AllPermissions And Not dbSecDeleteData
```

First, access the object's document by setting a Document variable equal to the proper document in the proper container. Then you choose a user or a group by assigning a string to the Document's UserName property (to assign a group, use the group name instead of the user name—you still use the UserName property). Then you're ready to check or assign permissions.

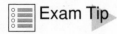 Exam Tip

> It is very important to understand the use of logical operators in checking and assigning permissions, and the operators can get a little confusing. Pay special attention, however—you're almost guaranteed to get a question on the exam about the syntax of checking and assigning security permissions through code.

Setting Permissions Through Code

Setting permissions through code depends on having the correct logical operators and syntax. Before you add or revoke permissions through code, you need to choose a document or container and then choose a user or group.

The examples in this section assume that Doc is a Document variable, that you have properly assigned Doc to the correct document, and that you have properly assigned Doc.UserName to the correct user or group (see code example in the section "DAO Permissions").

To add a permission without revoking any permissions the user already has, reassign previous permissions and then assign new permissions using the Or operator. Think of it as if you're telling the computer, "John can do what he could already do, *or* he can do this new thing, too." The following is an example of how to correctly add two permissions—to open the database at all and to open the database exclusively:

```
Doc.Permissions = Doc.Permissions Or dbSecDBOpen Or
➥dbSecDBExclusive
```

If you use And instead of Or in the preceding example, the Jet Engine tries to assign all current permissions, and then tries to assign dbSecDBOpen then dbSecDBExclusive, each of which represents only one permission. The result is the same as if you were trying to assign three states to one state field—the permissions do not work. To add permissions, you need to use the Or operator.

To revoke a permission without revoking all permissions the user already has, reassign previous permissions and then revoke permissions using the And Not operator. Think of it as if you're telling the computer, "John can do what he can already do, as long as it doesn't conflict with this action, which he cannot do." The following is an example of how to correctly revoke a permission—to open the database exclusively:

```
Doc.Permissions = Doc.Permissions And Not dbSecDBExclusive
```

If you use Or instead of And Not in the preceding example, you assign the permission rather than revoke it. If you use And instead of And Not, it fails for the same reason it fails when you try to add permissions.

Checking Permissions Through Code

Checking permissions through code also depends on having the correct logical operators and syntax, but the logic is a bit more complex. For example, you want to check to see whether John has permission to read the design of a form. If the answer is yes, you want to hear a Beep. If the answer is no, you want to see a Message Box that says "Too Bad." The following is an example of code showing how the permissions work:

```
Dim db as Database, Doc as Document, ReadDesignOK as Boolean,
Usr,Frm as String
Usr = "John"
Frm = "frmCustomer"
    Set db = dbEngine(0)(0)
    Set Doc = db.Containers!Forms.Documents(Frm)
    Doc.UserName = Usr

    'check permissions
    ReadDesignOK = (Doc.AllPermissions And acSecFrmRptReadDef)

    If ReadDesignOK > 0 Then
        Beep
```

```
Else
    MsgBox "Too Bad"
End If
```

The preceding code example assigns a value to the variable Read-DesignOK, which returns 1 if it is true or 0 if it is false. Therefore, to perform the logical operation, you can test ReadDesignOK for whether it is greater than 0 (you can also test for True and False).

The preceding example checks for *explicit* and *implicit* permissions by using AllPermissions, so the program properly checks for user-assigned and group-assigned permissions. If you want to check only those permissions directly assigned to the user, use Doc.Permissions rather than Doc.AllPermissions.

 Tip

The Access security constants are pretty self-explanatory (For example, dbSecDeleteData means the right to delete data), so you don't need to memorize all the security constants. You can familiarize yourself with them, however, by searching the Online Help Index for constants and then Security Constants.

DAO Passwords, Users, and Groups

Other than assigning and checking permissions through code, the primary security function for any database is modifying passwords and user and group information. The next sections discuss changing users' passwords and permissions.

Changing a User's Password

Use the NewPassword method of the user object to change passwords. Keep in mind that the only user's password that you can change is the user logged on to the active instance of Access. In other words, if you log on as John, you cannot change Jane's password. After you log on as the user whose password you want to change, the proper syntax you use to accomplish the task is NewPassword "OldPassword," "NewPassword." The following code shows you how to change the password:

```
Dim Usr as User
Set Usr = DbEngine.Workspaces(0).Users!John
Usr.NewPassword "OldPwd", "NewPwd"
```

As you can see, the process of changing a user's password in code is fairly straightforward.

Manipulating Users and Groups

Because users are associated with groups, and groups are associated with users, the interaction between users and groups in the DAO hierarchy is a bit mind-boggling, as shown in figure 12.7.

Figure 12.7

The interaction between the Users and Groups collections in the DAO hierarchy.

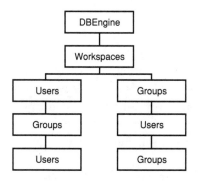

The following is an example of the interaction between users and groups. John is a user; therefore, a John object is in the Users collection. The John object has a Groups collection, which has one Group object for each group to which John is assigned. He's assigned to two groups: Users and Managers. Then both of those Group objects (Users and Managers) have a Users collection, which contain one User object for each user in those two groups.

When you use code to add a user to a group, you must remember to append that User object to the appropriate group, but you're not finished yet. After you append the User object to the appropriate groups, you then must refresh the User's Groups collection.

It works the same way if you choose to append the Group object to the appropriate user—then you need to refresh the Group's Users collection.

The following code is an example of appending a user to a group:

```
Dim Wrk As Workspace, Usr As User, Grp As GROUP, UsersName As String
Set Wrk = DBEngine(0)

UsersName = "John Doe"
Set Usr = Wrk.CreateUser(UsersName)
Wrk.Groups("Managers").Users.Append Usr
Wrk.Users(UsersName).Groups.Refresh
```

Without both of the last lines of code—appending the User to the Managers group in the workspace, and also refreshing the Groups collection of the User, the transaction is incomplete.

What exactly happens if you forget to refresh? The transaction still occurs, and the next time you start Access, you can see all the objects in the proper collections. You can't see all the objects in the proper collections right away, however, unless you refresh. If you don't refresh, you can cause big problems in any kind of looping code or with assigning permissions. Your best bet is always to refresh the collection you didn't append (Users or Groups).

In code, you can create a user who is not a member of the Users group. When you add users through the Access interface, the new user is automatically appended to the Users group, and the Users group is automatically appended to the new User's Groups collection. When you create a user in code, however, you must remember to do the necessary appending.

First you have to append the new user to the Users collection, so the user is a recognizable entity. The following code shows you the proper syntax:

```
Workspace.Users.Append UserName
```

Then you need to append the user to the appropriate groups, including the Users group. The following code shows you how to append the user:

```
Workspace.Groups("GroupName").Append UserName
```

Then you must refresh whichever collection you did not append, as follows:

```
Workspace.Users("UsersName").Groups.Refresh
```

The following is an example of the correct way to create a new user:

```
Dim Wrk As Workspace, Usr As User, UsersName As String
UsersName = "John Doe"
    Set Wrk = DBEngine(0)
    Set Usr = Wrk.CreateUser(UsersName, "UserPID", "UserPwd")
    Wrk.Users.Append Usr
        Set Usr = Wrk.CreateUser(UsersName)
        Wrk.Groups("Users").Users.Append Usr
        Wrk.Users(UsersName).Groups.Refresh
    Set Usr = Wrk.CreateUser(UsersName)
    Wrk.Groups("Admins").Users.Append Usr
    Wrk.Users(UsersName).Groups.Refresh
```

Remember that without appending both—one appending the user to the Users collection and the other appending the user to the appropriate groups—the transaction is incomplete.

The least complicated user/group code involves checking to see which users belong to which groups (or vice versa). The following is a straightforward example involving printing user names and group assignments in the Debug window:

```
Dim Wrk as Workspace, Usr as User, Grp as Group
Set Wrk = DBEngine.Workspace(0)
For Each Usr in Wrk.Users
    Debug.Print Usr.Name & " belongs to:"
    For Each Grp in Usr.Groups
        Debug.Print "      " & Grp.Name
    Next Grp
Next Usr
```

Checking Groups collections and Users collections works the same way as checking any other collection in DAO code.

Analyzing Security Code

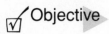 Objective ▶ In order to correctly answer all the Security questions on the exam, you need to look at code dealing with security issues and analyze it. This section shows examples of code, both correct and incorrect, and analyzes what is correct and wrong with the examples.

Analyzing Sample Code 1

You want to assign the right to view data to a user without revoking any permissions that the user already has. Will the following piece of code work (doc is a properly assigned Document object)?

```
doc.Permissions = doc.Permission And dbSecRetrieveData
```

The key to this question is the logical operator; the constant is correct (dbSecRetrieveData is the constant that assigns or revokes permissions to read data). But the logical operator is wrong—when you try to add permissions, you want to use the Or operator rather than the And operator. The preceding line of code, as it is, will not accomplish what you want it to do.

Analyzing Sample Code 2

If you want to write code that uses another user's permissions, you need to temporarily define another workspace, with another user. Which of the following lines of code is the correct syntax to create a new workspace (Wrk is a Workspace object)?

```
1. Set Wrk = DBEngine.CreateWorkspace("User Name", "User Pass-
word")

2. Set Wrk = DBEngine.CreateWorkspace("Workspace Name", "User
Name", "User Password")

3. Set Wrk = DBEngine.Workspaces.Add("Workspace Name", "User
Name", "User Password")

4. Set Wrk = DBEngine.Workspaces.Add("User Name", "User Pass-
word")
```

The syntax questions are always the trickiest, aren't they? When you use Access, you can just look up the syntax, but you don't have that luxury on the exam. The question doesn't even seem like a security issue because the question really asks about DAO syntax, but it counts as a security question anyway. The correct answer is the second line of code—CreateWorkspace is the correct method, and the arguments are Workspace Name, User Name, and User Password.

Analyzing Sample Code 3

What is the difference (if there is any) between these two lines of code (Usr is a properly defined User variable)?

```
1. DBEngine.Workspaces(0).Users.Append Usr

2. DBEngine.Workspaces(0).Groups(0).Users.Append Usr
```

There is a difference. The first line of code appends a user to the Users collection of the workspace. The second line of code appends the user to a specific group—the Users group. Users is always the default group in the Groups collection (Groups(0)), so to designate Groups(0).*Users* is the same thing as designating Groups("Users").

Analyzing Sample Code 4

If a user has permission to change the design of an object, how does this expression about that user's permissions evaluate?

```
(Doc.AllPermissions And Doc.dbWriteDef) > 0
```

The expression evaluates to True because dbWriteDef is the correct constant, and when checking permissions, you use the Permissions or AllPermissions property and the And operator. The AllPermissions property makes sure that explicit and implicit permissions are checked.

For more practice writing and analyzing code, go through the exercises and answer the sample exam questions at the end of the chapter.

Encrypting a Database

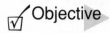 **Objective**

Encrypting a database compacts the database and then makes it unreadable to a word processor or other text-file utility program. You can gather some pieces of information by reading a database in a word processor—for example, if you know where to look, you can find the SID of the database owner or the SID of the Admins group.

More often than discovering a SID, however, people can use a word processor to access sensitive data in tables. The information is difficult to read, but it is in the table.

In an encrypted database, however, the entire file appears as a random series of meaningless characters. No patterns are left in an encrypted database. This explains why encrypted databases cannot be compressed with compression software because compression functions on repeated data patterns, and encryption removes patterns.

However, database performance pays a high price for encryption's security gains—the performance of an encrypted database is always 10 percent to 15 percent lower than the same unencrypted database.

Following are two ways to encrypt a database:

1. Run the Security Wizard, which creates a new, encrypted database from an unencrypted one. For details, refer to the section "Running the Security Wizard" earlier in this chapter.

2. Open Access without a database open, and choose the Tools menu, Security, Encrypt/Decrypt Database. You need to choose which database to encrypt and what to name the new encrypted database.

To decrypt a database, open Access without a database open. From the Tools menu, choose Security and then click Encrypt/Decrypt Database. You need to choose which database to decrypt and what to name the new decrypted database.

Key Terms and Concepts

Table 12.1 identifies key terms from this chapter. Review the key terms and make sure that you understand each term for the exam.

Table 12.1

Key Terms: Implementing Database Security	
Term	Covered in Section...
Share-level security	"Choosing the Appropriate Level of Security"
User-level security	"Choosing the Appropriate Level of Security"
Users	"Establishing User-Level Security"
Groups	"Establishing User-Level Security"
Workgroup database	"Workgroup Database"
User database	"User Database"
Security Wizard	"Running the Security Wizard (Optional)"
Object ownership	"Running the Security Wizard (Optional)"
Permissions	"Assigning Permissions to Appropriate Groups"
Documents	"DAO Permissions"
Containers	"DAO Permissions"
Encryption	"Encrypting a Database"

Lab Exercises

If you play around with the New Database wizards, you notice something very familiar about the databases used in these exercises. They are indeed wizard databases and are completely unaltered. You don't spend much time actually looking at them, however, because you create new Modules and work with the security interface.

Exercise 12.1: Implementing Security Through the Access Interface

To implement basic user-level security through the Access interface. In order to complete this lab, you need to understand how to do the following:

Objectives:

Create a workgroup database file.

Assign permissions and administrative rights.

Create new users and new groups.

Assign object ownership.

Time Estimate: 20–25 minutes

Steps:

1. Make sure that no copies of Access are running.

2. Start the Workgroup Administrator by navigating to the folder where Access is installed (using My Computer or Windows Explorer) and double-clicking Wrkgadm.exe.

3. Click Create to create a new workgroup database file. Type **Lilly** for your Name, **FlowersRUs** for Organization, and **Posies** for Workgroup ID.

4. The current path is fine, but do *not* leave the file named system.mdw! Instead, rename it to flowers.mdw and then click OK.

5. Click Exit to leave the Workgroup Administrator.

6. Open Access without a database open or active. From the Tools menu, choose Security, User and Group Accounts, and then go to the Change Logon Password tab.

7. Notice that you're logged on as Admin. The old password does not exist, so type **SoLongAdmin** for a new password in the New Password box and again in the Verify boxes. Click Apply.

8. Click the Users tab in the User and Group Accounts dialog box and click New to create the new administrator. Type **Lilly** for the new User Name and **Lilly Pad** for a Personal ID. Click OK.

9. With Lilly selected in the User Name box, select Admins in the Available Groups list box and then click Add.

10. Choose Admin from the User Name combo box. Select Admins in the Member Of list box, click Remove, and then click OK to close the dialog box.

11. Close and restart Access. The program prompts you for a user name and password. To log in as the new administrator, change the user name from Admin to Lilly, and leave the password box blank. Click OK.

12. You don't have to open a database, so click Cancel when prompted to open or create a database. From the Tools menu, choose Security, User and Group Accounts, and then go to the Change Logon Password tab. Notice that now you're logged on as Lilly. The old password does not exist, so type **Roses** in the New Password box and type **Roses** again in the Verify box. Click Apply.

13. Go to the Groups tab. Click New. Type **Designers** for the Group Name and **Artists** for the Personal ID. Click OK.

14. Go back to the Users tab. Make sure you select Lilly as the User Name, and Designers as the Available Group. Click Add.

continues

15. Open the sample database Wine List.mdb included on the CD. From the Tools menu, choose Security, User-Level Security Wizard. Click the check box OFF for Tables. Click OK. Accept the default path and name of Secure Wine List.mdb. Click Save.

16. Let the wizard do its thing. When the process is done, notice that the message box tells you that only user Lilly and members of the Admins group have rights to the database and the selected objects. Click OK.

17. Close the Wine List.mdb database and open the new Secure Wine List.mdb. Look around the database a bit, and notice that you can do anything, even modify a form's design, because you logged on as Lilly.

18. Exit and restart Access. This time, log on as user Admin with password SoLongAdmin (case-sensitive, the same way you typed it earlier). Open the new Secure Wine List.mdb and watch the errors. Notice that you can see the database window and do anything to the tables, including modify the design, but you can't open anything else.

19. Restart Access again and log on as Lilly with password Roses (case-sensitive). From the Tools menu, choose Security, User and Group Permissions. Make sure the Permissions tab is active. Click the Groups option button to change from looking at a list of users to looking at a list of groups.

20. Change the Object Type to Tables and select the table Switchboard Items. Select different groups and look at their permissions. Admins and Designers have no rights to anything, and Users have rights to everything.

21. With Switchboard Items still selected, select the Admins group. Click the Administer check box. Notice that all the other boxes fill in. Click Apply.

22. With Switchboard Items still selected, choose the Designers group. Click the Update Data check box. Notice that Read Data and Read Design fill in. Click Apply.

23. Go to the Change Owner tab. Notice that Admin owns everything, which explains why the user Admin has full rights to every object. Change the Object Type to Table and then select the table Switchboard Items. Change the New Owner to Lilly and click Change Owner. Click OK. Exit Access.

24. To make sure you don't have to always log on as Lilly as the default, go back to the Workgroup Administrator and click Join. Browse until you select the system.mdw in the directory where Access is installed. Click Open and then OK and then OK again. Click Exit to leave the Workgroup Administrator.

Comments:

If this were a real-world situation, you would want to assign administrative rights for all objects to the Admins group and make the Users group the most restrictive. You would also want to decrypt the database, if encryption were not necessary.

The exercise was enough to show you where items are and to give you a feel for implementing user-level security.

Reading Reference:

For more information about the concepts raised by the exercise, refer to the section "Implementing Basic User-Level Security."

Exercise 12.2:   Checking Security Through DAO Code

To learn to programmatically list users and groups. In order to complete this lab, you need to understand how to perform the following tasks:

Objective:

Analyze Security code.

Manipulate the Groups and Users collections in DAO.

continues

Time Estimate: 5–10 minutes

Steps:

1. Open the sample database Music Collection.mdb included on the CD. View the database window by double-clicking the minimized database window inside the Access window or by clicking the Database Window button.

2. Go to the Modules tab and click New. Then type in this code to programmatically list groups and users:

```
Sub ListGroupsUsers()
Dim Wrk as Workspace, Grp as Group, Usr as User
Set Wrk = DBEngine(0)
For Each Grp in Wrk.Groups
    Debug.Print "The " & Ucase(Grp.Name) & " Group has these
➥Members:"
    For Each Usr in Grp.Users
        Debug.Print "     " & Usr.Name
    Next Usr
Next Grp
End Sub
```

3. Open the Debug window by clicking the Debug Window button, or from the View menu, choose Debug Window. In the Debug Window, type **ListGroupsUsers** and press Enter.

4. You can accomplish this same goal in several ways, which points to all the ways available to access User and Group objects. Close the Debug Window and type in this code to programmatically list users and groups:

```
Sub ListUsersGroups()
Dim Wrk As Workspace, Usr As User, Grp As GROUP
Dim x, y As Integer
Set Wrk = DBEngine(0)
For x = 0 To Wrk.Users.Count - 1
    Set Usr = Wrk.Users(x)
    Debug.Print "The " & UCase(Usr.Name) & " User belongs to
➥the following Groups:"
    For y = 0 To Usr.Groups.Count - 1
        Set Grp = Usr.Groups(y)
```

```
        Debug.Print "      " & Grp.Name
    Next y
Next x
End Sub
```

5. Open the Debug window again, type **ListUsersGroups,** and press Enter. Notice that a few surprises are in this listing. The Creator User and the Engine User are hidden system Users. Because they do not belong to any groups, they are not included in the Groups to Users listing.

6. Save the module as basSecurity. You need the module in the next exercise.

Comments:

If you do this exercise while logged on to a workgroup with only the Admin user, you probably are thinking about adding another user and checking the code again. The odd thing is that if you add users through the Access interface, the users do not show up in your code right away—you must restart Access before they are listed.

The practical lesson you should learn from that fact is that after you do any work with users, groups, and permissions, your best bet is to restart Access—if you have the choice—before you do any more development.

Reading Reference:

For more information about the concepts raised by the exercise, refer to the section "Manipulating Users and Groups."

Exercise 12.3: Implementing Security Through DAO Code

To learn to programmatically add and manipulate users and groups. In order to complete this lab, you need to understand how to do the following:

continues

Objectives:

Analyze Security code.

Manipulate the Groups and Users collections in DAO.

Dynamically interact between the Groups and Users collections in DAO.

Time Estimate: 10–15 minutes

Steps:

1. Open the basSecurity module of the Music Collection.mdb database that you worked with in exercise 12.2. To complete exercise 12.3, you need some of the code you created in exercise 12.2.

2. Type the following code in the Module window to add a new user:

```
Sub AddNewUser()
Dim Wrk As Workspace, Usr As User, UsersName As String
UsersName = "Susie Q"
    Set Wrk = DBEngine(0)
    Set Usr = Wrk.CreateUser(UsersName, "UserPID", "UserPwd")
    Wrk.Users.Append Usr
        Set Usr = Wrk.CreateUser(UsersName)
        Wrk.Groups("Users").Users.Append Usr
        Wrk.Users(UsersName).Groups.Refresh
End Sub
```

3. Now open the Debug window and type **AddNewUser**. You probably do not see the computer processing the subroutine, but it has been accomplished.

4. To check what AddNewUser() accomplished, type **ListUsersGroups** in the Debug window and press Enter. Next, type **ListGroupsUsers** and press Enter. You should see Susie Q listed from both procedures.

5. To add another group, type the following code:

```
Sub AddNewGroup()
Dim Wrk as Workspace, Grp As Group
Set Wrk = DBEngine(0)
    Set Grp = Wrk.CreateGroup("Dancers", "RockNRoll")
    Wrk.Groups.Append Grp
End Sub
```

6. Now when you run ListGroupsUsers, the Dancers group has nobody assigned to it. To solve that problem, we assign Susie Q with the following code—in a different way than we assigned her to the Admins group:

```
Sub AppendGroup()
Dim Wrk As Workspace, Usr As User, Grp As GROUP, UsersName
As String
Set Wrk = DBEngine(0)
    UsersName = "Susie Q"
        Set Grp = Wrk.CreateGroup("Dancers")
        Wrk.Users(UsersName).Groups.Append Grp
        Wrk.Groups("Dancers").Users.Refresh
End Sub
```

7. Now Susie Q should be listed as a Dancers group member when you run ListGroupsUsers and ListUsersGroups. Save basSecurity, because you need it for the next exercise.

Comments:

Whichever collection you append—groups or users—you need to refresh the other collection, or you can run into trouble if you have any kind of looping code or if you attempt to assign permissions.

Reading Reference:

For more information about the concepts raised by the exercise, refer to the section "Manipulating Users and Groups."

Exercise 12.4: Manipulate Permissions Through DAO Code

To programmatically check and assign permissions. In order to complete this lab, you need to understand how to do the following:

Objective:

Differentiate between Permissions and AllPermissions.

Fully understand the distinction between OR, AND, and AND NOT in the role of checking and assigning permissions.

Differentiate between group and individual permissions.

Time Estimate: 10-15 minutes

Steps:

1. Open the basSecurity module of the Music Collection.mdb database that you worked with in exercise 12.3. To complete exercise 12.4, you need some of the code you created in exercises 12.2 and 12.3.

2. Susie Q, as a user, needs to be able to read or modify the data about the music, but she should not be allowed to delete data. First, check her permissions. Type the following code in the Module window:

```
Sub CheckPermissions()
Dim db As DATABASE, Doc As Document
Dim DeleteDataOK, ModifyDataOK As Integer
Dim Usr, Tbl As String
Usr = "Susie Q"
Tbl = "Recordings"
    Set db = DBEngine(0)(0)
    Set Doc = db.Containers!Tables.Documents(Tbl)
    Doc.UserName = Usr
        'check permissions
        ModifyDataOK = (Doc.AllPermissions And
        ➡dbSecReplaceData)
```

```
        DeleteDataOK = (Doc.AllPermissions And
    ➥dbSecDeleteData)
    If ModifyDataOK > 0 Then
        MsgBox Usr & " CAN modify data!"
    Else
        MsgBox Usr & " CANNOT modify data"
    End If
    If DeleteDataOK > 0 Then
        MsgBox Usr & " CAN delete data!"
    Else
        MsgBox Usr & " CANNOT delete data"
    End If
End Sub
```

3. Go to the Debug window and type **CheckPermissions**. Oops! Susie Q can modify *and* delete data. Reassign permissions by typing the following code in the Module window:

```
Sub AssignPermissions()
Dim db As DATABASE, Doc As Document, Usr, Tbl As String
Usr = "Users"
Tbl = "Recordings"
    Set db = DBEngine(0)(0)
    Set Doc = db.Containers!Tables.Documents(Tbl)
    Doc.UserName = Usr
            'revoke permissions
            Doc.Permissions = Doc.Permissions And Not
            ➥dbSecDeleteData
End Sub
```

4. Go the Debug window and type **RevokePermissions** to revoke Susie Q's permissions and then type **CheckPermissions** again and see whether the messages are more to your liking.

Comments:

Notice that we needed to revoke permissions from the Users group not just from Susie Q. The exercise does not work if we use Susie Q as the user rather than Users. If we add permissions instead of revoke them, we must type OR instead of AND NOT.

Reading Reference:

For more information about the concepts raised by the exercise, refer to the sections "Setting Permissions Through Code" and "Checking Permissions Through Code."

Review Questions

1. Which of the following are advantages to using user-level security over a database password? (Choose two.)

   A. User-level security enables you to efficiently manage a large number of users.

   B. User-level security enables you to use network security.

   C. User-level security does not enable people to read your database with a text editor or word processor.

   D. User-level security enables you to assign different permissions for each object for each group or user.

2. Which of the following statements is *not* true?

   A. Permission information about objects, such as tables and forms, is stored in the user database.

   B. Information about passwords is stored in the workgroup database.

   C. Permission is allowed or rejected based on a user's PID.

   D. When new users are added through the Tools menu, they are automatically added to the Users group.

3. You want to distribute a database and deny users the right to modify design on any object. You do not want most individual users to have to remember passwords or logon names. You are the only one administering or modifying design on any object. You use a custom workgroup file while developing your database. Which of the following security measures should you use?

A. Assign the Admin user ownership to all objects and then remove Modify Design permissions from the Admin user. Do *not* distribute your workgroup database file.

B. Remove the Admin user from the Admins group of your custom workgroup file. Then remove Modify Design permissions from the Admins and Users. Distribute your workgroup database file.

C. You cannot accomplish the task without users signing on as another user with a password. Create a generic user with a simple password and distribute the username and password with the workgroup database file.

D. Remove the Admin user from the Admins group of your custom workgroup file. Then remove Modify Design permissions from the Admins and Users. Do *not* distribute your workgroup database file.

4. To successfully re-create a workgroup database file, you need what pieces of information?

A. Workgroup Name, Organization, and Personal ID.

B. All Group Names, User Names, and Personal IDs.

C. Both A and B.

D. You do not need to re-create the entire workgroup database file identically, just the individual user accounts.

5. Which of the following tasks is possible in Access?

A. Deleting the Admin user

B. Synchronizing an encrypted database

C. Deleting the Admins group

D. Deleting a group with users assigned to it

6. Which of the following does *not* occur when you run the Security Wizard from an existing database?

    A. An encrypted database is created.

    B. The original database is deleted.

    C. The secure database is owned by the user who ran the Security Wizard.

    D. Table relationships are reestablished.

7. You have sensitive information in your Products table. You want your data-entry people to know how much to charge for an object, but not how much you paid for it. What is the best way to remove all permissions for the column that holds the sensitive data?

    A. Break the Products table into two tables with a one-to-one relationship—one table has sensitive information, and the other table has public information.

    B. Create a select query that returns all non-sensitive data, set the Run Permissions property of the query to Owner's, and deny all permissions for the Products table for the Users group.

    C. Set permissions for the Field object of the table to Not dbSecRetrieveData.

    D. Set permissions for the Field object of the table to Not dbSecFullAccess.

8. You want to enable a user named John the right to Add records to the Employees table, without revoking any permissions he already has. You have set the variables correctly using the following code:

```
Dim Doc As Document
Set Doc =
➥DBEngine(0)(0).Containers!Tables.Documents!Employees
Doc.User = "John"
```

Which line of code should come next?

A. Doc.Permissions = Doc.Permissions Or
   dbSecInsertData

B. Doc.AllPermissions = Doc.Permissions And
   dbSecInsertData

C. Doc.AllPermissions = dbSecInsertData

D. Doc.Permissions = dbSecInsertData

9. You want to add user John, who already exists, to the Accountants group. The variable Wrk is properly set to the current workspace, and the variable Usr is defined as a User variable. Which code listing should you use?

A. Set Usr = Wrk.Accountants.Append Usr

   Wrk.Groups(Accountants).Users.Append Usr

B. Set Usr = Wrk.User("John").Append "Accountants"

   wrk.Groups("Accountants").Append "John"

C. Set Usr =
   Wrk.Groups("Accountants").CreateUser("John")

   Wrk.Groups("Accountants").Users.Append Usr

D. Set Usr =
   Wrk.CreateGroup("Accountants").AppendUser("John")

Answers to Review Questions

1. A and D are correct. Refer to the section "Choosing the Appropriate Level of Security."

2. C is incorrect. Permission is based on a user's SID (Secure ID), which the Jet Engine creates from the user name and PID (Personal ID). Refer to the section "Users and Groups."

3. D is correct. Because you use the default Admin user, you do not need to distribute the workgroup database file. Refer to

the section "Redefining Administrative Accounts" and "Using Invisible Admin Security."

4. C is correct. You need every piece of information that you use to create the workgroup database and each group and user. Refer to the section "Creating or Joining a Secure Workgroup."

5. D is correct. You can delete a group with users assigned to it, but you can't perform any of the other actions listed. Refer to the section "Creating Groups and Users."

6. B is correct. The original database remains intact. Refer to the section "Running the Security Wizard (Optional)."

7. B is correct. Refer to the section "Assigning Owner Permissions for Queries."

8. A is correct. Refer to the section "Setting Permissions Through Code."

9. C is correct. Refer to the section "Manipulating Users and Groups" and "Analyzing Security Code."

Answers to Test Yourself Questions at Beginning of Chapter...

1. If you implement security for a database that will be replicated, you must choose user-level security and not share-level security. For more information, see the section "Choosing the Appropriate Level of Security."

2. The first step in implementing user-level security is to create or join a secure workgroup. For more information, see the section "Implementing Basic User-Level Security."

3. Permission information about objects, such as tables and forms, is stored in the user database. Information about passwords is stored in the workgroup database. For more information, see the section "Establishing User-Level Security."

4. The object's owner automatically has full permissions for an object, even if that user does not have full permissions for any other object in the database. For more information, see the section "Establishing User-Level Security."

5. No, you do not have to make your end-users remember a password in order to implement security. For more information, see the section "Using Invisible Admin Security."

6. This was a trick question. The Groups collection includes a Users collection, and the Users collection contains a Groups collection. For more information, see the section "Manipulating Users and Groups."

7. The Security Wizard reassigns ownership of all database objects to the current user. For more information, see the section "Running the Security Wizard (Optional)."

8. Encrypting a database compacts the database and makes it unreadable to a word processor or other text-file utility program. For more information, see the section "Encrypting a Database."

Chapter 13

Client/Server
Application Development

By the end of this chapter, you will be able to execute the following test objectives:

 Objectives

- ▶ Given a scenario, decide whether to use SQL pass-through queries or Microsoft Access queries

- ▶ Access external data by using ODBC

- ▶ Trap errors that are generated by the server

- ▶ Optimize connections

- ▶ Optimize performance for a given client/server application

1. Name a few reasons why you would want to design or convert a standalone database or file-server database to a client/server application.

2. In working with ODBC, which part of the ODBC layer links Access to all the defined ODBC data sources?

3. Explain how the FillCache method works.

4. What does ODBC stand for?

5. What is an SQL pass-through query?

6. List a few of the responsibilities of the ODBC Driver Manager.

7. Analyze this situation: You would like to utilize the CrossTab query in Access for a report that isn't supported by the server on the database. If processing speed is the most important aspect in the developing your client/server application, should using the CrossTab in Access be considered? If not, why? If so, under what conditions?

8. List a number of general guidelines for getting the most out of client/server.

9. What is the overall goal of the client/server architecture?

10. In the client/server architecture, what part of the model initiates a transaction by sending a message to a server where the database resides?

Answers are located at the end of the chapter...

Chapter 13 focuses on using Microsoft Access as part of a client/ server database solution as covered on the MSCD exam. This chapter begins by investigating the client/server architecture. The client/server architecture, illustrated in figure 13.1, is a distributed form of processing in which a client initiates a transaction by sending a message to a server on which a database resides. The server database performs the requested process on the database and then, if necessary, returns data to the client.

Figure 13.1.

The client/server architecture.

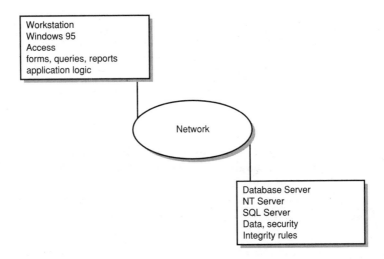

The client, or workstation, is connected to a server by a network through either a local area network or dial-up networking. The server portion is represented by a database that resides on a mainframe, mini, or personal computer.

In a client/server architecture, the *client* or *user's* workstation is sometimes called the *front end*. The *server* containing the database, which might be running on another computer, is sometimes referred to as the *back end* or the *database engine*. The server stores the data and processes the requested information initiated by the client.

Here's how a client/server system works. The client or workstation initiates a request for information in the form of a SQL query. The database processes the query and returns only the rows that are specific to those requested by the client.

In an efficient client/server system, the server helps with the processing and reduces the network traffic and work load usually needed to complete the transaction by the client. When the data is returned to the front, the client formats the data and then displays it to the end user.

An example of a client/server system is using Access as a front end to receive and process data from a Microsoft SQL server database that is running on an NT server or another computer.

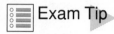 **Exam Tip**

Understanding the client/server model isn't specifically covered on the exam. However, a solid understanding of what Access' role should be and how all the pieces fit together in a well-designed client/server system is necessary.

Using Access as a client/server front end, as described earlier, differs from simply running Access on a file server. In the latter situation, the file server makes the database file available to the workstation or client so that they can share the data. When a client needs data, the client reads the data across network from the file server hard disk. The client must perform all the processing to select the data from a table or join multiple tables and perform any queries. The file server doesn't assist with any of the processing.

 Tip

Access is a very powerful tool in the client/server model because it can connect to database engines other than Access, such as SQL Server, Oracle, Informix, and so on.

Because this discussion of client/server application development pertains to the exam, this chapter focuses on the use of Access only as a front-end in the client/server architecture.

Choosing Access as a Client/Server Front End

There are some very good reasons why you would want to use Access as a front end or convert a current system to a client/server architecture for a database application. These benefits include the following:

▶ **Supports a large number of concurrent users.** If you have a database system that requires a large number of concurrent users, you might need to implement a client/server solution. A large number of users accessing a database on a file server can significantly reduce the processing power and response time of the server. An efficient client/server system utilizes the raw processing power and stability of a large main frame, mini, or personal computer.

▶ **Performs well even if large data requirements have been defined.** This benefit is similar to that of the preceding reason. Large amounts of data to be transferred over a network in a file server application can make a system very inefficient and less responsive. Access performs well with a few hundred or even a thousand records in a table. (Even Access' responsiveness is greatly reduced with hundreds of thousands, or perhaps millions, of records, however.)

▶ **Operates with superior speed and efficiency.** One valuable reason for migrating or building a client/server system is to improve the speed of searches and other database transactions. Database server software is highly efficient and provides much faster processing than the Microsoft Jet Engine.

▶ **Provides better security and reliability.** Microsoft SQL Server, Sybase SQL, Informix, DB/2, and a few other database engines can provide better security and reliability than that which Access can provide. Many database engines offer support for multiprocessor servers, as well. They also provide highly efficient algorithms and extended functions that do not exist within Access.

▶ **Offers an Open Systems computing environment.** Client/server computing offers the flexibility of developing an Open Systems computing environment, which provides enterprise-wide access to a database. Imagine that your company has hundreds of users working on PCs, Macintoshes, and UNIX workstations. These different computing platforms must have access the same data. A well-designed client/server system allows for the different operating systems to share the same data, reducing the number of systems to maintain and, therefore, reducing redundant data.

Tip

Access isn't available for UNIX or the Macintosh. Other software packages exist for UNIX and the Mac that allow access to the data on the server.

▶ **Provides an easy-to-use graphical interface in which to view and work with data from a mainframe system.** The old terminal-based system provides a simple text display of data. The client/server architecture provides a more responsive and easier-to-use graphical interface in which to look at data on a mainframe or mini system. The old terminal-based workstations cannot offer the productivity or the cost savings of Windows applications. Because mainframe or mini systems can contain valuable data that is vital to an organization, the need exists to graphically access the data. As stated earlier, the client/server architecture is the best solution because it offers a friendly, graphical, responsive tool with which to access the data.

Understanding Access in the Client/Server Architecture

Turn your attention to how Access works in a client/server architecture. Access works as a front end in a client/server model by means of linked tables. Linked tables in Access don't store actual data but simply contain a pointer to the location at which the data or information is physically stored.

Table 13.2 shows the layers in an Access client/server application:

Table 13.2

The Client/Server Application Layers in Access	
Layer	Functions
Access Front End	Appears on user workstations; interacts with users and servers.
Microsoft Jet Engine	Retrieves data requested by Access; enforces referential integrity and validation rules.

Layer	Functions
ODBC Driver and Driver Manager	Links from Access to all ODBC data sources. Driver can be provided by a third party such as Oracle, Informix, Sybase, and so on.
Network Communications Library	Network communications software that allows data to be exchanged between client and server.
Database Server	Software such as SQL Server that processes data requests and sends resulting rows or messages back to the client.

Utilizing Open Database Connectivity

Access utilizes the Microsoft *Open Database Connectivity (ODBC) application programming interface (API)* to provide data access connectivity to Microsoft SQL server, or to any database system for which ODBC drivers are available. Using the ODBC API in writing programmatic code enables a user to create a heterogeneous model that adapts to a wide variety of databases.

The ODBC API consists of a driver manager and one or more ODBC drivers. The ODBC API uses drivers to translate instructions passed from the application through the driver that are compatible with various RDBMSs (Relational Database Management System). When the ODBC driver manager receives instructions from Access that are intended for a particular data source, such as SQL Server database, the driver manager opens the appropriate ODBC driver for the database.

As you can understand, the ODBC driver manager and ODBC drivers must work together but maintain separate responsibilities. Take a look at their responsibilities.

The driver manager is responsible for the following:

▶ Loading the specified database driver as defined in the data source name entry

▶ Initializing the interface

▶ Providing driver entry points

▶ Validating parameters and managing serialization of ODBC functions

The ODBC driver is responsible for the following:

▶ Implementing ODBC API functions

▶ Establishing a connection and submitting requests to the remote database engines

▶ Translating and returning the results to the client

▶ Formatting errors into standard error codes

▶ Declaring and manipulating cursors

▶ Managing the transactions

 Tip

It is important to remember that an ODBC driver is required for each type of database that you link to an Access database.

ODBC doesn't possess its own networking capability. Therefore, you need a network library in addition to the particular ODBC driver. The network library is necessary for communication with the ODBC driver and the defined database that you want to access.

Setting Up the ODBC Connection

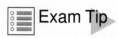 **Exam Tip**

The process of setting up the ODBC driver is not covered on the exam. You must understand, however, how the ODBC connection works in order to have a complete understanding of how Access connects to a remote database.

Fortunately, Access hides the complexity of the ODBC connection from the user and the developer. Before you can access the ODBC data source from Access, you must provide information to enable a connection to the remote server. The data source information needed to establish a connection can be provided by using the Control Panel ODBC Setup applet.

 Tip

An ODBC connection can also be established by using Data Access Objects coding. This is covered later in this chapter in the section "Using an ODBC Connection String."

To use the Control Panel applet to set up a SQL Server ODBC data source in Windows 95 or Windows NT, open the Control Panel folder and double-click on the ODBC icon.

The figures and examples used in this chapter are from a Windows 95 system. However, the ODBC setup discussed here is very similar to that in a Windows NT system. The Control Panel folder contains an icon that you can use to set up an ODBC data source, as shown in figure 13.2. Your application refers to this defined data source when it wants to make a connection to the database associated with the data source.

Figure 13.2

Use the 32bit ODBC icon to set up an ODBC data source.

The Data Sources dialog box lists the data sources, as shown in figure 13.3. You can use this dialog box to add or edit an existing driver or remove a data source or add a new one. It can also display information about the installed drivers, and set the ODBC trace options. Trace options can be used to fine-tune your data source and give you more detailed information about what the Microsoft Jet Engine is doing through ODBC to satisfy a request.

Figure 13.3

The Data Sources dialog box lists the data sources.

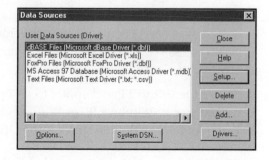

Click the Add button to add a data source to the list. The next screen displays the Add Data Source dialog box, as shown in figure 13.4.

Figure 13.4

The Add Data Source dialog box adds a data source to the list.

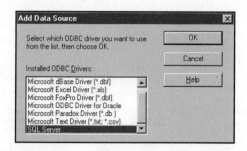

The Installed ODBC Drivers list box shows the drivers you can use from your Access application and the databases that you can access. If the database driver doesn't exist for the database that you want to access, you must install it before you can continue setup.

Choose SQL Server from the list of installed drivers and click on OK. This action will display the ODBC SQL Server Setup dialog box, as shown in figure 13.5.

Figure 13.5

*The ODBC SQL
Server Setup
dialog box.*

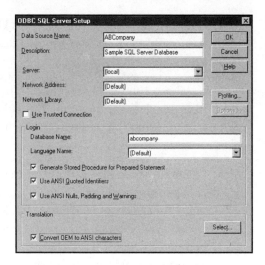

In this dialog box you have a number of fields that need to be set up. The fields and their definitions are as follows:

- ▶ **Data Source Name.** Type a user-determined name for the data source in the Data Source Name text box, and enter an appropriate description of the data source in the Description text box.

- ▶ **Server.** In the Server drop-down list box, select by using the mouse, or type the name of the server on which the server is installed. The name (local) indicates that the server specified is the local machine on which Setup is running.

- ▶ **Network Address.** The location of the server is specified by using the Network Address box. The actual address entered is dependent on the type of network running to which your computer is connected. For example, if you are using the TCP/IP protocol for your network the address specified should be an IP address.

▶ **Network Library.** In the Network Library text box specify the name of the Server Net-Library that the driver needs to communicate with the network.

▶ **Database Name.** Specify the database you want to associate with this data source name by clicking on the Options button and entering the database name in the Database Name text box.

▶ **Generate Stored Procedure for Prepared Statement.** Put a check in the Generate Stored Procedure for Prepared Statement check box to cause the SQL Server driver to create stored procedures for prepared statements. This option is beneficial when you use the statements frequently in your applications. When this option checkbox is clear, the creation of stored procedures for prepared statements is disabled. In this case, a prepared statement is stored and executed only when it is actually called.

▶ **Convert OEM to ANSI Characters.** Select the Convert OEM to ANSI Characters check box if the client computer and server are using the same non-ANSI character set. When this option checkbox is clear and the client machine and server are using different character sets, you must specify a character set translator.

When the preceding information is appropriately entered click the OK button to add the new defined data source. This step displays the Data Sources dialog box again, as shown in figure 13.3. Highlight the newly created source for server and click on the Drivers button to display information about the installed driver, as shown in figure 13.6.

You can have the ODBC calls that Jet makes written to a log file by clicking on the Options button in the Data Sources dialog box and then putting a check in the Trace ODBC Calls check box in the ODBC Options dialog box.

When tracing has been enabled, the ODBC Driver Manager writes to the file you specify in the ODBC Options dialog box the ODBC calls made by any application. The default SQL.LOG filename is created in the root directory.

Figure 13.6

*Information dis-
played about the
installed driver.*

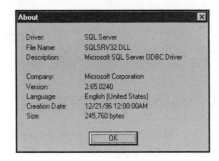

If you put a check in the Stop Tracing Automatically check box
(see fig. 13.7), the trace is turned off when the ODBC Driver Manager detects application termination. This steps clears the Trace
check box and forces you to reset it when you want to resume
tracing.

Figure 13.7

*The ODBC Op-
tions dialog box
indicates your
tracing options.*

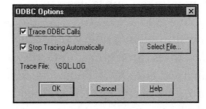

Understanding ODBC and the Registry

The Registry enables the user to change special features of the
ODBC Connection. Caution should always be taken when working
with the Registry.

When Jet accesses an ODBC data source, it uses the defaults that
are built into Microsoft Jet Engine. These default features control
ODBC Connection. For example, it might control the amount of
time to wait for an ODBC connection or the amount of time to
wait for a query to finish.

If the Jet defaults are unacceptable for your client/server application, you can build entries into the system registry to specify your
own options. You must add the registry tree to contain these values because the ODBC setup does not create them.

Tip

The preceding settings are only applicable to the Microsoft Jet Engine by Access applications.

Working with ODBC Connections

Now that we have properly set up the ODBC connection, it's time to work with it programmatically.

In most instances, Access hides the complexity of the ODBC connection from the user and the developer. This section discusses how to create and manipulate ODBC connections through the Access user interface and with Visual Basic for Applications code. We are now getting into the heart of what is covered on the exam.

When linked, the tables and queries act just as an internal Access table would act. A linked table or query in Access will serve as the row source for a query, report, or form. Remember that Access databases can connect to ODBC data sources through tables or queries. The *ODBC connections string* is stored in the Description property of a table. The connection string is created automatically when you attach a table from the Access menu. It can also be created or modified programmatically in Visual Basic for Applications code.

Here is an ODBC connection string for an attached Access table:

```
DATABASE=C:\ACCESS\SAMPLES\NORTHWIND.MDB;TABLE=Customers
```

The Access database filename and the table name are the only definitions that the connection string needs.

Here is a sample ODBC connection string used to attach to an SQL Server table:

```
ODBC;DSN=ABCompany;APP=Microsoft
➡Access;WSID=worksationid;DATABASE=abcompany;TABLE=dbo.names
```

If the connection string reads "ODBC;" or is blank, Access prompts you for the connection information at runtime. Managing your ODBC connections in this manner is not recommended.

Here is an example of how you can create and update ODBC connections with Access Basic:

```
'This code is an example and will not compile
Dim tf As TableDef
Dim fld As Field
Dim db As Database
Set db = DBEngine.Workspaces(0).OpenDatabase("MYDB.mdb")
'Create new TableDef
Set tf = db.CreateTableDef("Test"
'Add field to the TableDef
Set fld = tf.CreateField("TestComments",dbText)
tf.Fields.Append fld
'Save TableDef definition by appending it to the TableDefs col-
lection.
Db.TableDefs.Append tf
```

Working with SQL Pass-Through Queries

Pass-through queries enable you to write queries in the dialect of SQL used by the remote server RDBMS. SQL Server lets you write stored procedures that you can execute by name rather than sending individual SQL statements to the server. As stated earlier in the "Choosing Access as a Client/Server Front End" section, executing a stored procedure query on the server is much faster than executing the query through the Microsoft Jet Engine because of the reduced network traffic on and the processor speed of the server. Obviously, if a stored procedure exists on the server, writing a SQL pass-through query enables the user to execute it.

 Tip

Query result sets returned by SQL pass-through queries are Recordset objects of the SnapShot type, which are not updateable. Other query result sets against databases linked by ODBC, such as Recordset objects of the Dynaset type, can be updateable. However, the query design and index on the table will determine if the object is updateable.

Creating a SQL Pass-Through Query in Access

Now that you have learned about SQL pass-through queries, it's time to create one. Begin by creating a SQL pass-through query in Access and then use the Visual Basic for Applications code.

Here are the steps in Access that enable you to create a pass-through query:

1. Click the Queries tab in the Database Window, and then click New.

2. Click New Query. Because there is no Query Wizard for SQL pass-through queries, choose Design view.

3. Close the Show Table dialog box without choosing a table or query.

4. Choose Query, SQL Specific, Pass-Through.

5. The Query Properties sheet shown in figure 13.8 is normally displayed. However, if for some reason the Query Properties sheet cannot be seen, display it by choosing View, Properties or by clicking View Properties icon on the toolbar. Table 13.10 outlines the query properties.

Figure 13.8

Query Properties for the SQL pass-through Query.

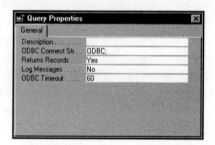

6. Enter the ODBC connection string in the ODBC Connect Str box.

Table 13.10

Pass-Through Query Properties	
Property	**Description**
Returns Records	Set to yes, the query returns rows; set to no, the query executes without returning any rows.
Log Messages	Set to yes, a table is created to store messages returned by the server.
ODBC Timeout	This property determines in seconds as to when the query will timeout.

Creating a SQL Pass-Through Query in VBA

You can also create a pass-through query in Visual Basic for Applications code. Follow these steps:

1. In the Database window, choose Modules and then New.

2. Create a new subprocedure by clicking the Insert Procedure button on the toolbar or by selecting the Insert, Procedure menu option.

3. Make the procedure a sub rather than a function and enter CreatePassThroughQuery as the subprocedure name. You use a subprocedure instead of a function because you won't be passing or returning any parameters.

4. Enter code that will work the Northwind.mdb database provided by Microsoft with Access. Enter the following in this procedure:

```
Public Sub CreatePassThroughQuery()

Dim db As Database
Dim qf As QueryDef
Dim strSql As String

Set db = CurrentDb
```

```
strSql="Select au_lname, au_fname * FROM Authors ORDER BY
➥au_lname"
Set qf = db.CreateQueryDef("qrySelectAuthors", strSQL)
DoCmd.OpenQuery qf.Name
      End Sub
```

5. Close the form module.

Passing Parameters in a SQL Pass-Through Query

You cannot pass parameters in a SQL pass-through query the way you can with other queries. Some stored procedures in the remote require one or more parameters to be passed into them. You need some way to specify them when you execute the pass-through query.

Here's an example:

```
'Code is only example and will not work or compile.
Set db = DBEngine.Workspaces(0).Databases(0)
Set qryQueryDef = db.CreateQueryDef("")
qryQueryDef.Connect = "ODBC;DSN=abcompany"
qryQueryDef.SQL = "dbCompanyParameter '" & txtCompany.Value & _
                  "'"
Set rs = qryQueryDef.OpenRecordset()
'Do something with results
rs.Close
db.Close
```

The preceding sample code creates a temporary QueryDef object. It then sets the Connect property to the data source name defined in the ODBC setup. The SQL property of the query is set to the name of the stored procedure you want to execute. The values for the required parameters are concatenated with the name of the parameter and its value. The QueryDef object is then opened.

The stored procedure in the next example takes one parameter to specify the company and returns the full name and phone number for the company:

```
'Code is only an example and will not work or compile
CREATE PROCEDURE dbCompanyParameter @companyin char(30)
As select full_name, phone where company = @companyin
```

Understanding the Server and Access

One of the so-called selling points of ODBC is that you can develop applications that are server independent. However, even though ODBC certainly makes it easier to move from server to server, it is still quite important to write your application with the target server in mind.

The server and the database on the server determine how Access will function and how to programmatically code your application.

References to the server also refer to the database, such as Oracle, Informix, DB/2, Microsoft SQL, Sybase, and so on. This is done to lessen the confusion between the Access Database and the remote server. Once again, Access in the client/server model is the front-end.

In developing a client/server application there are a number of characteristics that should be considered when choosing a server. If a server has already been chosen or predetermined, however, you will need to understand the server's limitations and strengths to determine how to develop and organize an efficient client/server system using Access.

Not only must you understand your server, but you will also need to understand Access. Access provides additional features that go beyond the ANSI and ISO standards found in other database systems.

For example, Access allows a query to retrieve the Top 10 customers or Top 10 Percent customers. Access also offers the capability to perform CrossTab queries—Distinct Rows, which hides duplicates, and OwnerAccess query rights, to name a few.

Access enables you to perform these functions on the client and not the server. This means that the processing will be done on the client.

If a user-defined function is frequently used in a client/server, it would be advantageous, if possible, to convert it to a stored procedure and move it to the server. It might be determined, however, that the functionality offered by Access outweighs the improved processing offered by the server.

Designing an Efficient Client/Server Application

In designing an efficient client/server application a good starting point is to clearly define and document all your transaction processing. Group together all related transactions processing to protect your data and allow you easy recovery.

When designing an efficient client/server system, you need to address several issues that you typically do not need to deal with when working with a standalone Access application. The following issues must be addressed because of rules that actually exist within the Microsoft Jet Engine when processing against an ODBC data source:

- ▶ Forms must use optimistic locking.

- ▶ Recordsets must use optimistic locking.

- ▶ ODBC uses only a single workspace.

- ▶ Action queries are processed in only a single transaction.

- ▶ Recordsets created inside a VBA transaction are processed under that particular transaction.

Client/Server Performance Optimization

After the client/server application has been built, the architecture provides a number of options for enhancing the performance.

The following sections discuss a number of general guidelines for getting the most out of your application that may be discussed on the exam.

These guidelines should be followed:

▶ Let the server do the work.

▶ Minimize unnecessary calls to the server.

▶ Create views on the server.

▶ Use attached tables whenever possible.

▶ Avoid operations that move the cursor through the record-sets.

▶ Use the CacheSize, CacheStart, and FillCache.

Letting the Server Do the Work

The overall goal of the client/server architecture is to divide the workload between the workstation and the server. This takes advantage of the strengths of each while avoiding their respective weaknesses.

The workstation is best suited for the following activities:

▶ Serving as an easy-to-use graphical interface

▶ Developing queries based on user input and submitting them to server

▶ Formatting data on the screen

▶ Formatting data on the report

▶ Performing calculations using retrieved data

▶ Utilizing Access functions and features not supported by the server

The server is best suited for the following activities:

▶ Providing raw transaction processing power

▶ Storing large amounts of data

▶ Retrieving, sorting, and updating shared data

▶ Optimizing queries

▶ Enforcing data integrity rules that apply to all applications

It stands to reason that the server should do as much as possible to manipulate the data in a user-specified manner, such as returning only the rows that the user wants to view or process on the workstation. If possible, all processing should be done on the server and not the client workstation.

Minimize Unnecessary Calls to the Server

The less often you retrieve data from the server, the faster your application will perform. The following suggestions can help reduce the frequency of requests of the server when working with Access:

▶ When you open a form, the underlying recordset for that form retrieves all rows, and displays the first record. This method is very inefficient in a client/server environment. For example, if you open a form that contains hundreds of thousands of records, the amount of network and server resources required is very inefficient.

The server would be better utilized to provide records based on criteria furnished by the user. The server retrieves only the records that you want to view or actually work with.

▶ Another tip to increase performance in the client/server architecture is to store reference tables on the workstation rather than on the server. The more frequently a table is accessed, the more likely that it should be located on the server. However, static tables are easy to update and you should consider a provision for synchronizing workstation copies of static tables with a master copy on the network.

The code in the following example updates a local parts reference table from a server-based reference table:

```
'Code is only example and will not work or compile.
Public Sub UpdateParts()
        Dim db As Database
        'Return database variable pointing to current database.
        Set db = CurrentDb
        db.Execute "Delete * from tblparts"
        db.Execute "INSERT INTO tblparts Select * from tblRemoteParts"

        End Sub
```

Creating and Linking Views on the Server

A powerful feature for controlling read-only access to specified rows and columns and joining tables as the server is a *view*. If your RDBMs supports this technique, you can link the view instead of the tables, and then attach the view in Access.

Using Attached Tables

Attached tables are faster, more convenient, and more powerful than database tables, although the latter can be opened using Visual Basic for Applications code. Attached tables are visible objects in the Database window and users can access them for queries, forms, and reports.

No indexes are created when exporting a table to SQL server. A unique index must exist on the export table in order for the server to identify the record to update.

Avoiding Operations That Move the Cursor Through Recordsets

Avoid moving the cursor through the recordsets. If you are working with 100,000 records, moving the cursor to the last row can be very time intensive. The reason for this is that the server must handle all the records between 1 and 100,000. Relational databases are not optimized for navigation operations like moving cursors. Relational databases are best suited for finding records based on their actual field values rather than their relative locations.

Using CacheSize, CacheStart, and FillCache

As stated in the preceding section, you should avoid, if possible, moving from record to record when working with relational databases. However, utilizing CacheSize, CacheStart, and FillCache can improve performance in a client/server architecture.

Cache is defined as an allocation of local memory used to store records retrieved from the defined remote data source.

Cache can help if it has been defined for your dynaset; it will be filled as you use MoveNext to move through the dynaset from the specified start of the cache. It will be limited to the specified cache size. When a record has been cached, the Microsoft Jet Engine completes the search for that record from the cache rather than from the data source.

After you have created a dynaset type record, you can set the recordset's CacheSize property to the number of records you want the cache to hold, from 5 to 1,200, or up to the limits of memory.

The first record to be cached is specified by setting the CacheStart property that equals the recordset BookMark property of the record you want. The record can be any record included in the defined recordset.

The FillCache method fills the cache with the number of records defined in the CacheSize property.

It is important to note that in order to use CacheStart you must specify the Binary Compare method for the module in which you are using the property. The current record will be set improperly if you don't use the Binary Compare method.

The following example shows how you can force the cache to fill with the FillCacheMethod:

```
Dim rs as Recordset
Dim db As Database
Set db = CurrentDb.OpenDatabase("",0,0,_
"ODBC;DATABASE=SQLDB;DSN=
oprSQL;UID=Guest;PWD=")
' Open ODBC Database
Set rs = db.OpenRecordset("OrderDetail",DB_OPEN_DYNASET)
' Open local recordset
rs.FindFirst "CustID = 1001"
rs.CacheStart = rs.Bookmark
' Start caching records at Customer ID 1001.
' Set cache size to 12 records.
rs.CacheSize = 12
' Fill cache
rs.FillCache
'…Display Rows
```

Using the Jet Errors Collection

This chapter on developing client/server applications concludes with an examination of the Jet Errors Collection. Anytime that Jet is processing data, runtime errors can be generated. Because Jet has the capability of reporting multiple runtime errors from a single operation that your code performs, it maintains a collection of those errors. Usually, you are concerned with the fact that an error has occurred and needs to be reported to the end user. However, in some cases, more detail for the error might be required. This is why you use the Jet Errors collection.

Recall from Chapter 4 that the collection is a property of the DBEngine object. When you handle an error in an error handler in your code, or in an error event handler, you can then browse the Jet Errors collection to determine specifically what Jet error or errors occurred while processing the data. The following code shows how you can accomplish this:

```
Sub JetErrorsCollection()
Dim db As Database

On Error GoTo JetErrorsCollectionErr
```

```
CurrentDb.Execute "appJetErrorsCollection", dbFailOnError

JetErrorsCollectionDone:
        Exit Sub
JetErrorsCollectionErr:
        Dim errCur As Error
        For Each errCur As Error
                Debug.Print errCur.Description
        Next
Resume JetErrorsCollectionDone
End Sub
```

In the preceding code, when Jet generates a set of errors, each of the error descriptions is printed to the Debug window. The Error object will reflect the topmost objects in the Errors collection. The Errors collection is cleared before the next Jet Engine operation is executed.

Lab Exercise

This exercise enables you to work with a few of the objectives that were covered in this chapter concerning developing client/server applications.

Exercise 13.1:   Illustrating an ODBC API Application

This exercise will illustrate a simple ODBC API application. The examples in this code are for demonstrative purposes only. You can use them by attaching to a SQL server database (for example). Obviously, the SQL server has not been included.

The code uses many of the basic ODBC functions to access a remote SQL server database. Generally, the type of database is irrelevant because the same code could be used to access a table on any type of database that is supported with an appropriate ODBC driver.

The code examples illustrate how the application does the following:

▶ Creates global variables to hold environment, connection, and statement handles

▶ Establishes a connection to an existing database

▶ Submits a SQL Select statement

▶ Displays results in an unbound combo box control

▶ Closes the connection

Note that the code in the following exercise is one continuous code example that takes you through creating storage for handles to closing connections.

Objective:

▶ Access external data by using ODBC.

Time Estimate: 25-30 minutes

continues

Exercise 13.1: Continued

Steps:

1. The following code creates global variables to hold environment, connection, and statement handles, in addition to result codes:

```
Dim henv As Long
Dim hdbc As Long
Dim hstmt As Long
Dim rc As Integer
```

2. The following code establishes a connection to an existing data source by using the SQLDriverConnect function with a connect string.

```
Private Sub OpenDatabase()
    Dim db As DATABASE
    Dim td As TableDef
    Dim ndx As Integer

    On Error GoTo errHandler

    Set db = DBEngine.Workspaces(0).Databases(0)
    For ndx = 0 To db.TableDefs.Count - 1
        Set td = db.TableDefs(ndx)
        If td.Connect <> "" Then
            td.RefreshLink
        End If
    Next ndx
    db.Close
    Exit Sub

errHandler:

    MsgBox "Error : " & Err.Description, 64, "Error Window"

End Sub
```

3. The following code submits a SQL Select statement using the pass-through query:

```
Dim db As DATABASE
  Dim rs As Recordset
  Dim qry As QueryDef

  Set db = DBEngine.Workspaces(0).Databases(0)

  Set qry = db.CreateQueryDef("")
  ' If you use SQL syntax of the remote engine in the _
  ' CreateQueryDef statement.
  ' Jet will complain.  Assign the SQL after setting the
  ➥Connect_
  ' property.
  qry.Connect = "ODBC;DSN=Chapter131"
  qry.SQL = "SELECT * FROM tblEmployee"

  ' Inform Jet that this query will return records.  Error
  ➥will _
  ' result otherwise.
  qry.ReturnsRecords = True
  db.QueryDefs.Refresh

  ' Now use the pass through QueryDef

  qry.SQL = "qryEmployee"
  Set rs = qry.OpenRecordset(dbOpenSnapshot)

End Function
```

4. The following code returns multiple result sets to the client. If your code isn't set up to handle these multiple sets, you see only the first result set return, which may not be the one you want:

```
Public Function MultipleResults()
  Dim db As DATABASE
  Dim rs As Recordset
  Dim qryQueryDef As QueryDef
  Dim qryQueryDef2 As QueryDef

  Set db = DBEngine.Workspaces(0).Databases(0)
```

continues

```
' Create a passthrough query that returns multiple
➥results.
Set qryQueryDef = db.CreateQueryDef("sp_dbproctest")
qryQueryDef.Connect = "ODBC;DSN=Pubs"
qryQueryDef.SQL = "dbproctest"

' Inform Jet that this query will return records.  Error
➥will _
' result otherwise.
qryQueryDef.ReturnRecords = True
db.QueryDefs.Refresh

' Create and execute a temporary make-table query that
➥stores _
' multiple results.
' from the SQLPassThrough query created above.
Set qryQueryDef2 = db.CreateQueryDef("")
qryQueryDef2.SQL = "Select * INTO [Multiset] from " & _
"[sp_dbproctest]"
qryQueryDef2.Execute

' Create recordsets from the resulting tables.
    Set rsRecordset = qryQueryDef.OpenRecordset("Multiset",
dbOpenDynaset)

' Open other tables according to number returned.
    rsRecordset.Close
    Set rsRecordset = db.OpenRecordset("MultSet1",
dbOpenDynaset)

End Function
```

5. The following code closes the connection, frees the allocations, and ends the application:

```
Public Sub Close_Form()
    Dim db As DATABASE
    Dim tblTableDef As TableDef
    Dim ndx As Integer

    On Error GoTo errHandler
```

```
    Set db = DBEngine.Workspaces(0).Databases(0)
    For ndx = 0 To db.TableDefs.Count - 1
        Set tblTableDef = db.TableDefs(ndx)
        If tblTableDef.Connect <> "" Then
            tblTableDef.RefreshLink
        End If
    Next ndx
' This is where we close the Database    db.Close
    Exit Sub
End Sub
```

Comments:

Parts of the preceding examples do work. However, trying to connect to another Access database is not allowed. The examples will give you good idea of working with ODBC.

Reading Reference:

For more information, please refer to the sections "Setting Up the ODBC Connection," and "Working with SQL Pass-Through Queries."

Review Questions

1. Your application includes the following code:

```
Dim db As Databse
Dim qf As QueryDef
Dim rs As Recordset
Dim tf As TableDef
Set db = CurrentDb()
Set qf = db.CreateQueryDef("qryCustomers",
  "Select * from Customers")
Set tf = db.TableDefs("Customers")
```

You want rs to be an updateable Recordset that is based on the linked Customers table. Which code fragment should you use?

A. Set rs = db.OpenRecordset("Select * from Customers")

B. Set rs = db.OpenRecordset("Customers", db_OpenTable)

C. Set rs = qf.OpenRecordset()

D. Set rs = tf.OpenRecordset(dbOpenSnapShot)

2. In a client/server application, you have a form that uses twelve connections to your server database. The server sometimes runs out of connections when multiple users are accessing the application. What can you do to reduce the number of connections used by the form?

A. Copy tables that are used as the row sources of combo boxes from the server to your local database.

B. Reduce the value of the Connection Timeout parameter that is in the registry.

C. Replace combo boxes with list boxes on the form.

D. Reduce the number of rows that Microsoft Access retrieves from the server in a single operation.

3. Your code links to a table to your database by using ODBC at runtime. If this fails, you want to retrieve error messages from the ODBC driver. Where can you retrieve the error information from?

   A. The properties of the Err object in Visual Basic for Applications

   B. The Errors collection

   C. The Err statement and Event variable

   D. The ODBCAPI.text type file

4. You want to be able to read and write records in a Microsoft SQL server table. What must the table have?

   A. A primary key

   B. A single field index

   C. A unique index

   D. A timestamp field

5. What is the default recordset for SQL pass-through query?

   A. Snapshot-type.

   B. Dynaset-type.

   C. Table-type.

   D. There is no default recordset type for SQL Pass-through queries.

6. When optimizing a client/server application, which of the following principles are important?

   A. Make sure the server gives you only what you need.

   B. Move data only once.

   C. Run only non-updateable queries.

   D. Do all processing on the client.

7. Which of the following are features of the ODBC?

   A. A programming interface that can access many database schema such as SQL Server, Informix, Oracle, Sybase, and so on

   B. Handles efficiently the parameters of stored procedures parameters

   C. Features registry options to modify specific features

   D. Provides cache modification to increase performance

8. What is one of the first items you need to add to an exported table after you have established a link to a SQL server database?

   A. A stored procedure

   B. A timestamp field

   C. At least one unique index for a column on the exported table

   D. All appropriate relationships

9. You have developed a client/server application that utilizes an unbound form to display information about your company's 350 leased vehicles. This information is retrieved by using a Recordset in your Visual Basic for Application code. The application currently retrieves one record at a time when users navigate through them on the form. Users normally view the entire recordset. If you want to display each record more quickly what should you do?

   A. Retrieve the records in groups of 10.

   B. Convert the application so that you are using a bound form.

   C. Use the FillCache method to retrieve all 350 records at once.

   D. Move all of your processing to the local computer.

10. What is stored in the description property of table that is linked into Access through ODBC?

    A. The actual name of the linked table

    B. Time and Date stamps for the table

    C. Data Source Description field name

    D. The ODBC connection string

Answers to Review Questions

1. B is correct. Queries are SnapShot by default and not up-dateable. The correct answer opens up the table as Open-Table, which allows the table to be updateable. For more information, please refer to the section "Working with SQL Pass-Through Queries."

2. A is correct. Even though it's possible to open tables directly in code, attached tables are faster, more convenient, and more powerful. Attached tables are visible as objects in the Database window, and users can access them for queries, forms, and reports. Referenced tables opened locally enhance the speed of the program. For more information, please refer to the section "Using Attached Tables."

3. B is correct. When Jet processes data, runtime errors can be generated. Because Jet has the capability of reporting multiple run-time errors from a single operation that your code performs, it maintains a collection of those errors. For more information, please refer to the section "Using the Jet Errors Collection."

4. C is correct. No indexes are created when exporting a table to SQL Server. A unique index must exist on the export table in order for the server to identify the record to update. For more information, please refer to the section "Using Attached Tables."

5. A is correct. The default recordset type for a SQL pass-through query is SnapShot. A snapshot is simply a static copy of a set of records retrieved from the database and copied into memory. Snapshots are not updateable. All SQL pass-through queries return snapshots. For more information, please refer to the section "Working with SQL Pass-Through Queries."

6. A and B are correct. Creating efficient client/server applications requires that you follow certain principles: try to move data only once, and make sure the server gives you only what you need. For more information, please refer to the section "Client/Server Performance Optimization."

7. All choices are correct. The ODBC API programming model provides the following features:

   ▶ A universal programming model that can access many database architectures.

   ▶ A native interface to Microsoft SQL Server

   ▶ Intelligent handling of stored procedure parameters.

   ▶ Keyset, dynamic, static, and forward-only cursor implementation

   ▶ Advanced result set management

   ▶ Complete post-call error management

   For more information, please refer to the section "Utilizing Open Database Connectivity."

8. C is correct. No indexes are created when exporting a table to SQL Server. A unique index must exist on the export table in order for the server to identify the record to update. For more information, please refer to the section "Using Attached Tables."

9. C is correct. Utilizing the FillCache method is part of cache. Cache can help if it has been defined for your dynaset; it will be filled as you use MoveNext to move through the dynaset from the specified start of the cache. It will be limited to the specified cache size. When a record has been cached, the Microsoft Jet Engine completes search for that record from the cache rather than from the data source. For more information, please refer to the section "Using CacheSize, CacheStart, and FillCache."

10. D is correct. The ODBC connection string is stored in the Description property of a table. For more information, please refer to the section "Using an ODBC Connection String."

Answers to Test Yourself Questions at Beginning of Chapter...

1. Following are a few of the reasons to design or convert an existing standalone or file-server database:

   ▶ Large number of concurrent users.

   ▶ Large data requirements have been defined.

   ▶ Improved speed and efficiency.

   ▶ Better security and reliability.

   ▶ Offers an Open Systems computing environment.

   ▶ An easy-to-use graphical interface in which to view and work with data from a mainframe system. For more information, please refer to the section "Choosing Access as a Client/Server Front End."

2. The ODBC Driver Manager links from Access to all ODBC data sources. The Driver may be provided by a third party such as Oracle, Informix, Sybase, and so on. For more information, please refer to section "Understanding Access in the Client/Server Architecture."

3. The FillCache method fills the cache with the number of records defined in the CacheSize property. For more information, please refer to the section "Using CacheSize, CacheStart, and FillCache."

4. Access utilizes the Microsoft Open Database Connectivity (ODBC) application programming interface (API) to provide data access connectivity to Microsoft SQL Server, or to any database system for which ODBC drivers are available. For more information, please refer to the section "Utilizing Open Database Connectivity."

5. Pass-through queries enable you to write queries in the dialect of SQL used by the remote server RDBMS. SQL Server enables you to write stored procedures that you can execute by name rather than sending individual SQL statements to the server. For more information, please refer to the section "Working with SQL Pass-Through Queries."

6. The Driver Manager is responsible for the following:

   ▶ Loading the specified database driver as defined in the data source name entry

   ▶ Initializing the interface

   ▶ Providing driver entry points

   ▶ Validating parameters and managing serialization of ODBC functioning

   For more information, please refer to the section "Utilizing Open Database Connectivity."

7. If a user-defined function is frequently used in a client/server, it would be advantageous, if possible, to convert to a stored procedure and move to the server. However, it might be determined that the functionality offered by Access outweighs the improved processing offered by the server. For more information, please refer to the section "Understanding Access in the Client/Server Architecture."

8. The following guidelines should be used when designing a client/server application:

   ▶ Let the server do the work.

   ▶ Minimize unnecessary calls to the server.

   ▶ Create views on the server.

   ▶ Use attached tables whenever possible.

   ▶ Avoid operations that move the cursor through the recordsets.

   ▶ Use CacheSize, CacheStart, and FillCache.

   For more information, please refer to the section "Client/Server Performance Optimization."

9. The overall goal of the client/server architecture is to divide the workload between the workstation and the server. This takes advantage of the strengths of each while avoiding their respective weaknesses. For more information, please refer to the section "Letting the Server Do the Work."

10. A client initiates a transaction by sending a message to a server where a database resides. For more information, please refer to the introduction to the chapter.

Chapter 14

Improving Database Performance

This chapter helps you prepare for the exam by covering the following objectives:

 Objectives

- ▶ Differentiate between single-field and multiple-field indexes

- ▶ Optimize queries by using Rushmore technology

- ▶ Restructure queries to enable faster execution

- ▶ Optimize performance in distributed applications

- ▶ Optimize performance for client/server applications

Test Yourself! Before reading this chapter, test yourself to determine how much study time you will need to devote to this section.

1. Ideally, how many indexes should you create for a small file?

2. Rushmore technology can alter the execution time of a query by doing what to the response time?

3. For faster execution of a query, fields used in joins should be what data type?

4. What tool for analyzing database performance is included with Access?

5. What command do you use from VB to define the starting point of a recordset cache?

Answers are located at the end of the chapter...

The topic of improving database performance is one of real merit in the everyday world. Because of this, Microsoft tends to thoroughly cover this area on the certification exam, and many students have had difficulty scoring well in this subject.

You must understand the different types of database performance improvements, and how they differ from one another. The questions usually provide a scenario and several possible solutions. You will need to be able to choose the appropriate solution, and know *why* it is appropriate.

You must know how indexes affect queries—positively and negatively—and the ways of altering indexes to increase query result speed. In short, study this chapter well and expect several related questions on the exam.

Differentiating Between Single-Field and Multiple-Field Indexes

 Objective

An index in a book helps the readers quickly find the information they seek. The purpose of an index in a database is to help your query get answered quickly. You can create indexes on single fields or multiple fields, depending on whether values are unique or not.

Access uses indexes to record unique values. If you do not index a field, Access reads all the values in the field. If you index the field, Access reads only the unique values. Therefore, if the field you most commonly search contains unique values—such as employee numbers, addresses, and so forth—you need to index only one field. If the field you commonly search contains shared values—such as departments, zip codes, area codes, and so forth—you should use multiple fields to distinguish among records where the first field has the same value.

As a rule of thumb, you should never create more indexes than absolutely necessary. Indexes do speed query operations, but they take up disk space and slow all other operations—such as adding new data, updating records, and so forth.

Creating Single-Field Indexes

To create a single-field index, complete the following steps:

1. Change to Design View, and click the field you want to index.

2. Choose the Indexed property box and choose Yes to either Duplicates OK or No Duplicates.

You created a single-field index.

Creating Multiple-Field Indexes

To create multiple-field indexes, complete the following steps:

1. You must first name the index.

2. From Design view, click the lightning bolt icon on the toolbar and enter an index name when prompted.

3. Choose all the fields you want to index at the Field Name prompt (you can select up to ten fields) and click the exit icon in the top-right corner when finished.

You created a multiple-field index.

Optimizing Queries by Using Rushmore Technology

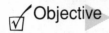 Objective ▶

Several years ago, FoxPro from Fox Software smoked all the competition in the amount of time the database took to return results from queries. FoxPro uses a patented search technology called Rushmore in order to perform the action. Microsoft purchased Fox Software, FoxPro became a Microsoft offering, and now Access uses Rushmore technology as well.

In short, Rushmore is a data-access technology that enables you to use certain types of expressions in query to get results very efficiently. To use Rushmore, you choose between simple expressions or complex expressions in your queries.

Using Simple Expressions

Example syntaxes for a simple expression are as follows:

> Indexed field Comparison operator Expression

> Expression Comparison operator Indexed field

The comparison operator is Boolean in nature and can be any of the following:

- ▶ <

- ▶ >

- ▶ =

- ▶ <=

- ▶ >=

- ▶ <>

- ▶ Between

- ▶ Like

- ▶ In

Following are simple examples of simple expressions:

> [zipcode]="47304"

> [birthdate]>#03/14/62#

Using Complex Expressions

You can create complex expressions in Access by using And or Or operators with simple expressions. Example syntaxes for a complex expression include the following:

> Simple Expression And Simple Expression

> Simple Expression Or Simple Expression

To quote official Microsoft documentation, "an expression created with a combination of simple optimizable expressions is fully optimizable. If one of the simple expressions is not optimizable and the two expressions are combined with And, the complex expression is partially optimizable. The following rules determine query optimization when combining simple expressions in query criteria." (See table 14.1.)

Table 14.1

Operators and Query Results			
Expression	Operator	Expression	Query Result
Optimizable	And	Optimizable	Fully optimizable
Optimizable	Or	Optimizable	Fully optimizable
Optimizable	And	Not optimizable	Partially optimizable
Optimizable	Or	Not optimizable	Not optimizable
Not optimizable	And	Not optimizable	Not optimizable
Not optimizable	Or	Not optimizable	Not optimizable
—	Not	Optimizable	Not optimizable
—	Not	Not optimizable	Not optimizable

In addition to the preceding, you can use parentheses to group combinations of simple expressions. After you turn simple optimizable expressions into complex expressions, you can combine the complex expressions to form even more complex expressions.

Examples of complex optimizable expressions are as follows:

((([town])="Evan")And((([county])="Kristin")

[town]="Evan"

OR [county]="Kristin"

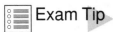 Exam Tip

Notice and remember for the exam the following about optimized expressions: AND and OR can make the expression optimized, although NOT does not.

Restructuring Queries for Faster Execution

 Objective

Microsoft recommends a number of actions to enable faster query execution. According to the official documentation included with Access (what you must memorize for the exam) you should consider the following actions:

▶ Index fields on both sides of a join, or create a relationship between these fields and index any field used to set criteria for the query.

▶ When defining a field in a table, choose the smallest data type appropriate for the data in the field. Also, give fields you use in joins the same or compatible data types.

▶ When creating a query, add only the fields you need. In fields used to set criteria, clear the Show check box if you don't want to display those fields.

▶ Avoid calculated fields in nested queries. If you add a query containing a calculated field to another query, the expression in the calculated field slows performance in the top-level query.

▶ When grouping records by the values in a joined field, specify Group By for the field that's in the same table as the field you're totaling (calculating an aggregate on). For example, if your query totals the Quantity field in an Order Details table and groups by OrderID, specify Group By for the OrderID field in the Order Details table, not the OrderID field in the Orders table. For greater speed, use Group By on as few fields as possible. As an alternative, use the First function where appropriate.

▶ If a totals query includes a join, consider grouping the records in one query and adding the query to a separate query that performs the join. The procedure improves performance in some queries.

▶ Avoid restrictive query criteria on calculated and nonindexed columns whenever possible.

▶ If you use criteria to restrict the values in a field used in a join, test whether the query runs faster with the criteria placed on the "one" side or the "many" side of the join. In some queries, you have faster performance by adding the criteria to the field on the "one" side of the join rather than the "many" side.

▶ Use field sorting judiciously, especially with nonindexed fields.

▶ If your data doesn't change often, use Make-table queries to create tables from your query results. Use the resulting tables rather than the queries as the basis for your forms, reports, or other queries.

▶ Avoid using domain aggregate functions, such as the DLookup function, in a query that accesses table data. Instead, add the table to the query or create a subquery.

▶ If you create a crosstab query, use fixed column headings whenever possible.

▶ Use the Between…And, the In, and the = operators on indexed columns. The operators help optimize queries.

Note that you can use the Jet Database Engine to optimize queries if you use a multiple-field index to join two tables.

Optimizing Performance in Distributed Applications

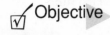 Objective ▶ One of the greatest tools for analyzing the performance of a database—the Performance Analyzer—is built into Access. Using

the Performance Analyzer, you can do a final analysis of your application prior to distributing it. Figure 14.1 shows the Analyze option on the Tools menu.

Figure 14.1

The Performance Analyzer on the Tools menu.

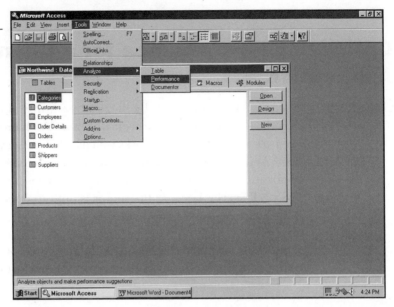

After you choose the Analyzer, select the object names you wish to examine, as shown in Figure 14.2, and a result of the analysis appears. The Analyzer suggests areas that can improve, along with recommendations and ideas. Continue refining the database until you can optimize it no more— a message similar to the one shown in Figure 14.3 tells you that the Analyzer has no more suggestions.

Figure 14.2

Selecting the categories for Performance Analyzer to examine.

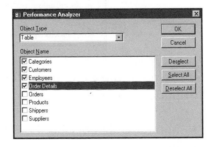

Figure 14.3

The message identifying a truly optimized database.

Optimizing Performance for a Client/Server Application

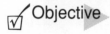

Client/servers—some of the biggest buzzwords of the past decade—are application servers optimized to handle intensive network requests. Access works well as a client/server database on any 32-bit operating system accepting SQL statements from client applications. The operating system of choice is Microsoft Windows NT Server, because the server is built to operate quite well in this capacity.

Optimization within this category requires two components: optimizing the server and optimizing SQL performance.

Optimizing the Server

Figure 14.4 shows the server configuration screen for Windows NT 4.0. You can access the screen on the server by choosing Network Neighborhood, Properties, Services, Server.

Figure 14.4

The NT Server configuration screen.

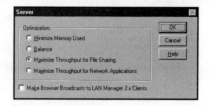

You have four ways to optimize the server, which are indicated by the option buttons:

▶ Minimize Memory Used is for a server that has ten or fewer users.

▶ Balance is the default; use it for a machine typically used as a server and a workstation.

▶ Maximize Throughput for File Sharing is the selection you should make if the server is an Access applications server.

▶ Maximize Throughput for Network Applications is the selection that you should make if the server is primarily a SQL server.

Making a change at this configuration screen can greatly improve the performance of your server on the network.

Optimizing SQL Performance

Keep in mind several considerations for the exam in relation to SQL performance optimization, most of which are common sense. The considerations are as follows:

▶ Restrict your results to only the information you want. Retrieving more information than you need slows down the query.

▶ Use cache memory whenever possible because it is quicker to read from than anything else, and it can improve performance on large recordsets. Access is designed to use cache, so you need be concerned only with directly writing to cache if you use data created in Visual Basic. If you use data created in Visual Basic, you can use several commands to control the cache:

CacheSize. Sets the number of records that the cache holds.

CacheStart. Identifies the record to start placing into cache.

FillCache. Fills the cache with the number of records defined in CacheSize from the starting point defined as CacheStart.

Note

A *recordset* is a logical grouping or set of records. You can choose three types of recordsets to use when working with VB. They are Dynaset, Snapshot, and Table. They differ in the following ways:

▶ **Dynaset.** Creates and returns a dynamic set of pointers to live data in records and fields. Dynaset differs from Table in that Dynaset can combine multiple tables into one table. You can update the returned records if the record is not locked and you set the Updatable property to True.

▶ **Snapshot.** As the name implies, Snapshot provides a static copy of records that you cannot update.

▶ **Table.** Provides a dynamic set of pointers to live data that you can update (if properties permit), but the data cannot be a combination of tables. Table recordsets cannot be used with linked ODBC tables, while Dynasets and Snapshots are used with linked ODBC tables.

▶ Use linked tables whenever possible rather than tables you have to open locally.

▶ Keep all queries on the server and try to avoid any processing on the local computer. When using SQL, queries that process locally are ones that include the words such as the following:

TOP

TOP PERCENT

GROUP BY (that cannot be processed remotely)

GROUP BY with a DISTINCT

GROUP BY used in conjunction with ORDER BY

ORDER BY (that cannot be processed remotely)

ORDER BY with a DISTINCT

ORDER BY used in conjunction with GROUP BY

DISTINCT (that cannot be processed remotely)

WHERE when used with DISTINCT

Locally processed queries also include joins between tables from different data sources.

Avoiding all the previous conditions and words reduces query processing time.

Key Terms and Concepts

Table 14.2 identifies key terms from this chapter. Review the key terms and make sure that you understand each term for the exam.

Table 14.2

Key Terms: Improving Database Performance	
Term	Covered in Section…
Rushmore	"Optimizing Queries by Using Rushmore Technology"
Single-field	"Creating Single-Field Indexes"
Multiple-field	"Creating Multiple-Field Indexes"

Review Questions

1. Using Multiple-field indexes, what is the maximum number of fields you can select for indexing?

   A. One

   B. Two

   C. Ten

   D. Unlimited, up to the total number of fields

2. Which of the following is *not* an operator allowed in a Rushmore-based query?

   A. <>

   B. !=

   C. <=

   D. =

3. Which of the following is *not* an operator allowed in a Rushmore-based query?

   A. Between

   B. Enter

   C. Like

   D. In

4. If a totals query includes a join and you want to execute the query as quickly as possible, what is one possibility for decreasing processing time?

   A. Use the NOT keyword.

   B. Restructure the Object class.

   C. Create a separate Name entity.

   D. Group the records in one query.

5. Which of the following is a recordset that is not updateable?

    A. Dynaset

    B. Snapshot

    C. Table

    D. ODBC

Answers to Review Questions

1. C is correct. Ten is the hard-coded limit on the number of fields that you can index. Please refer to the section "Differentiating Between Single-Field and Multiple-Field Indexes" for more information.

2. B is correct. The other three are legitimate operators, but != is not a valid operator in Access. Please refer to the section "Optimizing Queries by Using Rushmore Technology" for more information.

3. B is correct. The other three are legitimate operators, but Enter is not a valid operator in Access. Please refer to the section "Optimizing Queries by Using Rushmore Technology" for more information.

4. D is correct. Grouping the records in one query enables you to join executions to perform as quickly as possible. Please refer to the section "Restructuring Queries for Faster Execution" for more information.

5. B is correct. A snapshot is a recordset that you cannot update. Please refer to the section "Optimizing Performance for a Client/Server Application" for more information.

Answers to Test Yourself Questions at Beginning of Chapter...

1. You should create only one index, or the fewest number possible for a small file. For more information, see the section "Differentiating Between Single-Field and Multiple-Field Indexes."

2. Rushmore technology significantly alters response time by shortening it. For more information, see the section "Optimizing Queries by Using Rushmore Technology."

3. You should use compatible data types in joins for faster query execution. For more information, see the section "Restructuring Queries for Faster Execution."

4. Performance Analyzer is a tool included with Access for analyzing database performance. For more information, see the section "Optimizing Performance in Distributed Applications."

5. CacheStart is the VisualBasic command you use to define the starting point of a recordset cache. For more information, see the section "Optimizing Performance for a Client/Server Application."

Chapter

15

Distributing an Application

This chapter helps you prepare for the exam by covering the following objectives:

 Objectives

> ▶ Prepare an application for distribution by using the Setup Wizard
>
> ▶ Choose the best way to distribute a client/server application
>
> ▶ Distribute OLE Custom Controls with an application
>
> ▶ Provide Online Help in a Microsoft Access application

Test Yourself! Before reading this chapter, test yourself to determine how much study time you will need to devote to this section.

1. The Setup Wizard used with Access for Windows 95 consists of what one file?

2. Database connection information can be specified by what valid methods?

3. Custom Controls typically have what extension?

4. ControlTipText can be up to how many text characters within Access?

Answers are located at the end of the chapter...

So often, when thinking of Access applications, developers consider only its operation and pay too little attention to the details associated with distributing that application. The certification exam, however, considers distribution to be an integral component of Access development.

In reading this chapter, you will learn how to use the Setup Wizard to prepare an application for distribution, and then distribute it (with controls included, and with or without a client/server environment). You will also learn how to provide online help—a topic whose importance cannot be stressed enough. On the actual exam, you can expect one to two questions to come from this category—not a great many, but enough to make it worth studying.

While studying, pay particular attention to the Setup Wizard and the steps you must follow to prepare the application—that is quite often where exam questions come from.

Preparing an Application for Distribution by Using the Setup Wizard

 Objective

The Setup Wizard for Access 95 is included in the Access Developer's Toolkit and consists of the file WZSTP70.MDA. The Setup Wizard enables you to create distribution disks and distribute your application to other users.

The following steps illustrate how to use the Setup Wizard to create distribution disks and assume that you have an application created, optimized, and ready to share:

1. Compact the .mdb files and copy into the default folder any icons you want to use.

2. Start the Setup Wizard by choosing Start, Programs, Access Developer's Toolkit, Setup Wizard. Figure 15.1 shows the opening screen.

Figure 15.1

The opening dialog box of the Setup Wizard.

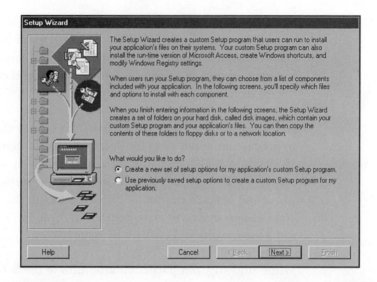

3. Choose Create a New Set of Setup Options and click Next.

4. In the Select Files dialog box, Select all the files that pertain to your application and then click Add. Figure 15.2 illustrates this process.

Figure 15.2

Adding the application files to the List of Files list box.

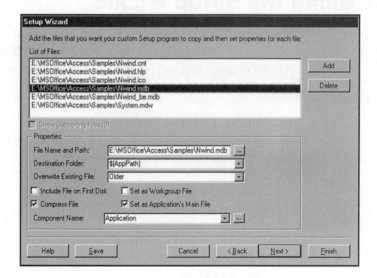

5. Select the main .mdb file and choose Set As Application's Main File in the appropriate check box. Click Next to continue. The Setup program enables you to specify whether the

system should prompt users before needed components are installed on their machines. If you do not give them a choice, a hidden *single-component setup program* is created. If you give users the choice, a *multiple-component setup program* is created.

6. The Setup Wizard compiles everything, including Registry entries. If you need to specify different Registry entries, you can do so by entering them at the prompt. Figure 15.3 illustrates this screen.

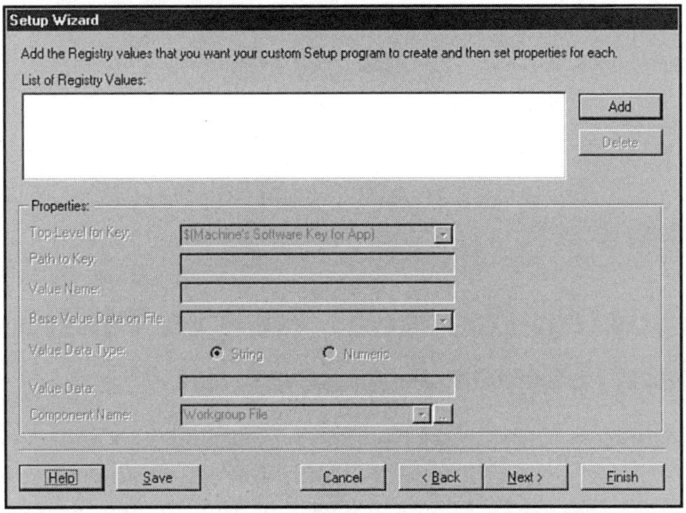

Figure 15.3

Add custom Registry keys to the application if you need them.

7. Verify that the components needed for your application to run are in all three installation types (Compact, Typical, and Custom) at the next screen and then click Next to continue.

8. Fill in the name and version number information for your application at the next screen and click Next to continue.

9. Enter a temporary path for the installation files to be compiled on your system and click Next.

10. Save your data as a template when the wizard prompts you, and the compressing begins. Figure 15.4 shows the bar chart that indicates the progress of the compression, and Figure 15.5 shows the message that appears after the process completes.

Figure 15.4

The progress bar indicates how far along the com-pression is.

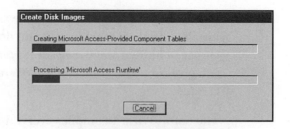

Figure 15.5

After the com-pression com-pletes, this mes-sage pops up to indicate success-ful compression.

You have now completed the compilation of necessary files for your application's distribution.

Choosing the Best Way to Distribute a Client/Server Application

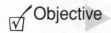 Objective ▶

Distributing client/server applications as opposed to other applica-tions differs primarily in the delivery mechanism. For large net-works, Microsoft's Systems Management Server (SMS) can simplify the installation. SMS is a member of the BackOffice family of appli-cations running on top of Microsoft Windows NT Server.

When using the Setup Wizard, you must include the Workgroup Administrator application with multiple-user applications. The Workgroup Administrator application enables the user to specify the location of the workgroup file before the application launch-es. Figure 15.6 illustrates how to select a file to use as the work-group file.

Figure 15.6

Selecting a file as the workgroup file for a multiple-user application.

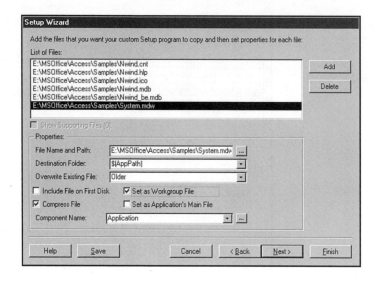

ODBC data sources are databases, or database servers, you use as sources of data, and you refer to them by their Data Source Name. ODBC database information is kept in the ODBC.INI file and the Windows Registration database, both of which you can use to create data sources.

You can specify database connection information by using the RegisterDatabase method. If the method succeeds, the ODBC.INI file updates automatically.

Distributing OLE Custom Controls with an Application

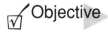

You can distrubute OLE Custom Controls with an application by adding the appropriate controls (identified by .OCX extensions) to the list of files installed with the Setup Wizard.

Chapter 9, "Custom Controls," discusses Custom Controls and the properties associated with them. To include them with the application, select them in the List of Files dialog box. Figure 15.7 illustrates the procedure.

Figure 15.7

Selecting the files to include in the distribution.

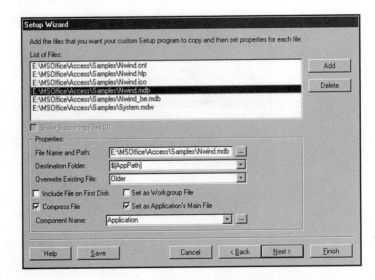

Providing Online Help in a Microsoft Access Application

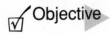

Online Help can complete an application and make it look more professional than any other feature that you can add. Not only does online help add to the application's appearance, but it also adds to the application's functionality and usability.

Online Help comes in many forms—from a Help file that is compiled with the Windows Help Compiler and attached via the HelpFile and HelpContextID properties to control tips that you configure using the ControlTipText property. This section looks at several of the most popular Online Help components and how to implement them in an application.

To create a Help file, you need the Windows Help Compiler. The compiler is included with the Microsoft Access Developer's Toolkit or most of the Visual languages, such as Microsoft Visual Basic and Microsoft Visual C++.

Using ControlTips

To create a *ControlTip* (a tip that appears when the pointer is over a control), complete the following steps:

1. Go to Form Design view.

2. Double-click the control for which you want to create a tip.

3. On the property sheet, select ControlTipText and type the message (up to 255 characters) you want to display for the control.

Adding Status Bar Text

To add status bar text for a control in the status bar, complete the following steps:

1. Double-click the control, and the control's property sheet opens.

2. Go to the StatusBarText property box.

3. Enter the message (up to 255 characters) that you want to display for the control.

 Note   You can enter up to 255 characters for the property, but Access can display only as much text as fits in the status bar, which is based on font and window size.

Creating a Custom Toolbar Button Tip

To create a tip for a custom toolbar button, you must complete the following steps:

1. Click anywhere on the toolbar.

2. Click Customize.

3. Right-click the button on the toolbar you want to change.

4. Click Choose Button Image.

5. Enter the new ToolTip in the Description box—again, up to 255 characters.

Creating a Compiled Help File

A compiled Help file displays help when a user presses F1. To create and implement the file, complete the following steps:

1. Create a source file from any text editor (such as Word), and save the file in rich-text format (.RTF).

2. Use the Windows Help Compiler to compile the file.

3. On the property sheet for the form, go to the HelpFile property box.

4. Specify the file name for the compiled Help file.

5. In the HelpContextID property box, enter the number of the topic (a number other than 0) that displays when users press F1.

 Note

You don't generally use the number 0 because it covers assistance for the whole form or report and not the specific item. If a control has focus when users press F1, but the control does not have a custom Help topic, the custom Help topic for the form (number 0) appears.

6. For every control, enter in the HelpContextID property the number of the topic that displays when users press F1.

Note Microsoft recommends putting the Help file in the same directory as your application for best results. Per their documentation, this placement ensures that you can keep the setting for the HelpFile property the same for each site using your application, and the placement enables users to install the application in the directory of their choice.

Creating What's This Tips

You can create Online Help that users receive when they reference the question mark button (What's This) by following the steps for creating a compiled Help file. The compiled Help file is referenced for What's This information.

Adding What's This to a Form

To add the What's This button (question mark) to a form, complete the following steps:

1. Go to Design view.

2. Double-click the form selector to get to the property sheet.

3. Go to the WhatsThisButton property and click Yes.

 Note If you have not listed a custom Help file in the HelpFile property box for the form, the Microsoft Access Help file displays by default.

Key Terms and Concepts

Table 15.1 identifies key terms from this chapter. Review the key terms and make sure that you understand each term for the exam.

Table 15.1

Key Terms: Distributing an Application	
Term	Covered in Section...
Setup Wizard	"Preparing an Application for Distribution by Using the Setup Wizard"
Compression	"Preparing an Application for Distribution by Using the Setup Wizard"
Help file	"Providing Online Help in a Microsoft Access Application"

Lab Exercise

This exercise gives you the opportunity to apply what you have learned about distributing an application to a real-life situation. By applying the concepts learned in this chapter, you are able to provide a solution to the exercise.

Exercise 15.1:   Using the Setup Wizard

This exercise walks you through using the Setup Wizard to prepare a database application for distribution.

Objective:

Prepare an application for distribution by using the Setup Wizard

Estimated Time: 15 minutes

Steps:

1. Select a database and compact the .mdb files.

2. Copy into the default folder any icons you want to use.

3. Start the Setup Wizard by choosing Start, Programs, Access Developer's Toolkit, Setup Wizard.

4. Choose Create a New Set of Setup Options and click Next.

5. In the Select Files dialog box, select all the files that pertain to your application and then click Add.

6. Select the main .mdb file and choose Set As Application's Main File in the appropriate check box.

7. Click Next to continue. The Setup Wizard compiles everything, including Registry entries.

8. Verify that the components needed for your application to run are in all three installation types (Compact, Typical, and Custom) and then click Next.

continues

9. Fill in the name and version number information for your application and click Next.

10. Enter a temporary path for where the installation files compile on your system and click Next.

11. Save your data as a template when the wizard prompts you, and the compressing begins.

Comments:

You have now successfully walked through the process of preparing a database application for distribution.

Reading Reference:

Please see the section "Preparing an Application for Distribution by Using the Setup Wizard" for more information.

Review Questions

1. The three types of installations the Setup Wizard creates for an application are:

    A. Typical

    B. Compact

    C. Custom

    D. Mobile

2. ODBC data sources are referred to by by what name?

    A. RegisterDatabase entry

    B. Data Source Name

    C. ODBCName value

    D. Application.Exe.Name

3. What does an extension of OCX predominantly indicate?

    A. A setup file

    B. A wizard

    C. A custom control

    D. A database extension

4. Help files are attached to a form via what two properties?

    A. RegisterDatabase

    B. HelpContextID

    C. HelpFile

    D. HelpDatabase

5. What is the property that determines the text displayed when the mouse is over a control?

    A. Pointer

    B. ControlTip

    C. ControlPointer

    D. MouseTip

6. What's This information displays from where?

    A. The compiled Help file

    B. The What's This text defined on the control's property

    C. The ControlTipText

    D. The ToolTip description

7. What is the HelpContextID property number indicating the entire form?

    A. 0

    B. 1

    C. 2

    D. 255

8. For the best results, Microsoft recommends placing the Help file in what directory?

    A. A Help subdirectory

    B. The WINDOWS directory

    C. The same directory as the application

    D. The root directory

Answers to Review Questions

1. A, B, and C are correct. Typical, Compact, and Custom are legitimate types of installs. Please refer to the section "Preparing an Application for Distribution by Using the Setup Wizard" for more information.

2. B is correct. Data Source Name is used to refer to ODBC data sources. Please refer to the section "Choosing the Best Way to Distribute a Client/Server Application" for more information.

3. C is correct. OCX extensions identify Custom Controls. Please refer to the section "Distributing OLE Custom Controls with an Application" for more information.

4. B and C are correct. HelpContextID and HelpFile are two properties used to attach Help files to a database. Please refer to the section "Providing Online Help in a Microsoft Access Application" for more information.

5. B is correct. ControlTip is the property that determines the text displayed when the mouse is over a control. Please refer to the section "Providing Online Help in a Microsoft Access Application" for more information.

6. A is correct. The compiled Help file provides the What's This information. Please refer to the section "Providing Online Help in a Microsoft Access Application" for more information.

7. A is correct. Use the HelpContextID number 0 to indicate the entire form. Please refer to the section "Providing Online Help in a Microsoft Access Application" for more information.

8. C is correct. Microsoft's recommendation is for you to place Help files in the same directory as the application. Please refer to the section "Providing Online Help in a Microsoft Access Application" for more information.

Answers to Test Yourself Questions at Beginning of Chapter...

1. Wzstp70.mda is the file constituting the Setup Wizard for Access for Windows 95. See the section "Preparing an Application for Distribution by Using the Setup Wizard."

2. RegisterDatabase is the method by which you specify database connection information. For more information, see the section "Choosing the Best Way to Distribute a Client/Server Application."

3. OCX is the default extension for Custom Controls. For more information, see the section "Distributing OLE Custom Controls with an Application."

4. 255 is the highest number of characters for ControlTipText. For more information, see the section "Providing Online Help in a Microsoft Access Application."

Chapter 16

Extending Microsoft Access

This chapter helps you prepare for the exam by covering the following objectives:

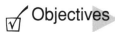
√ Objectives

- ▶ Implement error handling in add-ins
- ▶ Test and debug library databases
- ▶ Describe the purpose of the UsysRegInfo table

Test Yourself! Before reading this chapter, test yourself to determine how much study time you will need to devote to this section.

1. What utility should you use to load add-ins?

2. When an add-in uses two databases—a code database and an add-in database, for example—what are two causes for the Compile Error message?

3. Add-ins can consist of what items?

Answers are located at the end of the chapter...

As you read this chapter, you will learn about extending Access databases. This chapter covers the extending process and the rules you must follow when debugging a library or adding error handling to a database. Although you must understand the concepts of add-in error handling in order to answer the questions about extending Access, the exam will not ask a great many questions on this topic.

On the exam, you typically will encounter at least one question about the purpose of the UsysRegInfo table and how it is used. You must understand the different types of relationships between UsysRegInfo tables, library databases, and add-in error handling. Typically, you will be provided with a scenario and several possible solutions. You will need to be able to choose the appropriate solution, and know *why* it is appropriate.

Implementing Error Handling in Add-Ins

Objective

The concept of error handling was introduced in Chapter 5, "Debugging and Error Handling." You learned how to use the Errors collection and Error object to trap errors, use debugging tools, and write an error handler.

You treat add-ins in the same way. To implement error handling for an add-in, complete the following steps:

1. Use Design View to open the form.

2. Use either Visual Basic or a macro to write the error-handling routine for the add-in.

3. Select the add-in and assign the error-handling routine to the properties associated with the add-in.

Note

Note that you must use the Add-in Manager to load add-ins. If you do not, the add-in may not appear on the Add-in submenu.

Another possible problem that can occur with add-ins is the error message "Sub or Function not defined." This error is caused by the current .mdb (database) not having a reference to the add-in database, and the error is typically the result of creating add-ins with Visual Basic. You can solve the problem by creating a reference to the add-in database in the References option of the Tools menu.

Testing and Debugging Library Databases

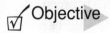 When working with library databases, you must always test and debug them before using them in a production environment. Access uses CodeDB() for opening library databases. CodeDB() works the same as CurrentDB() except CodeDB() returns the database object for the library database from which it was summoned, whereas CurrentDB() returns the database object from the current open user database. Aside from the differences, this section looks at some common problems and solutions associated with libraries.

One add-in problem occurs when an add-in uses two databases—a code library and an add-in database. When started, you can get the following error messages:

> "Compile Error"

> "Cannot find project or library"

When Access cannot find the code library, the second error occurs. Access looks in two places for the library:

▶ The folder of the add-in database

▶ The folder of the current database

If the code folder is located elsewhere, Access can't find the folder. You solve the problem by moving the code folder to either of these two known search folders.

Another problem that can occur is common when a database of generic functions calls a library of code functions. It is identified by one of the following error messages:

"Sub or Function not defined."

"Undefined function '<name>' in expression."

"#Name?"

When the current database does not have a reference to the code library database, the problem occurs. To solve this, you can manually add the reference by using the References command on the Tools menu. The following steps illustrate this concept:

1. On the Tools menu, choose References.

2. Click Browse from the References box.

3. In the Add Reference box, locate the database and then click OK.

4. Click OK to close the References box.

The final problem occurs when a user opens an add-in and the library takes a long time to load. You can rectify the problem by editing the Loadonstartup key in the Windows 95 Registry. Changing the key value forces the add-in's information to load when the database opens. To edit the Loadonstartup key—as documented in the Microsoft white paper Addinhlp.doc—complete the following steps:

1. In Windows 95, choose Run from the Start menu. In Windows NT, open File Manager and choose Run on the File menu.

2. In Windows 95, type **regedit** in the Open box and then click OK. In Windows NT, type **regedit32** in the Run box and then click OK.

3. Locate the HKEY_LOCAL_MACHINE Registry folder.

4. Expand the HKEY_LOCAL_MACHINE folder until you locate the Software\Microsoft\Access\7.0\Wizards folder.

5. Click Wizards.

6. On the Edit Menu in the Registry Editor, choose New and then click String Value.

7. The system creates a new value in the right pane of the Registry window. Type **Loadonstartup** and then press Enter.

8. While the Loadonstartup key is highlighted, choose the Edit menu and then choose Modify. Type **rw** (for read/write) as the data value and then click OK.

9. Close the Registry Editor.

You solved the problem, and the library loads much quicker.

Describing the Purpose of the USysRegInfo Table

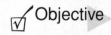 Objective ▶

You use the USysRegInfo table to register the values of an add-in with the Access Add-in Manager. Add-ins can consist of menu add-ins, wizards, or builders. When developing a custom add-in, you must set properties and create a USysRegInfo table in the add-in database (*.mda), so that it can be installed using the Add-in Manager.

To begin, you first import a copy of the USysRegInfo table from Wztool70.mda, and then you define the values in the records.

The following information defining the USysRegInfo table is quoted from the official Microsoft Help file documentation and is documented nowhere else.

Creating the first record

Creating the Registry key

The value in the Subkey field defines the names of the subkeys that will be created in the Windows Registry to register the add-in. This value must be the same for all records in the USysRegInfo table. The format of this entry depends on the kind of add-in you're installing. No matter what kind of add-in you're installing, for the first record, the value in the Type field must be 0 (which means "add this key"), and the ValName and Value fields must be left blank. The beginning of the Subkey entry can be either HKEY_CURRENT_ACCESS_PROFILE or HKEY_LOCAL_MACHINE. If you use HKEY_CURRENT_ACCESS_PROFILE and the installation is using a user profile (an alternate set of Registry keys that is invoked when Microsoft Access is started with the /Profile command-line option) the Add-in Manager will add the keys and values required to register the add-in in the user profile. If you use HKEY_CURRENT_ACCESS_PROFILE and a user profile is not in use, the Add-in Manager will add the keys and values required to register the add-in in the appropriate key below HKEY_LOCAL_MACHINE. If you use HKEY_LOCAL_MACHINE, the keys and values to register the add-in will always be added below HKEY_LOCAL_MACHINE.

Subkey format for control wizards, OLE custom control wizards, or builders

A control wizard is invoked from the toolbox when you click one of the control tools while designing a form or report. An OLE custom control wizard is invoked when you add an OLE custom control by clicking Custom Control on the Insert menu. A builder is invoked when you click the Build button next to a property box. To register a control wizard, OLE custom control wizard, or builder, the format for the Subkey field is:

HKEY_CURRENT_ACCESS_PROFILE\Wizards\WizardType\
WizardSubType\WizardName

The first part can be either
HKEY_CURRENT_ACCESS_PROFILE or
HKEY_LOCAL_MACHINE, as described earlier. The second part must be Wizards. Assuming there is no user profile in use, this will cause the Add-in Manager to write the
keys and values to register the wizard or builder in
HKEY_LOCAL_MACHINE\SOFTWARE\Microsoft\Access\
7.0\Wizards. WizardType defines whether the add-in is a
control wizard, or a builder (called a Property Wizard in
the Registry). OLE custom control wizards are registered
as control wizards. WizardSubType defines the specific
type of wizard. WizardName is the name of the key where
the values to register the wizard or builder will be added.
Note that WizardName must follow the Microsoft Access
object-naming rules. The following table describes the
possible values for WizardType and WizardSubType.

WizardType	WizardSubType
Control Wizards	For control wizards, the value of Wizard-SubType is the name of the control in the toolbox that you want to associate your wizard with. The names of the controls are:Label, TextBox, OptionGroup, Toggle-Button, OptionButton, CheckBox, Com-boBox, ListBox, CommandButton, Image, UnboundObjectFrame, BoundObject-Frame, PageBreak, SubformSubreport, Line, RectangleFor OLE custom control wizards, the value of WizardSubType is the value for the Class property of the OLE custom control. To see this value, open a form or report in Design view, use the right mouse button to click the OLE custom control, click Properties, and then read the value in the Class box. For example, DBOutl.DataOutline is the value of the Class property for the Microsoft Data Out-line Control 1.1 included with Microsoft Access.

Property Wizards	The name of the property that you want the builder to be associated with. This must be the name of the property with no spaces. For example, the names entered for standard Microsoft Access builders are:BackColor, BorderColor, FieldName, ForeColor, InputMask, LinkChildFields, LinkMasterFields, MenuBar, ODBCConnectStr, Picture, ShortcutMenuBar

Subkey format for object wizards

An object wizard is used to create a table, query, form, or report. An object wizard is invoked by clicking its name in the corresponding New Object dialog box. When you are registering an object wizard, the format for the Subkey field is:

HKEY_CURRENT_ACCESS_PROFILE\Wizards\WizardType\WizardName

The first part can be either HKEY_CURRENT_ACCESS_PROFILE or HKEY_LOCAL_MACHINE, as described earlier. The second part must be Wizards. Assuming there is no user profile in use, this will cause the Add-in Manager to write the keys and values to register the wizard in HKEY_LOCAL_MACHINE\SOFTWARE\Microsoft\Access\7.0\Wizards. WizardType defines what kind of object wizard is being installed. WizardName is the name that displays in the corresponding New Object dialog box and is also the name of the key where the values to register the wizard will be added. The following table describes the possible values for WizardType and WizardName.

WizardType	WizardName
Form Wizards	User-defined. The name you enter will be displayed in the New Form dialog box. For example, the names entered for standard Microsoft Access form wizards

continues

WizardType	WizardName
	are:AutoForm: Columnar; AutoForm: Datasheet; AutoForm: Tabular; Chart Wizard; Form Wizard; PivotTable Wizard
Query Wizards	User-defined. The name you enter will be displayed in the New Query dialog box. For example, the names entered for standard Microsoft Access query wizards are:Crosstab Query Wizard, Find Duplicates Query Wizard, Find Unmatched Query Wizard, Simple Query Wizard
Report Wizards	User-defined. The name you enter will be displayed in the New Report dialog box. For example, the names entered for standard Microsoft Access report wizards are:AutoReport: Columnar; AutoReport: Tabular; Chart Wizard; Label Wizard; Report Wizard
Table Wizards	User-defined. The name you enter will be displayed in the New Table dialog box. For example, the name entered for the standard Microsoft Access table wizard is:Table Wizard

Subkey format for menu add-ins

A menu add-in is invoked by clicking its name on the Add-ins submenu of the Tools menu.

HKEY_CURRENT_ACCESS_PROFILE\Menu Add-Ins\
MenuAddInName

The first part can be either HKEY_CURRENT_ACCESS_PROFILE or HKEY_LOCAL_MACHINE, as described earlier. The second part must be Menu Add-Ins. Assuming there is no user profile in use, this will cause the Add-in Manager to write the keys and values to register the menu add-in in HKEY_LOCAL_MACHINE\SOFTWARE\Microsoft\Access\ 7.0\Menu Add-Ins. MenuAddInName defines the name that displays on the Add-ins submenu and is also the name of the key where the values to register the add-in will be added. To define an access key for the menu add-in so that you can use the keyboard to choose the menu add-in, type an ampersand (&) before the letter that you want to be the access key.

Creating the second and subsequent records

Adding records to create values

The first record in the USysRegInfo table creates a key or keys used to register your add-in. Each record following the first record defines a value added to the last key in the subtree. The value in the Subkey field must be the same as the entry for the first record. The value in the Type field defines the type of the value created in the Registry: 1 to create a String (REG_SZ in Windows NT) or 4 to create a DWORD (REG_DWORD in Windows NT). The value in the ValName field defines the name of the value. The value in the Value field defines the value itself. The number of records you need to add depends on the type of add-in you are registering. The following tables define the records you need to add for each type of add-in.

Records required to define values for control wizards, builders, or OLE custom control wizards

Type	ValName	Value
4	Can Edit	Defines if a wizard or builder can be used to modify an existing control or property of the same type. 1=Yes, 0=No.
1	Description	User-defined. If more than one wizard has been defined for a control, or more than one builder has been defined

continues

Type	ValName	Value
		for a property, this string will display in the Choose Builder dialog box to allow users to select which wizard or builder to use.
1	Function	The function used to start the wizard or builder.
1	Library	Defines the path and name of the add-in database:|ACCDIR\MyAddInDb.mda. The first part is always the same. The Add-in Manager will substitute the path to the folder where Microsoft Access is installed.

Records to define values for object wizards

Type	ValName	Value
1	Bitmap	Defines the path to the bitmap (.bmp) that is displayed above the description on the left side of the New Object dialog box when the wizard is selected.
4	Datasource Required	Enter this record for form and report wizards only. Defines whether the user must choose a table or query from the Choose The Table Or Query Where The Object's Data Comes From box in the New Object dialog box before running the wizard. 1=Yes, 0=No.
1	Description	User-defined. Defines the text that is displayed on the left side of the New Object dialog box when the wizard is selected.
1	Function	The function used to start the wizard or builder.
4	Index	Defines the order in which the wizard is displayed in the list in the New Object dialog box, where 0 is the first item in the list.

Type	ValName	Value
1	Library	Defines the path and name of the add-in database:|ACCDIR\ MyAddInDb.mda. The first part is always the same. The Add-in Manager will substitute the path to the folder where Microsoft Access is installed.

Records to define values for menu add-ins

Type	ValName	Value
1	Expression	The function used to start the wizard or builder formatted as an expression:=MyAddIn_Entry()
1	Library	Defines the path and name of the add-in database:|ACCDIR\ MyAddInDb.mda. The first part is always the same. The Add-in Manager will substitute the path to the folder where Microsoft Access is installed.

Understanding What the Microsoft Documentation Says

Although the documentation is wordy, the information within the previous Microsoft documentation is as concise as it can be. For the exam, know that you must reference all add-ins to Access before they can be used, and you make the references in the USys-RegInfo table—users can create entries in the table of this library database to reference add-ins used in the database.

From a troubleshooting standpoint, if the following error message appears on your system when you try to open the object, you probably have an incorrect setting in the USysRegInfo table: "Can't start the wizard, builder, or add-in." This error can be as simple as an incorrect file name or path.

To correct the problem, complete the following steps:

1. Use the Add-in Manager to uninstall the add-in database.

2. Restart Access.

3. Open the add-in database.

4. Verify settings for the object in USysRegInfo.

Microsoft White Papers

Although it's not a specific test objective, exam questions have covered the migration of components between the previous version of Access and Access 7.0, as well as the differences between the full version of Access and the Run-Time version.

The following white papers address the preceding topics. The first (ACC95: Comparison of v 2.0 and 95 Wizards, Builders, & Add-ins) looks at the different versions, whereas the second—a summation of the paper—looks at the differences between full and run-time versions. Both are from Microsoft (©1997 Microsoft Corporation).

ACC95: Comparison of Version 2.0 and 95 Wizards, Builders, and Add-Ins

The article compares the add-ins, builders, and Microsoft Access Wizards in Microsoft Access version 2.0 and Microsoft Access version 7.0. It also provides an overview of each new add-in, builder, and wizard with a brief description of its purpose in Microsoft Access 7.0.

Name in Version 2.0	Name in Version 7.0
Add-In Manager	Add-In Manager
Add-Ins	Add-Ins
Archive Query Wizard	<Not Available>
Attachment Manager	Link Table Manager
AutoDialer	AutoDialer
AutoForm	AutoForm: Columnar
	AutoForm: Tabular
	AutoForm: Datasheet
AutoReport	AutoReport: Columnar
	AutoReport: Tabular
Code Builder	Code Builder
Color Builder	Color Builder
Combo Box Wizard	Combo Box Wizard
Command Button Wizard	Command Button Wizard
Crosstab Query Wizard	Crosstab Query Wizard
Database Documentor	Documentor
Expression Builder	Expression Builder
Field Builder	Field Builder
Find Duplicates Query Wizard	Find Duplicates Query Wizard
Find Unmatched Query Wizard	Find Unmatched Query Wizard
Graph Wizard	Chart Wizard
Groups/Totals Report Wizard	Report Wizard
Import Database Add-In	Import Table Wizard
Input Mask Wizard	Input Mask Wizard
List Box Wizard	List Box Wizard
Macro Builder	Macro Builder
Mailing Label Report Wizard	Label Wizard
Main/SubForm Wizard	Form Wizard

continues

Name in Version 2.0	Name in Version 7.0
Menu Builder	Menu Builder
Microsoft Word Mail	Office Links Command
ODBC Connection String Builder	ODBC Connection String Builder
Option Group Wizard	Option Group Wizard
Picture Builder	Picture Builder
Query Builder	Query Builder
Single-Column Form Wizard	Form Wizard
Single-Column Report Wizard	Report Wizard
Summary Report Wizard	Report Wizard
Table Wizard	Table Wizard
Tabular Form Wizard	Form Wizard
	AutoForm: Tabular
Tabular Report Wizard	Report Wizard
	AutoReport: Tabular
Wizards Customizer	<Not Available>
Zoom Box	Zoom Box

New Features in Microsoft Access 7.0

Name	Description of Purpose
Conflict Resolver	Resolves conflicts that occur during synchronization of replicated databases.
Database Splitter Add-in	Splits a database into two .mdb files: one for tables and one for queries, forms, reports, macros, and modules.
Database Wizard	Creates a new database for business or personal use. You can choose from more than 20 types of databases.
Import Spreadsheet Wizard	Helps you import spreadsheet data by choosing data types, date formats, and so on.

Name	Description of Purpose
Link Child/Link Master Builder	Helps you link subform or subreport data to the main form or report.
Macro to Visual Basic for Applications Converter	Converts macro actions to Visual Basic for applications code.
Performance Analyzer Wizard	Analyzes any object in your database and suggests changes you can make to improve performance.
Pivot Table Wizard	Creates a control on a form that enables you to summarize data using a format and calculation method you choose.
Simple Query Wizard	Creates single-table and multiple-table queries.
Subform/Subreport Wizard	Creates subform and subreport controls.
Switchboard Manager Add-In	Creates a switchboard form for easy navigation of your forms and reports.
Table Analyzer Wizard	Normalizes your tables to optimize the capabilities of relational databases.
Text Export Wizard	Helps you import and export text data by choosing field delimiters, data types, and so on.
User-Level Security Wizard	Starts securing a database by copying all objects to a new database, revoking users group permissions, and encrypting the database file.

Differences Between Retail and Run-Time Microsoft Access

Retail and run-time versions of Access differ in the following categories:

▶ **Database Windows.** Database, Macro, and Module windows are not visible in a run-time application.

▶ **Object Views.** The run-time version hides the Design views to prevent users from viewing or modifying your objects.

▶ **Menus.** Menus related to View, Tools, and Format are completely removed from the run-time version, as are items from Edit, Insert, and Records that enable users to make changes to the application design.

▶ **Toolbars.** All built-in toolbars are disabled in the run-time version, and you must create custom toolbars.

▶ **Unavailable keys.** Key commands relative to stopping execution or displaying programming windows are disabled.

▶ **Error handling.** In the retail version, errors return prompts and enable you to find the problems. In run-time versions, any error you leave unhandled shuts down the application.

▶ **Help.** You must write your own help files for the run-time version.

Review Questions

1. If a database does not have a reference to an add-in database, what error message commonly appears?

   A. "Sub or Function not defined"

   B. "Compile Error"

   C. "Cannot find project or library"

   D. "Undefined function '<name>' in expression"

2. When a library takes a long time to load, you can speed the process by doing what?

   A. Adding a RegisterDatabase entry

   B. Defining the Data Source Name

   C. Placing an ODBCName value in the Registry

   D. Adding a Loadonstartup entry to the Registry

3. The add-in database for use with USysRegInfo has what extension associated with it?

   A. OCX

   B. MDA

   C. MDB

   D. MCX

4. Which of the following are valid subkeys for menu add-ins?

   A. HKEY_CURRENT_ACCESS_PROFILE\Menu Add-Ins\MenuAddInName

   B. HKEY_LOCAL_MACHINE\Menu Add-Ins\MenuAddInName

   C. HKEY_CURRENT_USER_PROFILE\Menu Add-Ins\MenuAddInName

   D. HKEY_CURRENT_USER\Menu Add-Ins\MenuAddInName

Answers to Review Questions

1. A is correct. If a database does not have a reference to an add-in database, the most common error message is "Sub or Function not defined." Please refer to the section "Implementing Error Handling in Add-Ins" for more information.

2. D is correct. Adding a Loadonstartup entry to the Registry can reduce the amount of time it takes for a library to load. Please refer to the section "Testing and Debugging Library Databases" for more information.

3. B is correct. The USysRegInfo add-in database has an MDA extension. Please refer to the section "Describing the Purpose of the UsysRegInfo Table" for more information.

4. A and B are correct. Valid add-in subkeys include HKEY_CURRENT_ACCESS_PROFILE\Menu Add-Ins\MenuAddInName and HKEY_LOCAL_MACHINE\Menu Add-Ins\MenuAddInName Please refer to the section "Describing the Purpose of the USysRegInfo Table" for more information.

Answers to Test Yourself Questions at Beginning of Chapter...

1. You use the Add-in Manager to load add-ins. See the section "Implementing Error Handling in Add-Ins" for more information.
2. The Compile Error message can be caused by not having the code library in the Add-in database folder nor the folder of the current database. See the section "Testing and Debuging Library Databases" for more information.
3. Wizards, Controls, and Builders areconsidered add-ins. See the section "Describing the Purpose of the USysRegInfo Table" for more information.

Appendix A

Overview of the Certification Process

To become a Microsoft Certified Professional, a candidate must pass rigorous certification exams that provide a valid and reliable measure of his technical proficiency and expertise. These closed-book exams have on-the-job relevance because they are developed with the input of professionals in the computer industry and reflect how Microsoft products are actually used in the workplace. The exams are conducted by an independent organization—Sylvan Prometric—at more than 700 Sylvan Authorized Testing Centers around the world.

Currently Microsoft offers four types of certification, based on specific areas of expertise:

▶ **Microsoft Certified Solution Developer (MCSD).** Qualified to design and develop custom business solutions using Microsoft development tools, technologies, and platforms, including Microsoft Office and Microsoft BackOffice. MCSD is a second level of expertise, but in the area of software development.

▶ **Microsoft Certified Product Specialist (MCPS).** Qualified to provide installation, configuration, and support for users of at least one Microsoft desktop operating system, such as Windows NT Workstation. A candidate also can take additional elective exams to add areas of specialization. MCPS is the first level of expertise.

▶ **Microsoft Certified Systems Engineer (MCSE).** Qualified to effectively plan, implement, maintain, and support information systems with Microsoft Windows NT and other Microsoft advanced systems and workgroup products, such as Microsoft Office and Microsoft BackOffice. The Windows NT Workstation exam can be used as one of the four core operating systems exams. MCSE is the second level of expertise.

▶ **Microsoft Certified Trainer (MCT).** Instructionally and technically qualified by Microsoft to deliver Microsoft education courses at Microsoft-authorized sites. An MCT must be employed by a Microsoft Solution Provider Authorized Technical Education Center or a Microsoft Authorized Academic Training Site.

The following sections describe the requirements for each type of certification.

Note

For up-to-date information about each type of certification, visit the Microsoft Training and Certification World Wide Web site at `http://www.microsoft.com/train_cert`. You must have an Internet account and a WWW browser to access this information. You also can call the following sources:

▶ Microsoft Certified Professional Program: 800-636-7544

▶ Sylvan Prometric Testing Centers: 800-755-EXAM

▶ Microsoft Online Institute (MOLI): 800-449-9333

How to Become a Microsoft Certified Solution Developer (MCSD)

MCSD candidates need to pass two core technology exams and two elective exams. Passing the "Microsoft Access for Windows 95 and the Microsoft Access Developer's Toolkit" exam (#70-69), which this book covers, satisfies an elective requirement. Table A.3 shows the required technology exams, plus the elective exams that apply toward obtaining the MCSD.

Table A.3

MCSD Exams and Requirements	
Take These Two Core Technology Exams	Plus, Choose Two Exams from the Following Elective Exams
Microsoft Windows Architecture I #70-160	Microsoft SQL Server 4.2 Database Implementation #70-21
AND Microsoft Windows Architecture II #70-161	*OR* Developing Applications with C++ Using the Microsoft Foundation Class Library #70-24
	OR Implementing a Database Design on Microsoft SQL Server 6 #70-27
	OR Microsoft Access 2.0 for Windows-Application Development #70-51
	OR Developing Applications with Microsoft Excel 5.0 Using Visual Basic for Applications #70-52
	OR Programming in Microsoft Visual FoxPro 3.0 for Windows #70-54
	OR Programming with Microsoft Visual Basic 4.0 #70-65
	OR Microsoft Access for Windows 95 and the Microsoft Access Development Toolkit #70-69
	OR Implementing OLE in Microsoft Foundation Class Applications #70-25

How to Become a Microsoft Certified Product Specialist (MCPS)

You must pass one operating system exam to become an MCPS. Unfortunately, the "Microsoft Access for Windows 95 and the Microsoft Access Developer's Toolkit" exam (#70-69) does NOT apply toward this requirement.

The following list shows the names and exam numbers of all the operating systems from which you can choose to get your MCPS certification:

► Implementing and Supporting Microsoft Windows 95 #70-63

► Implementing and Supporting Microsoft Windows NT Workstation 4.0 #70-73

► Implementing and Supporting Microsoft Windows NT Workstation 3.51 #70-42

► Implementing and Supporting Microsoft Windows NT Server 4.0 #70-67

► Implementing and Supporting Microsoft Windows NT Server 3.51 #70-43

► Microsoft Windows for Workgroups 3.11-Desktop #70-48

► Microsoft Windows 3.1 #70-30

► Microsoft Windows Architecture I #70-160

► Microsoft Windows Architecture II #70-161

How to Become a Microsoft Certified Systems Engineer (MCSE)

An MCSE candidate needs to pass four operating system exams and two elective exams. The MCSE certification path is divided into two tracks: Windows NT 3.51 and Windows NT 4.0. The "Microsoft Access for Windows 95 and the Microsoft Access Developer's Toolkit" exam (#70-69), which this book covers, does NOT apply to either track of the MCSE certification path.

Table A.1 shows the core requirements (four operating system exams) and the elective courses (two exams) for the Windows NT 3.51 track.

Table A.1

Windows NT 3.51 MCSE Track

Take These Two Required Exams (Core Requirements)	Plus, Pick One Exam from the Following Operating System Exams (Core Requirement)	Plus, Pick One Exam from the Following Networking Exams (Core Requirement)	Plus, Pick Two Exams from the Following Elective Exams (Elective Requirements)
Implementing and Supporting Microsoft Windows NT Server 3.51 #70-43	Implementing and Supporting Microsoft Windows 95 #70-63	Networking Essentials #70-58	Implementing and Supporting Microsoft SNA Server 3.0 #70-13
AND Implementing and Supporting Microsoft Windows NT Workstation 3.51 #70-42	*OR* Microsoft Windows for Workgroups 3.11-Desktop #70-48		*OR* Implementing and Supporting Microsoft System Management Server 1.2 #70-18
	OR Microsoft Windows 3.1 #70-30		*OR* Microsoft SQL Server 4.2 Database Implementation #70-21
			OR Microsoft SQL Server 4.2 Database Administration for Microsoft Windows NT #70-22
			OR System Administration for Microsoft SQL Server 6 #70-26
			OR Implementing a Database Design on Microsoft SQL Server 6 #70-27

continues

Table A.1 Continued

Windows NT 3.51 MCSE Track

Take These Two Required Exams (Core Requirements)	Plus, Pick One Exam from the Following Operating System Exams (Core Requirement)	Plus, Pick One Exam from the Following Networking Exams (Core Requirement)	Plus, Pick Two Exams from the Following Elective Exams (Elective Requirements)
			OR Microsoft Mail for PC Networks 3.2-Enterprise #70-37
			OR Internetworking Microsoft TCP/IP on Microsoft Windows NT (3.5-3.51) #70-53
			OR Internetworking Microsoft TCP/IP on Microsoft Windows NT 4.0 #70-59
			OR Implementing and Supporting Microsoft Exchange Server 4.0 #70-75
			OR Implementing and Supporting Microsoft Internet Information Server #70-77
			OR Implementing and Supporting Microsoft Proxy Server 1.0 #70-78

Table A.2 shows the core requirements (four operating system exams) and elective courses (two exams) for the Windows NT 4.0 track. Tables A.1 and A.2 have many of the same exams listed, but there are distinct differences between the two. Make sure you review each track's requirements carefully.

Table A.2

Windows NT 4.0 MCSE Track

Take These Two Required Exams (Core Requirements)	Plus, Pick One Exam from the Following Operating System Exams (Core Requirement)	Plus, Pick One Exam from the Following Networking Exams (Core Requirement)	Plus, Pick Two Exams from the Following Elective Exams (Elective Requirements)
Implementing and Supporting Microsoft Windows NT Server 4.0 #70-67	Implementing and Supporting Microsoft Windows 95 #70-63	Networking Essentials #70-58	Implementing and Supporting Microsoft SNA Server 3.0 #70-13
AND Implementing and Supporting Microsoft Windows NT Server 4.0 in the Enterprise #70-68	*OR* Microsoft Windows for Workgroups 3.11-Desktop #70-48		*OR* Implementing and Supporting Microsoft System Management Server 1.2 #70-18
	OR Microsoft Windows 3.1 #70-30		*OR* Microsoft SQL Server 4.2 Database Implementation #70-21
	OR Implementing and Supporting Microsoft Windows NT Workstation 4.0 #70-73		*OR* Microsoft SQL Server 4.2 Database Administration for Microsoft Windows NT #70-22
			OR System Administration for Microsoft SQL Server 6 #70-26

continues

Table A.2   Continued

Windows NT 4.0 MCSE Track

Take These Two Required Exams (Core Requirements)	Plus, Pick One Exam from the Following Operating System Exams (Core Requirement)	Plus, Pick One Exam from the Following Networking Exams (Core Requirement)	Plus, Pick Two Exams from the Following Elective Exams (Elective Requirements)
			OR Implementing a Database Design on Microsoft SQL Server 6 #70-27
			OR Microsoft Mail for PC Networks 3.2-Enterprise #70-37
			OR Internetworking Microsoft TCP/IP on Microsoft Windows NT (3.5-3.51) #70-53
			OR Internetworking Microsoft TCP/IP on Microsoft Windows NT 4.0 #70-59
			OR Implementing and Supporting Microsoft Exchange Server 4.0 #70-75

Take These Two Required Exams (Core Requirements)	Plus, Pick One Exam from the Following Operating System Exams (Core Requirement)	Plus, Pick One Exam from the Following Networking Exams (Core Requirement)	Plus, Pick Two Exams from the Following Elective Exams (Elective Requirements)
			OR Implementing and Supporting Microsoft Internet Information Server #70-77
			OR Implementing and Supporting Microsoft Proxy Server 1.0 #70-78

Becoming a Microsoft Certified Trainer (MCT)

To understand the requirements and process for becoming a Microsoft Certified Trainer (MCT), you must obtain the Microsoft Certified Trainer Guide document (MCTGUIDE.DOC) from the following WWW site:

```
http://www.microsoft.com/train_cert/download.htm
```

On this web page, click the hyperlink MCT GUIDE (mctguide.doc) (117k). If your WWW browser can display DOC files (Word for Windows native file format), the MCT Guide appears in the browser window. Otherwise, you need to download the guide and open it in Word for Windows or Windows 95 WordPad. The MCT Guide explains the four-step process to becoming an MCT. The general steps for the MCT certification are as follows:

1. Complete and mail a Microsoft Certified Trainer application to Microsoft. You must include proof of your skills for presenting instructional material. The options for doing so are described in the MCT Guide.

2. Obtain and study the Microsoft Trainer Kit for the Microsoft Official Curricula (MOC) course(s) for which you want to be certified. Microsoft Trainer Kits can be ordered by calling 800-688-0496 in North America. Applicants from other regions should review the MCT Guide for information on how to order a Trainer Kit.

3. Pass the Microsoft certification exam for the product for which you want to be certified to teach.

4. Attend the Microsoft Official Curriculum (MOC) course for the course for which you want to be certified. This is done so you can understand how the course is structured, how labs are completed, and how the course flows.

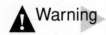 Warning

You should use the preceding steps as a general overview of the MCT certification process. The actual steps you need to take are described in detail in the MCTGUIDE.DOC file on the WWW site mentioned earlier. Do not misconstrue the preceding steps as the actual process you need to take.

If you are interested in becoming an MCT, you can receive more information by visiting the Microsoft Certified Training (MCT) WWW site at http://www.microsoft.com/train_cert/mctint.htm or by calling 800-688-0496.

Appendix

Study Tips

B

Self-study involves any method that you employ to learn a given topic, with the most popular being third-party books, such as the one you hold in your hand. Before you begin to study for a certification exam, you should know exactly what Microsoft expects you to learn.

Pay close attention to the objectives posted for the exam. The most current objectives can always be found on the WWW site `http://www.microsoft.com/train_cert`. This book was written to the most current objectives, and the beginning of each chapter lists the relevant objectives for that chapter. As well, you should notice a handy tear-out card with an objective matrix that lists all objectives and the page to which you can turn for information on that objective.

If you have taken any college courses in the past, you have probably learned what study habits work best for you. Nevertheless, consider the following:

- ▶ Study in bright light to reduce fatigue and depression.

- ▶ Establish a regular study schedule and adhere to it as closely as possible.

- ▶ Turn off all forms of distraction, including radios and televisions, or try studying in a quiet room.

- ▶ Study in the same place each time you study: your materials will be always readily at hand.

- ▶ Take short breaks (approximately 15 minutes) every two to three hours or so. Studies have proven that your brain assimilates information better when you allow for these breaks.

Here's something else to think about. There are three ways in which humans obtain information: visually, audially, and through tactile confirmation. That's why, in a college class, the students who take notes about the lectures have better recall on exam day; they take in information visually, audially, and through tactile confirmation—by writing it down.

Use study techniques that reinforce information in all three ways. For example, read the books to visually take in the information. Write down the information when you test yourself to benefit from tactile confirmation. And lastly, have someone test you out loud so you can hear yourself giving the correct answer. Having someone test you should always be the last step in studying.

Pre-Testing Yourself

Before taking the actual exam, verify that you are ready to do so by testing yourself a number of times in a variety of ways. Within this book, there are questions at the beginning and end of each chapter. On the accompanying CD-ROM, there is the TestPrep electronic test engine that emulates an actual Microsoft exam and enables you to test your knowledge of the subject areas. Continue to use these study aids until you are consistently scoring in the 90-percent range (or better).

 Note

This means, of course, that you can't start studying five days before the exam begins. You will need to give yourself plenty of time to read, practice, and then test yourself several times.

Macmillan Computer Publishing's TestPrep electronic testing engine on the enclosed CD-ROM, we believe, is the best one on the market. It is thoroughly described in Appendix D, "All About TestPrep."

Hints and Tips for Doing Your Best on the Tests

In a confusing twist of terminology, when you take one of the Microsoft exams, you are said to be "writing" the exam. When you go to take the actual exam, be prepared. Arrive early and be ready to show two forms of identification and sit before the monitor. Expect wordy questions. Although you have 90 minutes to take the exam, there are 57 questions you must answer. This gives you just over one minute to answer each question. This may sound like ample time to spend on each question, but remember that most of the questions are word problems that tend to ramble on for paragraphs.

Your 90 minutes of exam time can be consumed very quickly. It has been estimated that approximately 85 percent of the candidates fail their first attempts at taking a Microsoft exam. Although they can be prepared and quite knowledgeable, they don't know what to expect and are immediately intimidated by the wordiness of the questions and the seeming ambiguity of the answers.

For every exam that Microsoft offers, there is a different required passing score. The passing score for the Access 95 exam can change every day, depending on which pool of questions are being used. Scores in the high 700s or higher have been considered passing in the past.

Things to Watch For

When you take the exam, look closely at the number of correct choices you need to make. Some questions require that you select one correct answer; other questions have more than one correct answer. When you see radio buttons next to the answer choices, you need to remember that the answers are mutually exclusive and there is but one right answer. On the other hand, check boxes indicate that the answers are not mutually exclusive and there are multiple right answers. Be sure to read the questions closely for indications on how many correct answers you need to choose.

Also, read the questions fully. With lengthy questions, the last sentence often dramatically changes the scenario. When taking the exam, you are given pencils and two sheets of paper. If you are uncertain of what the question is saying, map out the scenario on the paper until you have it clear in your mind. You're required to turn in the scrap paper at the end of the exam.

Marking Answers for Return

You can mark questions on the actual exam and refer back to them later. If you get a wordy question that will take a long time to read and decipher, mark it and return to it when you have completed the rest of the exam. This will save you from wasting time on it and running out of time on the exam—there are only 90 minutes allotted for the exam and it ends when those 90 minutes expire, whether or not you are finished with the exam.

Attaching Notes to Test Questions

At the conclusion of the exam, before the grading takes place, you are given the opportunity to attach a message to any question. If you feel that a question was too ambiguous, or tested on knowledge you did not need to know to work with the product, take this opportunity to state your case. Unheard of is the instance in which Microsoft changes a test score as a result of an attached message. However, it never hurts to try—and it helps to vent your frustration before blowing the proverbial 50-amp fuse.

Good luck!

Appendix

What's on the CD-ROM

This appendix is a brief rundown of what you'll find on the CD-ROM that comes with this book. For a more detailed description of the newly developed TestPrep test engine, please see Appendix D, "All About TestPrep."

The TestPrep Test Engine

A new test engine was developed exclusively for New Riders. It is, we believe, the best test engine available because it closely emulates the actual Microsoft exam and because it enables you to check your score by category, which helps you determine what you need to study further. For a complete description of the benefits of TestPrep, please see Appendix D.

Exclusive Electronic Version of Text

Use the electronic version of this book to help you search for terms or areas that you need to study. It comes complete with all figures as they appear in the book.

Copyright Information and Disclaimer

New Riders's TestPrep test engine: Copyright 1998 New Riders Publishing. All rights reserved. Made in U.S.A.

Appendix

All About TestPrep

The electronic TestPrep utility included on the CD-ROM accompanying this book enables you to test your knowledge in a manner similar to that employed by the actual Microsoft exam.

Test Prep uses a unique randomization sequence to ensure that each time you run the program you are presented with a different sequence of questions—this enhances your learning and prevents you from merely learning the expected answers over time without reading the question each and every time.

Question Presentation

TestPrep emulates the actual Microsoft "Microsoft Access for Windows 95 and the Microsoft Access Developer's Toolkit" exam (#70-69); radio (circle) buttons are used to signify only one correct choice, and check boxes (squares) are used to imply multiple correct answers.

Scoring

The TestPrep Score Report follows, as closely as possible, the actual "Microsoft Access for Windows 95 and the Microsoft Access Developer's Toolkit" exam. Microsoft no longer makes available exact passing scores, but for exam #70-69, scores in the high 700s or higher have been considered passing in the past; the same parameters apply to the TestPrep. Each objective category is broken down into categories with a percentage correct given for each. Each test should include 57 questions, and each test session should last 90 minutes.

Note: Every effort has been made to maximize your test preparation by emulating the actual test experience as closely as possible. We cannot, however, guarantee that testing formats, or other details such as official passing scores, number of questions on an exam, or time given to take an exam, will not change.

Index

N

O